MW01255773

# THE WAR OF AMERICAN INDEPENDENCE, 1763–1783

*The War of American Independence, 1763–1783: Falling Dominoes* addresses the military, maritime and naval, economic, key personalities, key societal groups, political, imperial rivalry, and diplomatic dynamics and events from the post-Seven Years' War era in Great Britain's North American colonies through the end of the War of American Independence.

Beginning in 1763 and moving through the war chronologically, the authors argue that British political and strategic leaders failed to develop an effective strategy to quell the discontent and subsequent revolt in the North American colonies and thus failed to restore allegiance to the Crown. This book describes and analyzes events and the outcomes of central players' decisions—the British North American colonies, Great Britain, France, Spain, and the Dutch Republic—and the resultant actions. It examines events through the thematic lens of strategy, political and military leadership, public attitudes, economics, international rivalries and relations, and the role of traditionally less-considered groups: women, slaves, and Native American peoples.

This book is an enlightening and essential read for all history students, from high school through to those on postgraduate courses, as well as those with an interest in the American Revolution.

**Stanley D. M. Carpenter**, Emeritus Professor of Strategy and retired US Navy Captain, US Naval War College in Newport, RI, focuses on the American Revolution period, the British Civil Wars, and the twentieth-century world wars. His most recent work, *Southern Gambit: Cornwallis and the British March to Yorktown*, addresses the conflict from the British strategic perspective.

**Kevin J. Delamer**, retired US Navy Commander and aviator, is a former Naval War College Strategy Department Military Professor. Now a Department of the Navy consultant, he teaches the Naval War College Strategy and War non-resident seminar at the US Naval Academy and also publishes on naval aviation and World War II.

**James R. McIntyre**, Associate Professor of History at Moraine Valley College in Chicago, specializes in American Revolution German auxiliaries, the war in the middle colonies, and eighteenth-century irregular warfare. Recent works address the development of light infantry in the eighteenth century, the Philadelphia Campaign of 1777–1778, and a biography of Johann Ewald. He teaches the Strategy and War non-resident seminar in Great Lakes, Illinois.

**Andrew T. Zwilling**, Assistant Professor of Strategy at the Naval War College, teaches strategy as well as oversees the College of Distance Education's Strategy and War online curriculum. Specialties include the American Revolution, the British Mediterranean, the Royal Navy, and eighteenth and nineteenth-century naval history.

# Warfare and History

General Editor: Jeremy Black

**Israel's Wars**
A History since 1947, 4th edition
*Ahron Bregman*

**The Spanish Civil War**
A Military History
*Charles J. Esdaile*

**Military Thought of Asia**
From the Bronze Age to the Information Age
*Kaushik Roy*

**The First World Empire**
Portugal, War and Military Revolution
*Edited by Hélder Carvalhal, André Murteira and Roger
Lee de Jesus*

**Modern Insurgencies and Counterinsurgencies**
A Global History
*Kaushik Roy*

**The War of American Independence, 1763–1783**
Falling Dominoes
*Stanley D. M. Carpenter, Kevin J. Delamer, James R. McIntyre
and Andrew T. Zwilling*

For more information, or to place orders visit Routledge, Warfare and History
www.routledge.com/Warfare-and-History/book-series/SE0417

# THE WAR OF AMERICAN INDEPENDENCE, 1763–1783

## Falling Dominoes

*Stanley D. M. Carpenter , Kevin J. Delamer, James R. McIntyre and Andrew T. Zwilling*

Routledge
Taylor & Francis Group

LONDON AND NEW YORK

Designed cover image: 'Declaration of Independence:' Courtesy of the
Anne S.K. Brown Military Collection, Brown University Library

First published 2023
by Routledge
4 Park Square, Milton Park, Abingdon, Oxon OX14 4RN

and by Routledge
605 Third Avenue, New York, NY 10158

*Routledge is an imprint of the Taylor & Francis Group, an informa business*

© 2023 Stanley D. M. Carpenter, Kevin J. Delamer, James R. McIntyre
and Andrew T. Zwilling

*British Library Cataloguing-in-Publication Data*
A catalogue record for this book is available from the British Library

*Library of Congress Cataloging-in-Publication Data*
Names: Carpenter, Stanley D. M., author. | Delamer, Kevin J., author.Rev |
    McIntyre, James R., author. | Zwilling, Andrew T., author.
Title: The War of American Independence, 1763–1783 : falling dominoes /
    Stanley D. M. Carpenter, Kevin J. Delamer, James R. McIntyre and
    Andrew T. Zwilling.
Description: Abingdon, Oxon ; New York, NY : Routledge, [2023] |
    Series: Warfare and history | Includes bibliographical references and index.
Identifiers: LCCN 2022038916 (print) | LCCN 2022038917 (ebook) |
    ISBN 9780367484989 (hardcover) | ISBN 9780367484996 (paperback) |
    ISBN 9780367484989 (ebook)
Subjects: LCSH: United States—History—Revolution, 1775–1783.
Classification: LCC E230 .C29 2023 (print) | LCC E230 (ebook) |
    DDC 973.3—dc23/eng/20220822
LC record available at https://lccn.loc.gov/2022038916
LC ebook record available at https://lccn.loc.gov/2022038917

ISBN: 978-0-367-48498-9 (hbk)
ISBN: 978-0-367-48499-6 (pbk)
ISBN: 978-1-003-04127-6 (ebk)

DOI: 10.4324/9781003041276

Typeset in Bembo
by Apex CoVantage, LLC

*April 2023*

*The Stannus,*

Dedicated to Don Higginbotham, John Hattendorf,
and Piers Mackesy with the greatest respect.

*All the Best*

# CONTENTS

# ILLUSTRATIONS

## Figures

## Maps

# PREFACE

There has long been a tendency in War of American Independence histories and popular perception that the Patriot victory and the resultant establishment of an independent United States of America was inevitable and a foregone conclusion largely brought about by British political and military mistakes. More recent works have countered that perception and provided a broader analysis of the war in all its aspects. Traditional military narratives called "drum and trumpet" history tended to focus narrowly on campaign and battle narratives. While the particulars of campaigns and battles are critical in understanding the outcome of conflicts, these narratives obscured or failed to address the complex nature of societies at war. For the War of American Independence period, the roles played by women, African Americans, whether slaves or freedmen, and Native Americans, or as they were known then, Indians, have typically been underreported. In the mid to late twentieth century, the "War and Society" methodology of examining war and conflict came to dominate military history, with an expanded emphasis on how conflict impacts all aspects of a society and the roles of the people involved. In that light, while this examination is primarily an analytical, thematic, and chronological study of the period from the end of the Seven Years' War/French and Indian War (1763) through the ultimate peace of the Treaty of Paris (1783) that established an independent United States, the work folds in multiple aspects of a society at war.

In addition to the vital campaign narrative that largely is found in Chapters 2 through 9, the study incorporates important social, cultural, economic, political, and constitutional aspects where appropriate. In this way, the work creates a broader understanding of the conflict's dynamics, the roles played by all members of American society, the reasons for the ultimate Patriot victory, and the impact on the wider global environment. While each of these areas of study is inherently important in the overall historical analysis, the volume is first and foremost about the war itself and its place in shaping the future American Republic and British Empire. The constraints of space and length mean that many interesting and important topics cannot be addressed in the detail they deserve. For those seeking broader examinations of "War and Society" dynamics, there are numerous excellent studies of the American Revolution and War of American Independence period on issues of race, gender, culture, economics, politics, and so forth published in the past several decades, and the reader is encouraged to delve into those works.

This book's goal is simple—provide a concise, highly readable study of the War of American Independence that students of history from high school through post-graduate education will find useful and instructive. The monograph examines and narrates the War of American Independence and broader global struggle through the prism of the military actions, the politics (particularly the Lord North Ministry, Parliament, the Continental Congress, and Patriot political leadership), the diplomacy (especially Patriot attempts to win foreign support), as well as the economic aspects (e.g., privateering, colonial economy, commerce, and trade). The analysis provides insights for contemporary readers (including strategic, political, and operational planners/decision-makers), in terms of how a great power conducts a distant, irregular war, characterized by insurgency, rebellion, and internal civil strife, all complicated by a severe resource constraint within the context of international peer and great power competition.

There is a tendency to refer to the opponents as Americans (or colonials) and British. But, the war was both a rebellion against Britain and a civil war between Americans. With an estimated 430 different Loyalist units embodied at some point and with over 10,000 American Loyalists in arms in 1780 alone in Provincial regiments, it is erroneous to refer to the colonials in rebellion as the "Americans." Therefore, this study uses the terms "rebel," "Patriot," or "Whig" interchangeably to describe those Americans opposing Crown authority and "Loyalist" or "Tory" for those who remained loyal to Britain. Additionally, reference to "Crown" forces means not only regular British and Loyalist provincial units or German auxiliary hired troops but also irregular Loyalist militia and partisan groups.

Rank titles need to be noted. For compound ranks as in lieutenant general, vice admiral, lieutenant colonel, and so on, the British method was and still is to hyphenate as in lieutenant-general, vice-admiral, lieutenant-colonel, and the like. However, in America, the hyphen was dropped. Thus, these ranks are expressed as major general, lieutenant colonel, and so forth. In this narrative, if the character is a British or Loyalist officer-regular, provincial or militia-the title is hyphenated. For Patriot ranks, the hyphen is omitted.

As a textbook in the Routledge *Warfare and History* series, foot or endnote citations are held to a minimum, typically for direct quotations. Often, scholarly work citations can overwhelm the non-historian with minute details and explanations; the authors seek to avoid that trap. Additionally, while primary sources are the *sine qua non* of historical research and scholarship, for a comprehensive, concise text-book, the authors have drawn heavily upon the tremendous work of other scholars of the American revolutionary period. Many quotes, analytical concepts, and ideas are drawn from these previous works. All are cited, which is a special boon to students wishing to read further.

Not only is the war one of many peoples, it is one of many names. Often called the American Revolution, that term really describes the American "evolution" that began with the civil wars in England, Scotland, Wales, and Ireland that roiled the Three Kingdoms from the late 1630s to the ultimate establishment of parliamentary sovereignty by 1689. Those constitutional, political, economic, and Enlightenment or Age of Reason ideals drawn from the British and French Enlightenments percolated in the North American colonies throughout the century and ultimately came to fruition with the US Constitution by the late eighteenth century. Perhaps a more descriptive term might be "The American Evolution." That said, this work addresses the development of an armed rebellion from the end of the Seven Years' War/French and Indian War (1763) to the Peace of Paris (1783) that finally ended the fighting. Various titles are descriptive of that specific period—War of Independence, War of American Independence, Revolutionary War, American War of Independence, or simply the American War. The authors chose the War of American Independence and the American War as the most descriptive, but all the titles suffice as well.

Readers may notice a distinct focus on strategy and strategic decision-making. This dynamic should not surprise anyone since all four co-authors are United States Naval War College Professors of Strategy. Professor Stanley D. M. Carpenter is Professor Emeritus and former Department Head of the Strategy and Policy Department in the College of Distance Education. Professor Kevin J. Delamer is a former Military Professor of Strategy and Policy and is currently Fleet Professor (adjunct) of Strategy and War for Annapolis, Maryland. Professor Andrew T. Zwilling is Assistant Professor of Strategy at the Naval War College while Professor James R. McIntyre is the Great Lakes Naval Training Station, Illinois Strategy and War Fleet Professor. All four are specialists in the American War period. Having said that, there are going to be references to various theorists of war such as the Prussian General Carl von Clausewitz and the ancient Chinese philosopher of war, Sun Tzu, as well as the naval and maritime theorists, Rear Admiral Alfred Thayer Mahan and Sir Julian Stafford Corbett. That leads on to some basic strategic thinking terms that might not be understood by the reader. Here are some helpful definitions:

1) **Center of Gravity**—as Clausewitz explains, it is the "hub of all power" of an opponent against which one should exert their maximum effort.

2) **Culminating Point**—the point at which one reaches their maximum strength or objectives achievement beyond which strength or accomplishments diminish.

3) **Value of the Object**—a calculation to determine what the objective is really worth? Are the potential gains worth the cost in blood and treasure?

4) **Civil-Military Relations**—the relationship between the civil and military authority-legal, constitutional, or traditional. The institutional make-up of a military in a civil society.

5) **Strategy**—the overall plan of action that, if successful, establishes the conditions whereby the political objective(s) can be attained.

6) **Operations**—actions carried out in support of the strategy, whether campaigns, battles, or engagements.

7) **Joint**—multiservice as in the Royal Navy and British Army working together for an operation.

8) **Combined**—multinational as in the United States and France working together for an operation.

9) **Hybrid Warfare**—also known as irregular warfare, a combination of conventional force with an irregular element such as partisans, guerillas, or insurgents. Might also include irregular local militia.

10) **Limited War**—war fought for limited aims such as acquisition of territory. Unlimited war means the complete destruction of a society, state, kingdom, government, regime, and so on. A good example might be unconditional surrender as in World War II.

11) **Strategic Communication**—known variously as public relations or even propaganda, it is the perception that a military or political authority projects to the public.

12) **Situational Awareness (SA)**—an understanding of the situation, dynamics, or environment in which one operates and is often based on intelligence collection and analysis.

13) **CinC**—an acronym for Commander-in-Chief, the overall commander.

14) **Fog and Friction**—those forces that impact military operations and can range from actual weather to terrain to troop moral factors (fear, courage, hatred, motivation to fight, fatigue, etc.). Fog and friction can also hamper operations through poor SA, bad intelligence, successful deceptions, and environmental factors that interfere with operations.

Finally a word about the title. The outbreak of war and the events that drove the march to the eventual outcome can be viewed metaphorically like multiple rows of dominoes coming together at a key point and cascading down until all the pieces have fallen. In this case, the final falling domino for the rebellion and independence movement might be the Yorktown surrender. One might see the Battle of the Saintes and the lifting of the Siege of Gibraltar as the last dominoes to fall resulting in the end of global hostilities. Thus, the authors chose the title *The War of*

*American Independence, 1763–1783: Falling Dominoes* to capture that imagery of row after row of dominoes falling, leading to the eventual outcome—an independent United States of America and the ultimate domination of the world's empires by the United Kingdom.

Stanley D. M. Carpenter
Kevin J. Delamer
James R. McIntyre
Andrew T. Zwilling
*United States Naval War College*
*Newport, Rhode Island*
*February 2023*

# ACRONYMS

ADM—Admiralty Papers—National Archives, Kew, UK

C-CC—Benjamin Franklin Stevens, ed., *The Campaign in Virginia: Clinton-Cornwallis Controversy*, 2 Vols., 1888

HMC—Historical Manuscripts Commission, UK

LDC—Letters of Delegates of the Continental Congress, Library of Congress, Washington, DC

LOC—Library of Congress, Washington, DC

NA CO5—Letter Books of the Colonial Office, National Archives, Kew, UK (hereafter cited as NA CO5/vol. x/no. x)

NA HQ PRO 30/55—Headquarters Papers of the British Army in North America, 1775–1784 (Dorchester Papers), National Archives, Kew, UK (hereafter cited as NA HQ PRO 30/55/vol. x/no. x)

NA PRO 30/11—Cornwallis Correspondence, National Archives, Kew, UK (hereafter cited as NA CC PRO 30/11/vol. x/no. x)

WO 34—War Office Papers, National Archives, Kew, UK

# INTRODUCTION

## A War of Many Peoples

*Sir,*

*I have the mortification to inform your Excellency that I have been forced to give up the posts of York and Gloucester and to surrender the troops under my command by capitulation on the 19th instant as prisoners of war to the combined forces of America and France.*[1]

With these few words, Lieutenant-General Charles, 2nd Earl Cornwallis announced the British failure to subdue the rebellion in the North American colonies, pacify the populace, and restore colonial allegiance to the British Empire. Yorktown represented the culmination of British efforts to accomplish the policy objectives by military force. However, by 1778 with the intervention of France followed in 1779 by Spain and the Dutch in 1780, what started in 1775 as a colonial rebellion became yet another Anglo-Bourbon global maritime struggle. The War of American Independence might be described as the "war of many peoples." Men, women, whites, African Americans, both free and enslaved, Native American Indians, Loyalists, Patriots, Americans, Canadians, English, Scottish, Welsh, Irish, Germans, French, Spanish, Dutch, and so on all participated in what came to be yet another in the century and a half struggle for imperial domination between the British Empire and the Bourbon states. Woven into this narrative and analysis of key events are highlights of constituencies, including Loyalists and Patriots, soldiers and politicians, women, blacks, American Indians, and the decision-makers that shaped the outcome.

Throughout the War of American Independence, British leaders failed to develop an effective strategy to quell the discontent and subsequent revolt in the North American colonies and thus failed to restore allegiance to the Crown. By contrast, the American Patriots conducted a successful defensive war of attrition that, in combination with the intervention of European powers, countered and nullified all Crown political, military, economic, and diplomatic efforts to

DOI: 10.4324/9781003041276-1

end the rebellion. Despite losing the North American colonies by 1783, British naval and military forces successfully defeated French and allied efforts to conquer either the British homeland or the most significant colonial and imperial possessions.

British political and military measures undertaken in the wake of the Seven Years' War set the stage for conflict between the British colonists and the Crown. With the outbreak of open rebellion in Massachusetts in April 1775, the British Empire faced a daunting challenge—how does a distant imperial power conduct a war to suppress a colonial rebellion while simultaneously defending against peer competitors. Britain needed an effective military and political strategy to suppress the rebellion and return the colonies to allegiance, particularly after French, Spanish, and Dutch intervention turned the colonial affair into a global, great power conflict. Despite the state of communications, transportation, lack of sufficient naval and military manpower resources, and logistics, policy and strategy decision-makers embarked on an offensive strategy of annihilation (pacification by brute force). The result was a series of conventional operations designed to crush the Continental Army, suppress the Patriot militia and insurgents (often called partisans), allow the Loyalists to restore royal government in the colonies, and pacify the colonies, thus restoring allegiance. Several variations of this strategy emerged throughout the war often achieving operational success but ultimately resulting in strategic failure. From the American Patriot viewpoint, the war was largely reactive in that by fighting a strategy of defensive attrition (Fabian Strategy), the Patriots wore down British political will to continue the struggle following the surrender at Yorktown, Virginia, in October 1781. From the French and Spanish perspectives, the war represented revenge for the Seven Years' War humiliation. The war's outcome was neither the result of British errors nor a conflict won by American bravery and strategic insight. It was, rather, a complex mosaic composed of a colonial domestic discontent complicated by a dynamic international situation and an emerging and distinct American culture.

## The Machine Will Fail

Students of the American War are often confused by the eighteenth-century complex and seemingly inefficient British constitutional system, particularly the war administrative and decision-making apparatus. In the period, Britain stood in a transitory moment between a feudal household governance (i.e., administrators as essentially servants of the Crown) and the modern parliamentary constitutional monarchy whereby departments, ministries, bureaucrats, and officials have very defined roles and missions. The complex system of military administration, operating without a central organizing authority, proved disastrous for the British war effort in America. The modern departmental and cabinet governmental system had not yet fully developed with definitive roles and responsibilities. Many office-holders serving the monarchy, Cabinet, and the various departments were highly skilled and very professional. However, the modern civil service system had not developed; personality drove the government more than other dynamics. In terms of war administration and management, the Cabinet, made up of the king's principle ministers, established the national policy; however, it also influenced strategic and operational matters, including what operations or expeditions to embark upon, time frames, and troop allocations. Various Secretaries of State (Lord George Germain was Secretary of State for the Americas, commonly referred to as the American Secretary) actually executed the plans by issuing orders to the Treasury, Admiralty, Ordnance (artillery), and Commander-in-Chief of the Army (Executive Departments). Although these bureaucracies had responsibility for logistics, transportation, manpower, and force movements, they had little responsibility for operational planning or execution. The monarch, as captain-general, served as titular head of the army, but in reality, he might delegate a Commander-in-Chief (CinC), who commanded the home forces (but not overseas) and oversaw army administration. A Secretary at War, not a Cabinet member, assisted in military administration, particularly resources and finance. However, the Secretary at War had dubious authority and an ill-defined mission. Nonetheless, he might exercise great influence depending on his personality.

Actual operational control came under the Cabinet and the Secretaries of State. Once the Cabinet made strategic and operational decisions as transmitted through the appropriate geographic Secretary of State (North, South, and American Colonial), orders and instructions flowed directly to the field commanders. The Royal Navy's system differed vastly from the army. Rather than officials with ill-defined or dubious roles, the Lords Commissioners of the Admiralty, a mixed body of political appointees and professional naval officers, controlled all naval functions and decision-making. Led by the First Lord of the Admiralty and operationally commanded by the First Sea Lord, the Board exercised direct operational and administrative control. A subordinate Navy Board controlled shipbuilding, supply, and transport. Although the general outline of operations would be determined by the Cabinet and orders from a Secretary of State issued to the Board of Admiralty, unlike the army, the navy governed its own operations. Given the tight operational control over ships and movements, navy cooperation proved problematic. Typically, the navy held ships in port for weeks or months with spoiling cargo awaiting sufficient convoy escort. Since the Royal Navy deteriorated from its strength in the Seven Years' War to a dangerously low preparedness level by 1775, the Navy Board reluctantly released escort vessels from European, Channel, and Mediterranean duties for North American escort operations.[2] Given the Admiralty's control over naval force employment, there was little that a Secretary of State could do to force the issue. With the French threat by 1778, it became even more difficult to obtain escorts for supplies to America. Sir Henry Clinton in New York, CinC for North America, summed up the difficulty in supplying the forces in America and in working with the Royal Navy to William Eden of the Carlisle Peace Commissioner (1778):

> I have no money, no provisions, nor indeed any account of the sailing of the
> Cork fleet, nor admiral that I can have the least dependence on. In short,
> I have nothing left but the hope for better times and a little more attention![3]

British forces in theater relied on local foraging for food and fodder. Arthur Bowler nicely summarizes this troublesome connection between the need to forage, the danger of irregular force attack, and, ultimately, the relationship to the local population's loyalties:

> To obtain supplies it needed, the British army was forced throughout the war to engage in extensive forage operations. This allowed the often untrained rebel forces to fight the kind of battles for which they were best suited, and the brutality of these operations drove more and more Americans to the rebel side.[4]

A study by the United States Army Command and General Staff College captures the essence of the British logistical problem in America caused by distance and inefficient organization:

> The organization of the British administrative system was complex and initially ill suited for sustaining a war so far from England. The decentralized, civilian-led bureaucracy that effectively maintained far-flung colonies during times of relative peace was not prepared to support its army in a hostile environment. The lack of integration between the warfighting strategy and logistical design ensured that the army would suffer from a lack of provisions and supplies. Interagency cooperation was nonexistent . . . which compounded the inefficient use of transportation and other valuable resources. Corruption and profiteering simply made matters worse. These inadequacies formed a very unstable base for the entire logistics framework that extended from London and Cork to British garrisons in the colonies.[5]

Illustrative of the desperate supply situation is the commentary of Captain Robert Rotton in a letter to Lord Amherst:

> Our army moulders away amazingly: many die by the sword, many by sickness, brought on by bad provisions. . . . I wish government would look after the contractors, for without we are supplied with wholesome necessaries of life, it cannot be expected we will long fight their battles.[6]

## The War Machine

Given the nature of the British government in the late eighteenth century, the key to the effectiveness and efficiency of any British military undertaking lay in the talent of the responsible Secretary of State. Piers Mackesy's succinct description captures the essence of the role: "It was they who powered the war machine. They provided at once a Cabinet Secretariat and executive supervision. By their hands the complex of supply and transport, military movement and naval preparation was drawn together and given life."[7] Unfortunately for British field commanders, Lord George Germain, the Secretary of State for the Americas and the official charged with the suppression of the rebellion, lacked the extraordinary capabilities required to achieve victory in an irregular, unconventional, distant colonial war. Though noted for his administrative ability but not well liked, he lacked political support in Parliament, which might have overcome some obstacles. Germain often refused to cooperate, compromise, or accept expert advice. The Secretary felt that he had no role in operational planning or even military strategy and thus typically left all such planning to the field commanders. Germain saw his role as limited to that of the appointment of commanders, resource allocation and movement, and supply organization. However, he often suggested strategic and operational directions to field commanders, a habit that lacked the precision of definitive orders, further confusing and muddling strategic coherence.

A common sentiment in London as the rebellion dragged on advocated "One Great Director"—a war leader like William Pitt in the previous war, who could direct the machinery of British military administration, strategy, and operations. Though Germain's role was to oversee the war effort, he failed to pull all entities together for the common purpose. Mackesy says of Germain: "For all his talents, he lacked the magic gift . . . the power to frighten and inspire."[8] Germain's unrealistic expectations led to his undermanning forces in America, while simultaneously demanding results totally unachievable, given the war's nature, context, and geography. Clinton constantly complained of the Secretary's lack of support for troop needs coupled with unachievable expectations. Germain's most serious problem lay in his poor relations with the First Lord of the Admiralty and the Royal Navy.[9] When the nature of the conflict demanded cooperative, joint army-navy operations, and strategic planning, an adversarial relationship dominated. William Knox strongly advised him to take more positive control of the naval situation:

> to the insufficiency of their [Admiralty's] Instructions, when no directions are given them, much of our delays and disappointments are owing and if your Lordship does not determine to give the orders yourself instead of leaving it to Lord Sandwich . . . things will never be better.[10]

Germain did not press field commanders on operational details until after the war began to go badly. By this time, the profoundly weakened Lord Frederick North government lacked the power to make substantial changes in the status quo and force closer army-navy cooperation.

Complicating the problems of an adversarial, uncooperative joint relationship in the colonies, the less-than-adequate leadership of Vice-Admiral Marriott Arbuthnot, Royal Navy commander in North America during the early period of the Southern Campaign, deserves mention. William Willcox described the admiral as: "vacillating, irascible, and timid; his strategic sense was usually meager, and his tactical ideas . . . were in the worst tradition of the period."[11] Clinton feuded with

Arbuthnot over operational coordination for well over a year before the Admiralty acceded to his demands to replace him. Illustrative of the poisoned relations between the two commanders, Clinton referred to Arbuthnot as "an Old Dotard."[12]

From a strategic cohesion viewpoint, British decision-making suffered from a Secretary at War with ill-defined responsibilities; a Secretary of State charged with executing strategic direction who failed to coordinate the war effort effectively; and an Admiralty reluctant to cooperate with Cabinet and army officials. The constitutional arrangements for military and strategic matters from the political authority to operational field commanders consistently hobbled efforts to achieve victory. B. D. Bargar, Lord Dartmouth's biographer, captures the inefficiency and ineffectiveness of the American Department even before Germain arrived:

> The American Department continually suffered from certain constitutional defects and personality conflicts which prevented it from becoming a strong, permanent branch of the government. Until colonial policy could be concentrated in a modern Colonial Office, decisions which affected America were often taken in other offices or in cabinet meetings where Dartmouth was only one of five or seven ministers.[13]

As to the overall inadequacy of the Cabinet in prosecuting the war, Andrew J. O'Shaughnessy captures the problem:

> The consequence of North's leadership was a divided Cabinet that postponed decisions and often left military goals nebulous. In what he called government by departments, North was surrounded by strong personalities in the Cabinet who feuded with one another and pursued conflicting initiatives.[14]

Ultimately, the corrosive effect of Germain's strategic mismanagement complicated field operations. Alan Valentine captures the impact of the Secretary's actions:

> Thus as the year 1780 drew to an end, Lord George Germain had reduced his last commanding general [Sir Henry Clinton] in America to something like psychotic and military impotence. He had also aroused and stimulated enmity between Clinton and Cornwallis, and had encouraged Cornwallis to feel almost independent of his military commander. . . . If mutual trust and good will between statesmen and generals are essential to victory, Lord George had chosen a curious way to win a war.[15]

John Robinson, the Secretary to the Lords of the Treasury in 1777, captured the essence of the lack of a dominant and talented war leader and the inefficiencies of the chaotic Cabinet, stating:

> War can't be carried out in departments: there must be a consultation, union, and a friendly and hearty concurrence in all the several parts, which set the

springs at work and give efficacy and energy to the movements, without which the machine must fail.[16]

## Women and the American War

Women played a vital role. While relatively few took part in military operations as "camp followers," as men marched off to their respective forces, women and children maintained farms and businesses. Women formed knitting, spinning, and sewing clubs to supply clothing to the troops. In some locations, women manufactured saltpeter, a key ingredient of gunpowder. During the conflict, women often served as spies, the most notable was part of the Culper spy ring on Long Island, New York, which supplied intelligence of British troop movements and activities around New York City. Unfortunately, that lady's identity remains unknown to history. Women also participated in street protests against Loyalists and their interests, and, prior to the outbreak of military operations, in the anti-British protests and boycotts such as the anti-importation actions and events (e.g., the Edenton, North Carolina "Tea Party," 25 October 1774). One commentator, aghast at the overt political activities of New England women, commented: "A certain epidemical phrenzy runs through our fair country women which outdoes all the pretended patriotic virtues of the more robustic males."[17] Despite such protestations, many women became more outspoken on political matters, much to the chagrin of those who believed that women's role was purely domestic and familial.

Continental Army officers' wives in camp, particularly the more senior officers, were not uncommon even in harsh environments, such as the winter encampments at Valley Forge and Morristown. Martha Washington often wintered over with the general. Many officers' wives devoted time to knitting and sewing for the troops as well as partaking in a lively social scene. Balls, formal dinners, and dances occurred regularly, often as a match-making venue for senior officers' or local public officials' daughters and eligible junior officers. As an example, Alexander Hamilton, future cabinet secretary and light infantry commander, became engaged to the daughter of Major General Philip Schuyler at one such soiree. While the more senior wives lived relatively well during the winter months, many enlisted and junior officer wives joined their husbands when the armies were stationary and endured the harsh conditions alongside the troops. A few stayed with their husbands throughout the year and "followed" the army on campaign, hence the term, "camp follower." While that term has taken on the pejorative of prostitution, in the period, it simply meant wives and children, typically of the officer and senior non-commissioned officer ranks, who accompanied the force in camp and in the field, often serving in auxiliary roles as cooks, nurses, sutlers (merchants supplying the force), seamstresses, and other typically domestic endeavors.

John Ferling estimates that camp followers totaled about 3 percent of the total number of troops that served throughout the conflict.[18] The number of camp followers with the Continental forces represented a change that disturbed many senior officials. Given the traditional British anti-standing army attitudes, a direct holdover from the British Civil Wars and English Revolution experiences of the previous century as well as the centuries-old balance of power struggle between a centralizing monarchy and a country aristocracy jealous of their domains and governing prerogatives, that attitude is not surprising. The anti-standing army philosophy easily transferred across the Atlantic and took root in the colonies. North American colonists were expected to serve in the local militia commanded by local notables. When military force was required, as it was in the Mother Country, local militia stood up and marched to the fray. Notables such as Samuel and John Adams objected to a standing army as detrimental to liberty. Samuel Adams claimed that such a permanent force represented a threat to individual liberty. Cousin John Adams took an even dimmer view, believing that a man who would voluntarily enlist for long service was one of the "meanest, idlest, most intemperate and worthless" member of society.[19] George Washington, keenly aware of the need to depict the Continental Army as a temporary force of patriotic volunteers and not a standing army, viewed women in the field as a potential detriment and gave the impression of permanency or at least a long-term enlistment, rather than a citizen force raised for a short-term emergency. More practically, not only would women with the army represent a drain on the already paltry supplies, he saw them as "a clog upon every movement."[20]

But, reality being what it is, Washington had to accommodate the practice of wives and families in camp and on the march. Ferling provides a working estimate of up to 400 women at the 1777–1778 Valley Forge winter encampment. Despite his qualms, Washington came to accept their presence and eventually women and daughters were provided rations from the quartermaster stores at the rate of one woman for every 15 soldiers. Camp followers often supplemented their income by taking in laundry for a small fee. Other paid tasks included soap making, herding cattle, and tending to livestock. Enlisted wives might be hired as laundresses, cooks, and housekeepers. In a battle's aftermath, they also served as nurses assisting the surgeons with the wounded. In combat, women provided a vital function as water carriers not only to parched, thirsty troops but to the artillery. After each shot, the gun barrel had to be swabbed with a wet sponge to extinguish any remaining embers. Thus, a continuous water supply was vital. That aspect of female service led to the famous tale of Mary Ludwig Hayes, wife of a Pennsylvania artilleryman. Known as a rough, earthy woman, she rushed buckets of swabbing water to her husband's gun. Known in legend as "Molly Pitcher," when her husband went down with a deadly wound at Monmouth Courthouse, she reputedly took his place in the gun crew, an act that earned her an honorary sergeant's warrant from General Washington. True or not, the Molly Pitcher story underlines the critical role of women and families as vital auxiliaries for the armies whether in camp, winter quarters, or the field.

Sutlers—merchants who supplied various goods to the troops such as clothing, shoes, food and drink items, tobacco, and so forth—did a lively trade in the army camps providing little comforts to the soldiers. Sutlers might hire out family members to augment their staff. To control the prices and availability of goods, especially alcohol, the Continental Army licensed these merchants and determined their price structure, operating times, and locations. Inevitably, where a military force is posted, from time immemorial, women of a certain profession hawked their wares. Called "kippen" by the Continental troops, prostitutes operated on the encampment periphery. Near urban areas such as Philadelphia and New York, soldiers on leave or liberty could travel into town. Rural encampments proved most problematic; nonetheless, enterprising ladies still did a fair trade among the often bored, young soldiery far from home. Prostitutes found inside a camp would typically be unceremoniously expelled to the drum cadence of the "Whore's March" often with shaven head.

British forces had a long-standing history of camp following. It is estimated that women camp followers numbered perhaps as many as 10 percent of the total of British soldiers engaged in the war. This dynamic is not at all surprising in that as a volunteer professional force, troops often served for years on duty in some portion of the Empire far from home and hearth. Due to the high numbers of women and on remote stations, the Crown logistical system accounted for their presence and allotted enough rations to support six women per company. While on paper, a British infantry company fielded 80–100 men plus officers, musicians, and so on, the reality meant that a typical company on field service might be much smaller due to the normal combat and service attrition. Thus, even six female family members constituted a hefty percentage of those associated with the force. British Army camp followers performed the same functions as their Continental Army counterparts. Whether Patriot or Crown, the women of the armies lived a hard life alongside the soldiery.

## Slavery, African Americans, and the American War

For Africans in bondage, the war presented a brief but fleeting opportunity for freedom. An estimated half a million black slaves lived in the North American colonies at the war's start. With promises of emancipation if they supported the Crown forces, thousands of slaves fled farms and plantations. Clinton in his capacity as CinC issued a proclamation on 30 June 1779 promising freedom for slaves who fled their rebel owners. By early July 1780 with the capture of Charleston, South Carolina by Crown forces, over a thousand runaway slaves had fled for safety behind British lines. As the field commander in the South following Clinton's departure in June, Lord Charles Cornwallis enlisted hundreds of runaway slaves in the Crown service, mostly as laborers. Many became part of the pioneer and sapper units, the eighteenth-century troops responsible for road clearing, construction, and such vital military engineering tasks. An estimated 20,000 black slaves owned by Patriot masters escaped to British lines throughout the war. Many died of the usual causes of disease and not a few were re-captured and returned to their masters. Nonetheless, an estimated 10,000 freed slaves departed in 1783 with the British evacuations.

Attempts at raising slaves and freed blacks to fight for the Crown erupted early. John Murray, 4th Earl of Dunmore, Royal Governor of Virginia, raised the Ethiopian Regiment in Tidewater Virginia. In November 1775, Dunmore proclaimed that all slaves and indentured servants who enlisted in the Crown forces would be totally freed from their contractual obligations and servitude. Appeals went out to all groups, including runaway slaves and Indians. Norfolk became a refuge. An estimated 800 or more runaway slaves formed the Ethiopian Regiment with white officers and senior non-commissioned officers. The unit saw action first in November at the Battle of Kemp's Landing (present-day Virginia Beach, Virginia). With a potent force supplemented by two companies of regulars (14th Regiment of Foot), Dunmore sought to inflict great economic pain on land and business owners in rebellion. The quest ended in defeat at the Battle of Great Bridge, south of Norfolk, on 9 December 1775 in which the Ethiopian Regiment participated and suffered casualties. Subsequently, Dunmore fled to New York with roughly 500 black soldiers. Although disbanded in 1776, many former Ethiopian soldiers continued serving the Crown, particularly in the pioneer units based in New York. Following the evacuation of all Crown forces in 1783, many black veterans migrated to Canada, especially Nova Scotia and Newfoundland. The Dunmore policy failed unequivocally. Richard Henry Lee commented on the reaction of Virginians to Crown black recruitment: "Lord Dunmore's unparalleled conduct in Virginia has . . . united every man in that large Colony [against the British]."[21]

Further South, freedom for those runaway slaves who served the Crown proved especially appealing. In the first attack on Savannah in September 1778, Quamino Dolly, a former slave of deposed Royal Governor James Wright, showed the invading force a pathway around the Patriot right flank, an action that precipitated a stunning Crown victory and Savannah's capture. The city then became the linchpin of Crown activities in the South until Charleston fell to siege in May 1780. With the coming of the Southern Campaign, many landowners fled their estates leaving black slaves behind. With the promise of freedom offered by the British, thousands joined the Crown forces or served in auxiliary roles as cooks, scouts, spies, laundresses, nurses, and butchers. An estimated 1,500 former slaves fled into British lines within a few months of the Savannah occupation. In Virginia, as Lord Cornwallis thrashed about the countryside prior to taking station at Yorktown, an estimated 4,000 runaway slaves came into the British camps. Not all who came under British control gained freedom. Under a British commission, many slaves continued as property of the plantations abandoned by Patriot owners. British authorities also refused to free any slaves owned by Loyalists. Physical support in some form for the Crown cause trumped any altruistic notions of slave emancipation.

The specter of a massive slave revolt and of runaway blacks serving the Crown in great numbers especially terrified Southern Patriots. Continental Army leaders understood the value of this dynamic in terms of alleviating the Crown logistics and manpower problem. Congressman John Henry of Maryland wrote: "[T]he greatest source of Danger [to the Patriot cause] . . . is the accession of strength they [Crown forces] will receive from the black inhabitants." Others realized the danger to the British of enlisting blacks, whether runaway slaves or freedmen. South Carolinian Edward Rutledge commented that Dunmore's actions would "more effectively . . . work an external separation between Great Britain and the Colonies . . . than any other expedient."[22] Indeed, although relatively few blacks were armed and brought into Crown military units in the South after 1778, the damage was done. A Loyalist captured the frustration over the British practice of employing Indians and blacks, commenting that:

> The lower part of the people . . . particularly in South Carolina, originally attached to the British Government, have suffered so severely, & been so frequently deceived, that Great Britain has now a hundred enemies, where it had one before.[23]

Several freed blacks served in the Patriot forces besieging Boston, and many fought at Bunker Hill but could not formally enlist in the new Continental Army. The New England colonies recruited some 200 black soldiers for the Boston siege before Washington prohibited their enlistment. In reaction to Dunmore's proclamation, Washington responded by allowing black recruitment. Congress, still wary of the implications, required service in the besieging force at Cambridge to formally enlist. Congressional efforts to exclude or at least limit black enlistment continued throughout the war; however, manpower demands made a mockery of those efforts. Simply put, the Continental Army, continually struggling with limited enlistments and the normal travails of a period organized military force—desertion, combat casualties, and disease—needed able-bodied troops willing to fight. By summer 1778, as the Continental Army matured into a potent fighting force, regimental muster returns across the army show an average of 54 blacks serving in each brigade.[24] In the South, French forces under the *compte* D'Estaing in the failed October 1779 Patriot-French attempt to recapture Savannah, included the 600-man Volunteers of San Domingo, the first free black unit in the French Army along with over a hundred West Indian Volunteers.

As many as 5,000 African Americans served in the Continental Army throughout the war. While initially prohibited by Congress from formally serving, by 1779 with the growing manpower shortage, many states actively recruited blacks into the state regiments. Many were runaways from their masters or already freedmen; some were recruited as substitutes, an ancient practice in Europe whereby a substitute was hired in place of someone not desirous of serving. Many substitutes were slaves offered freedom at war's end for their service. Most notably was the 1st Rhode Island Regiment composed of white officers but made up of former slaves or freedmen. With numbers desperately low, General James Varnum of Rhode Island proposed combining two Rhode Island Continental Line regiments into one and sending the officers out as recruiters. Though initially reluctant, Washington forwarded the proposal on to the state and at least 250 black soldiers enlisted for the war's duration in the newly amalgamated 1st Rhode Island Regiment. Seeing the success of "Little Rhody," neighboring Connecticut and Massachusetts followed suit. By August 1778, almost 800 blacks served in the Continental Army, mostly in segregated, but many in integrated units. As the war progressed and the natural attrition of disease, end of enlistments, battle casualties, desertions, and so on exacerbated the manpower problem, more black soldiers enlisted and served admirably in the Patriot forces. By the end of the war, as many as 10 percent made up the Continental Army soldiery. In late 1780, Virginia (and earlier in South Carolina), seeing the dearth of young white men joining the Continental Army, the legislature proposed providing a slave and 100 acres of land to each white recruit. The effort failed to raise many more enlistees and the system of providing a slave as a substitute on condition of freedom at war's end persisted. Despite the roadblocks to black soldiers in the Patriot forces, the ones that did serve did so admirably. On the march from New York to Virginia in late summer, 1781, one French officer commented on the high number of blacks in the Continental force: "a quarter of them were negroes, merry confident, and sturdy."[25]

## Native American Indians

American Indian alliances proved a thin reed upon which to craft a successful pacification strategy. As the war progressed, efforts to incorporate Indian allies into operations added little to the Crown's chances for victory, most notably in the Hudson Valley campaign of 1777 and the South early in the struggle. That effort resulted in the destruction of the Cherokee in the Carolinas in 1776. There were some successes in bringing in Indian forces, For example, the Mohawks under Joseph Brant, traditional British allies, saw the maintenance of British colonial sovereignty as the only hope for the restoration of their traditional tribal lands and for restraining the westward settler movement. Brant even raised a unit called Brant's Volunteers, a mixed Loyalist and Mohawk unit that terrorized Patriot communities. Despite efforts to raise forces from among the upper New York and Canadian tribes, little recruitment resulted. One reason lay in Sir Guy Carleton's attitude. As governor-general of Canada, he refused to enlist Indians for fear that such action would rile up Hudson Valley and frontier residents. He had cause for concern. Any hint of Indians acting on the Crown's behalf stirred the populace against the Crown all along the "Indian Boundary." In the South, British Indian agent John Stuart commented: "Nothing can be more alarming than the idea of an Attack from Indians and Negroes."[26]

Still, as the war evolved, Crown officials attempted to employ their tribal allies but ultimately to no real gain. Seeing no advantage to allying with either side, many tribes such as the Six Nations confederation in the Mohawk Valley region vainly attempted to remain neutral. But, by 1779, a savage war engulfed the northwestern frontier (modern Western New York and Pennsylvania). A bitter internecine civil war with Indians and Tories on one side against Patriots and their Indian allies brutalized the frontier settlements. Killing, burning dwellings, rape, razing homes and fields, and stealing livestock, actions carried out by both sides, roiled the frontier resulting in the Sullivan Expedition of 1779 against the Iroquois Confederation.

The majority of tribes that chose to ally with either the Crown or Patriot side chose George III. The reasons seem clear—the crown at least attempted to protect traditional lands from colonial expansion and economic exploitation. Conversely, a Patriot victory could only escalate the westward-moving incursions. Some tribes such as the Oneida in New York and the Catawbas in Piedmont North and South Carolina sided with the Patriots and took an active part in military operations at Ninety Six and Stono and provided supplies to the partisans. The Catawbas paid dearly for their participation. British forces destroyed villages, homes, and crops. As Ferling points out, "[T]he common thread in Indian Experience in the Revolution was loss."[27] Aside from battlefield casualties, American Indian tribes lost land, homes, and crops. Brant and some followers did flee to Canada, but most tribes whether siding with the Patriots or the Crown lost all. With the Peace of Paris in 1783 and ultimate Patriot victory, the destruction of the Eastern American Woodland Indian culture and independence soon followed.

## Economics of the American War

The war devastated the American economy. The most heinous problem was inflation, typically caused by too many entities chasing too few goods or services. Thus, the currency devalues as prices rise, causing economic chaos. There is an expression from the period to the effect that something is "not worth a Continental," meaning the value of the Continental dollar was nil. There was no real backing for the currency issued by Congress or individual states. Vendors, suppliers, sutlers, and merchants demanded hard cash.

One of the principal precipitants of the revolt was economic. The Navigation Acts, implemented first in the 1650s, required that certain colonial trade, particularly the more valuable agricultural commodities, pass first through British ports where tariffs were paid and then transferred to other hulls for transport to locales such as Spanish America or the continent. Other trade goods might go directly. All goods originating from the European continent had to pass first through British ports and pay a tariff, which certainly aided royal revenue, but drove up prices. The Acts effectively closed colonial ports to much of the valuable foreign trade. Additionally, many trade and tariff laws sought to protect Home Island industries from North American competition. Other trade restrictions evolved with the mercantilist system. Based on the zero-sum game economic theory, mercantilism holds that the world's wealth is finite and the only way to expand one's piece of the wealth pie is at another's expense. Thus, trade was highly regulated and controlled, a dynamic that aggravated colonial merchants desirous of breaking into the Spanish and other markets. While this description is simplistic and certainly does not address all the aspects of mercantilism, the point here is that colonists (e.g., southerners providing commodities such as timber, naval stores, rice, indigo, and tobacco) were agitated by the trade restrictions. And, all colonists likely objected to the price of manufactured goods from Britain. In short, trade restrictions played a large role in firing colonial discontent along with taxes, parliamentary interference in local govern-ance, admiralty courts, and the raft of post-Seven Years' War complaints.

States raised taxes for military expenses. Congress, without the ability to tax at the national level, could not help the states resulting in a chronic shortage of mili-tary funding. Owing to a number of factors, not just economic, by early 1781, the Continental Army was near dissolution. Even with the injection of French funds, the army was always short of money for such basics as uniforms, victuals, and all manner of logistics. Congress proved particularly inept at providing basic necessi-ties to the forces, particularly in the Commissary and Quartermaster Departments. Although Major General Nathanael Greene did a magnificent job as Continen-tal Army quartermaster-general during the harsh times at the Valley Forge and Morristown winter encampments, he barely kept the army logistically afloat. Alan Taylor aptly describes the problems: "confusion, corruption, and incompetence brought rancid meat, spoiled flour, or nothing at all to the encampments. For want of proper uniforms, soldiers often looked like ragged beggars."[28]

In response to the fiscal crises, Congress and the states printed paper currency, essentially a promissory note for later payment. Not surprisingly, hyperinflation followed. Price controls, sale of sequestered Loyalist property, and penalties for refusal to accept the paper currency as legal tender all followed to prop up the paper currency. Riots and attacks on merchants erupted as inflation roiled the populace. By late 1779, the value ratio of a Continental dollar to gold stood at 100 to one. Desperate measures ensued. In March 1780, Congress declared that 40 Continental dollars equaled one gold dollar. Woe to the common soldier who had been paid in Continental dollars. Woe to the small farmer who had supplied the forces with goods and services and had been paid in the hyper-inflated Continentals. And woe to those merchants that were owed in Continentals. Though the intent was to choke off the increasing inflation and stabilize the currency, one can only imagine the economic chaos. Venders eventually demanded hard currency or double the price in Continentals for goods and services. Washington lamented on the soldier's plight: "The long and great sufferings of this army is unexampled in history."[29]

The British blockade, porous at best but nonetheless hurtful to the Ameri-can economy, made the formerly abundant British and imperial trade goods dear. While smuggling still went on, especially in New England, with British forces controlling key seaborne trade ports at various times, including Boston, Newport, New York, Philadelphia, Wilmington, Charleston, and Savannah, trade in quantity ceased. As an example of the tremendous expansion in commerce between the col-onies and Britain, total trade from the colonies to the Mother Country from 1700 to 1775 expanded seven times. As with all financial and economic crises, specula-tors and price gougers ran rampant. Washington expressed his disgust at those who took advantage of the country's economic woes. He stated bluntly:

> I would to God that one of the most atrocious of each State was hung in Gib-bets upon a Gallows. . . . No punishment . . . is too great for the man who can build his greatness upon his Country's ruin.[30]

By 1781, price controls collapsed. Merchants and farmers often refused to sell goods and services at a loss, thus spiraling inflation even higher. One by one, Congress and the states ceased printing the worthless currency and required debt and tax payments in hard cash (coinage). With a low money supply of hard currency, one sees the obvious trouble. Debts could not be paid, creditors lost out as hyperinflation exploded. Inevitably, the inflation balloon burst and deflation set in crashing markets, particularly for farm products. To pay debt interest, taxes soared to, in some places, three or four times the pre-war rates. Desperate citizens sold their promissory notes for desperately low prices. The result was catastrophic. To then pay the new holders of the debt the full value of the promissory note (their right to demand), taxes soared. Former debt owners then had to cover the cost of the notes they had just sold for pittance on the dollar. A massive recession rocked the post-war economy.

Following the Peace, upward of 60,000 Loyalists departed, a further blow to the shaky economy. Many Loyalists had been substantial farmers and merchants and thus consumers of products from farms and businesses. Many settled in Canada and the West Indies. Some returned to Britain or Ireland. Others, particularly from the South, migrated to East or West Florida despite the fact that the Floridas reverted to Spain in the settlement. Both colonies remained loyal throughout and offered safe haven to deposed Loyalists. With an estimated 25,000 deaths in military service throughout the conflict (primarily disease), with farms and businesses devastated, families bereft of the primary earner, and trade disrupted, the economic devastation was profound. American national income declined by as much as a third by the late 1780s.

It is beyond the scope of this study to address in depth the economic aspects of the American War; nonetheless, readers should bear in mind that economics often determine attitudes, actions, prejudices, and in this case, many loyalty choices. A recent US election slogan captures the criticality of economics: "It's the economy, stupid!" By the 1790s, the economy rebounded dramatically. Trade resumed with Britain in even greater quantities of goods bought and sold. Professor Adam Smith's "invisible hand" of free market economics whereby each individual strives to improve his economy benefits the economy as a whole increasingly dominated economic activity.[31] Secretary of the Treasury Alexander Hamilton stabilized and restored confidence in the currency. State debts, absorbed by the new Federal Government with the power to raise taxes, allowed the reduction in state tax rates. The Wars of the French Revolution and Napoleon roiled the continent but brought expanding markets for American goods, especially in Spanish America as Spain descended into chaos. In short, within a decade after the guns of Yorktown fell silent, the American economy blossomed once again.

## Notes

1  Cornwallis to Clinton, Yorktown, Virginia, 20 October 1781, *Cornwallis Correspondence,* NA CC PRO 30/11/74/105; *Letter Books of the Colonial Office* (National Archives, Kew, UK) CO5/103/268.

2 From 90K personnel in 1763 to 16K by 1775; from 100 ships-of-the-line in 1763 to 66 in 1775, many of which were old, decrepit, and in bad repair. For example, after the French entered the war in March 1778, the Royal Navy had 41 percent of its assets on American station with 47 percent in European waters. By 1779, only 9 percent remained on American station with 33 percent in the West Indies. Thus, a difficult situation in terms of supplying convoy escorts from Britain became far more complicated.

3 Clinton to Eden, New York, 1 September 1780, Sir Henry Clinton, *The American Rebellion: Sir Henry Clinton's Narrative of His Campaigns, 1775–1782, with an Appendix of Original Documents*, ed. William B. Willcox (New Haven, CT: Yale University Press, 1954; reprint, Hamden, CT: Archon, 1971), 456.

4 R. Arthur Bowler, "Logistics and Operations in the American Revolution," in *Reconsiderations on the Revolutionary War: Selected Essays, Contributions in Military History, Number 14*, ed. Don Higginbotham (Westport, CT: Greenwood Press, 1978), 71. For analysis of the British supply and logistical problems, see R. Arthur Bowler, *Logistics and the Failure of the British Army in America, 1775–1783* (Princeton, NJ: Princeton University Press, 1975). Other excellent studies on the logistical dynamics include David Syrett, *Shipping and the American War* (London: The Athlone Press, 1970); Norman Baker, *Government and Contractors: The British Treasury and War Supplies, 1775–83* (London: Athlone Press, 1971); and John Brewer, *The Sinews of Power: War, Money and the English State, 1688–1783* (New York: Alfred A. Knopf, 1989).

5 John R. Tokar, *Redcoat Resupply! Strategic Logistics and Operational Indecision in the American Revolutionary War, 1775–1783* (Fort Leavenworth, KS: Army Command and General Staff College, 1999), 16.

6 Rotton to Amherst, 12 February 1780, quoted in Alan Valentine, *Lord George Germain* (Oxford: Clarendon Press, 1962), 433.

7 Piers Mackesy, *The War for America, 1775–1783* (Lincoln, NE: University of Nebraska Press, 1992), 17.

8 Ibid., 54.

9 The best biography of the Earl of Sandwich and one that captures the essence of strategic leadership and coordination with the Cabinet, Germain, and the army, is N. A. M. Rodger, *The Insatiable Earl: A Life of John Montagu, Fourth Earl of Sandwich, 1718–1792* (New York: W. W. Norton & Company, 1993).

10 Knox to Germain, Whitehall, London, 31 October 1780, *HMC, Stop-Sack*, 2/215.

11 William B. Willcox, "The British Road to Yorktown: A Study in Divided Command," in *The American Historical Review* 52, no. 1 (October 1946): 3.

12 Quoted in Andrew Jackson O'Shaughnessy, *The Men Who Lost America: British Leadership, the American Revolution, and the Fate of the Empire* (New Haven, CT: Yale University Press, 2013), 232.

13 B. D. Bargar, *Lord Dartmouth and the American Revolution* (Columbia, SC: University of South Carolina Press, 1965), 164.

14 O'Shaughnessy, *Men Who Lost America*, 67.

15 Valentine, *Germain*, 375.

16 Quoted in Willcox. "Yorktown," 3.

17 Quoted in Alan Taylor, *American Revolutions: A Continental History, 1750–1804* (New York: W. W. Norton & Company, 2016), 111.

18 For a more in-depth look at the role of women in the war, see John Ferling, *Almost a Miracle: The American Victory in the War of Independence* (New York: Oxford University Press, 2007).

19 Quoted in Don Higginbotham, *The War of American Independence: Military Attitudes. Policies, and Practice, 1763–1789* (New York: Macmillan, 1971), 390.

20 Quoted in Ferling, *Almost a Miracle*, 129.

21 Quoted in Taylor, *American Revolutions*, 149.

22 Quoted in Ferling, *Almost a Miracle*, 325.

23 Quoted in Taylor, *American Revolutions*, 249.

24 From unit muster returns for August, 1778 as cited in Robert Leckie, *George Washington's War: The Saga of the American Revolution* (New York: HarperPerenial, 1993), 181.
25 Quoted in Ferling, *Almost a Miracle*, 523.
26 Quoted in Taylor, *American Revolutions*, 228.
27 Ferling, *Almost a Miracle*, 578.
28 Taylor, *American Revolutions*, 196.
29 Quoted in Leckie, *George Washington's War*, 506.
30 Ibid., 505.
31 Adam Smith, *An Inquiry into the Nature and Causes of the Wealth of Nations* (London: W. Strahan and T. Cadell, 1776).

# PART I

# Blowing the Matches

# 1

# "IN A FIT OF ABSENCE OF MIND"

> The Revolution was effected before the War commenced. The Revolution was
> in the minds and hearts of the people; a change in their religious sentiments of
> their duties and obligations.[1]
>
> —*John Adams in a letter to Hezekiah Niles in 1818.*

The American Revolution may have shaken the world, but it did so as a slow,
deep tremor that still resonates today. Whether we consider the revolution to be
the open combat that began at Lexington Green and ended at Yorktown or the
broader social, religious, and intellectual transformation, as did Adams, the first
faint vibrations can be traced to the conflict that preceded the War of American
Independence. The Seven Years' War, popularly known in North America as the
French and Indian War, represented a conflict on a global scale. Fought across the
Indian Ocean, Mediterranean, West Africa, Atlantic Ocean, the Americas, and
Europe, the conflict left Britain "Master of the World" but also deeply in debt.[2]
It sheared France of its North American possessions, leaving it and Spain burning
for retribution. It also produced instability in the British colonies, both those long
established and those newly acquired. While the effects crossed lines of culture,
society, and economy, the origins were primarily military and arose from the manner in which the earlier war was fought and from the military requirements that
victory imposed.

## Seven Years' War

The Seven Years' War established Great Britain as the dominant Atlantic power.
It also set the stage for a continuing series of wars on the Indian sub-continent
that culminated with Arthur Wellesley's victory over the Maratha Confederacy

DOI: 10.4324/9781003041276-3

in 1803, which secured British control of India. While the Seven Years' War set Britain on a course to become the dominant, global maritime power, that rise was not without complications. The primary domestic problem for British leaders lay in the enormous debt incurred during the war. Both the army and navy had expanded enormously. Britain also earned a reputation as the "paymaster of Europe" by subsidizing Continental allies, forcing France to allocate resources to raising, equipping, and supplying its army, thus diverting her from concentrating on building a robust navy. Britain provided enormous sums to Prussia and indirectly to other French enemies. Additionally, the Crown spent vast sums to arm and pay colonial militia, troops more commonly employed in support activities rather than direct combat; the fiscal burden was significant, regardless of the assigned tasks. A massive shipbuilding program further taxed the Crown's financial resources. Naval estimates, the contemporary term for the naval budget, reached almost £5.9 million in 1762. Naval expenditures totaled over £6 million that year.[3] The tremendous increase in the navy's size saw a concomitant rise in the costs of manning the fleet, necessitating a huge number of sailors and a dramatic increase in the number of officers. While sailors were paid off at the end of their ship's commission and the government's financial obligation ended, the officers went ashore on half pay, a continuing burden on expenditure already stretched to the limit.

All told, the national debt at the end of the Seven Years' War stood at over £132 million, a staggering amount, particularly as Crown revenue amounted to only £8 million annually.[4] During Britain's eighteenth-century wars, between 75 and 85 percent of total national expenditures were dedicated to the army, navy, or paying off debt from earlier conflicts.[5] Aside from the monarchy's personal expenses, the only other considerable expenditures went to diplomatic efforts, largely associated with the conflict. The government under William Pitt committed to an unsustainable spending level to obtain French lands in the new world. The obvious corollary to this acquisition was that newly acquired territories needed to prove profitable enough to recover the incurred expenses. This dynamic created problems in itself, starting with the debate over which territories to keep and which to return to France and Spain in peace agreements.

Spanish and French possessions fell into two categories: the North American continent and islands in the Caribbean Basin. France lost Canada on the North American continent and a number of West Indies islands. Spain, conversely, did not suffer continental losses but saw British encroachments on its island possessions. The dilemma facing British diplomats negotiating the Treaty of Paris (1763) involved a decision as to which captured possessions to cede back to the defeated powers and what to demand in return. The "cabinet wars" of the seventeenth and eighteenth centuries were not fought to overthrow other great powers. The understanding implicit in this arrangement was that while some captured territory would be retained by the victor, some possessions would be returned. They were taken, in effect, to serve as bargaining chips in the peace negotiations. This idea was most famously articulated by the nineteenth-century military theorist Carl von Clausewitz in describing what he termed limited war.[6] Decisions regarding captured territory were hotly debated in Parliament.

In the aftermath of the twentieth century, to the United States, having twice served as the "arsenal of democracy" and with an industrial capacity that dwarfed the rest of the world at mid-century, it would seem that the retention of the continent at the expense of returning the islands would have been a simple decision. In 1763, however, the choice was not nearly so clear. Canada was primarily a source of furs brought to market by the *coeurs de bois*, traders who collected pelts from native hunters. Thinly populated and economically marginal, Canada often acted as a drain on French resources rather than a source of national wealth.[7] By contrast, the Caribbean "Sugar Islands" represented a source of enormous commercial wealth and served as the driving force behind an economically valuable, if morally repugnant, triangular trade system involving sugar products, slaves, and finished products. The final decision was to retain the French possessions on the North American continent proper. Several captured islands in the West Indies were surrendered to France. Spain recovered its island possessions and gained French Louisiana, but it did so at the expense of Florida, which became the British royal colonies of East and West Florida. This arrangement removed the pressing threat that bound the colonies to Britain and the constant fear of France and her Native American allies. While Cherokee, Mingo, Ottawa, and Potawatomi warriors, among others, still posed a significant threat to frontier communities, the withdrawal of direct French support limited the scope and extent of their raids. The departure of French forces greatly increased the security of the more densely settled areas along the coast. The origins of the revolt that erupted in Massachusetts in April 1775 lay in the military strategies employed sequentially to deal with the challenges created when French power on the North American continent was extinguished.

## A Fit of Absence of Mind

The American colonies, as with most of the British Empire of the time, were not acquired as a result of a grand design. Most were established by private companies or individuals operating under a Crown charter. Historian Sir John Robert Seeley wrote that England had "conquered and peopled half the world in a fit of absence of mind."[8] While written a century after the end of the American War, the assessment raises questions about how effectively any empire so acquired could develop an effective strategy for expansion or defense. British leaders faced a number of strategic challenges following the Seven Years' War. Having alienated allies on the European continent, the diplomatic environment in that quarter was decidedly unsettled. Stability in Europe was based on a balance of power. The alignment of the various great powers and a series of smaller states limited the extent of intramural contests among the European powers. Two factors radically changed this dynamic and unbalanced this system.

The first issue was the realignment that shuffled traditional alliances leading to the Seven Years' War. Prussia, traditionally a French ally, switched places with Austria, which now sided with France and Russia. King Frederick II of Prussia aligned his nation with Great Britain, at least as long as British subsidies continued to flow to Berlin. The decision in London to discontinue those subsidies further disrupted the tenuous equilibrium. British foreign policy traditionally relied on at least one continental ally and frequently an entire coalition. The objective had always been to prevent the strongest power in Europe from dominating the continent. British statesmen used naval power to exert pressure on colonial and economic interests while supporting continental allies financially and with small land force contingents. For almost a century, the main European rival had been France. The shift in allegiances sparked by the Seven Years' War and the subsequent cooling relationship between Britain and Prussia left London without an alliance partner except for the relatively weak German possessions of the British ruling house (notably, Hannover).

The other critical factor lay in the accumulation of overwhelming British influence outside of Europe. In acquiring possessions and concessions, London sparked both fear and jealousy in European capitals. These gains, primarily at the expense of France and Spain, were accomplished largely by a dominant Royal Navy without regard for the impact on the existing diplomatic balance. France and Spain were left burning for revenge. Most other European powers, greater and lesser, were concerned with the breadth and range of British acquisitions, and not just the acquisitions. The maritime dominance established by the Seven Years' War eventually led to the formation of the League of Armed Neutrality during the American War, another diplomatic complication.

Prussian alienation represented a problem of a different sort as it was the only remaining firm major power ally. Prussia, not likely to resume the earlier alignment with France, did not represent an active threat to Britain. It had no naval forces of note. But Prussia was uniquely positioned to provide a counterweight on the continent. During the American War, a conflict between Prussia and Austria erupted over the succession of the elector of Bavaria. A combination of reticence on the part of Frederick and a dedication by French leaders to remain aloof of continental entanglements eliminated the possibility that Britain could employ its preferred strategy of embroiling France in a continental war to siphon resources from the maritime and colonial struggle. Prussia was absorbed with the 1772 partition of Poland among Prussia, Austria, and Russia. The partition diverted the attention of the only remaining great power that could have changed the strategic dynamics in Europe as the crisis in North America evolved.

The final actor that might have altered the diplomatic and military balance was Austria. As a traditional British ally throughout the first half of the century, the Hapsburg Monarchy might have served as a useful strategic distraction by posing a threat to France from the east. Austria, however, had aligned with France against Prussia by mid-century. While changes in the period's diplomatic kaleidoscope seemed a regular feature of European politics, another shift did not benefit Britain. Like Prussia, Austria was absorbed with matters to the east. The acquisition of many smaller European states in the early 1770s left Austria with a host of ethnic and diplomatic issues more pressing than the far-off struggle between Britain and its rebellious colonies.

Britain acquired vast extra-European holdings as a result of the Seven Years' War, continuing a pattern of random imperial growth. In doing so, it also acquired a vast array of strategic problems while simultaneously diminishing any hope of support within Europe. George III and his loyal servant Lord North had to balance possible European challenges against the need to both protect and maintain control in the far-flung colonies. Doing so with strained finances proved challenging. Strategic mistakes by officials in North America created even greater trials (see Figure 1.1).

**FIGURE 1.1** King George III

*Source:* Courtesy of the Anne S.K. Brown Military Collection, Brown University Library, Providence, Rhode Island

## Dealing With Native Challenges

The first and greatest of the military problems facing Major-General Thomas Gage when he succeeded to command of His Majesty's forces in North America (1763) lay in dealing with the various Native American Nations, whether they fought for France, remained neutral, or sided with Britain. The challenges, as diverse as the peoples who posed them, ranged from open warfare to feeding large numbers of refugees from the fighting in the previous conflict. Overlaying these issues, the relentless pressure of colonists seeking land in the West regardless of royal proclamations prohibiting settlement sparked conflict with native populations and created friction with the Crown.

Some of the wounds suffered by the British government were self-inflicted, none more so than the "penny-wise, pound-foolish" approach that General Sir Jeffrey Amherst took in dealing with Native Americans who fought in Pontiac's Rebellion (1763). As the British commander during the final war years, his reversal of promises made by British authorities represented the root of the problem. Instigation by rogue French officials who either had not been informed or refused to accept the Peace of Paris terms contributed to violence as well. The most profound factor, however, lay in the complete revision of Indian diplomacy effected by the departure of French power from North America. As long as France maintained control of Upper and Lower Canada, various leaders of Indian nations had a wide variety of diplomatic options. The dichotomy between British and French philosophies regarding how the North American colonies were peopled and administered made France a more appealing partner to many Native leaders. Waves of British and German immigrant settlers pushed relentlessly westward. By contrast, French Canada was thinly peopled in part because French immigrants did so more in search of trade than for land.[9] These traders, the *coeurs de bois*, tended to live among the Indians, took local brides, and only disrupted the native lifestyle to the degree that their demand for pelts distorted the traditional hunting patterns. By contrast, English and later Scottish, German, and Irish migrants came primarily in search of agricultural land. In spite of the obvious threat posed by these British settlers, some Native American leaders sought accommodation or cooperation. In each case, they played off one imperial power against the other to retain as much sovereignty and land as possible. The Treaty of Paris ended most such maneuvering.

Contentious relations between settlers and the Native Nations in the South had a long history. The conflict along the southern frontier involving the Creek and Yamasee dated to the founding of South Carolina. Further north, the Cherokee warred with Native rivals to their north and south. Trading relationships with British colonies became a critical part of the Cherokees' ability to defend their territory. Despite this factor, open war with the southern colonies erupted. The Anglo-Cherokee War of 1761 is more properly classified as a part of the conflict between Britain and France, but it prepared the ground for a resumption of hostilities in 1776.

The Cherokee, an Iroquoian people living in a series of towns in Virginia, North and South Carolina, and Georgia, had a population about equal to that of

Georgia, although about 40 percent of Georgia's population was enslaved. Traditionally aligned with the British, the Cherokee clashed with Creek, Yamasee, and Choctaw who were aligned with either France or Spain as the situation suited them. Cherokee disaffection came as a swift and unexpected turn of events. The theft of horses by warriors traveling north to support British efforts sparked an escalating cycle of violence and reprisal. When South Carolina Governor William Henry Lyttleton undertook to force Cherokee leaders to surrender individuals involved, he precipitated open hostilities. The mercurial nature of the relationship between Indian Nations and the colonists was not unique to the southern frontier, but it was along that boundary that the change in the military and diplomatic balance was most evident.

The Catawba, another nation that traditionally relied on balancing diplomatically between the rival European powers and who resided along the river of the same name near the border between South and North Carolina, suffered a catastrophic decline. It was once among the most powerful of the southeastern tribes. Smallpox, encroachment by settlers, and constant wars with rival Indian nations reduced this proud people to dependency upon the settlers. Their fate became an object lesson for their regional rivals, a fate the Cherokee, Creek, Chickasaw, and other nations sought to avoid.[10] Unique conditions in the South may have led directly to hostilities, but common themes underpinned all of the conflicts, including Pontiac's Rebellion.

## Pontiac's Rebellion

During the Seven Years' War, a Leni Lenape Delaware religious leader known as Neolin began preaching a new doctrine that focused on returning to traditional practices. He rejected the use of alcohol, wished to end trade with whites, and sought a return to traditional forms of agriculture and hunting. His rise to prominence in Native communities coincided with his prophecy that a war approached between settlers and Natives.[11] As his influence spread, the Ottawa leader Pontiac became an avid convert.

By the spring of 1763, encroachments on Native lands in the Great Lakes Basin became increasingly widespread. In response, a meeting among war leaders of the Ottawa, Potawatomi, and Wyandots was convened at which Pontiac convinced fellow leaders that the time was propitious and that Fort Detroit should be the target. The planned surprise attack in April failed to take the fort. Instead, a siege ensued. Word of the siege circulated along with war belts, strings of beaded shells also known as *wampum*, which served as diplomatic overtures. Within weeks, of the British garrisons in the Northwest, only Forts Detroit, Niagara, and Pitt held out. Dozens of smaller posts and the blockhouses protecting the lines of communication had been overwhelmed.

By June 1763, Amherst faced a widespread revolt across the entire Trans-Appalachian region. He instructed Colonel Henry Bouquet, "The post of Fort Pitt, or any others commanded by officers, can certainly never be in danger from such a wretched enemy." Amherst could not have been more wrong. In June, he was still ordering commanders to hold posts such as Forts LeBoeuf, Venango, and Presque Isle, all lost already.[12] The siege intensity at remaining forts was directly related to how deep into former French territory it lay. Fort Pitt, at the Forks of the Ohio, the most heavily defended with the largest garrison, had a degree of early warning. The closest fort to the more heavily populated coast, it was the first to be reinforced and resupplied. The defenders also benefitted from two blankets deliberately given to Native visitors taken from the hospital where smallpox victims were being treated.

Bouquet, ordered by Amherst to take charge of the war in the West, was the British Army's most experienced practitioner of what today is called irregular warfare. The first task lay in raising a relief force. Much of the army had been disbanded following the conflict with France. Amherst could spare only one understrength regiment recently returned from the Caribbean. The end of the previous war freed troops for service in North America; however, he chose to send these troops to coastal cities. Bouquet had to make do with the meager force of just over 500 troops, a mix of regulars and provincials. Despite the dearth of numbers, victory at the Battle of Bushy Run (5–6 August 1763) broke the siege.[13] After the long string of disasters, it proved welcome news, but the respite was short-lived as a relief column for Fort Niagara was ambushed in September.

British attempts to pacify the West were further complicated by the behavior of Pennsylvania frontiersmen. During earlier North America conflicts, support from Native American factions was often critical. During King Philip's War, Mohegan, Mohawk, and Pequot intervention on the behalf of the British colonists turned the tide. The shift of the Six Nations of the Iroquois from neutrality to active support of British forces had a pronounced impact on the French and Indian War. In December 1763, however, settlers from Paxton, Pennsylvania, attacked Christianized Susquehannock Indians in the town of Conestoga and subsequently killed survivors who were under the protection of the colonial government in Lancaster. The frontiersman then marched on Philadelphia to hold the legislature accountable for failing to protect settlers along the frontier against earlier attacks for which the Susquehannocks had been wrongly blamed. Benjamin Franklin led a delegation to meet them at Germantown, northwest of the capital, to hear their grievances. The group dispersed.[14] The damage was already done. Sir William Johnson, Superintendent for Indian Affairs in the northern colonies and a key figure in negotiating Iroquois support for Britain, was already in negotiations with the Iroquois to prevent other members of the Six Nations from following the Western Seneca in aligning with Pontiac. These negotiations were complicated and delayed by the incident. Johnson eventually successfully negotiated the treaty of Fort Niagara in 1764, defusing the threat in western New York. Johnson's success also provided a contingent of Native American warriors for the ensuing dual campaigns that ended the rebellion.

Further west, the rebellion was broken by a combination of military maneuvering and diplomacy undertaken by Colonel John Bradstreet that led to negotiated settlements. Pontiac faced divided opinions among the rebellion leaders near Detroit, the majority of whom favored making peace. Pontiac initially refused peace overtures and did not attend the council but eventually sent a "peace belt," which Bradstreet destroyed with a hatchet to indicate his displeasure at the Ottawa leader's absence. This act, violating cultural norms to which French officials had adhered, complicated the negotiations.[15] Local leaders eventually agreed to a peace settlement in spite of the transgressions. Pontiac and some from the Illinois Country moved west across the Mississippi. Further south, Bouquet led an expedition that took a more punitive approach. It succeeded. George Croghan, William Johnson's deputy, was sent west in 1765 to negotiate a settlement with the holdouts, the principal feature of which was an agreement that British posts, as had been the case with the French posts, were in effect leased and did not confer ownership of the lands on which they were built.[16]

Pontiac has been portrayed as the guiding intelligence behind a pan-Indian war for independence from all of the European powers. Alternatively, he is depicted as a purely local leader whom historians later transformed into a more influential figure. The truth lies somewhere between these extremes. While "war belts" traveled widely through the region announcing the agreements to begin hostilities and the prophet preaching war to restore traditional practices was Leni Lenape Delaware, the links between the centers of rebellion were at best nebulous. Timing and distance also argue against Pontiac having influenced events at Forts Niagara and Pitt. He did, however, hold sway over those individuals with whom he came into personal contact. That impact diminished as the interests of the parties diverged. The relationships among the Native American leaders were not hierarchical, not one of patrons and clients. Complex dynamics dominated the interactions and, ultimately, interest outweighed personal considerations. Pontiac, unable to hold the local coalition together in the Great Lakes, saw his standing fade and collapse when he broke with leaders in the Illinois Country and agreed to terms with George Croghan. Never a single conflict driven by a national figure in the European sense, Pontiac's Rebellion represented a series of local conflicts that sought the same end, security from encroaching European settlement. Each segment of that struggle waxed and waned independently and did so for local reasons. Pontiac, and Neolin, the religious figure who inspired him, wielded influence that fluctuated with time and distance.[17]

Pontiac's War is often portrayed as the watershed event that created concern about the cost of maintaining an army in the colonies. As the narrative goes, that expense precipitated the parliamentary decision to levy taxes, which in turn sparked the rebellion. Like a series of dominoes falling one after another, each event was a link in a chain of events. The problem with the narrative was the diverse factors that led to each successive event. Rather than a singular path, a network of interconnected incidents influenced the growing dissension in the colonies. While a specific sequence might have led to the outbreak of hostilities, the result was more a function of the cumulative effects of varied events, at times only marginally related. The events leading to war were more like a complex demonstration in which multiple lines of dominoes converge to precipitate some spectacular collapse. Pontiac's War was one of a series of incidents that combined with many others to produce a synergistic effect.

## Paying the Cost

The fiscal toll of this rebellion was significant. But in the broader scheme, these expenses were only part of the equation. The annual cost of administering the colonies and maintaining the army in North America hit over £350,000 for 1763. Against the broader expenditures, amassing approximately £60 million in additional debt over a period of nine years, this sum is relatively low. By 1767, the portion for the entire British Army in the colonies represented a smaller figure still, particularly once budget constraints forced London to cut the force from 20 battalions to 15. Even a force so diminished proved an expensive proposition and amounted to roughly 4 percent of the entire national budget. The cost of dealing with the frontier was a separate matter. Of the 20 battalions, many were posted in company-sized units and only a fraction in areas contested in the recent rebellion or in disputed areas in the South. The majority remained in the more populated regions nearer the Atlantic coast, in Canada, or in West Florida.[18]

The allocation of military force raises more issues concerning the underlying Crown objectives in the North American colonies. In October 1763, the Grenville Ministry passed the Proclamation Act, effectively prohibiting settlement between the Appalachian Mountains and the Mississippi River. The proclamation spurred Lord Barrington, the Secretary at War, to question the need for even the limited troop assignment in the Trans-Appalachian West. He queried Gage on the reason for the garrisons in light of the prohibition on settlement. In response, Gage suggested that the forts prevented Indians from falling on the settlements east of the Appalachians. His primary rationale was that the traders operating in the region required monitoring. The various treaties that ended Pontiac's War stipulated a return to practices that pre-dated the outbreak and included lifting restrictions on trade goods between merchants and the tribes. Unscrupulous merchants used alcohol to induce questionable arrangements, particularly in the transfer of land.[19] Gage's response did have a ring of truth if only partially accurate.

The broader question concerned force distribution. Had fears of renewed rebellion been the driving factor, the regiments should have been posted in regions where rebellion had recently been suppressed. Surviving maps detailing the cantonment of British troops paint a very different picture. In the aftermath of Croghan's successful negotiations, four regiments were arrayed across the region where fighting had occurred. By contrast, four regiments occupied Quebec. Two more regiments garrisoned Nova Scotia with three posted to Florida.[20] Troop strength in Canada and Florida changed little in the ensuing months, but in the colonies originally settled by England, posts were established in coastal towns like Philadelphia and New York at the expense of garrisoning the interior.[21] These reallocations suggest that London's fears centered not upon further conflict with Native Americans but rather with mischief made by agents of European rivals in their former possessions and by British colonists. In the latter case, the fears were well founded.

## Taxation, Troops, and Unrest

Clearly, frontier security represented only part of the need for troops in the colonies. At the behest of British planters with interests in the West Indies, the 1733 Molasses Act imposed high duties on the importation of molasses from non-British sources to North America to provide British planters with a competitive advantage. The act suppressed *ad hoc* barter arrangements common between the British North American colonies and other European powers' island colonies. Many American merchants responded by smuggling in cheaper molasses. Whether by bringing the goods in surreptitiously or bribing customs officers, avoiding the taxes was commonplace. During the Seven Years' War, British officials proved particularly disinclined to alienate colonials as the success of the campaigns in the colonies depended largely on funding, manpower, and material support from the various colonial legislatures.

George Grenville sought to deal with the fiscal problems on becoming prime minister in 1763. When the Seven Years' War ended, the Grenville ministry asserted more control over the colonies. Taxation levied to recoup the costs of securing North America began while Pontiac's Rebellion still raged. From the official perspective in London, initial efforts appeared reasonable. The American Duties Act of 1764, often referred to in America as the Sugar Act, lowered duties on molasses and other sugars. Grenville sought to assert Parliament's right to control the colonies even more than he sought to raise revenue. The act, however, did far more than change the tax on various forms of sugar. The legislation added duties on a number of other commodities, including wine imported from Portugal and Spain. In doing so, it created a black market where none previously existed. Of greater concern to the colonists, it also changed the legal framework for enforcing these duties. It established severe penalties for customs officials who failed to enforce the laws. It allowed prosecutors to choose the legal venue for prosecutions. Previously, offenses were tried in local court. In Rhode Island, infamously dependent on smuggling, local citizens also involved in similar activities frequently failed to return a guilty verdict regardless of the evidence. Under the American Duties Act, the prosecutor could now opt for a vice-admiralty court in Halifax. Smugglers now faced impartial judges, not local juries. Operating from Canada, those judges would not be subject to local coercion.[22]

Another important change in the legal framework involved immunity for the customs men. The tendency of juries to nullify customs law proved inconvenient and costly for the government and economically devastating for those charged with enforcing the laws. Previously, defendants found not guilty had recourse to bring legal action against officials who brought the original charges. The American Duties Act granted an exemption for the customs officials provided they had reasonable cause for the original charges. It also denied defendants restitution for legal costs, even if found not guilty. An earlier law commissioned naval officers to serve as customs officers and provided handsome rewards out of the proceeds of seized goods.[23] In colonial societies deeply imbued with a sense of rights and obsessed with legal precedent, these new laws were of greater concern than the tax itself.[24] In short, the taxation represented a threat to the self-government that had existed since the colonization at Jamestown, Virginia, in 1607. The American Duties Act merely raised the curtain on a succession of attempts to establish control through revenue measures.

In addition to levying a tax on sugar in 1764, Parliament outlawed the use of paper currency for private debts in colonies south of New England. Specie was in short supply in the colonies; officials looked the other way when colonial legislatures issued paper currency during the recent war. In New England, legislatures backed the paper currency with gold and silver reserves. In other colonies, most notably Virginia, colonial treasuries made no such provisions. Complicating the problem, the law was not a product of ministry policy but was forced through by merchant Members of Parliament (MPs) who feared that inflation might result in colonial debtors settling their accounts with worthless colonial paper currencies. Customs officials who interpreted the statute as also barring the payment of public debts with colonial paper money exacerbated the problem. The ambiguities created more problems than they solved.

## Sparking Paramilitary Organization

The Stamp Act sought to establish authority in the colonies by imposing the will of Parliament through a direct tax. But, it intended to raise only a fraction of the defense and administrative costs. Stamp acts were not new devices for raising revenue. Originally conceived in the United Provinces in the seventeenth century, it raised revenue by requiring an embossed seal on certain documents, affixed after the duty had been paid.[25] Imported to Britain during the "Glorious Revolution of 1688," it was first imposed in England in 1694 and then only on vellum. Products to which the duty was applied gradually expanded over time and by 1712 included newspapers and pamphlets.[26] The tax expansion did elicit some political opposition, more so because the duty was alleged to suppress outlets that did not support the ministry. The tax regime's gradual imposition in Britain may have accounted for the paucity of resistance, but such was not the case in America.

As with so many ill-conceived policies regarding the colonies, the Stamp Act united disparate elements of colonial society. Individual colonies generally had stronger ties to London than to each other. In this instance, politically active New Englanders made common cause with Virginian and Pennsylvanian land speculators, a combination that arose repeatedly during the escalating crises. In New England, particularly in Massachusetts, literacy was extremely high. Communities centered around a Calvinist faith required individuals to read the Bible, and literacy rates were likely above 90 percent.[27] In addition to promoting piety, the ability to read shaped a culture where the citizenry actively participated in political affairs;

newspapers and pamphlets represented a critical aspect of that participation. In New England, opposition to the stamp duty was pronounced and perceived, not unlike the 1712 expansion of the Stamp Act in England, as an assault on opposition newspapers. Alone, the resistance among the politically minded in northern colonies might not have proved decisive. Combined, however, with opposition from colonists whose wealth was tied to the buying and selling of land and added to the impact on men engaged in legal affairs, the result constituted a critical mass.

Influential Virginia gentry involved in land speculation were already disaffected as a result of the Royal Proclamation of 1763, decreed to prevent future wars with the Native American tribes. The Stamp Act now imposed additional costs on the transfer of land, even in the regions where settlement was permitted. Where New Englanders had been concerned with the perceived suppression of ideas, colonists whose wealth was tied to real estate objected to the costs associated with the act. Little affinity existed between small land holders and merchants of New England and the owners of immense plantations in the South. Relationships among people from different geographic regions were marked by suspicion and hostility. Culturally, different regions of British North America remained distinct owing to the different times at which regions were settled and to specific areas from which settlers originated. Nonetheless, the act's impact on different populations gave colonists common cause where none existed before.

Overlaying this union of disparate peoples, the Stamp Act disproportionately burdened printers and publishers, adding another group aggrieved by the impositions on their purses. Benjamin Franklin, then serving as a colonial agent in London, warned his business partner in Philadelphia that the duties on newspapers and advertisements would "go near to knock up one Half of both."[28] While advertising rates varied throughout the colonies, tax stamp costs represented at least 40 percent of the going rate for an advertisement and could be more than 60 percent in more competitive markets. The added expense threatened to drive smaller printers out of business or reduce the income of larger establishments. To protect their own interests, these businesses amplified the unrest in other areas of society. Resistance took a number of forms. Political action took the lead with colonial legislatures offering a series of resolves condemning Parliament's attempt to impose direct taxes on the colonies, the most famous being the Virginia Resolves. Debates in the Virginia House of Burgesses marked the rise of Patrick Henry, whose rhetoric would crescendo with another debate a decade later.

Economic effects played a role as well. While the era of formal non-importation agreements still had not yet arrived, many consumers were unwilling to accept any goods involving tax stamps. Some such as playing cards, books, and dice were directly taxed. Other imports were indirectly affected as the goods themselves were not subject to the duties. Documents associated with legal transactions were taxed. In American scholarship, Benjamin Franklin has long been considered the key figure in moving Parliament to reconsider the Stamp Act, but the eloquence of the "First American" would not likely have carried more weight than the contemporaneous testimony of British merchants who informed MPs of the loss of entire businesses due to the cessation of colonial exports. They blamed these conditions on the Stamp Act.[29]

The act also provoked a military response. The growth of committees of correspondence throughout the colonies provided the impetus for organizations that later assumed a martial character. In unsuccessfully opposing passage of the Stamp Act, MP Lieutenant-Colonel Isaac Barré rose to warn against imposing harsh measures on the colonies. Barré coined the phrase "Sons of Liberty," a moniker later adopted by colonists opposed to Crown policy. In December 1765, Connecticut and New York colonists formally agreed to support each other as groups formed to organize and develop techniques for mobilizing the population. Interestingly, the signatories also pledged themselves to "the support of his majesty's just prerogative and the BRITISH CONSTITUTION."[30]

A primary weapon was the threat of violence. Most active in New England, the same coordinated threats spread. They often developed into actual violence, but these events were rarely, if ever spontaneous. Governor William Bull, Jr. of South Carolina noted, "Yet there is great reason to apprehend they [the Sons of Liberty] were animated and encouraged by some considerable Men, who stood behind the Curtain."[31] As with armies of the time, the rank and file came from the lower orders of society while the guiding intelligence came from the upper strata. While not explicitly military in character, as the series of crises deepened, these affiliations transformed into military units incorporating elements of the colonial militia system. The first sparks of the conflagration that began at Lexington and Concord in April 1775 were struck in 1765 resulting from Stamp Act opposition.

## Fanning the Flames

Repealed in the face of growing violence and due to the testimony of British merchants suffering from the loss of trade, the process was complicated. The Grenville ministry fell over other issues and the scramble to form a new government involved negotiations that included coaxing the ailing William Pitt, Earl of Chatham, to form a cabinet. Failing in that endeavor, the Marquis of Rockingham formed a government, but his inexperience produced the ill-advised Declaratory Act. His eventual fall ushered in the period of political instability that allowed Chancellor of the Exchequer Charles Townsend to push through the disastrous set of duties that bear his name. Townsend became "a loose cannon on the deck of the ship of state."[32] The Townsend Acts imposed duties on a list of items, most perceived as luxuries. The Rockingham ministry lasted less than two years followed by Pitt. Briefly invigorated when asked to form a new government, he quickly retired back to the country as his health once again declined. In his absence, no other member of the cabinet had sufficient standing to divert Townsend from his purposes. The Townsend Duties included a tax on tea, later described by Edmund Burke as "the most important object, of any in the mighty circle of our commerce."[33] Government intervention in the tea trade, designed to benefit the East India Company, resulted in a quite different effect; it destabilized the market leading to further crises and provoked colonial responses that mirrored reaction to the Stamp Act. Political reaction focused on formalizing non-importation agreements. Colonial leaders once again sought to punish influential merchant interests such as the East India Company by diminishing profits derived from colonial trade through restrictions on importing the various goods on which duties had been laid.

As secretive organizations, the committees of correspondence and Sons of Liberty left little in the way of centralized documentary records. Each major city, however, did have substantial numbers of working-class men seemingly ever-ready to fill the streets to coerce Crown representatives or merchants reneging on agreements to forgo dealing in proscribed commodities. Circumstantial evidence suggests that these groups were structured, capable of coordinated effort, and had identifiable leadership. Boston was emblematic. There, activities conducted by revolutionary organizations were directed and synchronized. The destruction never devolved into widespread ruin but tended to focus on political targets. During the Stamp Act disturbances, Thomas Hutchinson's home was completely gutted while those of other officials damaged to varying degrees. Vandalism was limited to the residences of a few prominent officials. Given that a large percentage of the adult male population turned out for these events, the restraint in limiting the targets speaks to a degree of both organization and discipline. Were those facts not sufficient to suggest the working of a coordinated effort, the demonstrations in reaction to the Townsend Duties certainly did.

Parliament simultaneously enacted two other provisions that proved equally damaging to colonial relations. Various acts of Parliament, originating during the recent war, required the colonies to provide accommodation for troops stationed in the colonies known as "quartering." One law involved self-government in New York. Gage became embroiled in a dispute with the legislature over payment for billeting troops. The complex issue involved the disproportionate number of troops stationed in New York. Parliamentary reaction to the colony's unwillingness to provide the necessary funds led to the legislature's suspension until accounts were settled. The decision to temporarily end self-government accomplished the goal. Funds to billet the troops were disbursed by the legislature. However, obtaining a relatively insignificant sum to supply the troops had unintended consequences. New Yorkers formerly dedicated to the Empire slowly started to distance themselves from the Crown. The other initiative—Customs Act of 1767—created a new organization with the authority to execute the new trade and revenue laws. One particular Townsend Act intended to ease the burden on colonial merchants by resolving disputes in the colonies rather than in Britain. The American Board of Customs was sited in Boston, already the scene of considerable unrest. The commissioners arrived in December 1767. Obscured by the protest against the duties scheduled to be imposed and the appearance of the tax officials, the commission's arrival initially received little notice. That condition would change.[34]

Tight discipline distinguished many Boston demonstrations against the new laws. Guy Fawkes Day and St. Patrick's Day were particular occasions for demonstrations. According to Governor Francis Bernard, the displays "produced terror only, and not actual mischief."[35] Violence directed against stamp officers and attacks on officials' homes were not repeated. Instead, leaders kept a tight rein on the mob. Organizers believed that the repeal of the offending duties was imminent; violence might compromise those developments. When Parliament did not act as expected, targeted violence resumed focused on merchants who did not abide by the non-importation agreements.

The normal British reaction to unrest was to deploy the army. As formal police forces had not yet been organized, large disturbances were commonly met by sending out troops. The Riot Act was read aloud by a civil official, at which point the army employed any measures necessary to restore order.[36] Martial engagement became the approach taken by Lord Hillsborough, Secretary of State for the Colonies, in response to the Boston disturbances. Political dynamics internal to Massachusetts aggravated the process. Governor Bernard had been involved in a power struggle with the General Court, the provincial legislature. Throughout 1767, the governor sent a stream of correspondence to London requesting troops. By early 1768, the appointment of Wills Hill, Earl of Hillsborough as Secretary of State for the Colonies brought to power a decided opponent of any concessions to the colonists. A member of the faction known as the King's Friends, he was a hardliner with regard to the colonies and a man of little political talent or judgment.[37] He quickly sent orders to Gage to deploy a regiment "or such Force as you shall think necessary."[38] Before the letter left England, events spun out of control. The newly established Commissioners of Customs seized *Liberty*, a merchant vessel belonging to John Hancock. In response, young men were called into action and the ensuing disturbance became known as the *Liberty* Riot. Rumors of the impending arrival of troops further heightened tensions, but Gage still hesitated. In late summer two regiments arrived from Halifax. The troops, ultimately supplemented to over 3,000 men, served as a catalyst for the insurrection rather than suppressing it.[39] Matters became even more chaotic in the South.

The first stirrings of the Regulator movement erupted in the Carolina backcountry. The Regulators developed on very different paths in North Carolina and South Carolina. In South Carolina, the movement was a reaction to the rise of banditry. When authorities in Charleston failed to suppress these lawless elements, local citizens banded together to provide for their own security. South Carolina Governor Charles Montagu ordered the bands of armed citizens to disperse. With little authority in the backcountry, his orders were ignored. Petitions from respected citizens in the inland counties went unheeded. Coastal elites objected to the growing influence of the small, up-country planters. They did not, however, rally to the calls from the governor to arm against the Regulators, limiting the conflict to skirmishing between rival backcountry factions. The local opposition to the Regulators styled itself the Moderators. In the end, a pair of respected backcountry citizens mediated the dispute between the armed groups. Both Regulators and Moderators returned to their homes without bloodshed. The issues between the low country and the inland counties were not resolved but, unlike North Carolina, it did not degenerate into intersectional violence.[40]

In North Carolina, the Regulator movement took a very different path. The conflict centered on the friction between the coastal counties and the more populous inland counties. Along the coast, large plantations dominated the landscape, and the owners dominated politics. In the legislature, the disproportionate representation of the eastern counties contributed to the dispute despite the western counties being more populous. An influx of migrants from Virginia, Pennsylvania, and Maryland, as well as from Europe, trebled the colony's population in the decade preceding the uprising. These new residents had few ties to the coastal gentry. The large coastal plantations relied on trade with Britain while inland small landholders traded locally. As a result, the conflict based on sectional interests and occupations pitted western farmers against coastal merchants, large landholders, and lawyers. The resistance smoldered through the Townsend Act controversy but did not explode in a full-blown conflagration until other events intervened.

Across the colonies, resistance to the Townsend Duties grew slowly. Merchants suffered from the trade interruptions connected with the Stamp Act and remained reluctant to repeat that experience. Colonial agents such as Franklin convinced many influential colonists to forego dramatic reactions to the duties. The unexpected death of Townsend (1767) removed the only advocate for the duties within the ministry. Never popular in Parliament, the duties survived only due to the need to confirm the Declaratory Act, previously enacted to assert the right of Parliament to tax the colonies. With their chief supporter dead, the acts became untenable. Intervening events and a brewing financial crisis preserved a narrow segment of the tax regime but caused further damage to the transatlantic relationship. The duties remained while the Chatham ministry floundered without the firm hand of William Pitt, absent due to failing health. Colonial leaders, unaware of the chaos within the ministry, did not await the inevitable repeal.

When the repeal did not proceed as expected, colonial attitudes hardened. Non-importation took hold with a vengeance. Enforcement of the agreements was largely in the hands of working-class men, whose direction was unclear as to leadership or that any coordination was governed by the confluence of interests. Whatever the case, the violence was not limited to Boston and the Carolinas. Throughout the colonies, the Sons of Liberty and other opposition groups used targeted violence against anyone who defied the non-importation agreements. Offending shops were destroyed in Philadelphia and elsewhere. Customs officials were harassed in every port and a general, growing "ambiance of violence prevailed."[41]

## Flashpoints

Parliament repealed all but one of the Townsend duties in April 1770, already too late. Blood had been shed. Equally troublesome, gunpowder was stored up and down the Atlantic seaboard. Originally acquired as security against hostile Native American attacks and in some colonies against fears of slave rebellion, the colonials increasingly saw the supplies as insurance against British military efforts to dominate the colonial political landscape. British officials, on the other hand, saw the powder in colonial hands as a threat to the garrisons originally sent to protect the colonies but increasingly seen as adversaries by colonists. Nowhere was this situation tenser than in Boston.

Boston's population amounted to about 15,000 souls. Three thousand troops stationed in the city's narrow confines represented a significant population increase. With little to occupy their time when not on duty and given the common soldiers' notoriously low pay, these men became competitors for scarce jobs in a town that had seen a decided decline in its economic fortunes. In the late war, operations to seize Canada had been a boon to New England. The conflict's conclusion ended the hard currency with which the army purchased local produce and goods. Tensions heightened due to the economic competition, primarily with the common laborers. Those working-class men, already mobilized as shock troops from the earlier political violence, now competed with off-duty soldiers. To add to the tension, the Quartering Act required the colony to expend scarce revenue to house and feed the very troops who now depressed wages by working for lower rates since the colony paid their room and board.[42] This intolerable condition could not continue indefinitely. A series of escalating incidents led to a pair of fatal tragedies. Social unrest led to repeated confrontations. Opponents of government policies clashed with soldiers as well as with colonists who supported the government. Overlaying this tableau of violence, depressed wages, and the unhappy lot of bound laborers, whether slaves, indentured servants, or apprentices, this friction provided another source of mischief. Apprentices tended to gather in unruly groups during their free moments, which led to the first death, that of 11-year-old Christopher Seider.

Ebenezer Richardson was a customs official and a man of volatile temper. In late February 1770, a group of young men harassed his neighbor for alleged violations of the non-importation agreement, and he intervened. Unsuccessful, he retreated toward his home, engaging in a running verbal dispute along the way. That argument attracted the attention of a group of youths, who started with verbal abuse and escalated to throwing trash and stones. Richardson eventually responded by firing birdshot at the crowd. Two youths fell, one mortally wounded. Both were merely spectators. Richardson was convicted of murder by a Boston jury but later pardoned and reinstated in the customs service. The funeral for young Seider attracted a crowd of 2,000 people.[43] The ensuing tensions embroiled off-duty troops in addition to the disputes with Boston residents. In early March, events turned explosive.

Boston was not the only locale that experienced unrest. In January, disputes between British soldiers and New Yorkers boiled over when a group of soldiers made public their grievances against the townspeople. Posting a broadside describing their ill-treatment, a gaggle of New Yorkers surrounded the troops. Off duty, unarmed, and outnumbered, the soldiers retreated with the exception of two men, who were physically restrained and hauled before a magistrate on the charge of libel. While injuries suffered in the fracas were minor, it was reported as the Battle of Golden Hill; the news contributed to the increasing tensions throughout the colonies.[44] Violence in New York provided another spark for the political kindling in Boston. Social and economic unrest combined with what many perceived as a military occupation soon sparked a tragedy.

By introducing troops into Boston and allowing those men to seek employment while off duty, Britain almost guaranteed violence. While proficient at military tasks, soldiers generally did not have marketable civilian skills. One industry prevalent in seaports did offer opportunities. Ropewalks manufactured line for rigging ships. The labor was hard but did not require any expertise. Anti-government sentiment ran high in the ropewalks. An incident in March set the powder alight. Seeking employment, a soldier entered the ropewalk unaware that the proprietor and many of the rope workers were members of the Sons of Liberty. Physically accosted and ejected from the business, he returned with other members of his company. Finding the rope workers reinforced, the soldiers retreated following another scuffle. The regimental lieutenant-colonel interceded with the owner to defuse that particular situation, but nothing diminished the general hostility between the workers and soldiers, which set the stage for tragedy.

In March 1770, New England still lay in winter's full fury. Snow and ice made walking treacherous. Streets lined with oyster shells churned into a frozen mix of shell, ice, and snow. A lone sentry in front of the Customs House was accosted verbally by a group of young men, most likely apprentices finished with their work for the day. Verbal taunts escalated to throwing snowballs (more likely chunks of ice laden with oyster shells). Captain Thomas Preston, informed of the gathering crowd, ordered the main guard to turn out. Taking charge, he followed the corporal of the guard and six grenadiers who charged down King Street to reinforce the beleaguered private guarding Customs House. Far from the fanciful Henry Pelham drawing made famous when Paul Revere appropriated it as the basis for the prints that spread word of the incident, what transpired was neither orchestrated nor ordered.

The tragic evening began with a squad of soldiers interrogating any group larger than two persons. The action effectively cleared the area around Customs House, which was usually guarded to secure the official documents and specie stored there. When that body of troops withdrew for the night, the young men who had been dispersed returned to resume the harassment of a lone sentry. Reckless behavior by soldiers was also on display. Bells rang at three nearby churches at quarter past nine in the evening, normally indicating a fire. The sound turned out a great many more Bostonians. Preston, informed that the citizens were preparing to attack, hurried to the troop quarters, and initiated the final, fatal sequence of events.

Upon arriving at Customs House, the corporal of the guard arranged the soldiers in a rough arc with their backs to the building. They had marched hurriedly through the streets with bayonets fixed, wounding a number of people in the process. Two of these men had been involved in the altercation at the ropewalks. They now loaded their muskets in full view of the gathered crowd. The trailing Preston was delayed, pressed by bookseller Henry Knox, a future Continental Army major general, and sea captain Richard Palmes. Both men made ominous remarks intended to sow doubt in Preston. The crowd continued to jeer at the soldiers while throwing snowballs, ice, and oyster shells, daring them to fire. At that point, the story becomes muddled by differing accounts. Without question, a soldier lost his balance and fired. After a delay variously described as a few seconds or up to half a minute, other soldiers discharged a ragged volley. Preston regained control—too late. Three men lay dead already. Two more later died.[45]

Officially reported as the Riot on King Street, Boston radicals seized on the incident. The Pelham original drawing proved inflammatory. Before Gage completed his investigation, businessman and reputed leader of the Sons of Liberty John Hancock dispatched a packet boat to London carrying accounts of the event. The first word that arrived in London was framed by government opponents and arrived amid political chaos surrounding the imprisoned John Wilkes, the radical former MP. The "massacre" narrative had been set earlier when seven Wilkes supporters were killed in 1768 in the St. George's Fields Massacre. Newly released from prison in 1770, he continued to cause a political stir when news of another "massacre" broke. The soldiers involved in the London deaths were not convicted. The same could not be said in Boston. Two soldiers found guilty of manslaughter had their punishments reduced to a few weeks in prison and the branding of their thumbs. By the first anniversary of the Riot on King Street, all of the soldiers returned to their regiment. Others were found not guilty, including Captain Preston, somewhat ironically defended by attorney John Adams. Not all events in 1770 were resolved with so little bloodshed.

The North Carolina struggle against the Regulators was brought to a head by the decision of Royal Governor William Tryon to launch a suppression campaign against the movement. The governor, largely at the insistence of anti-Regulator interests, may have intervened to curry favor with coastal elites who supported construction of a lavish official residence funded by tax revenue. The Regulators derisively labeled the governor's new home "Tryon's Palace." The Battle of Alamance in May 1771 represented the final spasm of violence in suppressing the Regulator movement. As battles go, it was a small affair with 1,000 militia facing a Regulator force of about twice their number. Better armed, better equipped, and better disciplined, the militia placed the Regulators in an untenable tactical position and called on them to disband or surrender. Most fled. Seven insurgents were captured and executed. The later stages of the impending war in the South devolved into a barbaric internecine civil war with the contending factions—Whigs and Tories—prefigured by the adversaries in this struggle. In many ways, the Battle of Alamance represented the first military engagement of the American War.[46]

## Shoring Up the Government

Lord North took the reins of government in January 1770. A member of the Irish peerage, North assumed the post as Chancellor of the Exchequer following the death of Charles Townsend. Amiable and self-effacing, North enjoyed a warm relationship with King George III, who saw him as a kindred spirit. Dedicated to their families, they also shared a common outlook on government issues. The close relationship stood Lord North in good stead early in his tenure. The degree to which the king trusted and relied upon him also made it almost impossible for North to resign as the American War soured. The antithesis of so many other leading ministers who served with him, preceded him, or followed him, he possessed neither the swaggering, charismatic bravado of Pitt nor the licentiousness of Fox or the Duke of Grafton. Through his steady hand and the absence of personal drama coupled with a talent for managing the Commons, he commanded large majorities in the House even during the worst crises of the war. King George only allowed him to retire after the disaster at Yorktown, and even then reluctantly. He met two crises in his first year in office, one diplomatic and military and the other financial. In the former, he performed superbly. In the latter, he reignited the fires that flared briefly in the winter and spring of 1770.

The first crisis came in June 1770 when the Spanish governor of Buenos Aires sent a naval force to seize the Falkland Islands. Taking action in the dead of the austral winter, the governor doubtless expected his *fait accompli* to stand. In 1768, France had taken the island of Corsica and even the protracted campaign that dragged on until May 1769 did not induce Britain to intercede. At that point, the chaos of the Chatham ministry and the successor Grafton ministry could not muster the political capital to intercede militarily nor to use diplomacy to force France to relent. In the Falklands, the North ministry proved far more resolute. The Spanish governor may not have acted independently. Étienne François, duc de Choiseul, French Minister for Foreign Affairs during the Seven Years' War, negotiated the 1761 renaissance of the Bourbon Family Compact, drawing Spain into the war. His diplomatic maneuvers failed to reverse the eventual outcome. From the moment the war ended, however, he began planning a new war of vengeance. His patron, Madame de Pompadour, the king's former mistress, remained a powerful political influence even after she had been supplanted in the king's chambers. When she died in 1764, Choiseul's enemies at court plotted revenge. In the Falklands crisis, Choiseul mobilized the French military and navy in preparation for the war of revenge. He did not, however, consult King Louis XV before doing so. The king was not inclined to bold action and encouraged by Choiseul's court enemies, his chief minister bore the brunt of the royal displeasure. When France declined to support Spain's attempt to grab the islands, the Spanish king disavowed his governor's actions, diffusing the looming conflict. Choiseul was dismissed and exiled from Paris.

The Falklands affair boosted British prestige throughout Europe. That benefit did not come without cost. The Royal Navy mobilized for war, but such preparations did not come cheaply. In peacetime, ships were laid up in ordinary, the eighteenth-century version of the modern process of placing ships in "mothballs." Masts and guns were removed and stored ashore. Only a skeleton crew maintained the hull. Recruiting crews, re-rigging ships, loading stores, and munitions were all expensive propositions. The naval estimates voted by Parliament for 1771, the year in which the bills for the mobilization came due, stood just short of twice those for the previous year. Adding an additional £1.4 million to the already overwhelming debt incurred in the late war further complicated the task facing Lord North, particularly in his role as Chancellor of the Exchequer.[47]

## Scorching the Foundations

The other crisis besetting North was financial, rather than diplomatic. The East India Company, a chartered joint stock company, included as investors many of the most prominent men in the kingdom. Run speculatively, early in its existence, the Company generated enormous profits. Those profits bred increased speculation and led to the acquisition of more ships for the tea trade, a major part of its operations. Two factors eventually undercut this prosperity. Foreign competition challenged profits and the increased number of ships in response to the challenge produced a glut of tea on the market. Together, these issues nearly brought down the Company. Had that collapse been permitted, a great many London banking houses might have followed, as the investors had borrowed heavily. Dutch traders undercut the closed British markets, particularly in North America while British merchants saw a decline in their share of the general European market. The critical problem erupted with the increase in the number of ships carrying tea to London. In late spring 1771, 13 tea ships arrived in London. Collectively, these merchantmen carried 50 percent more tea than the London market usually absorbed in an entire year. The price collapsed, triggering a series of bankruptcies, and setting in motion events that led to war between Britain and her colonies.[48]

North shepherded a government intervention that prevented an immediate economic collapse. When the Townsend Duties were repealed, the tax on tea had been retained. In practice, most of the objectionable aspects of the Townsend Acts remained in place. The tea duty was the only tax that generated significant revenue. Royal officials were still paid by the Crown rather than the colonies and the customs procedures remained, as did the authority of admiralty courts. The tea market collapse drove a move to allow the direct sale of tea in the colonies, rather than forcing the Company to first auction the tea in London. With the Tea Act of 1773, the collection of the duty was still required and the onus placed on colonial officials, already objects of derision. The provisions commissioning Royal Navy officers to act as customs enforcers made matters worse. That arrangement led to the first naval casualties of the war (see Figure 1.2).

Rhode Island had a long-standing reputation for free thinking and freewheeling commerce. Founded by religious dissenters who viewed the Puritan strictures of Massachusetts as too limiting, Rhode Islanders took a similar attitude toward commercial laws. Narragansett Bay is dotted with dozens of islands, its shores carved into dozens of coves and inlets—a smuggler's paradise. Smaller warships were brought to the bay to suppress the illicit commerce but to little avail. One sloop, *Liberty*, previously confiscated from John Hancock, came into the bay to enforce the customs laws under which it had been seized. At one point, *Liberty's* crew fired point blank at a detained vessel's master. A Newport mob boarded the sloop and coerced the master into ordering his crew ashore, retook two detained

**FIGURE 1.2**  The Tea Tax

*Source:* Courtesy of the Anne S.K. Brown Military Collection, Brown University Library, Providence, Rhode Island

vessels, and scuttled the offending customs sloop, which subsequently washed up on a beach and burned. The crew's rash action in firing upon the master and the *Liberty's* checkered history combined to dampen the official response. Three years later, the destruction of another vessel elicited a different response.

The destruction of the schooner *Gaspee* represented an altogether different affair. Built for the customs service and commanded by a Royal Navy lieutenant, its loss could not be blamed on tides or mischance. The ship was deliberately lured into treacherous waters near Providence. A shallow draft vessel suspected of illicit commerce led the schooner across an uncharted sandbar whose position was locally known. *Gaspee* stuck fast. After dusk, small boats approached by stealth and subterfuge. Boarders stormed onto the deck, wounded the captain, and ordered the crew off, then burned the ship. The *Liberty* incident had occurred in Newport harbor. The stories were muddled. The crew had legal disputes with town officials and the burning was attributed to the wreck of a derelict vessel. None of these conditions applied in the case of the *Gaspee*, deliberately attacked in the open bay. If the Battle of Alamance represented the first shots of the war, the *Gaspee* represented the first naval action.[49]

These incidents illustrated a larger pattern created by resistance to the customs laws. The most famous opposition to the duties became known as the Boston Tea Party. The American Revenue Act repeal was only partial. It left the duty on tea in place, given the need to prevent an East India Company collapse. The Company could send tea directly to the colonies but the duties had to be paid. That fact remained the sticking point, not the price or amount of the tea tax. The Tea Act actually reduced the price of tea paid in the colonies. The precedent that London could enact laws for America roiled the colonists. In 1773, seven tea ships crossed the Atlantic in hopes of lifting the Company's sagging fortunes. In Boston, three of the four ships bound for the port arrived over a period of weeks. One ship wrecked off Cape Cod, but the tea and other goods were saved and later sold. The first ship to arrive, the *Dartmouth*, and two other vessels together carried 342 chests of tea amounting to something over 130,000 pounds (59,000 kilograms) and valued in contemporaneous letters at £18,000. The law required that the duties on imported goods be collected within 20 days after entering the harbor. As that deadline approached, a group of men, described in some accounts as having disguised themselves as Mohawks boarded the ships. Tea chests were carefully, even expertly, raised from the holds, broken open, emptied into the harbor, and the containers themselves followed. No other cargo damage or injury was suffered. Even a padlock that had been damaged to access the tea was restored. The entire evolution was carried out with military precision, not the action of a lawless mob such as the riot on King Street.[50] Samuel Adams is believed to have directed the action. Warned by Hancock that Boston merchants would be alienated by the type of violence that had surrounded the Boston Massacre, a concerted effort was made to shape perceptions. In short, crowd actions were regulated.

Not only in Boston, but similar "tea parties" erupted up and down the coast. Public pressure, often accompanied by threats of organized violence, prevented East India Company tea from coming to market. In South Carolina, Charleston's Sons of Liberty made it clear to the consignees that their persons, homes, and businesses would be unsafe should they accept delivery of the 257 chests of tea shipped on the vessel *London*. The tea went unclaimed and duties not paid, thus the Collector of Customs seized and stored the tea in a damp warehouse unsuited to the purpose—destroyed as effectively as if it had been dumped into the harbor. In November 1774, the consignees actually dumped recently arrived tea from another vessel into the harbor. South Carolina conducted a tea party every bit as destructive as its more famous predecessor in New England (see Figure 1.3).[51]

In New York, threats induced the captain of the *Nancy* to depart without paying the duties or landing the tea. Governor Tryon, who previously had suppressed the Regulator movement in North Carolina, made a secret agreement with the Sons of Liberty. The organization's prominent members paid to re-provision the vessel for the return voyage and the governor issued a permit for the ship to clear the port without landing the cargo or paying the duty. In Philadelphia, no such accommodations occurred. Delaware River pilots were warned against guiding an inbound tea ship up the river and the captain was hauled before a meeting of

**FIGURE 1.3**   The Boston Tea Party

*Source:* Courtesy of the Anne S.K. Brown Military Collection, Brown University Library, Providence, Rhode Island

Philadelphia citizens and threatened. The *Polly* provisioned and departed without assistance from the local non-importation advocates. Perhaps the most unusual tea party occurred in October 1774 in Maryland at Annapolis where the consignee was one of the owners of the brig *Peggy Stewart*. After consulting with leading Maryland citizen Charles Carroll, the owners were informed that the only way to avoid violence to their persons and homes was to destroy the ship and the tea. It was run aground and destroyed.[52] The destruction of tea at various locations was not the death knell of the East India Company. While a heavy blow, the actual losses amounted to less than £60,000 burned, spoiled, or left to rot. An equal amount was sent back to London to be sold in the saturated market. The problem for the Company and investors lay in that an entire market had closed.

## Laying the Fuse

The year 1774, a coherent sequence of inseparable events, has been labeled "The Long Year of Revolution." It began with the first of the tea parties in December 1773 and continued through most of 1774. The cycle did not end until the psychic shock of the "shot heard 'round the world." Throughout that extended cycle of seasons, the Crown's reaction to the provocations in Boston exacerbated the situation and gave the disparate societies that made up the North American colonies common cause.[53] Parliament enacted a series of punitive measures in the wake of the Boston Tea Party. The Coercive Acts sought to punish Boston and prevent any recurrence of the lawless behavior that had precipitated the crisis. The laws did not have the desired effect. The first statute—the Boston Port Act—closed the port to all commerce until the East India Company had been reimbursed for the destroyed tea. Closely thereafter came the Massachusetts Government Act, which revoked the colony's royal charter and substituted direct rule by the royal governor. The Administration of Justice Act allowed governors to send royal officials to Britain for trial. Then came the Quartering Act of 1773. In American mythology, it allowed the government to displace families and billet soldiers in private residences. Hyperbole aside, it neither allowed such harsh measures nor was it the first act of the kind. It clarified earlier statutes, allowed the use of public and unoccupied buildings to house troops, and included provisions for punishing officers who overstepped the authorities granted. Nonetheless, the damage to public perception and what has been called the "hearts and minds of the people" had been done. In the American colonies, these measures became known as the Intolerable Acts.[54]

Another law that further roiled America emerged during the same period. Not intended as a coercive statute, rather, the Quebec Act had its origins in an inquiry conducted by the Rockingham ministry. The same conditions that had made French Canada difficult to defend and economically marginal still existed. A series of ministries had sought a solution, but the North ministry finally acted. Nothing suggests that this statute represented a direct response to the unrest in Boston, yet the act was perceived in America to be as intolerable as the legislative responses to the tea party. The law sought to secure the newly won colony against French intrigues and to make it more economically viable. To this end, all land north and west of the Ohio River was added to the Province of Quebec. The law also allowed Catholics free exercise of their faith while remaining eligible for government positions. Catholics in Canada enjoyed rights not shared by their co-religionists anywhere else in the empire. Seemingly a reasonable set of measures, the perception in the American colonies proved quite different.[55]

New England, populated by people with a deep and abiding antipathy toward all things Catholic, resented the Quebec Act on religious grounds.[56] Further south, attitudes were more economic. For land speculators in Pennsylvania and Virginia, the region west of the Ohio River promised untold wealth. Land speculation companies hoped to reverse the strictures imposed by the Proclamation of 1763. By giving Catholics rights that New England Congregationalists found egregious and coupling those rights with the permanent transfer of western lands to the government of Quebec, the Crown once again united groups that had little in common, just as it had in the immediate aftermath of the Seven Years' War. The statute became another glue that bound the regions together in dissent. But, other parliamentary measures also sparked hyperbolic reactions. George Washington referred to the Administration of Justice Act as the "Murder Act," implying that royal officials would never be held accountable. The hardships imposed on Boston spurred outpourings of support from other colonies. The Massachusetts Government Act stoked anger at the revocation of rights previously granted by the Crown in perpetuity. Previous actions by London had sparked outrage that had abated over time. In the Quebec Act, religious sentiments and fiscal motives collided with the more transient sources of antipathy to light a fuse that would not be extinguished.[57] Like the multiple rows of dominoes coming together, the situation only demanded a spark to light the conflagration.

American reactions to parliamentary interventions were both political and martial. The political responses were mixed. Even the other port towns in Massachusetts were less than unified when it came to refusing to trade with Britain. The further the distance from Boston, the more reticent merchants were to sacrifice their businesses out of solidarity with the beleaguered town. Various colonial legislatures were dismissed by royal governors or, in the case of Massachusetts, disbanded entirely. Members continued to meet anyway. In Virginia, 89 members of the House of Burgesses met in a Williamsburg tavern after the legislature was suspended and "recommended to the committee of correspondence, that they communicate, with the several corresponding committees, on the expediency of appointing deputies from the several colonies of British America, to meet in general Congress."[58] As in the move for the Stamp Act Congress, Virginia took the lead. Other colonies responded. Only Georgia, the most recently founded colony of the 13 that eventually rebelled, declined to send delegates to Philadelphia to meet in Congress. The gathering's tenor was political and conciliatory, save for one aspect. Congress adopted The Suffolk Resolves, drafted by Joseph Warren. The 11th article of that document, distinctly martial, admonished colonists to "use their utmost diligence to acquaint themselves with the art of war as soon as possible, and do, for that purpose, appear under arms at least once every week."[59] The stage was set for a military struggle.

## Blowing the Matches[60]

The fortunes of General Thomas Gage are, perhaps, the best indicator of the growing conflict's trajectory. When he departed New York in 1773, he was praised and given the "freedom of the city." His arrival in Boston was met with approbation by none other than noted radical Dr. Joseph Warren. Even into August 1774, he enjoyed cordial relations with locals. That condition changed in September with the "powder alarm." Gage reported that he required a naval blockade, the withdrawal of all troops from the rebellious colonies, and a return later with a much larger force to quell the growing dissent. By the time his dispatches sent in November arrived, London had ceased to value Gage's advice and three major-generals were dispatched to assist him as he appeared to have lost confidence in his ability to control the situation. British officials engaged in a series of military actions, mostly related to the possession and storage of gunpowder and shot. Largely focused on New England, a series of confrontations escalated the crisis. On 1 September 1774, just days before the opening of the First Continental Congress, Gage sent soldiers to remove 250 barrels of gunpowder from a house outside Boston. The action provoked outrage and exaggerated stories. News of blood in the streets of Boston reached the Congress but cooler heads prevailed, and the reports proved to be in error. That action, however, primed other towns to prepare against similar confiscations.

British troops or militia loyal to the colonial governors seized cannons in Rhode Island and Maryland. In New Hampshire, Paul Revere, pre-figuring his more famous April 1775 ride, arrived in Portsmouth warning of the imminent landing of soldiers from warships to seize the powder and stores at Fort William and Mary. Four hundred armed citizens stole a march on the raid and removed the powder. The raid was a phantom, but the local citizens gained confidence in their ability to stand against military intervention. Similar incidents occurred through the autumn and winter. In some cases, government forces seized powder or cannon while groups of colonists successfully deterred or forestalled action by removing weapons and powder. The final powder alarm occurred after blood was spilled at Lexington and Concord. The Royal Governor of Virginia, John Murray, Lord Dunmore, became increasingly concerned with the tenor of the public discourse. When the Virginia legislature voted a day of prayer and fasting in the wake of the Coercive Acts, Dunmore dissolved the Assembly. Across Virginia towns began raising independent companies. When the Virginia Convention convened in March and Patrick Henry famously thundered that he would only countenance liberty or death, the governor thought it prudent to remove the powder in the Williamsburg magazine to a Royal Navy vessel. He arranged for sailors to move the munitions. When the "gunpowder incident" was discovered, members of local companies prepared to storm the governor's residence. Calming words from rebellion leaders prevented harm to Dunmore and his family, but the tension led the governor to flee to the safety of a naval vessel in the ensuing weeks. By the time these events transpired, the war had begun in Massachusetts.

## Notes

1 John Adams, *The Works of John Adams, Second President of the United States: With a Life of the Author, Notes and Illustrations,* vol. 10, ed. Charles Francis Adams (Boston, MA: Little, Brown and Co., 1856), 266.

2 Frank McLynn, *1759: The Year Britain Became Master of the World* (New York: Atlantic Monthly Press, 2004), 388–91.

3 N. A. M. Rodger, *The Command of the Ocean: A Naval History of Britain, 1649–1814* (New York: W. W. Norton, 2004), 644.

4 Brewer, *Sinews of Power,* 30.

5 Ibid., 40.

6 In his master work, Clausewitz defined limited, offensive war as an attempt to seize enemy territory for just such purposes. See Carl von Clausewitz, *On War,* indexed edition, ed. and trans. Michael Howard and Peter Paret (Princeton, NJ: Princeton University Press, 1984), 69, 601, and 611–2.

7 David Hackett Fischer, *Champlain's Dream: The European Founding of North America* (New York: Simon & Schuster, 2008).

8 John Robert Seeley, *The Expansion of England* (London: Macmillan, 1883), 10.

9 See Fischer, *Champlain's Dream,* for a detailed account of French colonial policy.

10 For a broad history of the Catawba Indians in this era, see James H. Merrell, *The Indians' New World: Catawbas and Their Neighbors from European Contact Through the Era of Removal* (Chapel Hill, NC: University of North Carolina Press, 1989).

11 Alfred A. Cave, "The Delaware Prophet Neolin: A Reappraisal," in *Ethnohistory* 46, no. 2 (1999): 265–90.

12  Walter O'Meara, *Guns at the Forks* (Englewood Cliffs, NJ: Prentiss-Hall, 1965), 233; Colin G. Calloway, *The Scratch of a Pen: 1763 and the Transformation of North America* (New York: Oxford University Press, 2006), 71.

13  Ibid., 236–44.

14  Kevin Kenny, *Peaceable Kingdom Lost: The Paxton Boys and the Destruction of William Penn's Holy Experiment* (New York: Oxford University Press, 2009), 130–55.

15  Ibid., 622–3.

16  Calloway, *Scratch of a Pen*, 75–6.

17  These arguments are drawn largely from Richard Middleton, "Pontiac: Local Warrior or Pan-Indian Leader?," in *Michigan Historical Review* 32, no. 2 (2006): 1–32.

18  Estimates, even at the time, varied widely from as low as £111,000 to figures above £400,000. £350,000 represents a best estimate, see Peter D. G. Thomas, "The Cost of the British Army in North America, 1763–1775," in *William and Mary Quarterly* 45, no. 3 (1988): 511–12, 516.

19  Colin G. Calloway, *The American Revolution in Indian Country: Crisis and Diversity in Native American Communities* (Cambridge and New York: Cambridge University Press, 1995), 7.

20  *Cantonment of the forces in North America 11th. Octr.* [1765] Map.

21  *Cantonment of His Majesty's forces in N. America according to the disposition now made & to be completed* [sic] *as soon as practicable taken from the general distribution dated at New York 29th. March* [1766] Map.

22  On Rhode Island, see Steven Park, *The Burning of His Majesty's Schooner Gaspee: An Attack on Crown Rule before the American Revolution* (Yardley, PA: Westholme, 2016), 2–3.

23  Thomas C. Barrow, *Trade and Empire: The British Customs Service in Colonial America, 1660–1775* (Cambridge, MA: Harvard University Press, 1967), 177.

24  On the general tenor of the society, see Karl-Friedrich Walling, *Republican Empire: Alexander Hamilton on War and Free Government* (Lawrence, KS: University Press of Kansas, 1999), 24–6.

25  Jan M. Novotny, "Stamp Duties," *The Journal of Economic History* 15, no. 3 (1955): 289.

26  Joseph M. Thomas, "Swift and the Stamp Act of 1712," in *PMLA* 31, no. 2 (1916): 247.

27  David Hackett Fischer, *Albion's Seed: Four British Folkways in America* (New York and Oxford: Oxford University Press, 1989), 131–3.

28  Arthur M. Schlesinger, "The Colonial Newspapers and the Stamp Act," in *The New England Quarterly* 8, no. 1 (1935): 65.

29  Stuart A. Green, "Notes and Documents: Repeal of the Stamp Act: The Merchants' and Manufacturers' Testimonies," in *The Pennsylvania Magazine of History and Biography* 128, no. 2 (2004): 179–97.

30  Edmund S. Morgan, ed., *Prologue to Revolution: Sources and Documents on the Stamp Act Crisis, 1764–1766* (Chapel Hill, NC: University of North Carolina Press, 1959), 117.

31  Edmund S. Morgan, *The Stamp Act Crisis: Prologue to Revolution*, 3rd edition (Chapel Hill, NC: University of North Carolina Press, 1995), 187.

32  Don Cook, *The Long Fuse: How England Lost the American Colonies, 1760–1785* (New York: Atlantic Monthly Press, 1995), 115.

33  Ibid., 32.

34  Barrow, *Trade and Empire*, 221.

35  Governor Bernard to Lord Shelburne, 19 March 1768, quoted in John C. Miller, "The Massachusetts Convention 1768," in *The New England Quarterly* 7, no. 3 (1934): 447.

36  Stanley H. Palmer, "The Military, the Law, and Public Order in England, 1650–1850," *Journal of the Society for Army Historical Research* 56, no. 228 (1978): 200.

37  Cook, *Long Fuse*, 128.

38  Hillsborough to Gage, quoted in Richard Archer, *As If an Enemy's Country: The British Occupation of Boston and the Origins of Revolution* (Oxford and New York: Oxford University Press, 2010), 90.

39  For a detailed account of the rising tensions in Boston, see Archer, *Enemy's Country*.

40  Walter Edgar, *South Carolina: A History* (Columbia, SC: University of South Carolina Press, 1998), 213–6.

41  Joseph S. Tiedemann, "A Tumultuous People: The Rage for Liberty and the Ambiance of Violence in the Middle Colonies in the Years Preceding the American Revolution," in *Pennsylvania History: A Journal of Mid-Atlantic Studies* 77, no. 4 (2010): 387–431; Glenn Curtis Smith, "An Era of Non-Importation Associations, 1768–73," *The William and Mary Quarterly* 20, no. 1 (1940): 84–98.

42  Archer, *Enemy's Country*, 176; Serena Zabin, *The Boston Massacre: A Family History* (Boston, MA and New York: Houghton Mifflin Harcourt, 2020), 148–9.

43  Archer, *Enemy's Country*, 179–81; Hiller B. Zobel, *The Boston Massacre* (New York: W. W. Norton, 1970), 172.

44  Richard M. Ketcham, *Divided Loyalties: How the American Revolution Came to New York* (New York: Henry Holt, 2002), 272.

45  More detailed accounts are found in Archer, 185–99.

46  For discussions of the Regulator movement and its origins, see George R. Adams, "The Carolina Regulators: A Note on Changing Interpretations," in *The North Carolina Historical Review* 49, no. 4 (1972): 345–52; James P. Whittenburg, "Planters, Merchants, and Lawyers: Social Change and the Origins of the North Carolina Regulation," *The William and Mary Quarterly* 34, no. 2 (1977): 215–38.

47  Rodger, *Command of the Ocean*, 369–72, 644; Rodger, *Insatiable Earl*, 126–7.

48  Nick Bunker, *An Empire on the Edge: How Britain Came to Fight America* (New York: Alfred A. Knopf, 2014), 41–2.

49  For a more complete account of the incident, see Park, *Schooner Gaspee*.

50  Francis S. Drake, *Tea Leaves: Being a Collection of Letters and Documents Relating to the shipment of Tea to the American Colonies in the Year 1773, by the East India Tea Company* (Boston, MA: A.O. Crane, 1884), LXV–LXIX.

51  George C. Rogers, "The Charleston Tea Party: The Significance of December 3, 1773," in *The South Carolina Historical Magazine* 75, no. 3 (1974): 157–62; Drake, LXXXIV; "Charleston Tea Party," *South Carolina Gazette*. Page 2. 21 November 1774.

52  Joseph A. Cummins, *Ten Tea Parties: Patriotic Protests That History Forgot* (Philadelphia, PA: Quirk Books, 2012), 105–9, 72–7, 155–7.

53  See Mary Beth Norton, *1774: The Long Year of Revolution* (New York: Alfred A. Knopf, 2020).

54  Ian R. Christie and Benjamin W. Labaree, *Empire or Independence, 1760–1776: A British-American Dialogue on the Coming of the American Revolution* (New York: W. W. Norton, 1976), 187–94.

55  Details of the legislation are found in the official record, 14 George III, ch. 83, The Quebec Act.

56  For an example, see Article 10 of the Suffolk Resolves in Worthington C. Ford, et al., eds., *Journals of the Continental Congress, 1774–1789* (Washington, DC: Library of Congress, 1904), 1:35.

57  Christie and Labaree, 194–97; Harlow Giles Unger, *American Tempest: How the Boston Tea Party Sparked a Revolution* (Cambridge, MA: DaCapo Press, 2011), 187–8.

58  Julian P. Boyd, ed., *The Papers of Thomas Jefferson*, vol. 1, 1760–1776 (Princeton, NJ: Princeton University Press, 1950), 107–9.

59  *Journals of the Continental Congress*, 1:35.

60  Before the invention of flintlock mechanisms for cannon, sailors blew slow-matches, lengths of rope that were soaked in tar and lit. "Blowing the matches" was a preparatory command used to get the embers actively burning before they ignited the powder that primed the guns. See Christopher McKee, *Edward Preble, A Naval Biography, 1761–1807* (Annapolis: Naval Institute Press, 1972), 141.

# 2

# THE SHOT HEARD 'ROUND THE WORLD

Our disgraces have been great and repeated in America.[1]
—*John Montagu, 4th Earl of Sandwich, December 1775*

George Washington made a grand entrance at the Second Continental Congress in Philadelphia. The founding myths suggest Washington was the only man so clad—certainly the most striking figure. Tall, athletic, and wearing an impeccably tailored uniform of blue with buff facings, he exuded a martial presence. A veteran of the French and Indian War, he served with General Edward Braddock during the disastrous Fort Duquesne expedition and with John Forbes' later campaign that ejected France from the Forks of the Ohio River. He likely initiated the entire war with a misadventure in the Pennsylvania backcountry known as the Battle of Jumonville Glen when his mixed force of Indians and Virginia troops attacked a French party from Fort Duquesne.[2] Perhaps due to his attire, his congressional colleagues eagerly sought his advice. He had been little noted in the First Continental Congress perhaps due to what John Adams described as a gift for silence.[3] He participated in the second gathering to a much greater degree, sitting on nine committees, most dealing with military issues. Adams observed that Washington: "by his great military experience and abilities in military matters is of much service to us."[4]

## Opening Reverses

Washington did not actively seek command of the newly created Continental Army. He famously informed Patrick Henry: "From the day I enter upon the command of the American armies, I date my fall, and the ruin of my reputation."[5] He confessed to several individuals that he did not believe himself equal to the task although he

DOI: 10.4324/9781003041276-4

served in numerous occasions in the previous war and commanded the Virginia Regiment defending against Native American war parties along the frontier.[6] Self-taught in military matters as in all things, he had never commanded a formation larger than a regiment, and a badly understrength unit at that. His commission as a field grade officer on the provincial establishment officially carried less authority than that of the newest subaltern possessed of a royal commission. His battle experience taught him the dangers that awaited an unprepared army. All these reasons could have led to his carefully considered appraisal that disaster loomed. But different individuals carry different weight in events. In a display in which dominoes of different sizes create a cascading effect, a larger piece will have a greater impact and is harder to tumble. Washington, despite his doubts and trepidations, proved a very large domino.

Washington should have been the last individual of concern to the Crown. A scion of the Virginia planter elite, wealthy and connected, he had sought a royal commission like his brother Lawrence, a commissioned officer of the 43rd Regiment of Foot. Rejected, he settled for service in the provincial forces. His social circles included powerful men with interests on both sides of the Atlantic. His allegiance to the nascent rebellion represented an enormous problem for Britain. Some observers have suggested that his initial demure when asked about command was false modesty; others have deemed his behavior a form of political maneuvering. Appearing in uniform signaled an indication of willingness to serve in a military capacity.[7] Reconciling the seeming contradictions is critical as his strategic insights were fundamental to the success of what he termed "the Glorious Cause."

A few rivals campaigned for the post, some actively and some behind the scenes. John Hancock made no secret of his desire to lead the army, a poor choice on a number of accounts. He had no real combat experience. Hailing from Massachusetts represented a more significant problem. Success in the fight depended on a unified effort supported by all the colonies. An army comprised of New England troops led by a Boston radical did not cry out that the colonies were unified. Virginia, the most populous colony, provided the most active advocates of opposition except for Massachusetts. A Virginian would almost certainly have to lead the united army. Two former British officers, Charles Lee and Horatio Gates, had ties to the colony and might have been viable alternatives. Both men served as Continental Army general officers, but neither succeeded in supplanting Washington.

Lee was an anomaly. Serving in the British Army with some distinction during the Seven Years' War, he never rose above the rank of major. He shared the hardships of Braddock's campaign with Washington and fought at Fort Ticonderoga. After the war, he offered his services to the King of Poland as a military advisor with the titular rank of major general. Lee quarreled with his superiors, however, and left Poland before partition by the great powers. Returning to England, he managed to have his half-pay rank elevated to lieutenant-colonel before arriving in Virginia in 1773. His experience and the cache of service as a regular officer convinced many that he was a credible candidate for overall command. Even Washington, normally a superb judge of men, was beguiled. Lee, however, a newcomer, an unsociable loner, and quarrelsome, ultimately caused more problems than he solved for the Continentals.[8]

Horatio Gates also aspired to the highest position in the new army. He served in the disastrous Braddock march as well but was injured early in the campaign and afterward not actively engaged. He proved an excellent military administrator and became the brigade major under Generals John Stanwix and Robert Monkton, including service in the capture of Martinique in 1762. The war's end stalled his career. Gates had neither wealth with which to purchase a more senior rank nor political influence. He sold his major's commission and, like Lee, settled in Virginia. Ultimately, his lack of "interest," as political influence was then known, blocked his ambition.[9] His resentment festered, eventually leading to association with participants in the alleged Conway Cabal. His disastrous performance late in the American War at Camden, South Carolina, justified the selection of the Master of Mount Vernon over his "professional" rival.

## Tactical Blunders and Strategic Reverses

Before the formation of a Continental Army and Washington's appointment as its CinC, the first battle of the American War occurred when a junior officer took a wrong turn. A simple mistake brought British troops face to face with armed colonists intent on blocking the advance to Concord where the troops were ordered to search for a weapons cache. The morning might well have ended in bloodshed in either case, but other factors were in play on that April morning in 1775. Hancock and Samuel Adams quit the crowded confines of Boston and the ever-present, red-coated soldiers. They traveled west to Lexington preparing to represent Massachusetts in the forthcoming Continental Congress. The First Continental Congress adjourned the previous October as rumors abounded of blood in Boston streets when gunpowder had been seized at Charlestown. While untrue, the potential for harassment or even arrest made Hancock and Adams depart for safer country environs. On 19 April, Lieutenant-General Thomas Gage sent a column of troops marching to Concord with orders to seize arms, ammunition, and powder—an *ad hoc* force comprised of companies drawn from Boston garrison regiments. British regiments of the time each included two elite companies, one of grenadiers and one light company. The former acted as shock troops, the latter in open order fighting and skirmishing. For the march to Concord, the light companies were separated from their parent formations and brigaded as were the grenadiers. The arrangement added more disorder to a confused situation. Some subordinates decried the commander, Lieutenant-Colonel Francis Smith, as overweight, slow, and lacking imagination. Gage saw him as prudent and cautious. These characteristics are not mutually exclusive. He did not, however, lead from the front, a dynamic that had serious repercussions early that morning (see Figure 2.1).[10]

GENERAL GAGE.

Printed for T. Robson, Newcastle upon Tyne.

**FIGURE 2.1** Lieutenant-General Thomas Gage

*Source:* Courtesy of the Anne S.K. Brown Military Collection, Brown University Library, Providence, Rhode Island

The entire venture was ill-advised. Surprise facilitated the gunpowder removal from Charlestown the previous September in the "powder alarm." The Massachusetts town had been taken unaware and the deed done before an effective repost could be made, a lesson not lost on other towns. By December 1774, a system to monitor troop movements had been devised by the committees of correspondence. Somewhat effective, but certainly not perfect, another march to seize weapons and ammunition occurred in February 1775 when Lieutenant-Colonel Alexander Leslie brought a force of regulars across the harbor without detection. But, the general intent had already been discerned and the countryside alerted. Salem, Massachusetts, most famous for its witch trials, might have been famous as the first battle of the rebellion had Leslie not been a man of sound military judgment. Upon arriving in Salem, he was confronted by a small force as more militia streamed into the village. His decision to disengage and withdraw preserved the peace, at least in the near term. Together, these incidents should have represented a warning to Gage. The veteran of the bloody suppression of rebellions in Ireland and Scotland did not, however, discern the danger into which his troops stood (see Figure 2.2).[11]

Strategy can be held hostage by tactical decisions. In the late twentieth century, a US Marine Corps Commandant wrote of the "strategic corporal," a relatively junior military member whose actions could have outsized effects. Jesse Adair was not a corporal, but he was a Marine. A hard-charging lieutenant, Major John Pitcairn selected him to lead the vanguard of six light companies rushing ahead of the main column to offset the time lost when the British force landed in a swamp that morning. The assignment-reach Concord as quickly as possible to paralyze any local resistance that might assemble. The road divided as it approached Lexington. Adair might well have chosen to bypass the village. While leaving an organized military force in the rear of the advanced guard might seem foolish, describing the 80-odd militia men as an organized force would be overly generous. Alerted by Paul Revere's famous ride, these men had been active for hours; some had already straggled away. Those who remained spent the intervening time in the nearby Buckman Tavern. Instead of pressing on recognizing the critical need for speed, Adair marched on to Lexington Green. Pitcairn soon gained the head of the column, but too late. With the soldiers drawn up in rough lines, some of the militiamen withdrew when commanded to do so by the British major (see Figure 2.3).

The confrontation might have eased had not a single shot been fired, most likely from inside Buckman Tavern. It may well have been part of the alarm spreading through the countryside. The troops' response was to open fire. Their volley killed eight and wounded ten more, at the cost of a single wounded man. A small skirmish in which the strength of both sides combined totaled less than 350 men set in motion another row of dominoes whose cascade eventually spread across much of the globe and became legendary as "The Shot Heard 'Round the World."[12]

Pitcairn pressed on and rendezvoused at Concord with the main column. Initially, they gained possession of the town and conducted a search, albeit with little to show for the effort. In the interim, however, thousands of "minutemen," members of the

**FIGURE 2.2** Grenadier, 10th Regiment of Foot

**FIGURE 2.3**   The Fight at Lexington Green

*Source:* Courtesy of the Anne S.K. Brown Military Collection, Brown University Library, Providence, Rhode Island

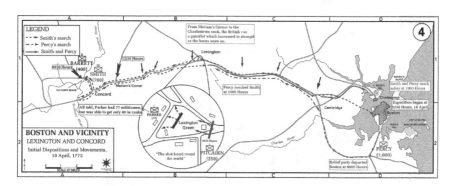

**MAP 2.1**   British March to Concord

*Source:* Map Courtesy of the United States Military Academy Department of History, West Point, New York

town militia designated to respond most quickly to emergencies, streamed toward Concord taking up positions along the road the column would have to retrace. North of Concord, the militia withdrew across North Bridge, held at bay by a few dozen soldiers. Smith's force might have withdrawn with less bloodshed but for another of those small tactical accidents that produced major strategic effects. While searching a blacksmith's shed, the troops upset a brazier and started a fire. Militia across the stream saw only the smoke and assumed the town was being set to the torch. They goaded their reluctant commander into action, forcing the retreat of the outnumbered regulars on the bridge. Falling back on the main body, these troops precipitated a general retreat. Converging militia from surrounding towns joined the fight in small groups, firing from cover along the road back to Lexington. The retreat became a rout.[13] Despite the complaints of some subordinates, Smith proved prudent, having already sent for reinforcements earlier in the morning. The original force suffered roughly 300 killed, wounded, or missing. Losses might have been greater still had it not been for the swift actions of Brigadier Hugh Percy. Leading a relief column, he established a secure perimeter at Lexington into which the survivors of Smith's column fell back in disorder, saved only by this sanctuary (see Figure 2.4).

British troops had been garrisoned in Boston since the Stamp Act crisis, yet the commanders demonstrated a startling lack of knowledge about the local topography. Cartography, one of the most basic skills cultivated by later staff organizations, represented a basic form of intelligence about the environment without which successful operations cannot be assured. Intelligence on the opposing forces was

**FIGURE 2.4** Retreat from Concord

*Source:* Courtesy of the Anne S.K. Brown Military Collection, Brown University Library, Providence, Rhode Island

not effectively gathered. Perhaps British commanders were lulled into a false sense of security by the unprofessional appearance of the militia at musters who "made a miserable appearance on parade."[14] While their appearance may have been unimpressive, some of their number had seen active service in previous wars. Gage once wrote to Washington that New Englanders were "the worst Soldiers on the Continent," but the sheer number of citizens training with weapons should have forced him to pause and reconsider his plans. The ancient Chinese theorist of war, Sun Tzu, would have admonished Gage to know the enemy and to know his own force.[15] He may have understood the strengths and weaknesses of his own troops, but he clearly did not understand the adversary. On the day of the battle, almost 4,000 men turned out to oppose the troops marching toward Concord. Dozens of surrounding towns sent contingents who kept continuous pressure on the beleaguered regulars all along the return route.[16]

If Gage acted rashly, his actions were spurred by a letter from Lord Dartmouth, the colonial secretary, who directed him: "to arrest and imprison the principal actors & abettors in the Provincial Congress" and an admonition that: "in such a Situation, Force should be repelled by Force."[17] It is not clear whether Gage was aware of the impending arrival of a trio of major-generals or that one of them, William Howe, held a dormant commission to succeed Gage as commander of all troops in the colonies. One of the great ironies was that Dartmouth did not act out of spite or hatred. Not an advocate of making concessions to the colonists, nonetheless, he was one of the voices of moderation. As the Cabinet saw matters, the time for moderation had passed. Leaders in London viewed the Boston radicals as a rebellious rabble and expected that "any efforts of the People, unprepared to encounter with a regular force, cannot be very formidable . . . it will surely be better that the Conflict should be brought on."[18]

Not all Cabinet members remained so optimistic. Two officials, in particular, foresaw the difficulties should violence erupt. Adjutant General to the Forces Edward Harvey had seen the suppression of rebellion firsthand as aide-de-camp to the Duke of Cumberland during the final Jacobite rising in 1745–1746. Lord Barrington, Secretary at War, though limited in his responsibility for army administration, had served as a member of the Lords of the Admiralty during the War of the Austrian Succession (1740–1748). He understood both the requirements of an army in the field on the far side of the Atlantic and the difficulties of transporting supplies across the ocean. Barrington and Harvey believed that a naval blockade of Boston represented the only option.[19]

## Cascading Effects

The "rude rabble" proved to be almost 20,000 strong. Exact numbers are impossible to determine as George Washington later noted; the militia tended to come and go as they pleased.[20] In the aftermath of the Lexington-Concord affair, colonial militia effectively laid siege to Boston. Men pouring in from surrounding Massachusetts towns bolstered troops from neighboring colonies. Nathanael Greene, who would do more for the cause than any officer except Washington, brought in 1,500 Rhode Islanders. John Stark led 2,000 men from New Hampshire. Connecticut sent 6,000 with Benedict Arnold at the head of one small contingent. Three problems plagued these forces. First, the troops came to the encampment with minimal resources with ammunition in critically short supply. Second, no single authority governed all of the troops. Finally, the rebel forces lacked artillery.[21] The first problem troubled the Continental Army throughout the conflict. The last two issues found more immediate solutions.

Benedict Arnold is, in the United States, synonymous with treason. His fate was not preordained. A prominent New Haven merchant with a thirst for military glory, he brought troops to the encampment at Cambridge, Massachusetts, but quickly realized that neither the limited prospects for battle nor his relatively junior rank offered much chance to distinguish himself. Leaving the company he brought, Arnold sought authority from the Massachusetts Committee of Safety to take control of forts along the Lake Champlain corridor. Armed with nothing more than a warrant to raise troops in the western part of the colony, he set off on the expedition. Concurrently, Ethan Allen led a militia group into the New Hampshire Grants, a disputed region east of Lake Champlain claimed by both New York and New Hampshire. Residents did not recognize the sovereignty of either colonial government. Allen, with a price on his head before the American War began, had a long history of resisting attempts by New York to impose authority; he and his Green Mountain Boys had done so forcefully. A Connecticut delegation entreated him to accomplish the same task undertaken by Arnold. The strategic value of the forts at Ticonderoga and Crown Point was clear to everyone. Arnold, hearing of another force bound on the same errand, arrived on the eastern shore of Lake Champlain to find Allen and over 200 men already at work securing boats. With only a handful of troops under his authority and recognizing the attachment of the Green Mountain Boys to Allen, the two struck a deal for shared command. A tenuous situation at best, neither commander had much respect for the other. Arnold's scathing report to the Massachusetts Committee of Safety reported that: "Colonel Allen is a proper man to head his own wild people, but entirely unacquainted with military service." Arnold went on to show his prickly nature in stating his intention to assert authority at Ticonderoga (see Figure 2.5).[22]

With only enough transport for less than half the force, a hundred men set off across the lake, achieving complete surprise. The sleeping garrison was unaware of the outbreak of hostilities. The commander of forces in Canada, from which they were detached, would not hear of the events in Massachusetts for another four days. With the structural damage from the earlier war never fully repaired and a garrison of less than 50 officers and men, Fort Ticonderoga lay in decrepit condition. The fort was taken by stealth, not assault. The fort at Crown Point was also seized and a subsequent expedition against St. John captured an armed sloop, giving the rebel force complete command of the lake (see Figure 2.6).[23]

**FIGURE 2.5**   Benedict Arnold

*Source:* Courtesy of the Anne S.K. Brown Military Collection, Brown University Library, Providence, Rhode Island

**FIGURE 2.6**   Capture of Fort Ticonderoga

*Source:* Courtesy of the Anne S.K. Brown Military Collection, Brown University Library, Providence, Rhode Island

Leadership on both sides recognized the importance of the "Great Warpath"— the waterways of upstate New York. Movement by water has always been the most effective method of transporting large bodies of troops and significant equipment. A chain of lakes and rivers, bridged by portages and short stretches of road linked Canada with New York City. The Lake Champlain—Lake George—Hudson River corridor represented either a profound advantage or a lethal vulnerability depending on the balance of power in northern New York. In the Seven Years' War, these waterways provided an avenue for a French advance that threatened Albany. As the war progressed, it facilitated the British campaign against Montreal. The highway for raiding parties and military campaigns since before European settlers, the American War saw this pattern continue with each army taking its turn.[24]

## Elbow Room

Washington was appointed to command the Continental Army on 14 June 1775. The forces arrayed around Boston and those occupying the forts in the northern wilderness were all incorporated into the newly created Continental Army. The first and most formative of the early battles would be fought, however, before the army knew its new commander or its new name. Ticonderoga was taken by stealth. Lexington and Concord had been haphazard affairs, meeting engagements where troops blundered into contact. Militia used cover, concealment, and movement before melting back into the population, now known as "irregular warfare." Such tactics characterized those first skirmishes but would not win the war. Events on the hills surrounding Boston Harbor were far more traditional affairs reflecting the standard military doctrine of the time. These events also shaped the perceptions of senior leaders on both sides with dramatic repercussions throughout the war.

Boston represented the principal point of contention in the years preceding the war and through the March 1776 British withdrawal. Not the sprawling web of neighborhoods today, it occupied a small, clenched fist protruding into the harbor. The Back Bay to the west covered a greater area than the town. Linked to the mainland by a narrow neck that barely rose above the high tide line, it was a prison for the inhabitants and the government troops occupying the town, dominated by high ground across the water both north and south. To the south lay Dorchester Heights, the summit of which would eventually be crowned with cannon making the harbor untenable for the Royal Navy. The high ground to the north—the Charlestown peninsula—effectively became an island during high tides and the ground for the war's first set-piece battle. Charlestown peninsula formed a rounded projection thrusting southward dominated by three hills with Bunker Hill lying closest to the land bridge and rising the highest. The hill had been initially occupied by British troops who withdrew in the weeks following Concord.

Peaking at an estimated 20,000 men, the militia strength rapidly dropped as men from nearby towns returned home. The remainder still outnumbered Gage's small force trapped in Boston. With isolated detachments withdrawn, everything beyond the barricade across Boston Neck was ceded to the rebels.[25] Lord Percy, commander of the relief column in April, wrote describing the rebels to Lord Dartmouth: "Whoever looks upon them as an irregular mob will find himself much mistaken. They have men amongst them those who know very well what they are about."[26] The balance of forces shifted as fresh blood was injected into the British command structure. The frigate HMS *Cerberus* sailed into Boston Harbor on 25 May 1775. It delivered what one member of the group termed a "triumvirate of reputation," sent to bolster Gage's increasingly defeatist tone. Perhaps the vessel was the warship most readily available, but the choice seems to speak of a wicked sense of humor at the Admiralty. A ship named for the three-headed hell hound of Greek mythology delivered a three-headed group of leaders intended to guard the Crown's interests. Upon arrival, Sir Henry Clinton is reported to have quipped about the close confines of Boston: "Well, let us in, and we shall make elbow room."[27] Had these men expended as much effort cooperating in that task as they did undermining each other, the outcome might have been very different.

The rebellion's prospects were far from the deterministic inevitability of some American popular histories. Gunpowder remained in short supply as over half the local stores had been expended between Lexington, Concord, and the attacks on the retreating soldiers.[28] Troop numbers reported at the Cambridge encampment ebbed and flowed from day to day, representing a polyglot assembly with a variety of weapons. While Arnold and Allen had captured the cannon and mortars at

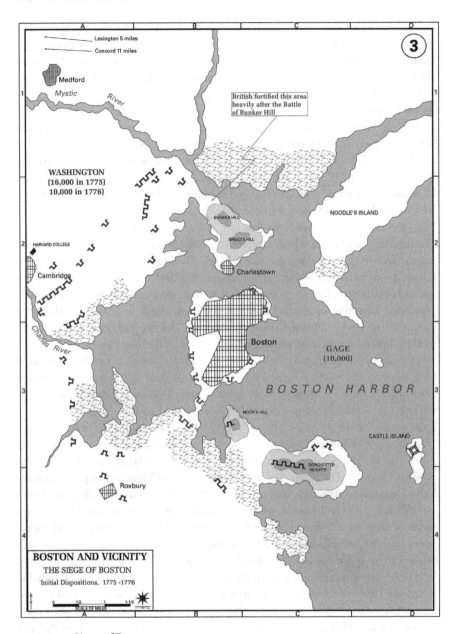

**MAP 2.2**  Siege of Boston

*Source:* Map Courtesy of the United States Military Academy Department of History, West Point, New York

Ticonderoga, artillery in the Boston area was sparse. Firing even those few pieces would have quickly exhausted rebel powder stores. To complicate matters, the trio of aggressive subordinates in the British camp began to drive the agenda in Boston.

William Howe was senior and regarded as one of the finest officers to have served in the colonies during the Seven Years' War, particularly in James Wolfe's victory at Quebec in 1759. Clinton, son of an admiral and governor of the Province of New York, earned a stellar reputation in Germany during the same war. John Burgoyne served in Portugal during the late war and raised the 16th Light Dragoons, popularly known as Burgoyne's Light Horse, a unit remarkable for the modern and humane treatment of the troops, and was a Member of Parliament, a playwright, and a notorious gambler. Having sold his commission after the war, he was both the oldest of the three and the most junior in date of rank. Together these men represented a wealth of military expertise. They quickly set to work seeking to force the decisive battle that London sought. Influential government members suggested that a single battle would suppress the rebellion. Many, including Lord Suffolk, Secretary of State for the Northern Department, and Lord Sandwich, First Lord of the Admiralty, predicted that the colonials would run at the first sound of the guns. General Jeffrey, Lord Amherst, who preceded Gage as CinC in North America, believed he could sweep all of the American opposition before him with only 5,000 troops.[29] This profound failure to understand the nature of the rebellion produced profoundly ill results for Crown forces. London did not just dispatch new leaders, it sent troops. The force in Boston eventually swelled to 17 infantry regiments, four cavalry squadrons, and five artillery companies, all supported by four ships-of-the-line, three frigates, and various smaller vessels.[30] As the newly arrived major-generals planned to create "elbow room," their opponents stole a march and occupied one of the hills on the peninsula to the north.

On 13 June, the Massachusetts Committee of Safety received intelligence that Gage intended to occupy the heights at Charlestown and Dorchester and ordered Colonel William Prescott to establish a defensive position on the peninsula. Prescott chose Bunker Hill. The lead element commander differed with his superior on the best place to build a fortification and began construction on Breed's Hill to the southwest with the nominal purpose to establish a battery to bombard Boston. Breed's Hill, closer and thus a more advantageous position, was, however, exposed to fire from ships anchored in the harbor. Reinforcements would have a perilous path, not only crossing Charlestown Neck but also moving from Bunker Hill to the redoubt further down the peninsula. All these factors contributed to the subsequent rebel defeat.

Gage mounted a swift response and mobilized an infantry force when the redoubt was sighted on the morning of 17 June. By mid-afternoon, 3,000 troops under the overall command of Howe ferried across the harbor to Charlestown. The fight that ensued changed the perceptions of many leaders on both sides. Howe did not expect the stiff initial resistance and thus mounted a frontal assault. When it failed, he launched another, and finally a third. The last assault carried the fortification, but largely because its location made reinforcement and resupply almost impossible. The frigate HMS *Lively* early on opened a cannonade against the redoubt even as it was being built. Other Royal Navy ships made passage of the Neck extremely hazardous. With powder and shot almost exhausted, tradition holds that one of the rebel officers gave the order not to fire at the oncoming redcoats until they could see "the whites of their eyes." Whether the words were actually spoken or by whom remains unclear. What is clear is that the incident, as well as perceptions of the events, became enshrined in American mythology. More immediately, the day's events shaped the perception of American commanders regarding the capabilities of their troops and those of their adversary.[31]

The troops fighting on the hill did not yet know that they had been officially designated the Continental Army. The doctrine of that army would be shaped by interpretations of the battle. Discipline and adherence to orders, already long inculcated in George Washington's psyche, remained paramount as he shaped the new army.

Had the battle occurred on Bunker Hill, the outcome might have been different. Captain Richard Gridley, the lead element commander, had credentials that made his choice for the redoubt persuasive. Like Prescott, he had long military experience stretching back to King George's War. His service at Louisbourg in 1746 and subsequently under Wolfe and Amherst earned him a royal commission as an engineer, specializing in siege artillery. But with no artillery, the Breed's Hill choice was questionable. Though exposed on three sides, it had been stoutly defended. If one of the lessons from Bunker Hill involved following orders, another certainly confirmed the colonial militia's ability to stand firm in the face of British regulars, at least when protected by fortifications. Finally, the men themselves learned to fear the "cold steel" of British bayonets. Throughout the war's first half, the Continental Army lacked both the edged weapons and training in using them. British bayonets also claimed one of the rebellion's foremost intellectual supporters, Doctor Joseph Warren. Among the leading Boston radicals, he had been appointed as a brigadier general in the Continental Army. His commission not yet having arrived, he fought in the redoubt and was killed there serving as a private soldier. The American troops were not the only side to suffer notable casualties (see Figure 2.7).

Howe's losses were frightening. Overall, 227 officers and men were reported killed on the field, including Major John Pitcairn who had led the light infantry and grenadiers at Lexington and Concord. Over 800 soldiers of all ranks were wounded, 250 dying of their wounds after returning to Boston. One lieutenant-colonel, two majors, seven captains, and nine lieutenants were among the dead with 62 more wounded officers. The casualties proved the worst suffered by the British Army in any single engagement of the war. The carnage left Howe so shocked that he avoided further frontal assaults. Clearly stunned by the losses, he might have been more aggressive at other times and in other places where a more assertive decision might have ended the rebellion. In September, HMS *Scarborough* arrived with orders recalling Gage to London for "consultations." William Howe's dormant commission to succeed him was activated. The psychic wounds of Bunker Hill not only served as the foundational mythology for American arms but it also resonated through both armies in ways no one at the time could have predicted.

**FIGURE 2.7**    Bunker Hill, Death of Dr. Warren

*Source:* Courtesy of the Anne S.K. Brown Military Collection, Brown University Library, Providence, Rhode Island

## "That Peace and Good Order May the Sooner Be Restored"[32]

Far to the south, very different events unfolded. John Murray, Lord Dunmore, enjoyed a brief flurry of popularity in 1774 in Virginia. Disputes arose between colonists seeking to extend the boundaries of the colony into Shawnee and Mingo tribal lands. A series of provocations eventually led to a punitive expedition under the royal governor. The campaign's success initially placed Dunmore in a favorable light, but his attempts to profit financially from the newly acquired territory soon turned powerful Virginia political interests against him. His attempts to profit from the conflict, combined with the unrest in New England, alienated most of the politically powerful men in the colony. Patrick Henry, a barrister and political radical, famously intoned, "Give me liberty or give me death!" Henry's March 1775 speech and Dunmore's decision to dismiss the legislature marked the final collapse of royal government in Virginia. It also precipitated another "powder alarm" when Royal Navy sailors emptied the Williamsburg magazine. When Henry led a force of several hundred men of the Virginia independent companies toward Williamsburg demanding that the seized powder be returned or recompensed, Dunmore fled with his family for the safety of the 44-gun frigate HMS *Roebuck*.[33]

The governor never returned to his palatial residence in the capital. He continued to issue orders and edicts from his shipboard sanctuary and a series of bases ashore established under the navy's guns. Dunmore saw one particular proclamation as a military necessity. With no royal troops headed to Virginia in the foreseeable future and few Loyalists willing to take up arms, he tapped the only source he deemed available: "I shall be forced and it is my fixed purpose to arm all my own Negroes and receive all others that will come to me whom I shall declare free."[34] In November, he further included: "all *indented servants, Negroes,* or others (appertaining to rebels) *free,* that are able and willing to bear arms, they *joining his Majesty's troops.*"[35] The decision proved militarily unprofitable. The troops never re-established royal authority. Politically, the proclamation proved disastrous. Most large landowners had a significant stake in continued commerce with Britain particularly in tobacco, and these individuals initially remained committed to this arrangement. Landon Carter, one of the richest men in Virginia, represented the shift in political opinion that occurred in late 1775. A firm opponent of independence, he favored the British mixed monarchial form. Dunmore's proclamation, among other factors, convinced him that the British government had turned tyrannical. Many more such as Carter soured on royal governance forcing governors in North and South Carolina to flee.

## "It Was Apparent That We Must Surrender"[36]

Benedict Arnold, rebuffed in his quest to command the forces at Ticonderoga, returned to Cambridge with another scheme designed to bring military glory. He proposed an expedition to seize Quebec by proceeding overland through what is now Maine. By ascending the Kennebec River and then coming down the Chaudiere River, his force would emerge at Point Levis, opposite Quebec. Arnold initially approached Adjutant General Horatio Gates and, through him, the commanding general. Arnold was familiar with Canada as a result of his mercantile enterprises before the war. His energy and knowledge of the area made him appear an ideal candidate to lead the expedition. Unfortunately, his knowledge of Canada did not confer a similar familiarity with the backwoods along the proposed route of march. Arnold's force suffered grievously on that account. One of his columns turned back, reducing his force by almost a third. His men suffered from a lack of food, destruction of their equipment, and the absence of adequate maps. Arnold's force of will drove his diminished army toward the St. Lawrence River, arriving with only 600 men, five rounds of ammunition per man, and no artillery.[37] Another expedition proceeding from the Lake Champlain Valley experienced difficulties of a different sort. The departure was delayed by Philip Schuyler's indecision. Appointed a major general in June 1775, he was instructed to seize St. John, Montreal, and the surrounding territory. The order was framed in wording that offered Schuyler discretion as to whether to carry out the operation. Plagued by ill health and not aggressive by nature, he demurred until pressured to relinquish command of the expedition to newly appointed Brigadier General Richard

Montgomery. The opposite of Schuyler, he possessed substantial military experience and had campaigned with Amherst's army at Ticonderoga, Crown Point, and Montreal during the previous war. Schuyler squandered the entire summer before Montgomery assumed command and imposed order on the undisciplined New York and Connecticut militia that comprised his force. He did not begin his march north until September, well after Arnold began his epic struggle across modern Maine.

The two small armies converged on Quebec; Montgomery having swept aside token detachments along the way. By the time the two bodies merged, winter arrived. The army proceeding from New York had shed much of its manpower with many militiamen refusing to leave the colony. Montgomery did bring captured winter clothing, artillery, and ammunition, but the cannons were far too small to breach Quebec's walls. Lacking the heavy artillery to batter down the walls, sufficient troops to encircle the city, and not enough food to keep his army in place long enough to force a surrender, his storming of Quebec though heroic, floundered. Montgomery was killed by grapeshot in the assault's first surge in a snowstorm on the last day of 1775. A diversionary attack by friendly Canadians never materialized. The 900 attackers were outnumbered two to one by the defenders who also possessed more and heavier cannons. But Montgomery had to act. Most enlistments expired the next day; only a few agreed to reenlist. Bravely storming the citadel in two separate thrusts, one led by Montgomery and the

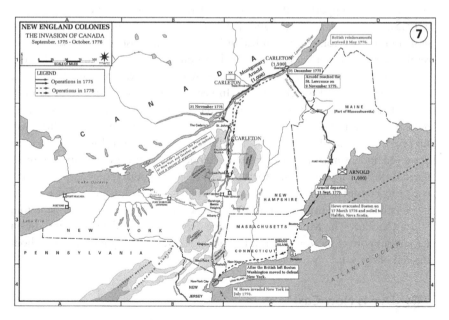

**MAP 2.3**  Invasion of Canada

*Source:* Map Courtesy of the United States Military Academy Department of History, West Point, New York

other by Arnold, the survivors were eventually driven back or surrounded. Among those taken prisoners included the eventual victor at Cowpens, Daniel Morgan. The campaign, properly supported, might have changed the war's calculus. Canada remained loyal and served as a staging point for two Crown expeditions down the lakes corridor toward Albany and ultimately New York.

The army sent against the fortress faced a capable, if cautious, adversary who possessed vast military experience.[38] Major-General Guy Carleton, a veteran of the War of the Austrian Succession and the Seven Years' War, ironically was wounded in the campaign to take Quebec in 1759. He also knew his adversary having served alongside Montgomery in Cuba during the same war. Informed by his native caution, he husbanded his available troops at Quebec, the lynchpin of the Canadian defensive system. Carleton committed only token forces to delay the advance from New York, thus providing him with a force at Quebec that outnumbered the invaders. Carleton's professional skill contrasted with the rebel's amateurish effort. A concerted, adequately provisioned campaign might have been irresistible. It might have added a 14th colony to the rebellion, but Canada was one domino that remained standing, in large part thanks to Guy Carleton.

## A Deceptive Coda

The final acts of the first year of open warfare appeared to favor the rebellion's prospects. In North Carolina, Loyalists drawn mainly from upcountry Scottish Highlanders rose in support of the Crown. Largely composed of discharged soldiers who had taken the land bounty afforded them for service in the earlier conflict and settled in the interior, these men had little love for the coastal elites or the former royal governor. Nonetheless, they rallied to London's call for volunteers. Marching toward the coast to meet an expected army bringing weapons and equipment, they were intercepted by rebel militia. In February 1776, at the Battle of Moore's Creek Bridge, several miles north of the rendezvous port of Wilmington, clansmen armed with broadswords charged the Patriots blocking their way. They were shattered, just as the Jacobite army, in which some of them had served, had been destroyed under similar circumstances at Culloden 30 years earlier. Commodore Sir Peter Parker finally arrived in April with the British troops intended to combine with the Loyalist militia to control the Carolinas. Upon learning of the defeat, he re-embarked the troops and initiated the failed attempt to capture Charleston, South Carolina. The Moore's Creek Bridge debacle presented a lesson not lost on Crown supporters in North Carolina who largely remained quiescent throughout the rest of the war.[39]

## "The Dye Is Now Cast"

While Arnold and Montgomery marched through the snow to attack Quebec and struggled to execute their final assault, another winter march echoed their heroic efforts. Henry Knox mounted a different march. The self-taught artillery commander (designate), an imposing presence standing six foot, three inches (just under 2 meters), the former Boston bookseller arrived at Ticonderoga in early December with orders to bring the usable artillery to Cambridge. Choosing 55 pieces, Knox set off on 9 December by boat to float the weapons down Lake George then overland by ox-drawn sleds (called sledges). He arrived in Cambridge 47 days later, having conquered the Hudson River, the Berkshire Mountains, and deep snows, and without losing a man or a weapon. His effort, combined with a maritime success, set the stage for the final act that forced Howe to quit Boston.[40]

The schooner *Lee*, commissioned by Washington to interdict British supplies bound for Boston, departed Beverly, Massachusetts, in late November 1775. Cruising for prizes on 29 November, she was mistaken for a pilot boat by the ordnance brig *Nancy*, bound for Boston with flints, cannonballs, and other ammunition, which was attacked and taken. Her confiscated cargo combined with the artillery brought by Knox solved a pressing problem.[41] Gunpowder had been captured through other agencies. All that remained to force Howe to evacuate Boston was to mount the artillery on Dorchester Heights, the headland south of Boston. Once positioned atop the heights, the artillery made the main anchorage untenable. The army could not remain in Boston without a secure maritime supply link.[42] The final crescendo came in March 1776. With sufficient powder and the cannon from Ticonderoga, a bombardment of Boston began on 2 March 1776—a subterfuge. The distracting bombardment covered the movement of troops to Dorchester Heights. The operation, unlike the building of the redoubt on Breed's Hill, was meticulously planned. Gabions, wicker baskets filled with earth, were loaded into frames. Knowing the frozen ground would not easily be excavated, the earthworks were built above ground. Bombardment noise covered the movements. At Bunker Hill, Colonel Prescott asserted that the works were best defended by those who constructed them. At Dorchester Heights, the Continental Army demonstrated mastery of at least some of the lessons of Bunker Hill. Fresh troops replaced those that had built the fortifications. They brought cannons. Howe had no alternative. Boston had to be evacuated.

Howe had already been ordered to evacuate Boston. His instructions came a month earlier. He hesitated. Even in the face of the new position on Dorchester Heights, his first inclination was to repeat the folly of Bunker Hill. Weather intervened, so the seriousness of the intent was never put to the test. He quickly moved, instead, to load troops, supplies, and about a thousand Loyalists into transports. People were prioritized over supplies; a pall of smoke hung over the town when military equipment that would not fit on the transports was burned. The loadout was completed on 17 March. The town, having suffered badly under British occupation, was in no mood for the sectarian squabbles of earlier times. Even Washington was in no hurry to claim the prize. The population had been devastated, not only by occupation and evacuation but by a smallpox outbreak. The armada cleared the harbor ten days later, sailing for Halifax in preparation for the next great act in the drama.[43]

Clausewitz wrote that "the only source of war is politics . . . war in itself does not suspend political intercourse."[44] Political activities did not end with Lexington and Concord. Even as Arnold trudged through the wilderness toward Quebec, the Continental Congress furiously debated a measure to defuse the crisis without further bloodshed—the Olive Branch Petition. Hancock signed it as prominently as he later signed the Declaration of Independence. It did not matter. George III wrote to Lord North in response to events around Boston: "the New England Governments are in a State of Rebellion, blows must decide whether they are to be subject to this Country or independant [sic]."[45] The king's attitude hardened before the arrival of the Olive Branch Petition. He refused to receive it. His earlier letter on a Quaker petition urging Britain to relent on taxes suggested his future attitude: "the dye [sic] is now cast, the Colonies must either submit or triumph."[46] It became clear in the spring of 1776, that such triumph or submission would be at the point of a bayonet.

## Notes

1 Sandwich, quoted in Mackesy, *War for America,* 61.
2 Washington's misadventures are detailed in Alex Axelrod, *Blooding at Great Meadows: Young George Washington and the Battle that Shaped the Man* (Philadelphia, PA: Running Press, 2007) and David A. Clary, *George Washington's First War: His Early Military Adventures* (New York: Simon & Schuster, 2011), 54–90.
3 Ron Chernow, *Washington: A Life* (New York: Penguin Press, 2010), 185.
4 Ibid., 183.
5 Washington, quoted in Edward G. Lengel, *General George Washington: A Military Life* (New York: Random House, 2005), 88.
6 Ibid., 87–8; Clary, George *Washington's First War.*
7 Lengel, *Washington,* 85–9, 182–7.
8 Dominick Mazzagetti, *Charles Lee: Self Before Country* (New Brunswick, NJ: Rutgers University Press, 2013); Charles Lee, *The Life and Memoirs of the Late Major General Lee* (New York: Richard Scott, 1813).
9 Paul David Nelson, *General Horatio Gates: A Biography* (Baton Rouge, LA: Louisiana State University Press, 1976), xi, 41.
10 David Hackett Fischer, *Paul Revere's Ride* (New York and Oxford: Oxford University Press, 1994), 117–21.
11 Ibid., 54, 58–60.
12 Ibid., 189–91; John Ferling, *Independence: The Struggle to Set America Free* (New York: Bloomsbury, 2011), 111–2.
13 Fischer provides an excellent overall account of the events both during the battle and in the period leading to the engagements. A more concise account can be found in George F. Scheer and Hugh F. Rankin, *Rebels and Redcoats* (New York: World Publishing, 1957), 17–40.
14 Fischer, *Paul Revere's Ride,* 154; Higginbotham, *War of American Independence,* 51–2.
15 Sun Tzu, *The Art of War,* trans. Samuel B. Griffiths (New York: Oxford University Press, 1963), 129.
16 Gage quoted in W. W. Abbot, ed., *The Papers of George Washington: Colonial Series* (Charlottesville, VA and London: University Press of Virginia, 1984), 3:115; for the strength of the forces opposing the march, Ward lists 3,763 men who participated while the earlier examination of muster rolls by Coburn counted over 3,900. In so fluid a situation, exact numbers can never be determined; Frank Warren Coburn, *The Battle of April 19, 1775* (Lexington, MA: Lexington Historical Society, 1922); Christopher Ward, *The War of the Revolution* (New York: Macmillan, 1952), 50.
17 Dartmouth to Gage, 27 January 1775, Thomas Gage Papers, Series II, Subseries I, 767, William L. Clements Library, The University of Michigan, Ann Arbor, Michigan.

18  Ibid.

19  John Shy, *A People Numerous and Armed* (New York: Oxford University Press, 1976), 99.

20  Washington to Arthur Lee, *The Writings of George Washington,* vol. 3, ed. John Clement Fitzpatrick (Washington, DC: Government Printing Office, 1931), 450.

21  Higginbotham, *War of American Independence,* 66.

22  Arnold to Massachusetts Committee of Safety in *The Spirit of Seventy-Six,* ed. Henry Steele Commager and Richard B. Morris (New York: HarperCollins, 1967), 104–5.

23  Ibid., 102–5.

24  The term "Great Warpath" is taken from Eliot A. Cohen, *Conquered into Liberty: Two Centuries of Battles along the Great Warpath That Made the American Way of War* (New York: Free Press, 2011), which argues that the events along this watershed were central to the history of North America.

25  Paul Lockhart, *The Whites of Their Eyes: Bunker Hill, the First American Army, and the Emergence of George Washington* (New York: HarperCollins, 2011), 39–42; Scheer and Rankin, *Rebels and Redcoats* 41–7.

26  Percy to Dartmouth, quoted in Scheer and Rankin, *Rebels and Redcoats,* 43.

27  Ibid., 55.

28  Kevin Phillips, *1775: A Good Year for Revolution* (New York: Viking, 2012), 297.

29  Higginbotham, *War of American Independence,* 52; Ira D. Gruber, *The Howe Brothers and the American Revolution* (Chapel Hill, NC: University of North Carolina Press, 1972), 22.

30  Arthur Swinson, ed., *A Register of Regiments and Corps of the British Army* (London: Archive Press, 1972).

31  For detailed accounts of the battle, see Lockhart, *The Whites of Their Eyes* and Richard M. Ketchum, *Decisive Day: The Battle for Bunker Hill* (New York: American Heritage, 1962).

32  John Murray, Lord Dunmore, Proclamation of 7 November 1775, Dunmore's Proclamation, printed in the *Pennsylvania Journal and Weekly Advertiser,* December 6, 1775 (New York: The Gilder Lehrman Institute of American History), GLC01706.

33  James K. Swisher, *The Revolutionary War in the Southern Back Country* (Gretna, LA: Pelican, 2010), 47.

34  Dunmore to Dartmouth, 1 May 1775, *Documents of the American Revolution,* Vol. IX, ed. G. K. Davies (Shannon: Irish University Press, 1972), 108.

35  Dunmore, Proclamation of 7 November 1775.

36  The end of the account of Arnold's expedition by John Joseph Henry in Commager and Morris, *The Spirit of Seventy-Six,* 206–9.

37  Kenneth Roberts, ed., *March to Quebec, Journals of the Members of Arnold's Expedition* (Garden City, NY: Doubleday, 1938).

38  Detailed accounts of the campaign can be found in Thomas A. Desjardin, *Through a Howling Wilderness: Benedict Arnold's March to Quebec, 1775* (New York: St. Martin's Press, 2006); Robert McConnell Hatch, *Thrust for Canada: The American Attempt on Quebec in 1775–1776* (Boston, MA: Houghton Mifflin, 1979); from the British perspective, George F. G. Stanley, *Canada Invaded, 1775–1776* (Toronto: A.M. Hakkert, 1973).

39  Stanley D. M. Carpenter, *Southern Gambit: Cornwallis and the British March to Yorktown* (Norman, OK: University of Oklahoma Press, 2019), 38–41.

40  Ferling, *Almost a Miracle,* 102–5.

41  James L. Nelson, *George Washington's Secret Navy: How the American Revolution Went to Sea* (New York: McGraw Hill, 2008), 210–5.

42  Ferling, *Almost a Miracle,* 106.

43  Scheer and Rankin, *Rebels and Redcoats,* 107–10; Ferling, *Almost a Miracle,* 105–7.

44  Clausewitz, *On War,* indexed edition, eds. Michael Howard and Peter Paret (Princeton, NJ: Princeton University Press, 1984), 605.

45  John Fortescue, ed., *The Correspondence of King George the Third from 1760 to December 1783,* Vol. III (London: Macmillan, n.d.), 153.

46  Ibid., 131.

# 3

# HIGH WATER MARK

In a word, my dear Sir, if every nerve is not strained to recruit the new army
with all possible expedition, I think the game is pretty nearly up.[1]

—*George Washington to his brother John Augustine Washington,*
*18 December 1776*

As Christmas 1776 approached, William Howe had many reasons to be satisfied (see
Figure 3.1). He commanded the largest force ever employed by Britain on overseas
service. The second-largest city in the colonies—also the largest port—lay firmly in
hand and served as this headquarters. His opponent, George Washington, had been
driven from the most important strategic position in North America. Howe accomplished the feat without a frontal assault and the consequent losses. While many
subordinates chaffed under the restrictions on such aggressive actions imposed by
the commander, his outlook was different than many of the officers in the colonies.
Some critics even went so far as to suggest that Howe's indolence and dissipation
had resulted in missed opportunities.[2] He took a mistress, the wife of a provincial
officer whom Howe appointed as the commissary of prisoners. His dalliance in the
safe confines of New York led to derisive ditties that made the rounds of the taverns:

> Awake, arouse, Sir Billy
> There's forage in the plain.
> Ah, leave your little Filly,
> And open the campaign.[3]

Such criticism did not represent an accurate reflection of the reasons for his
restraint. The Howe brothers had personal connections to the colonies. Their
older brother was killed in battle during the Seven Years' War. Massachusetts commissioned the monument to him at Westminster Abbey. An opponent of using

DOI: 10.4324/9781003041276-5

**FIGURE 3.1**    Lieutenant-General Sir William Howe

*Source:* Courtesy of the Anne S.K. Brown Military Collection, Brown University Library, Providence, Rhode Island

force in North America, he ran for Parliament on a promise not to accept command. Why, then, did he accept command? The Howe brothers, William and Lord Richard, were believed to have a familial connection to the royal family. Loyalty inspired them. They were also inspired by their personal connection to the colonists. Howe accepted command, as did his brother, on the condition that they were also appointed as peace commissioners with the goal of restoring colonial loyalty. They reasoned that a crushing military defeat inflicting massive casualties would be counterproductive, breeding resentment, rather than reconciliation. This insight informed the entire 1776 campaign.[4]

## Southern Rebuff

The opening moves of the summer campaign did not bode well for British arms. Even in the aftermath of the abortive North Carolina Loyalist rising that ended at Moore's Creek Bridge in February, Admiral Sir Peter Parker and Major-General Henry Clinton pressed on to Charles Town (Charleston), South Carolina. The plan called for landings on Sullivan's Island, the barrier island immediately north of the harbor entrance. Occupying the partially completed Fort Moultrie on the island would close the harbor and force the city to surrender. Initial landings on the island north of Sullivan's Island offered hope for a quick resolution. Loyalists and Native Americans were expected to descend on the frontier concurrent with coastal operations. These operations, mutually supporting, created the appearance of a coordinated and thoughtful campaign to reclaim the southern colonies whose governors assured Lord George Germain that a vast reservoir of support for the Crown could be tapped, an illusory impression. Ignorance of the local terrain, physical and human, that had complicated operations in Massachusetts was more pronounced and more detrimental in South Carolina.[5]

The attempt to draw rebel forces inland by fomenting a Cherokee attack on the frontier miscarried from the start. John Stuart, Superintendent for Southern Indian Affairs with long experience along the frontier, was well liked by the Cherokee and honored with the title "Beloved Father." He argued against activating Britain's Cherokee allies. The devastation that the campaigns against the Cherokee wrought during the French and Indian War (primarily in 1761) had also been the training ground for irregular warfare practitioners such as Andrew Pickens and Francis Marion. Sequential colonial offensives destroyed the Cherokee towns forcing many to flee westward, seeking sanctuary with other Nations. As a result, Cherokee war parties released against the frontier would be unlikely to discriminate between settlers loyal to Britain and those supporting the rebellion. Finally, internal Cherokee politics also made an offensive problematic. Leaders who had fought the war and made peace in 1761 struggled to maintain influence and were in danger of being supplanted by a younger, more aggressive generation. Stuart warned that the delays incumbent on the debates between older chiefs and rising leaders would delay any action until after any campaign along the coast was complete. Stuart proved prescient on all accounts.

The plan for seizing Sullivan's Island involved a coordinated assault beginning with a naval bombardment and followed by an assault launched from the adjacent island. The attack would begin after a pre-arranged signal from the fleet. According to Clinton, that signal never came. According to Parker, the signal was made. The attack would likely have failed even if attempted. The initial bombardment did little damage to the palmetto palm log redoubt (a form of fortification). Even if the cannonade succeeded, the channel between the islands was not fordable especially at low tide. Clinton did have boats but made no attempt to cross.[6]

The harbor's contours led to Royal Navy attempts to force the passage to enfilade Fort Sullivan (later renamed Fort Moultrie in honor of the commander). Where the ford from the north was too deep, the waters through which the ships sailed were too shallow. The ships struck hard on a shoal. Two were floated off and escaped, but HMS *Actaeon* stuck fast and was burned by her crew. It cost Britain a newly commissioned frigate and gave the rebels an incremental victory that buoyed spirits in a period of foreboding.[7]

The failure and the subsequent disputes regarding responsibility for the defeat permanently poisoned relations between the two commanders. Parker was not the last admiral with whom Clinton would fall out. He was not the only general whose flaws were foreshadowed in this battle and the aftermath. His nominal opponent, Major General Charles Lee, showed his mercurial disposition during the defense. By turns, he caromed between defeatism and overly optimistic aggression. His letters to Moultrie on Sullivan's Island instructed him to be prepared to spike the guns and withdraw and then within days to prepare to attack the British troops across the same channel that would ultimately protect Fort Sullivan's northern flank.

## A Grand Armada

Clinton and Lee were recalled by their respective commanders to prepare for the descent upon New York. Preparations by both sides were undertaken with urgency. Clinton and Lee served under their respective commanders, who would each wield unprecedented military instruments. Washington commanded an army larger than any colonial force ever amassed. Howe commanded the largest British amphibious expedition in history until the twentieth century. He directed a series of engagements that brought Britain to the brink of victory only to have that triumph snatched away by the same type of incremental victory that the rebellion had enjoyed in Charles Town. Washington had the more daunting task. His army of 30,000 men formed as he campaigned. It consisted primarily of militia from New York, New Jersey, Pennsylvania, and Connecticut. Less than one-third were Continental Army soldiers and only marginally better trained. Some units did stand with incredible bravery. A regiment of Marblehead, Massachusetts, fishermen repeatedly applied their seamanship skills to rescue the rebellion. Other battalions disintegrated on contact with the enemy. The uneven quality plagued Washington throughout the conflict.[8] The New York militia were a particular concern. Whereas the New England militia had organized detachments of "minutemen" prepared to respond on short notice, the middle colonies represented a different dynamic. The New England militia tradition was borne of seventeenth-century conflicts with Native American tribes and French troops. King Philips' War resulted in the death of roughly 7 percent of the regional colonial population.[9] Thus, colonists focused on military preparedness. While conflicts with France included substantial fighting in northern New York, the remoteness of the theater insulated the more populous coastal areas. The level of training and equipment of the more coastal militiamen can only be described as primitive.[10] These unreliable units constituted half of Washington's force.

By contrast, the Crown forces that began landing on Staten Island on 23 June 1776 were the lead elements of an army that swelled to over 31,000 officers and men. It included over 12,000 German auxiliary troops contracted from Brunswick and Hessen-Kassel.[11] Howe had substantial Long Island Loyalists numbering perhaps 1,500 men and a contingent of 2,000 Royal Marines that nominally answered to his brother, Admiral Richard, Lord Howe. The close cooperation between the brothers made the command conflict issue moot and ensured that the British Army would be supported by the fleet's firepower and freedom of operational maneuver throughout 1776 and 1777. Army and the navy synchronization during this period proved the exception during the war. The fundamental problem during the balance of the conflict was the fact that each service answered to a different master in London. The American Secretary, Lord George Germain, directed army operations (see Figure 3.2). The Royal Navy was controlled by the First Lord of the Admiralty, John Montagu, 4th Earl of Sandwich. While both were advocates for dealing harshly with the colonial rebels, the strategic visions animating the actions of each were irreconcilable.

Sandwich, a controversial figure often defamed as a gambler and libertine, nonetheless served as First Lord for the third time, having directed the Royal Navy during previous wars. He endeavored to prepare for the inevitable clash with France by reforming the purchase of naval stores. The measures proved insufficient, as the king and the majority of the Cabinet focused all available military and naval power on the recalcitrant colonies. Sandwich opposed the deployment of major naval units to North America, viewing the traditional role of the navy as "Britain's Wooden Walls" defending the homeland as a more appropriate employment.[12] His desire to concentrate the fleet in European waters clashed with Germain's intent, which focused on dedicating all available assets to prosecuting a "hard war" against the rebels.

Germain was a famously disloyal colleague, behavior that had led to his court martial and dismissal from the army for an egregious failure to execute attack orders at the Battle of Minden (1759) during the Seven Years' War. He proved no more accommodating in the Cabinet once politically rehabilitated. Bent on establishing himself as a dominant war minister, obstacles to his goal were three: the Secretary of State for the Southern Department, the First Lord of the Admiralty, and the principal minister who was also Chancellor of the Exchequer. Lord Frederick North did not see himself as a war leader and tried to step down on numerous occasions. Lord Weymouth was an intimate friend of Charles James Fox, who famously opposed using military force against the colonies. Noted more for sharing Fox's dissolute lifestyle than his politics, he offered little resistance to Germain's designs. Sandwich thus represented the principal stumbling block to

**FIGURE 3.2**   Lord George Germain

*Source:* Courtesy of the Anne S.K. Brown Military Collection, Brown University Library, Providence, Rhode Island

Germain's ascendancy. Even when Germain successfully secured Cabinet assent for specific naval deployments, Sandwich managed to delay or subvert the American Secretary's intent.[13] The strategic incoherence was not limited to his relations with the Admiralty.

Germain opposed the appointment of the Howe brothers as peace commissioners. When overruled, he crafted their instructions in a manner that made the failure of any negotiations a foregone conclusion. He also sought to enforce a blockade in addition to vigorous campaigns ashore. Lord Howe, as jealous of his prerogatives as was Sandwich of his authority, proved to be another insurmountable obstacle to Germain's designs. He sought to ensure the success of his brother's campaign in New York by providing direct naval support. Dedicating assets to the army's operational designs did have several detrimental effects. Chief among these was the limited number of ships available for blockade duty with only 15 frigates and sloops to cover the entire coast between Canada and East Florida. This paltry force made the failure of the blockade as certain as Germain had made the failure of the negotiations.[14] Germain's relationships remained strained with not only the principle but many of the key commanders, men who had garnered fame and reputation in the Seven Years' War. Howe was once described as the finest officer in the British Army. Both Clinton and Guy Carleton had served as aide-de-camp to the allied commander who had dismissed Germain. On this inauspicious foundation, Germain built a complex plan that required initiative from Carleton, who chafed at not receiving higher command in the colonies, and vigorous action by Howe and his subordinate commanders, who sought reconciliation. The grand design thus required both principal commanders to act in a manner inconsistent with their inclinations.

Lord Howe arrived on 12 July 1776 with a powerful squadron and 85 transports carrying reinforcements from Britain, including German auxiliaries. Parker's arrival from South Carolina further strengthened Howe's forces. He commanded the largest contingent of warships anywhere in the world. With over 40 percent of the active ships in the Royal Navy, his force included half of the ships-of-the-line (the battleships of the day). Lord Howe immediately set about contacting Washington to arrange negotiations. His entreaties were rebuffed over a matter of protocol. Lord Howe was willing to address his letter to Washington in any manner acceptable to the colonial leader except that which was demanded— General George Washington.[15] In the end, the admiral did meet with a Continental Congress delegation consisting of Benjamin Franklin, John Adams, and John Rutledge. The meeting was held on 11 September 1776 while William Howe contemplated the next move, having already driven Washington from Long Island.

William Howe's army arrived on Staten Island throughout July and early August. The final two convoys from Europe disembarked troops, including the Hessian contingent on 19 August 1776. Upon the arrival of the last regiments, the Hessian commander informed Howe that his men required a week to recover from the long Atlantic passage. They were given six days. All totaled, the force amounted to over 25,000 troops. While the German troops recovered, most of the army moved to Long Island. The Crown force came ashore at Gravesend Bay at the southwestern-most end of Long Island. Aptly named, the island stretched slightly less than 120 miles (193 km) from that landing site to Montauk Point at the far eastern end.

Strategically, the rich farmlands fed the city and every maritime approach to New York was dominated by the Long Island coast. Washington understood the military value of the position but was also concerned about a direct assault on Manhattan Island launched from Staten Island, which Howe had occupied without resistance upon his arrival in June.[16]

The challenge was heightened in July by the ease with which the frigates HMS *Rose* and HMS *Phoenix* passed up the Hudson River and sailed past the American batteries without suffering meaningful damage. The defenders also attempted to block the river by sinking hulks in the channel, attaching trees to the sunken vessels to form a sort of maritime *chevaux-de-frise*. The warships and accompanying tenders swept past the obstacles and anchored in Haverstraw Bay, over 30 miles upriver. Local militia made repeated attacks using row galleys, each mounting a large caliber

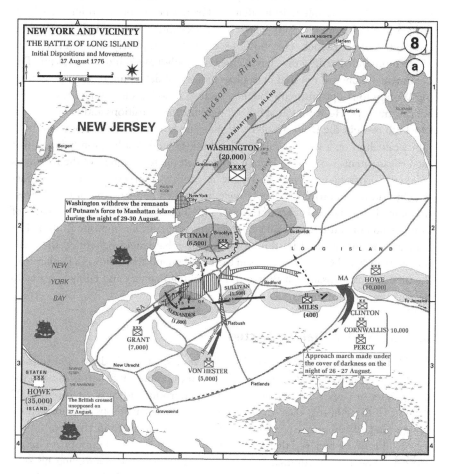

**MAP 3.1**    The New York Operation

*Source:* Map Courtesy of the United States Military Academy Department of History, West Point, New York

cannon in the bow. The attacks failed to capture or destroy the British vessels but did inflict sufficient damage to induce the captains to depart in early August when favorable winds and an ebbing tide allowed the ships to return back to the lower harbor. The frigates and their tenders again passed the gauntlet between Fort Lee on the New Jersey shore and Fort Washington on Manhattan Island, suffering some damage but brushing through the river obstacles with ease again.[17] Nonetheless, the point was made—the Royal Navy ruled the water.

## American Strategy

The strategic options open to Washington were limited. The Continental Army included two major generals who had previously served in the British Army as field grade officers. They offered conflicting opinions regarding the appropriate strategy for resisting the inevitable British offensive. Charles Lee favored turning New York into a charnel house, blockading streets and exacting a Bunker Hill-like cost for the capture of each block. Horatio Gates offered a completely different approach. He recommended ceding the coastal cities and withdrawing into the interior. The Continental Congress rejected both plans in favor of defending the city, constraining Washington's options, who sought a "war of posts" (a variation on the classical Fabian strategy). He would establish strongly fortified positions and invite Crown attacks to re-fight the Bunker Hill battle on more favorable terms. Hoping to both inflict casualties on a similar scale and hold the ground, Washington believed that such engagements would lead Britain to abandon the re-conquest of the rebellious colonies. Surprising for a man who spent his youth as a surveyor, his choice of battlefields had not improved markedly since his ill-sited construction of Fort Necessity in the Pennsylvania backcountry in 1754.[18] The rolling hills and open spaces of Long Island bore little resemblance to the confined peninsula opposite Boston. The maneuver room afforded by the more expansive battlefield benefitted the well-trained British and German regulars in the engagements that followed. Rather than the bloody frontal assaults of Bunker Hill, flanking marches and enfilading attacks became the order of the day.

## In Better Order Than I Expected

Shielded by a dozen frigates, several smaller vessels, and backed by eight ships-of-the-line, hundreds of vessels circulated between the camp on Staten Island and the sandy shore of Gravesend Bay during the late morning and early afternoon of 22 August. In three hours, over 15,000 British and German troops disembarked on Long Island. Washington, receiving incomplete or inaccurate intelligence from a variety of sources, believed that Howe had landed roughly 9,000 troops at Gravesend Bay. The Patriot commander remained cautious about reinforcing his own position in Brooklyn; he feared the move to Long Island might be a feint and "not knowing but the fleet may move up with the remainder of their army, and make an attack here [Manhattan], at the next flood tide." His opinion remained unchanged until the eve of the battle, when a hastily penned note informed the Continental Congress that it appeared the bulk of Howe's army had redeployed to Gravesend Bay. By then, his option of reinforcing his position in Brooklyn had foreclosed.[19]

A most interesting strategic question remains as to why Admiral Howe did not interdict the transfer of Continentals to Brooklyn. Several possible explanations exist for the decision by the British commanders not to interfere. Unfortunately, neither the general nor the admiral left details regarding their plans for New York. The absence of detailed correspondence is perhaps understandable. The Howe family valued education, but ruinously expensive political campaigns left the family in financial straits; the untimely death of the patriarch, Emanuel Scrope Howe, left them nearly destitute. The oldest son, George Augustus Howe, was considered a model officer and an educated gentleman. The eldest sister, Caroline, was not formally educated but her keen intellect made her formidable and a fixture in London society. Richard Howe, on the other hand, was never intellectually inclined in a formal sense. He left school at 14 to accompany Commodore George Anson on his circumnavigation of the globe. He also experienced merchant marine service that began at ten. Whatever the truth, Admiral Howe was noted for clear thinking but found articulating those ideas difficult and capturing them in writing almost impossible, not surprising for one of so limited a formal education.[20] His younger brother William benefitted from brief matriculation at Eton but was appointed as a royal page one year after arriving, a post frequently bestowed on sons of impoverished noble families. Noted early in his career for his drive and dedication, he penned a manual for light infantry based on his experiences in the American campaigns during the Seven Years' War. However, by the time he assumed the American command a fellow officer described him as "illiterate and indolent."[21] While certainly not actually illiterate, the sentiment likely illustrates why the Howes did not leave the detailed correspondence typical of many contemporaries.

Possibly, Washington was allowed to freely transport soldiers to Long Island to simplify the task of destroying his army. With the Royal Navy controlling the waterways, the Continental Army could be trapped and destroyed completely. Such a stratagem would, however, be inconsistent with declarations made by William Howe while standing for parliamentary election. The Howe brothers accepted command only on the condition that it carry with it authority to negotiate peace as well as prosecute the war. A design to maximize Patriot force casualties would be inconsistent with their sentiments. Thus, it appears likely that they believed a crushing defeat might permanently alienate the very subjects they were charged with returning to allegiance.[22]

If not meant to crush the rebellion by brute force, then what could have been the objective of allowing American forces free movement across the East River? Most likely, a combination of unique geography and inadequate intelligence combined to stay Lord Howe's hand. New York Harbor was challenging from an operational perspective. The East River is narrow; currents generated by the confluence of that waterway and its tributaries, mixing intermittently with tidal waters flowing from Long Island Sound, give part of the treacherous river the evocative name

"Hell's Gate."[23] While the Royal Navy dominated the waterways, not all of the rivers, bays, and sounds encircling the islands of southern New York are navigable. To complicate matters, General Howe believed Washington's army on Long Island to be much larger than it actually was. Clausewitz commented, "Many intelligence reports in war are contradictory; even more are false, and most are uncertain."[24] The observation perfectly captured the problems facing both commanders. Even after the campaign's opening phase, General Howe believed that the force defending the Brooklyn Heights was twice the number actually manning those lines.[25] Units that remained in Manhattan also gave British commanders pause, uncertain about their strength and intentions. Clausewitz assessed the challenge faced by officers in the period: "The only situation a commander can know fully is his own; his opponent's he can know only from unreliable intelligence."[26] Thus, it was better to allow Washington to reinforce a position that the Royal Navy could completely isolate. In the end, it did not matter.

Washington deployed only 9,000 of the 19,000 available troops to defend Long Island. He had not yet developed an acumen for operational art and never mastered tactics. The decision might have been appropriate had those troops been concentrated in the high ground dominating the East River and Lower Manhattan. Concerned with the logistics problem of maintaining his army, Washington directed that the troops spread out to defend the long ridge extending eastward, known then as the Heights of Guan (or sometimes Guana). The ridge, a terminal moraine seven miles in length, was penetrated by four passes. Continental commanders attempted to draw British troops into attacking strong positions defending the passes while spreading the remaining troops more sparsely along the connecting high ground. Even this expedient left too few troops to garrison all of the passes. Only a handful of militia held the easternmost defile, known as Jamaica Pass. The tactical disposition represented an invitation to disaster.

Howe accepted the invitation but had no wish to see the carnage of Bunker Hill repeated. With over 20,000 troops and aid from local Loyalists serving as guides, he fixed his adversary in place and sent a large force on a flanking march. A mobile column under Clinton marched off to the east on the evening of 26 August. Brigadier James Grant's troops, meanwhile, inadvertently initiated the fight in the early morning hours at the eastern end of the line. Foraging between the lines, British troops were fired on by Continental pickets. Patriot commanders perceived the random firing as the opening move of the anticipated attack. Major General John Sullivan, newly appointed by Washington to command the troops on Long Island, rushed battalions forward to meet the threat. After dawn, Hessian troops under General von Heister began a bombardment of the central pass, known afterward as the Battle Pass. Brushing aside the militia guarding Jamaica Pass, the British mobile column fell on the flank and rear of the Continental line. Chaos ensued in the Patriot lines. Heroes were revealed and Washington learned to improvise.

William Alexander claimed his inheritance as a descendant of the Earl of Stirling. Scottish courts agreed. The House of Lords did not. He nonetheless claimed the courtesy title of Lord Stirling, the only member of the titled hereditary nobility to fight for the American cause. His brigade of 1,600 troops, caught south of Gowanus Creek as Clinton's column rolled up the Continental positions from east to west, fought valiantly. The 1st Maryland Regiment gained posthumous laurels. The "Maryland 400" repeatedly assaulted a stone farmhouse captured by British troops that had been turned into an artillery position and rained fire on the Patriot troops withdrawing across the tidal waterway. The Marylanders' sacrifice allowed the balance of Stirling's troops to escape back to fortified lines on the Brooklyn Heights. All told, about 9,000 troops managed to withdraw within those fortifications.[27] The Continentals now faced a perilous decision with the army potentially isolated by the Royal Navy. The position was extremely strong and might have formed an ideal extended redoubt to inflict severe casualties on assaulting forces but only if Howe consented to a frontal assault. Instead, he paused. Unsure of the rebel strength, he resorted to a classic siege to limit casualties. A steady, inexorable advance without unnecessary loss of life or property destruction might be the only way to force the colonists to negotiate on Britain's terms and restore the bond between the colonies and the mother country.[28] Before the siege lines were completed, Washington and fate changed the entire landscape.

An old military adage advises commanders not to call a council of war if they want to fight a war. While senior officers can be paralyzed by indecision, raising innumerable troubling problems, an exceptional leader rises above the cacophony, discerns the best course of action from the proffered advice, and makes a decision. Clausewitz referred to this quality as the inward eye or *coup d'oeil*.[29] Washington did not yet exhibit this quality, but he was fast learning. Out of the council of war on 29 August, he determined that the troops on the Brooklyn shore had to be extracted. He employed a series of tactical ruses that were common for the day, but he also enjoyed the intervention of the elements. A "nor'easter" storm brought winds that kept Admiral Howe's frigates and sloops out of the East River. As the winds dropped after the storm passed, a dense fog descended. It blanketed the area until well into the following morning, by which time the rebel army had departed.[30]

Meteorological intervention was not the only factor. Washington viewed the army as the center of gravity of the struggle for independence and was determined to preserve it. Losing roughly 40 percent of the force in its first major engagement might well have proven fatal to the American cause. While the council of war debated, Washington set in place the critical pieces to execute the move. Among his troops were two regiments of Massachusetts mariners, mostly fishermen. The 14th Continental Regiment, commanded by Colonel John Glover, received the task of organizing the evacuation of over 9,000 troops as well as the irreplaceable artillery. The regiment was an odd choice. The sea is a hard master and seafarers care little for a man's skin color or heritage. What mattered was competence. Glover's troops were ethnically diverse, including Native American Indians and men of African descent.[31] For a Virginia planter and slave owner who had spent much of the previous war battling Native American war parties, to select such a unit for one of the most critical tasks of the war spoke of either profound insight or desperation, or perhaps both. Washington wrote to John Hancock, President of the Continental Congress, of Glover's accomplishment: "Our Retreat was made without any Loss of Men or Ammunition and in better order than I expected."[32] This event would not be the last desperate crossing the Marblehead mariners executed.

Howe decided not to risk a frontal assault to avoid British casualties. Defending his decision during later parliamentary inquiries, he offered his rationale: "On the other hand, the most essential duty I had to observe was, not to wantonly commit his majesty's troops, where the object was inadequate."[33] The self-serving nature of retrospective analysis aside, this belief clearly animated strategic decisions for the remainder of 1776. Howe exhibited a preference for using his brother's squadron to outmaneuver the Continental Army whenever possible. The next phase of the campaign followed this pattern precisely.

## Cascade of Calamities

Washington faced a dilemma. Operationally, New York City was no longer a tenable position. The hinterland that supplied much of the subsistence for the city and the forces stationed there lay in enemy hands. The geography of Manhattan Island was problematic as well. Narrow and aligned north and south, and bounded on both sides by deep water channels, it gave the Royal Navy ready access along both shores. Both Nathanael Greene and Charles Lee, Washington's most trusted subordinates at the time, advocated burning the city and retreating northward.

Washington agreed with his subordinates and sent the Continental Congress the secret message advising his political superiors of the loss of Long Island and his proposed course of action. In response, Congress forbade him to burn the city. Symbolically, the loss of the second-largest city in the colonies and its large secure harbor were as politically and strategically unpalatable as defending the city was operationally. Washington pondered his options and split the difference. Stores and ammunition, as well as the wounded, were moved northward up the Hudson River by boat while troops manned defensive positions around the island. Howe did not wait while Washington pondered.

Having secured Long Island, Howe next sought to drive the Continental Army from Manhattan Island. British forces employed an effective feint sending a small flotilla up the Hudson to demonstrate against the northwest corner of the island. Howe thus managed to draw Washington and his available reserves to defend the Harlem River crossings to preserve an escape route. Howe struck instead on the eastern side of the island on the morning of 15 September 1776. Five British warships navigated up the East River and anchored overnight off Kip's Bay, about five miles up the channel (near present 33rd Street in Manhattan). The main body of Crown troops lay hidden across the river hunkered down in flat-bottomed boats. Their landing was preceded by a cannonade from the ships, which scattered the rebels, a brilliant operational and tactical success costing only a single British casualty. Howe ordered the initial body of troops to hold a short distance inland and await the next wave before advancing.[34] An immediate advance would have trapped much of the Continental Army at the southern tip of Manhattan Island and forced them to either attempt to fight their way out or surrender. The cautious strategy instituted by the Howes cost the Crown another opportunity to crush the rebel army and possibly the rebellion as well.

Washington's army made a reasonable stand the next day at Harlem Heights near the position he had originally expected to defend. After the initial skirmish, the Continentals fortified their position and awaited a renewed assault. It did not come. Howe surveyed the works he inherited. Another complication erupted—the fire that broke out on the evening of 20 September. Suspicious that the fire was a ruse to facilitate an attack by the rebels, the army remained in the lines and did not render any assistance until the morning. By then, most of the buildings between Broadway and the Hudson River had been consumed. Perhaps a quarter of the city's buildings were lost. Howe reported to London that it had been arson but the claim has never been substantiated. Washington opined: "Providence, or some good honest fellow has done more for us than we were disposed to do for ourselves."[35] The fire was sufficient to divert Howe from his pursuit of Washington's battered army for almost a month.

While the American general awaited the blow that did not fall, Howe agreed to a compromise regarding his next move. His army subordinates and the naval officers differed on the landing site. The final decision was not informed by an adequate knowledge of the terrain. The troops were landed on Throgs Neck, a swampy finger of land and an island at high tide. Not only did British staff officers choose poorly, but their opponents had also begun to learn. Causeways and bridges had been pulled down and reliable sentries posted along the East River shore. The British troops were contained. On 18 October, Washington abandoned Manhattan and force-marched his troops north to White Plains, a village a dozen miles farther north. He left behind a contingent holding a fort bearing his name. On the same day, Howe extracted his troops, landing them again three miles upstream at Pell's Point. Their Patriot adversaries stood ready. Colonel Glover led a brigade that included local militia and his own Massachusetts regiment. Three Hessian regiments eventually drove Glover back but not before his force inflicted more casualties on Howe's troops than they had suffered in the entire conquest of Long Island. The British pursued Glover's brigade back to the main American line at White Plains. Washington awaited. The Continental Army and supporting militia were drawn up in a strong position partially protected by the Bronx River and dominated by a central height. Three Hessian regiments executed the main thrust that eventually drove Washington from the heights but not before suffering almost double the casualties that had been incurred at Pell's Point. The dwindling Continental Army was again forced to retreat, but it did so in good order.[36]

Howe still had one problem to resolve in Manhattan. The Continental regiments defending Fort Washington could not be left in the British rear unguarded. The size of the British force in New York did not allow for a simultaneous pursuit of the defeated rebels and a cordon around the isolated fort. The threat to the British rear was not the only consideration. Washington's army was not the only thing dwindling. The campaigning season was also drawing to a close. Howe did not wait. Contrary to his usual predilections, he mounted an assault on the fortification. An American traitor delivered the plan of the fort and reported that the men defending it were inadequate for the extent of the lines.[37] The assault was again undertaken by Hessian regiments, who assaulted from the landward side, taking heavy casualties. The outer works were carried, and the inner fort became untenable. Until British officers intervened, Hessian troops denied quarter to many surrendering Continental soldiers. Those who managed to surrender were consigned to the prison hulk *Jersey* from which few emerged. Washington watched from across the Hudson as his army dissolved. On the eve of White Plains, he commanded over 14,000 effectives. Fort Washington cost him over 2,700. Contingents under Gates and Lee drifted north and west. By the time Washington completed his flight across New Jersey, he reported a muster of only: "Fourteen to Fifteen hundred effective Men. This handfull [sic], and such Militia as may choose to join me, will then compose our Army."[38] He reported to Robert Morris that he had only 1,200 men, although he expected the arrival of 2,000 men under Sullivan, the remnants of Lee's force. Lee himself was taken prisoner as he traveled south separately from his troops.

British commanders differed regarding the proper course of action in response to the enemy's collapse. Clinton advocated a vigorous pursuit and suggested that he be appointed to command the chase. His contentious relationship with Howe did not facilitate his ambitions. He was sent, instead, to seize Newport, Rhode Island to obtain the deep water, ice-free harbor that Admiral Howe desired. The move was strategically insightful and simultaneously obtained a fleet anchorage not constrained by tides or sandbars while eliminating rebel access to the supplies that this famous hub of smuggling had been providing. It had the corollary effect of removing Clinton from New York and relieving Howe of dealing with a subordinate whom he found obnoxious.

As Washington retreated across New Jersey, he saw that the war of posts had clearly failed. Defending key positions and inviting the British forces to attack them proved impractical. The casualties inflicted in such assaults would, in theory, induce Britain to renounce the struggle. Instead, British operational art won victories through maneuver and avoided casualties. Washington next embraced a true Fabian strategy that required him to reject general engagements until British strength had been whittled away through small actions. A Fabian strategy, however, required a counteroffensive and decisive culminating battle, which would come but only after the correlation of forces shifted in favor of the Continental Army.

## Retreat and Renewal

A complete collapse of the refugee army that fled New York might have led to the rebellion's demise. Lee, before his capture, openly disparaged Washington in a letter to Gates. Both men believed that their experience as former British officers made them much better qualified to command the new nation's army. Lee would later be court-martialed in 1778 for his performance at Monmouth Courthouse. Gates became a more persistent problem due to his involvement with members of the Continental Congress who sought to remove Washington.[39] Neither aspirant was politically astute. One of Washington's greatest strengths was his ability to navigate the difficult confluence of politics and military affairs. Clausewitz observed that "war cannot be divorced from political life; and whenever this occurs . . . we are left with something pointless and devoid of sense."[40] Washington, formerly a member of the Continental Congress, understood this fact implicitly.

The retreat saw the army hemorrhage manpower due to desertion and the inability of many of the sick and wounded to keep pace. One man who did remain with the army had already had a profound impact on the course of the rebellion. Not a commander or even a soldier, he was an author. Thomas Paine, a transplanted Scot, offered the rationale for rebellion in his pamphlet *Common Sense*. Paine's 46-page tract changed Washington's thinking on the war. He deemed it so important that he ordered it distributed through the army and read to those who could not read. It shaped the debate on independence and led to the second great strategic communication document of 1776, the Declaration of Independence (see Figure 3.3).[41] The declaration was not primarily for the politicians who signed it or for the king to whom it was nominally directed. It was a document to garner foreign support. It was a warning to Crown supporters at home and abroad and a plea for men to defend the newly declared nation.[42]

Neither document was explicitly military, but both had military implications. Paine and his pen would go another round in the cause of independence. Reflecting on what he saw along the retreat, Paine wrote *The American Crisis*, which begins with familiar words: "These are the times that try men's souls." As Paine had previously made an argument against monarchy in general and the rule of the British Crown over America, he now made an argument against abandoning the fight. His words and the events of the months following the retreat combined to renew the rebellion and chart a new course.

The fall of Fort Washington was the first in a series of dominoes, each cascading into the next. The intricate patterns spread in multiple directions. Gates and Lee questioned Washington's leadership. Those questions led them to resist his instructions, or at least delay execution. At first, Lee was difficult, slow to respond to Washington's instructions and thus foreclosing a chance to make a stand behind the Raritan River in central New Jersey. He was subsequently captured. His relatively benign captivity raised suspicions regarding his loyalty to the American cause. Gates also was slow to respond to his commander's summons. Resultantly, Washington led fewer than 2,000 troops when he crossed the Delaware River into Pennsylvania.

Even before dispatching the army to pursue Washington's depleted force, the Howe brothers issued a proclamation offering amnesty to anyone who would

**FIGURE 3.3** Declaration of Independence

*Source:* Courtesy of the Anne S.K. Brown Military Collection, Brown University Library, Providence, Rhode Island

return to loyalty. The people of the newly occupied territories seemed disposed to accept the pardons. Washington lamented to his cousin Lund Washington, "A large part of the Jerseys have given every proof of disaffection that they can do, and this part of Pennsylvania are [sic] equally inimical."[43] His pessimism was a bit overstated.

In spite of the benevolent policies decreed by General Howe, some subordinate commanders, and many British troops were not so favorably disposed toward the people of New Jersey. In many cases, those who had taken Howe's pardon came out to welcome the government forces only to be badly used. Incidents ranged from uncompensated requisitioning of food and firewood to murder and rape. Severe punishments were meted out in cases where the transgressions were brought before senior officers. Men were executed, but the public relations damage had already been done. The disaffection toward the rebellion about which Washington had complained quickly became disaffection with the occupiers. Strategically, the behavior of the British and Hessian troops was as disastrous for Crown interests as Washington's retreat had been for the rebellion. The mismatch between the strategy of reconciliation and the tactical application of violence used to secure supplies raised a new force with which General James Grant, commanding the forces in southern and central New Jersey, now had to contend.[44]

While Washington decried the lack of loyalty displayed by the people of the territory through which he retreated, the occupiers' harsh measures upended Howe's plans. Huntingdon County, New Jersey, sits north of the bend in the Delaware River where Pennsylvania protrudes eastward into its neighbor. The local militia embodied itself to deal with the increasing violence inflicted on the area by the occupiers. Another similar uprising occurred further south. Together with raids launched from Pennsylvania, the unrest kept the southernmost posts in the string of winter quarters that Howe established, in a constant state of uproar. The Hessian troops garrisoning these posts were exhausted by constant alerts. The approaching Christmas holiday offered no respite.

## Incremental Victory

Modern strategic theory holds that a weaker adversary can defeat a stronger opponent but must do so by protracting the war and avoiding a catastrophic defeat.[45] Washington had eluded his British pursuers or was perhaps allowed to escape. Howe appears to have restrained his subordinates. When Hessian Captain Johann Ewald sought to destroy units of the retreating Continental Army, he was ordered to refrain by Cornwallis himself:

> I began to skirmish with them and sent back a *jäger* to fetch more men, but instead of the *jägers*, I received an order from Lord Cornwallis to return at once. I had to obey, and informed him what I had discovered—'Let them go my dear Ewald, and stay here. We do not want to lose any men. One *jäger* is worth more than ten rebels.'[46]

Pondering the orders, the German officer concluded that the strategy involved defeating the rebel army without shedding so much blood that the colonists would be permanently embittered.[47] Howe would come to regret his leniency.

The constant alerts worked to the advantage of rebel forces. The Hessians wore down while Washington slowly built upon the army of less than 3,000 men with which he had crossed the Delaware River into Pennsylvania. Contingents formerly commanded by Lee and several hundred soldiers under Gates came into camp. Preserving the army was a critical task, but enlistments set to expire within weeks complicated the effort. Men enlisted for a single year. In a letter to his brother, Washington expressed the belief that an entirely new army would have to be recruited. The associated delays would cripple what he termed the "Glorious Cause." Men who have known nothing but defeat are unlikely to re-enlist. Citizens who have only seen their army retreat are unlikely to rally to the cause. Washington needed a victory.

The story of the Delaware crossing on Christmas Day is well worn. Three separate columns composed of a mix of Continentals, militia, and a volunteer formation called the Pennsylvania Associators marched toward a number of crossing points. The river defeated the rebels at two of the three locations. Ice floes and adverse winds prevented these columns from advancing on Trenton. The northernmost group under Washington made it to the Jersey shore largely due to the herculean efforts of John Glover's Marbleheaders. Glover and his mariners combined forces

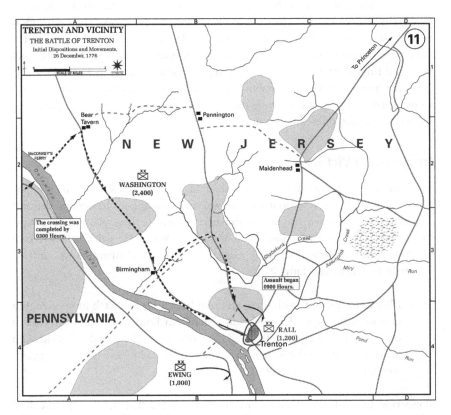

**MAP 3.2**   Attack on the Crown Post at Trenton

*Source:* Map Courtesy of the United States Military Academy Department of History, West Point, New York

**FIGURE 3.4**   Battle of Princeton

*Source:* Courtesy of the Anne S.K. Brown Military Collection, Brown University Library, Providence, Rhode Island

with Philadelphia dockworkers and New Jersey watermen to defeat the river and the storm.

Washington's force fell on the Hessian garrison at Trenton, New Jersey. The mythology of the rebellion holds that the German troops had enjoyed too much Christmas cheer. They had not. On alert for days on end, the Hessians were caught unawares because the storm masked the rebel approach. A short, sharp battle left the Hessian commander dead and most of the battalion captured or killed. The Patriots slipped back across the Delaware before a relief column could react. It was precisely the incremental victory that the rebellion required.[48] Washington returned to Trenton in the new year to lure British forces into an attack on a prepared position. Faced with a far superior force, he slipped away and struck at Princeton instead. Informed that the treasury for British forces was a short distance away, he weighed the possible gain against the risk to his fragile army. Washington chose instead to slip away again (see Figure 3.4).[49]

The year 1776 was a rocky road for the rebellion but ended on a high note at Trenton and Princeton. The failed assault on Quebec boded ill, but rebel fortunes rose when the British abandoned Boston. Despite overwhelming Crown victories at Long Island, Manhattan, White Plains, and Fort Washington, cascading disasters followed. On Christmas night, Washington and his Continentals rescued the flailing rebellion in central New Jersey. The cascade of British disasters gathered momentum in the ensuing year.

## Notes

1 Jared Sparks, ed., *The Writings of George Washington* (New York: Harper & Brothers, 1847), 229.
2 Christopher Hibbert, *Redcoats and Rebels: The American Revolution Through British Eyes* (New York and London: W. W. Norton, 1990), 135.
3 Scheer and Rankin, *Rebels and Redcoats*, 208.
4 Ira D. Gruber, *The Howe Brothers and the American Revolution* (Chapel Hill, NC: University of North Carolina Press, 1972), 49, 67; Mackesy, *War for America*, 75–6, 96–8.
5 Modern military operations often include consideration of the political, social, and cultural affiliations and affinities, generally described by the short-hand notation "human terrain." For amplification, see Douglas E. Batson, *Registering the Human Terrain: A Valuation of Cadastre* (Washington, DC: National Defense Intelligence College, 2008).
6 Amphibious landings under fire were not normally undertaken during this era and would not be considered acceptable practice until World War II. A redoubt is usually a square or triangular fortification where a trench was dug out and wall formed from the dirt. The trench and wall would be supplemented by various obstructions and typically a log palisade erected atop the dirt mound.
7 An incremental victory is a critical element of a Fabian strategy. Endlessly avoiding pitched battle and surrendering territory will demoralize a belligerent population. Emblematic victories, like Sullivan's Island and those at the end of 1776, are necessary to preserve an insurgency. For a detailed description of the battle, see Scheer and Rankin, 130–41.
8 David Hackett Fischer, *Washington's Crossing* (New York: Oxford University Press, 2004), 385–8.
9 Nathaniel Philbrick, *Mayflower: A Story of Courage, Community, and War* (New York: Viking, 2007), xiv.
10 John J. Gallagher, *The Battle of Brooklyn 1776* (New York: Perseus Books, Da Capo Press, 1995; reprint, Edison, NJ: Castle Books, 2002), 14.
11 Fischer, *Washington's Crossing*, 388–90; Rodney Atwood, *The Hessians* (Cambridge: Cambridge University Press, 1980), 25.
12 Rodger, *Insatiable Earl*, 222; David Syrett, *The Royal Navy in European Waters During the American Revolution* (Columbia, SC: University of South Carolina Press, 1998), 18–22.
13 Rodger, *Insatiable Earl*, 220–3.
14 Gruber, *Howe Brothers*, 100–3, 136.
15 Lengel, *General George Washington*, 137–8.
16 Sparks, *Writings of George Washington*, Vol. IV, 41–2.
17 Ibid., 16–8; George C. Daughan, *If by Sea: The Forging of the American Navy from the Revolution to the War of 1812* (New York: Basic Books, 2008), 92.
18 During the Seven Years' War, Washington constructed a fort during his initial attempt to drive French soldiers from the Forks of the Ohio, modern Pittsburg, in 1754. It was so poorly situated as to be indefensible. See Fred Anderson, *Crucible of War: The Seven Years' War and the Fate of Empire in British North America, 1754–1766* (New York: Alfred A. Knopf, 2000), 59–60.
19 Sparks, *Writings of George Washington*, Vol. IV, quotes, 61, 66–7.
20 Gruber, *Howe Brothers*, 47; Julie Flavell, *The Howe Dynasty: The Untold Story of a Military Family and the Women Behind Britain's Wars for America* (New York: Liveright, 2021), 15–7.
21 Cited in Maldwyn Allen Jones, "Sir William Howe: Conventional Strategist," in *George Washington's Opponents*, ed. George Billias (New York: Morrow, 1969), 64.
22 Gruber, *Howe Brothers*, 107.
23 Gallagher, *Brooklyn*, 27.
24 Clausewitz, *On War*, 117.
25 Daughan, *If by Sea*, 95.
26 Clausewitz, *On War*, 84.

27  For a detailed account of the battle, see Gallagher, *The Battle of Brooklyn 1776*.

28  Gruber, *Howe Brothers*, 107.

29  Clausewitz, *On War*, 102–3.

30  Account of Benjamin Tallmadge in Commager and Morris, *Spirit of Seventy-Six*, 444–6.

31  Fisher, 101–2; New England Historical Society, "The Red Black and White Men of Glover's Regiment Take Washington Across the Delaware."

32  Washington to Hancock, dated 31 August 1776, in Fitzpatrick, vol. 5, 506.

33  William Howe, *The Narrative of Lieut. Gen. Sir William Howe in a Committee of the House of Commons on the 29th of April, 1779, Relative to His Late Command of the King's Troops in North America* (London: H. Baldwin, 1781), 5.

34  For a more detailed account of the landing at Kip's Bay, see David Hackett Fischer, *Washington's Crossing* (New York: Oxford University Press, 2004), 101–4.

35  Quoted in Scheer and Rankin, *Rebels and Redcoats*, 189.

36  For a detailed account of the battles at Pell's Point and White Plains, see Patrick K. O'Donnell, *The Indispensables: The Diverse Soldier-Mariners Who Shaped the Country, Formed the Navy, and Rowed Washington across the Delaware* (New York: Atlantic Monthly Press, 2021), 260–77.

37  Commager and Morris, *Seventy-Six*, 492.

38  Washington to President of Congress, dated 24 December 1776, in Fitzpatrick, 6:432.

39  For an example, see Thomas Fleming, *Washington's Secret War: The Hidden History of Valley Forge* (New York: Smithsonian, Collins, 2005), which details the Conway Cabal.

40  Clausewitz, *On War*, 605.

41  For a more complete analysis of *Common Sense*, see Scott Liell, *46 Pages: Thomas Paine, Common Sense, and the Turning Point to Independence* (New York: MJF Books, 2003).

42  For a more complete analysis of the Declaration of Independence, see Pauline Maier, *American Scripture: Making the Declaration of Independence* (New York: Alfred A. Knopf, 1997).

43  George Washington to Lund Washington, dated 17 December 1776, in Fitzpatrick, 6:

44  For the treatment of civilians in New Jersey, see Fischer, *Washington's Crossing*, 160–81.

45  A superb articulation of this concept can be found in Mao Tse-Tung [Mao Zedong], "On Protracted War" in *Selected Works of Mao Tse-Tung*, Vol. II (Peking [Beijing]: Foreign Languages Press, 1967: 113–94.

46  Johann von Ewald, *Diary of the American War: A Hessian Journal*, ed. and trans. Joseph P. Tustin (New Haven, CT: Yale University Press, 1979, 18.

47  Ibid., 26.

48  For a discussion of incremental victory, see Thomas Mahnken, "A Strategy for Protracted War" in *Unrestricted Warfare Symposium, 2006: Proceedings on Strategy, Analysis and Technology* (Laurel, MD: Johns Hopkins University Applied Physics Laboratory, 2006), 35–64.

49  For complete accounts, see Fischer, *Washington's Crossing*, 206–61 and O'Donnell, *Indispensables*, 297–336.

**PART II**

# Stalemate in the Middle

# 4

# DIVIDE AND CONQUER

In 1777, the British ministry, or more accurately, George Germain, initiated two campaigns, each designed to break the back of the colonial rebellion. The first encompassed a drive south down the Lake George-Lake Champlain-Hudson River route. The second involved an attack on the rebel capital in Philadelphia. These were not, however, separate parts of a coherent strategy. Instead, they reflected the goals of two very different commanders, as well as the lack of a clear strategic vision from London.

## Drums Along the Hudson

Lieutenant-General John Burgoyne (1722–1792) represented the driving force behind the Hudson Valley Campaign. Burgoyne hailed from the landholding gentry of Sutton in Bedfordshire. The Burgoynes increased their worth by purchasing land during the dissolution of the monasteries under Henry VIII in the early sixteenth century. As a result of their real estate acquisitions, they sat in Parliament since the latter sixteenth century. During the British Civil Wars (1639–1660), they sided with Parliament against Charles I, all of which added up to a solid pedigree for the gentleman in his youth. The general's father was an army captain, who gambled away the family's fortune and died a debtor. After completing his education, young Burgoyne followed in his father's footsteps and joined the army, entering the Horse Guards as a cornet. This position would have been a good posting from which to launch a career in arms; however, his service included several significant interruptions, each of which cost him seniority. The first occasion came in November 1741 when he sold his commission in the Horse Guards but then returned to the service as a cornet in the 1st Royal Dragoons, known as the Royals. He saw service on the continent during the War of the Austrian Succession (1740–1749), participating in the Battle of Fontenoy in 1745. Burgoyne's propensity for gambling and high living

DOI: 10.4324/9781003041276-7

led to the accumulation of substantial debts. To escape his creditors, he once again sold his commission and fled to the continent.

Burgoyne established his reputation as a commander during the Seven Years' War. He returned to the army as a captain in the 11th Dragoons and earned distinction during the landings on Saint-Malo off the coast of Brittany in 1758. Afterward, he received an appointment as lieutenant-colonel of the 2nd Regiment of Foot Guards (Coldstream Guards). An even greater honor, as well as an opportunity for financial gain, came when Burgoyne was selected to raise a new cavalry regiment, the 16th Light Dragoons, a rare mark of distinction for an officer of his junior status. Economic opportunity derived from raising a new unit, which allowed its commander to sell the officer billets at a handsome profit. Burgoyne served in Portugal during the latter stages of the Seven Years' War in what was referred to as the *Guerra Fantastica*. The unit served in an expeditionary force sent to support Britain's Portuguese ally in repelling the 1762 Franco-Spanish invasion. During the campaign, Burgoyne planned several daring assaults that undermined the Spanish advance. Burgoyne returned to England and became involved in politics as well as engaging in his passion for the theater, writing several well-received plays. He remained interested in military affairs and toured the continent, interviewing many of the veteran commanders of the Seven Years' War and writing down their perceptions, as well as his opinions of the relative capabilities of the various militaries of the major continental powers.[1] Throughout his early military experience, Burgoyne demonstrated his innovation, tactical acumen, keen grasp of military theory and doctrine, and great physical courage, characteristics that heralded future command success.[2]

As relations with the North American colonies soured, Burgoyne favored taking a hard line. When tensions erupted into open violence in 1775, Burgoyne once again entered the British military, coming to America in 1775 on HMS *Cerebus* in the company of fellow generals Howe and Clinton. He served under the former through 1775 and 1776, all the while chafing for his own command. Following the New York 1776 campaign, Burgoyne returned to London, ostensibly to attend the winter session of Parliament in which he continued to hold a seat. He landed at Portsmouth in the afternoon on 9 December 1776 and sat in Lord Germain's office by noon the following day. Piers Mackesy's assessment that Burgoyne "had no lack of energy, which he employed in pushing his own claims to high employment," certainly seems valid.[3]

Once in London, Burgoyne quickly gained a sense that Sir Guy Carleton, the royal governor of Quebec province who had initially attempted a descent from Canada, was out of favor with Germain. While Carleton received the red ribbon of a Knight of the Order of the Bath the previous year, this distinction only fueled the ire of his political enemies, one of whom was Germain. At the same time, Carleton possessed the king's patronage. As a result, the political leadership split on who should lead any future expedition from Canada into New York. Still, Burgoyne understood London politics and realized that Carleton had made him a party to the continuing feud between himself and Germain. While Burgoyne always professed loyalty to Carleton, he likely felt vindicated in tempering that loyalty by being depicted as an ally of Carleton against Germain. Furthermore, in early 1777, Burgoyne's popularity with the Secretary of State for the colonies had risen dramatically.[4]

Regardless of who would lead the campaign, the invasion plan originated in a memorandum submitted by Burgoyne on 28 February 1777.[5] Titled *Thoughts for Conducting the War from the Side of Canada*, the memorandum essentially re-stated British strategic thinking regarding Canada's role. Within a week, he sent a further elaboration to Germain. The plan called for an invasion from Canada to seize Ticonderoga, the strategically crucial fort at the head of Lake George. Crown Point served as the temporary springboard for this initial phase of operations. Ticonderoga provided the staging area for subsequent movements. From Ticonderoga, invading troops would move either down the Hudson River Valley or through the Green Mountains to the Connecticut River and link up with troops moving north out of Rhode Island. The former meant moving south as far as Albany along the Hudson River and there meeting troops marching north under Howe from New York City. Such a move reflected Howe's draft strategic plan for 1777 submitted in November 1776. The New England alternative entailed forming a junction on the Connecticut River with a force moving from Rhode Island meant to reduce the New England colonies' ability to support logistically the rebellion in the Middle Colonies. Essentially, the plan represented a strategy of divide and conquer, echoing an approach taken by the French in various wars for empire in the region. At the same time, it included several innovations such as a supporting column from New York meeting the invasion force at Albany. Such a move would cut communications between New England, long acknowledged as the radical center of the revolutionary movement, and the remaining colonies. The assumption, largely unquestioned, was that with the remainder of the colonies once cut off from New England would lose their zeal for the revolt and revert to loyalty to the Crown.[6]

The second aspect in which Burgoyne's proposal differed from previous invasion plans was the diversionary movement of a force of regulars, provincial Loyalists, and allied Indians under the command of Colonel Barry St. Leger. That force would move east from Oswego on Lake Ontario through the Mohawk Valley. This force would tie down rebel units in western New York and prevent them from reinforcing resistance to Burgoyne's invasion. In essence, it would force the defenders to divide their forces to meet the coming Crown onslaught. If all went according to plan, St. Leger would rendezvous with Burgoyne in Albany, where the two would then be joined by a column marching up from New York under Howe. In making the case for his operational plan, Burgoyne noted that a seaborne invasion would be less likely to threaten the Americans. Likewise, it was not "so effectual to close the war, as an invasion from Canada by Ticonderoga. This last measure ought not to be thought of, but upon positive conviction of necessity."[7]

The plan actually originated from Sir Guy Carleton (1724–1808, later Baron Dorchester). Carleton hailed from an Ulster Protestant family. After completing his education, he entered the army at age 17, commissioning as an ensign in the

25th Regiment of Foot in 1742. He took part in the suppression of the Jacobite Uprising of 1745–1746, including at Culloden. In 1751, Carleton joined the 1st Regiment of Foot Guards (Grenadier Guards) with a captaincy the following year. At some point between the 1748 Peace of Aix-la-Chapelle and the outbreak of the Seven Years' War, Carleton met and enjoyed the patronage of the 3rd Duke of Richmond, a factor that heavily influenced his subsequent military and political career. In 1766, Carleton was named acting Lieutenant-Governor and Administrator of Quebec, somewhat surprising in that Carleton possessed no previous administrative experience and came from a politically insignificant family. He succeeded to the governorship in April 1768. Promoted to major-general in 1772, Carleton did much to secure the former French colony and win over the residents with his support of the 1774 Quebec Act. The Act ensured freedom of religion for the Catholic French-Canadians. But being out of favor with Lord Germain, he was not considered for command of the campaign. His efforts to pursue Benedict Arnold the preceding year and the disappointing expedition that closed with the Battle of Valcour Island (October 1776) on Lake Champlain with the subsequent retreat back to Canada resulted in his being passed over for the command of the Hudson Valley expedition. Promoted to lieutenant-general the following year. Carleton played an important role in supplying locally recruited manpower for the expedition.[8]

Several assumptions undergirded Burgoyne's plan as presented to Lord Germain and the king. First and foremost was the idea that Howe would remain somewhere in the vicinity of New York and therefore make a junction with Burgoyne at Albany. This assumption did not take into account Howe's plans for a thrust southward into Pennsylvania aimed at Philadelphia. Further, the plan assumed that by moving through the Hudson Valley corridor, Crown forces would sever rebel communications. With support from Royal Navy warships on the Hudson and in the lakes, this objective might be possible. While there existed some settled areas, much of this territory encompassed forested frontier. Beyond the river system, there were few roads, only several footpaths. Successfully interdicting all of these on a regular if not constant basis presented a significant challenge. Previously, colonists resorted to fixed fortifications to interdict indigenous people's movements; this approach failed. The native raiding parties merely bypassed the fortifications.[9]

These issues aside, another consideration lay in the coordination of the Hudson Valley advance with that of the forces presumed to be moving northward from New York. Communications presented a major hurdle. Any troops moving north into the interior would operate in areas with divided loyalties. A lack of reliable communications between Burgoyne and Howe added an additional critical problem, perhaps exacerbated by personal antipathy between the two. Additionally, Germain failed to coordinate the two divergent initiatives. There is the oft-repeated story that Germain was headed for a weekend at his country estate when he learned that a final letter informing Howe of Burgoyne's plan had not been

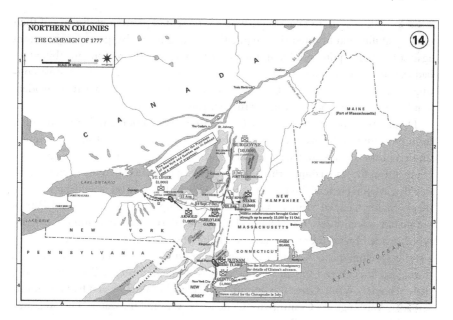

**MAP 4.1**   Hudson Valley Campaign

*Source:* Map Courtesy of the United States Military Academy Department of History, West Point, New York

prepared. Not wanting to be late, the Secretary trusted his staff to handle the matter and the communication was not sent.[10] Howe, therefore, remained unaware of the scope of Burgoyne's plan and continued to implement his own, as was his prerogative as overall commander in North America.

Burgoyne's plan was predicated on numerous Loyalist formations from New York and Canada as well as Native auxiliaries. It assumed that the King's Friends would flock to the standard. However, old rivalries that impeded cooperation between regular and militia formations during the French and Indian War persisted. Regular army officers looked down on militia leaders. Likewise, they discounted the intelligence provided by local leaders with long experience in regional affairs, preferring to write their own scripts for the expected behavior. These issues of mistrust particularly plagued St. Leger's expedition.[11]

The final factor was the Native American presence. Neither Burgoyne nor St. Leger truly understood the motivations and methods of the Native Americans. Part of the interest for Native warriors in taking part in the expeditions was plunder. This dynamic contributed meaningfully to the Native economy, especially in goods such as firearms, lead shot, and gunpowder. When Burgoyne and St. Leger issued proclamations and general orders forbidding native troops to plunder, they deprived these warriors of their economic motivation. Young men also joined to demonstrate their warrior prowess and thus enhance their standing in the tribe.

They fought, as well, to take scalps, which represented prominent displays of their military ability and boosted their reputation among peers. Burgoyne's injunctions against looting—quite sensible in the effort to win over the region's inhabitants—had the unintended consequence of undermining the morale of the Native contingent. Likewise, an attempt by some Natives to gain a scalp spawned an incident that had profound repercussions for the campaign's success.

Despite these negative dynamics, Crown forces were not the only ones to suffer from profound problems in their institutional organization. The Patriots were not unified in their command arrangements either. In the campaign's opening stages, competition for leadership of the Northern Department between the current commander, Major General Philip Schuyler (1733–1804), and his would-be replacement, Major General Horatio Gates, severely complicated and degraded Patriot command effectiveness (see Figure 4.1). Gates derived from common origins, which made him far more popular among the New England troops who possessed a strong leveling spirit. A former British officer who had served in North America during the French and Indian War, he possessed much greater military experience than Schuyler. While Gates was certainly an able administrator and had previously served as Washington's Commissary General, he was no "fire-eater." His own men called him "Granny Gates."

Schuyler, on the other hand, descended from the old Dutch Hudson River Valley *patroon* class of whom he was quite well-connected. He received a quality education, demonstrating an affinity for both mathematics and French. At the outset of the French and Indian War, he was commissioned a captain in the New York forces and took part in the fighting on Lake George in 1755. Soon thereafter, he became involved in Crown forces logistics. The appointment proved an apt assignment, as Schuyler suffered from rheumatic gout, and was often too sick to serve in the field. In 1757, he resigned his commission but continued to take an active role in supplying the army; he earned a substantial income in provisioning the king's forces. Following the peace in 1763, Schuyler expanded his business and land holdings. He became deeply enmeshed in politics as well, being elected to the New York Assembly in 1768, where he became involved in a boundary dispute between New Hampshire and Massachusetts. Schuyler supported the claims of the New York settlers. This position and his moderate stance in the growing dispute with British policies earned him the bitter enmity of many New Englanders. Still, his prominence among the New York political elites led to him being named a major general in 1775 and given command of the Northern Department. His appointment, especially his insistence on strict discipline, further alienated New England troops.[12] Schuyler, while a talented organizer, was not one to make aggressive moves in the field; his talents lay more in organization and logistics. His lack of aggressive activity represented one of the factors leading to his replacement by the more popular Gates, which created a cleavage in the New York Patriot movement. Clearly, the command structures on both sides were divided to various extents.

**FIGURE 4.1**   Major General Horatio Gates

*Source:* Courtesy of the Anne S.K. Brown Military Collection, Brown University Library, Providence, Rhode Island

## More to His Satisfaction

Burgoyne's force consisted of 4,135 British regulars, 3,116 German auxiliaries, mainly Brunswickers, and 150 Montreal Canadian militia. Eventually, approximately 500 French Canadians took part in the expedition. Only about 500 Native Americans, mostly from the Algonquin, Abenaki, and Huron tribes, joined the force.[13] Much smaller than what Burgoyne hoped to lead into northern New York, the turnout from among the French Canadiens and Native Americans was particularly disappointing. Despite the low numbers, Burgoyne left St. John's, Canada, on 17 June and first moved down the Richelieu River, then Lake Champlain in a variety of watercraft. On 20 June, Burgoyne issued to his troops the General Orders:

> Lieut. General Burgoyne takes the Occasion of the Army assembling to express publicly the high Opinion he entertains of the Troops which his Majesty has been graciously pleased to entrust to his Command; they could not have been selected more to his Satisfaction.[14]

With their commander's motivational words still resonating, the army marched out. Initial movements went fairly easily as his troops made their way down Lake Champlain. A lack of enemy opposition stemmed from the confusion in the Patriot ranks over command. Burgoyne arrived at Crown Point on 26 June. As his troops prepared to move out from Crown Point, Burgoyne embraced his flair for the dramatic, giving his men a rousing exhortation:

> The Army embarks tomorrow to approach the enemy. We are to contend for the King and Constitution of Great Britain, to vindicate the Law and relieve the Oppressed. A cause which His Majesty's Troops and those of the Princes his Allies, will feel equal Excitement.[15]

The bombastic exhortation is an example of strategic communication on Burgoyne's part as well, in that it was clearly aimed at the regional Loyalists. He hoped that his appeal might lead some to take up arms, thus augmenting his manpower and offsetting the lackluster showing of the French Canadiens and Natives. He continued, focusing more particularly on the expectations he held of the troops:

> The services required of this particular Expedition are critical and conspicuous. During our progress occasions may occur, in which nor difficulty nor labour nor life are to be regarded. THIS ARMY MUST NOT RETREAT.[16]

Later in the campaign, Burgoyne adhered to the final declaration long after prudence and common sense dictated a withdrawal. Initially, however, his march seemed more a victory parade than a plunge into the wilderness.

On 3 July from his camp near Fort Ticonderoga, Burgoyne included the follow-ing in his orders to the army:

> It is known that there are many men in the Rebel Army who are well affected to the Cause of the King. Some have been compelled into the Service, oth-ers engaged only with a view of joining the King's Troops. The Savages are therefore cautioned against firing upon any single man or small parties that may be endeavouring to come over, and the Army in general will consider these men in a very different light from the common Deserters, and treat them with all possible encouragement; and should it unfortunately happen that any Soldier of this Army should fall into the hands of the Enemy, it will be his Duty to let this Order be known in the Enemy's Army.[17]

Here, again, Burgoyne engaged in strategic communication. The message in his General Orders was clearly meant more for the adversary's consumption than for his own troops. He sought to tamp down prohibited actions by the Native Ameri-can contingent, feared by the inhabitants for their brutality in previous conflicts. The general did not want the warriors to do anything to stir these ghosts, since they certainly were quite useful to his opponent's propaganda. In addition, there was the admonition to spread the idea that those who rejoined the king's side would receive good treatment. Clearly, this initiative aimed at undermining rebel morale. In this, one sees the "win the hearts and minds" argument as an effective counter-strategy to the rebellion's appeal.

From Crown Point, he proceeded on to Fort Ticonderoga, arriving on 2 July. The fort, situated at the confluence of Lakes George and Champlain, represented a key strategic point for the defense of the New York frontier. Though garri-soned and well-provided, the Patriots failed to fortify neighboring Mount Defi-ance believing the incline too steep to bring up heavy artillery. The misconception created a vital and exploitable gap in the rebel defenses. British sappers constructed a road and cleared a firing position atop the peak. With British guns emplaced on Mount Independence and the fort now untenable, the Patriots withdrew the bulk of their forces from Fort Ticonderoga on the night of 5–6 July. Some 600 men sailed up the lake in a flotilla of river galleys and small craft, while the remainder of the garrison retreated overland.[18] The first key objective had been attained at little cost to Burgoyne.

The noise as they evacuated alerted Burgoyne's besieging forces, who then launched a pursuit. Some of the garrison remained at the fort, too drunk on the rum supplies to join in the retreat, and were taken prisoners. On the morning of 7 July, British forces caught the retreating Patriots at Hubbardton in the Hampshire Grants.[19] In the resulting clash, a force of some 2,000 American rebels was routed by a British contingent half the size. The bulk of the rebel force retreated through Hubbardton to Castleton. While the campaign appeared to be highly successful up to this point, supply lines grew more strained, resulting in random foraging. If a key aspect of the divide and conquer strategy was to "win the hearts and minds" and draw in Loyalist support, marauding injected an evil element. Recognizing the danger of unchecked pillage and plunder, Burgoyne issued a strong statement in his General Orders of July 7:

> It is of the utmost prejudice to the King's Officers to molest or terrify persons Coming in to surrender; the attempt to take anything from such people, as well as every other kind of Plunder, will be punished with the greatest severity.[20]

Movement onward from Skenesborough became difficult. Local militia routinely blocked the trail by felling trees, destroying bridges, and damming and diverting streams. Some 40 bridges and causeways had to be rebuilt as Burgoyne advanced. As a result, the march from Skenesborough, a distance of only 20 miles consumed 20 days.[21] As Crown forces slowly advanced, Schuyler withdrew to Stillwater, 30 miles above Albany. Piers Mackesy observed in his classic study: "If the army could have advanced at once, Burgoyne could have driven the Americans before him and reached Albany with scarcely a pause."[22] Thus, the operational tempo slowed significantly, a clear benefit to the Patriots.

A factor that slowed Burgoyne's advance from the outset was his insistence on bringing a large train of guns into an area where few roads existed; the roads that did exist were often glorified dirt tracks. He justified this action, claiming that artillery represented the chief weapon of war. Field artillery was necessary to combat the rebel propensity to throw up field fortifications and fight from prepared defensive positions. Likewise, he needed guns to defend the entrenched camp he planned to construct on reaching Albany. One recent historian noted that bringing the artillery was "a correct decision but one for which he was and still is criticized."[23] Whether prudent or not, given the harsh environmental conditions, the weight of excess and wagons, baggage, field guns, cannon shot, and the accoutrements to support such a robust artillery train slowed the advance to barely a crawl, granting the defeated Patriot forces time to rally, collect, reinforce, and arrange for the coming engagements.

On 8 July, a force of some 200 British regulars faced off against 1,000 Continentals and militia at Fort Anne on the eastern side of Lake George, the same force that had evacuated Fort Ticonderoga by boat via Lake Champlain. The flotilla carried numerous camp followers, sick and wounded, as well as significant quantities of supplies. Believing that the maritime obstructions at Ticonderoga, which included a log boom and pontoon bridge, would delay the British pursuit for some time, the rebels conducted a leisurely withdrawal down the river. The British caught the rebels portaging their boats. An encounter engagement ensued with the Patriots losing five vessels—three destroyed and two forced to surrender. The defeated rebels retreated overland to Fort Anne but not before setting a fire that eventually engulfed much of Skenesborough. As the British continued their advance, they rounded up more Patriot wounded and stragglers as more skirmishes ensued.[24]

The abandonment of Fort Ticonderoga without a fight caused much consternation in the Continental Congress and led to Schuyler's replacement. While abandoning the post was not his decision, it occurred in Schuyler's area of command and fed Congressional opposition. Samuel Adams wrote of Schuyler's performance: "[I]t is probable you will have heard of the untoward Turn our Affairs have taken at the Northward. I confess it is not more than I expected when Genl Schulyer was again intrusted [sic] with the Command there." He then identified his choice to lead the Northern Department: "Gates is the Man I should have chosen."[25] Initially, Congress asked Washington to name a replacement. The CinC demurred, choosing to avoid a confrontation with the civil authorities.[26] Consequently, on 28 July, Jonathan Sergeant of New Jersey put forward a motion to replace Schuyler with Gates, which carried the majority.

Early in Gates' tenure, a key event occurred known as the rape of Jane McCrea. The young woman, fiancée of a Loyalist officer serving in Burgoyne's force, lived with her brother in Saratoga, New York. At the beginning of hostilities, her fiancée made his way north to Canada. On learning that he was with Burgoyne's army, the young woman headed north to join him. She traveled as far as Fort Edward when a group of Native Americans entered the village. A number of residents were killed, however, McCrea was taken captive and marched off to the British camp. There remains some controversy concerning what occurred next; however, it appears that two of the warriors argued over who could claim Jane as their prisoner. In the resulting scuffle, she was murdered and scalped. When the men returned to the British camp, an officer recognized Jane's scalp and demanded to know what transpired. Initially, the Natives remained silent but the story soon made its way to Burgoyne. Recognizing the importance of dealing with the affair, Burgoyne initially sought to identify the murderers and intended to execute them, both for justice and to maintain discipline in his composite force. At this point, the Mohawk leader Joseph Brant intervened. He informed Burgoyne that if he prosecuted the malefactors, he risked losing the entire Native contingent. Rather than risk this outcome, Burgoyne let the matter drop. In doing so, he essentially handed the Patriots a propaganda victory. His inaction cost Burgoyne the hearts and minds of the local population, including Loyalists.[27]

For local inhabitants on learning of Jane's fate, the conflict was no longer about vague notions of sovereignty. It became a challenge to defend kith and kin. Fewer and fewer men came out to support the advance as the perception that the Crown would not protect them from Native attacks spread. Conversely, local militiamen turned out in the hundreds for the Patriots after the McCrea incident. The reaction presents the complex and frustrating interaction of white settlers and Natives along the frontier in microcosm. Conflict had waxed and waned for decades along the Mohawk and Hudson River areas. The Natives accused the colonists of bad faith agreements, while the colonists accused the Natives of savagery and blatant attacks on innocent farmers with elements of truth on both sides. The incident added to the perception that the Crown cared little for the frontier's safety. Rebel propagandists played on the perception that British forces used Indian allies to terrify and cow the population. In truth, the fear of Native Indian attack far outweighed the constitutional notions of freedom and independence on one side and loyalty to the Mother Country on the other. Local settlers typically banded together for the common cause despite their political loyalties, associations, or sensibilities as had happened earlier in the Cherokee War of 1776. There, Loyalist and Patriot subordinated their animosities and marched west into the mountains under Brigadier General Griffith Rutherford to crush Cherokee power. The Cherokee, like the Mohawks in New York, remained Crown allies throughout the century, a factor that now turned against Burgoyne.

Not only was Burgoyne losing the public relations battle, but his chances of receiving aid from any force marching north from New York dwindled as summer progressed. On 30 July, Clinton received a letter from Howe, then on his way to Pennsylvania with the bulk of the New York garrison. Howe reminded his subordinate that any diversion that could aid Burgoyne would be useful. At this juncture, Clinton and the designated southern reinforcement force engaged in several defensive fights to maintain Crown control over New York and key defensive posts.[28] Meanwhile, St. Leger advanced by crossing Lake Ontario to Oswego where he received Native American reinforcements under chiefs Joseph Brant, Sayenqueraghta, and Cornplanter. The enlarged force marched east along the Lake Oneida-Mohawk River line, as a diversion to split Patriot forces.

## Rendezvous at Albany

Like Burgoyne, St. Leger commanded a composite force of British regulars, Loyalists from Butler's Rangers and the King's Royal Regiment of New York, Hesse-Hanau *Jaegers*, Native Americans, mostly from the Mohawk and Seneca tribes, and Canadien laborers.[29] The Native Americans were seen as indispensable for scouting and screening the movements of the Crown force. In addition, the force included a small complement of artillery and small mortars. Fort Stanwix, the only major obstacle along St. Leger's axis of advance, covered the "Oneida carrying place," an important portage between Lake Oneida and the Mohawk River. The artillery would not be sufficient for a formal siege of a well-defended post; however, his intelligence indicated that the fort was held by a meager garrison of 60 troops. Constructed in 1758 during the French and Indian War, the fort had fallen into disrepair. The disparity between the supposed and actual number of defenders illustrates a chronic problem for Crown forces throughout the war—a lack of reliable, accurate, and actionable intelligence. In this regard, the Patriot opponents typically had a far better "situational awareness" than did Crown commanders, a factor that severely compromised Crown operations.

St. Leger's invasion force quickly made their way to the Oneida carrying place, encountering only nominal opposition, arriving before Fort Stanwix on 1 August. The garrison actually consisted of roughly 700 men under Colonel Peter Gansevoort. Exacting and methodical, he earned the respect of both officers and enlisted men. While he could be sensitive to slights of his personal honor, real or perceived, he could laugh at his own foibles as well.[30] In essence, a combination of local connections and personality helped him weld the men under his command into a cohesive fighting force. Schuyler dispatched Gansevoort to occupy the post and repair its defenses in April. After learning from Gansevoort that the fort lacked ammunition and other critical logistics, Schuyler sent additional supplies. Gansevoort's leadership provided a key element in the failure of the St. Leger expedition mission. Combined with the strategic incoherence at all levels of command from London to New York to Canada resulting in Howe departing for Pennsylvania rather than providing substantial support to Burgoyne, the failure of St. Leger to reach Albany left Burgoyne's forces struggling through the Hudson Valley wilderness while the Patriots coalesced in ever great numbers.

Gansevoort delayed St. Leger's march by felling trees along his route of march. The tactic slowed the movement of artillery and required substantial troops to clear the obstructions. Initially, St. Leger sought to overawe the fort's defenders into surrendering without a fight by parading in front of the defenders, hoping to impress them with his numbers. When this tactic failed, he surrounded the post and initiated regular siege operations. Since clearing the road to bring up his artillery occupied many of his regular troops, St. Leger left the encirclement of the fort to his Native allies. The proficiency of Native troops in sniping at the garrison from concealed positions made them ideal for this work.

On 5 August, St. Leger received intelligence from Molly Brant, Joseph Brant's sister, that a relief column of roughly 800 militia commanded by Nicholas Herkimer, chairman of the local Committee of Safety, approached Stanwix. Based on the information, St. Leger dispatched his Native Americans, along with a small contingent of regulars and provincial rangers to set an ambush for the relief column. On 6 August, Patriot militia stumbled into the ambush. Hit with an initial volley with Herkimer among those wounded, the Patriots rallied and fought briskly until driven back. Herkimer eventually succumbed to his wounds in this engagement known as the Battle of Oriskany. While much of St. Leger's force engaged Herkimer and the militia, Gansevoort seized the opportunity to launch a sortie from the besieged fort, an action illustrative of his aggressive and proactive leadership. Patriot raiders broke into the poorly defended British camp and seized several wagonloads of supplies, carting them into the fort. On their return from Oriskany, Crown troops, and especially the Native Americans, came on a camp ravaged and pillaged of vital supplies. Not surprisingly, many of the Native contingent abandoned the siege.

Schuyler received word of the reverse at Oriskany and dispatched a relief column. Benedict Arnold led the relief force and by late August assembled some 700 men. He attempted to augment the relief force with Oriskany survivors. Understandably, only a hundred of these citizen soldier militia responded to the call. The siege finally broke when Arnold approached the besieged post. Employing a clever ruse, he dispatched a captured Loyalist to the British camp with information that a much larger force marched to relieve the fort. On hearing this information, many of the remaining Natives abandoned St. Leger. Now lacking sufficient manpower to continue the siege, he broke camp on 22 August and marched back toward Lake Ontario. The plan to aid Burgoyne had failed. Likewise, it cost the British substantial support from Native Americans and regional Loyalists; Crown forces failed to secure what seemed a fairly easy target.[31]

The inability of Crown forces throughout the war to pacify the countryside, and, more critically, ensure Loyalist security as illustrated by the St. Leger failure came to be a constant and debilitating theme throughout the war's remainder, particularly chronic and ultimately catastrophic in the Southern Campaign of 1778–1781. British leadership should have paid more attention to the dynamic of falling active Loyalist and Native support illustrated by the failed St. Leger expedition. Despite Crown success in field actions such as Oriskany, so long as the Patriot forces remained in the field and active, there was no Loyalist security, even in locations such as the Carolinas and upstate New York where arguably, Loyalism dominated. Though a small event relative to the greater engagements such as Long Island, White Plains, Monmouth Courthouse, Brandywine, Germantown, and others in the campaigns of 1776–1778, the Fort Stanwix-Oriskany episode played large in the events to follow and ultimately in the war's eventual outcome. Politically and economically, the affair contributed to the singular most important outcome of the Hudson Valley Campaign that soon culminated at Saratoga, New York, only weeks after Oriskany—the French Alliance.

## Fog and Friction of War

Burgoyne's advance continued though much slowed by the Patriots' disruptive activities. They felled trees and destroyed bridges in the path of the advance. These actions led to significant supply difficulties as the army reached Fort Edward on the Hudson River just beyond the lower end of Lake George. Compounded by his long baggage train as well as the large artillery park, Burgoyne seized supplies from the local settlements. The supply difficulties led to the failed expedition to Bennington in August. General Friedrich Adolph Baron von Riedesel first suggested that a foraging expedition focus on Manchester, New Hampshire, an important Patriot supply center. When he presented his idea to Burgoyne, the latter vacillated but warmed to the plan when he learned of St. Legers retreat. Believing intelligence that claimed the country to the east teamed with Loyalists, Burgoyne approved the foraging mission, which turned out to be an erroneous perception leading to a disastrous Crown defeat—the Battle of Bennington.[32]

Lieutenant-Colonel Friedrich Baum commanded the expedition and marched out on the morning of 9 August headed for Bennington, thought to be only lightly defended. Baum commanded a composite force of over 800 men that included dismounted Brunswick dragoons, Hesse-Hanau artillerymen to serve a pair of three-pounders, British infantry, a detachment of *Jäger* (German riflemen who served as scouts and skirmishers), French-Canadians, Loyalists, and Mohawks. While such a disparate force is not necessarily inefficient, the fact that at least four different languages were spoken certainly risked muddled command, control, and communications when in action.[33]

The Patriots received word of a British force moving into the region and mustered some 1,500 men, including Massachusetts and New Hampshire militia under General John Stark, a veteran of Lexington, Concord, and Bunker Hill. Troops under Seth Warner joined as well. Initial skirmishes between Baum's column and a patrol sent out by Stark confirmed the composite force's approach. Stark called for reinforcements. A further engagement grew out of the need to acquire mounts for the dragoons. Manchester, the original target, was guarded by Colonel Seth Warner's Continental Regiment and between four and five thousand militia. The clash actually occurred at Walloomsac, New York, about ten miles from Bennington. It rained heavily on the night of 15–16 August, but by the afternoon of 16 August, the weather cleared. Both sides received reinforcements as they prepared to square off. Some skirmishing occurred in the morning, but fighting erupted in earnest in mid-afternoon. Surrounding the outnumbered Crown forces, who established a defensive position on a raised hillock, rebels poured in fire from all sides. Crown forces sustained over 200 killed along with roughly 700 captured and lost two 3-pounder and two 6-pounder guns as well. The Patriots suffered only 30 killed with another 40 wounded. Beyond the tactical success, Bennington held strategic implications. The loss of nearly a thousand troops significantly reduced Burgoyne's expeditionary force. In addition, the defeat led many Native Americans to abandon the expedition as defeat now seemed inevitable.

While many factors combined to lead to Baum's defeat, a clear plan did not exist for Baum, rather, "[a]n objective was designated and everything in between was accomplished through snap decisions."[34] While a decentralized command can be successful, in this case, it was impeded by a clear lack of intelligence on the terrain and the level of resistance Baum was likely to encounter. The force's composite nature compounded the command and control problems. For the unfortunate Crown soldiers, the "fog of war" hung heavy over Bennington. While the affair constituted a major setback, Burgoyne soldiered on hoping for support from Clinton. His goal became reaching Albany before the onset of winter. Exacerbating the loss of men at Bennington, Burgoyne diverted troops to garrison Ticonderoga. Initially, he asked Carleton to provide a garrison to the post; however, strained relations flummoxed the increasingly dire situation. Carleton, "still wearing the mask of civility, had stood by the letter of his instructions."[35] His orders granted no authority outside the Canadian border. Accordingly, he refused to provide Burgoyne with the garrison troops. Here, again, the internal friction between personalities exerted a deleterious effect on a campaign's conduct, a dynamic that consistently undercut Crown expeditions and efforts to restore authority and allegiance and pacify the roiled countryside.

As summer progressed, it grew clearer that the expedition was not likely to rendezvous with additional forces coming out of New York. Burgoyne grew concerned with securing potential winter quarters. By September, the campaign's momentum clearly turned against him. Nor was he likely to receive any aid from

Howe, now engaged in securing Philadelphia. Even if Howe gained control of Philadelphia in a timely fashion, he would have to embark a significant portion of his force, sail back down the Delaware River, up the Atlantic coast, and up the Hudson, a significant feat. Even after the British gained Philadelphia on 26 September, they still had to reduce the Delaware River defenses, an operation that took until mid-November to complete. Burgoyne became even more concerned when word arrived that rebels had captured the British shipping at the head of Lake George as well as the troops guarding it. With his communications with Canada effectively severed, even Ticonderoga lay vulnerable.[36] With his rear threatened and little hope of reinforcement, Burgoyne now faced greater resistance in front as well. Gates, commanding a Continental Army force augmented by numerous militia formations barred the line of march.

By now, Burgoyne had lost most of his Native American contingent depriving him of vital intelligence on Patriot positions and strength. Still, he continued his advance reaching a point four miles north of the American defensive lines at Saratoga by 18 September. The two armies first came to grips at the Battle of Freeman's Farm on 19 September. Burgoyne ordered an advance on the American positions in three columns, the left commanded by Riedesel, the center by Brigadier-General James Hamilton, and the right under Brigadier-General Simon Fraser. Fraser had the key mission of turning the Patriot left situated on Bemis Heights. The British began their advance mid-morning. Arnold, ever aggressive, sought Gates' permission to move off the heights and take up a more advantageous position in the woods. Gates, grudgingly, allowed Arnold to make a reconnaissance in force of the British advance using Colonel Daniel Morgan's riflemen along with some light infantry. Heavy fighting ensued through much of the day with a brief lull followed by renewed heavy fighting through mid-afternoon.

In the end, Burgoyne held the field of battle but sustained 600 casualties, men he could ill afford to lose operating deep in hostile territory with only the most tenuous logistics. The Patriot forces sustained only about half the casualties of their British opponents. At the end of the day, it appeared clear to the belligerents on both sides that while Burgoyne could claim a victory technically based on his occupation of the battlefield, he had in fact suffered a significant reverse that placed his campaign in dire jeopardy. This dynamic occurred commonly throughout the war, notably at Guilford Courthouse in March 1781. While Lord Cornwallis held the field, a sign of victory in the Early Modern Era, he lost 25 percent casualties in the process, a disastrous figure for any force at any point in the history of conflict.

Simultaneously, Major General Benjamin Lincoln launched an attack on Fort Ticonderoga. Patriots surprised the defenders at the end of the portage trail that connected Lakes George and Champlain. Retaking the fort severed completely the thin logistical and communications link that kept Burgoyne connected to Canada. For the next month, the two forces faced off warily over the same ground they fought so furiously to claim on 19 September. The Crown force situation grew more and more perilous, especially as American militia contingents, sensing that Burgoyne had penned himself in, came out in great numbers. Likewise, desertions, the common metric of morale, increased among Crown forces. For the Patriots, tensions between Gates and Arnold reached a breaking point, and the former relieved the latter of command. Arnold requested permission to go to Pennsylvania, a move clearly meant to send the message that he would plead his case directly to the Continental Congress. Though Gates readily accepted, Arnold remained in the camp.

Hoping to break out of the trap, Burgoyne ordered a reconnaissance in force for 7 October. He sought to turn the Patriot left flank and proposed to use roughly one-third of his available troops in the attempt. Not all of Burgoyne's senior officers supported the plan. Riedesel in particular, thought the wiser course lay in retreat. Since the 19 September battle, Burgoyne's forces shriveled while Gates' increased. Burgoyne could likely call on only about 5,000 effectives against a total of some 12,000 Patriots.[37] This discrepancy in numbers no doubt influenced many senior officers' reluctance to attempt further offensive actions. The British advance began in mid-morning of 7 October. Gates, learning of the British movements, dispatched Morgan and several other units into the woods below the American position on Bemis Heights to engage the British left. The initial British assaults were broken by the Patriots, adding an additional 400 casualties Burgoyne's army could ill-afford.

At this juncture, Arnold, ordered by Gates to remain in his tent, fulminated with rage. Unable to remain out of the action and demonstrating the bold action that characterized his military career (and led in many ways to his downfall), he charged out of his tent, seized command of the Patriot left, and led an assault on two key redoubts that anchored the British left. The outermost of these, the Breymann with the innermost Barlcarres redoubts, anchored the Crown line. The loss of either seriously jeopardized the entire Crown position. Arnold's forces took the Breymann redoubt by frontal assault. Burgoyne's position became untenable. He could neither retreat north nor cross the Hudson River against stiff opposition.[38] There followed another period of tense waiting between the two forces lasting for six days. By 13 October, Burgoyne's army was totally surrounded as the Patriots kept his camp under constant harassing fire. A council of war supported asking for terms. Negotiations began on 13 October and led to the Convention of Saratoga, signed on 16 October after Burgoyne made one final attempt to play for time in the hopes a relief expedition under Clinton might come to his aid. He asserted that Gates had dispatched numerous troops, and therefore no longer possessed the numerical superiority he once had. Burgoyne requested the opportunity to inspect his adversary's troops to establish their numbers, a gambit immediately rejected. Finally, Burgoyne agreed to Gates's terms. One significant aspect was the naming of the agreement as a convention, as opposed to a surrender. The primary reason Gates agreed to such an agreement lay in the simple fact that as it grew clear that the Crown forces were penned in, many of the militia contingents left for home, their agreed times of service up. Gates was thus under significant pressure to conclude the victory as quickly as possible (see Figure 4.2).

**FIGURE 4.2** Burgoyne's Surrender at Saratoga

*Source:* Courtesy of the Anne S.K. Brown Military Collection, Brown University Library, Providence, Rhode Island

Article two of the Convention later generated some controversy and was overturned by the Continental Congress:

> A free Passage to be granted to the Army under Lieut. General Burgoyne, to Great Britain, on Condition of not serving again in North America during the present Contest; and the Port of Boston is assigned for the Entry of Transports to receive the Troops whenever General Howe shall so order.[39]

In effect, the Convention agreement placed Burgoyne's army on parole. When it learned of this provision, the Continental Congress refused to accept it. Concerned that the troops would simply return to Britain and be replaced by other units currently based there, Congress repudiated the convention and held the Crown forces as prisoners of war.

Burgoyne's surrender marked the first major defeat for Crown forces in North America. It also provided a powerful propaganda tool for Americans in their bid to gain foreign recognition and alliances. Shortly after it received word of Burgoyne's surrender, Congress informed their emissaries in France.[40] The victory exacerbated some internal dissent in the Patriot ranks as well. Gates reported the victory directly to Congress, not bothering to inform Washington. While Gates, holding an independent command, was within his prerogatives to act in this manner,

Washington could not help but feel the slight. Further, Gates highlighted his own role in securing the victory at the same time denigrating those of Arnold and Morgan. His actions alienated two of the best tactical leaders on the Patriot side. The surrender effectively ended Burgoyne's military career. While he returned to his seat in Parliament, he never again held a field command.

## Culminating Point

The Saratoga campaign is often depicted as a turning point in the conflict; this view holds merit. It contributed in no small way to the French Alliance in the following year. At the same time, it is worth noting that in the Hudson Valley region, the war continued unabated through the following years. It could be argued that following Ticonderoga, Burgoyne's invasion surpassed its culminating point. Following his success in taking that post with such ease, the friction of operating in an area lacking a significant road network, and where there was a hostile population, grew more and more telling. Following the capture of Ticonderoga, the advance slowed to a crawl as local residents felled trees and destroyed the bridges. Nor can Burgoyne be exonerated. While he possessed no experience in operating on the colonial frontier, he did possess experience campaigning in difficult terrain. In Portugal, he worked in a difficult operating environment, but much of the local population was supportive. The same could not be said for the Hudson Valley.

In this campaign, both Crown forces and rebels relied heavily on Native allies to gather intelligence, patrol, and disrupt their opponents. Both sides courted the Native Americans, in this case, the Six Nations of the Iroquois Confederacy.[41] Consequently, members of the confederacy had to choose sides. This dynamic disrupted the confederacy and led to a civil war between the various indigenous groups. As the ancient Chinese theorist of war, Sun Tzu, observes, if one cannot attack an enemy's strategy, "Next best is to disrupt his alliances."[42] While the Patriot efforts did not sever the majority of the tribes from their support of the British, they did reduce their overall combat effectiveness, as much of their energy was expended in internecine warfare.[43] Both Burgoyne and St. Leger misjudged the depth of commitment of their respective Native allies. Likewise, they failed to understand their motivations. Using Native allies as force multipliers proved in all theaters to be a thin reed upon which to build a successful strategy and subsequent operations to restore allegiance and pacify the population.

Finally, in his comparative analysis of military thinkers, Michael Handel noted how Clausewitz discerned a number of factors that work against an invader's success. These included the necessity of garrisoning fortresses, hostility in the theater of operations, the lengthening of supply lines and consequent shortening of them for the defender, the threat of allies coming to the aid of the defender, and the invader's slackening of effort versus the defender's increasing exertion.[44] This typology, applied to Burgoyne's drive, illuminates a number of the factors that brought about his eventual surrender.

## Notes

1 Edward Barrington De Fonblanque, *Political and Military Episodes in the Latter Half of the Eighteenth Century: Derived from the Life and Correspondence of the Right Hon. John Burgoyne, General, Statesman, Dramatist* (London: Macmillan, 1876), 62–83.
2 For Burgoyne's biography, see: Max M. Mintz, *The Generals of Saratoga* (New Haven, CT: Yale University Press, 1990); O'Shaughnessy, *Men Who Lost America,* 123–64.
3 Mackesy, *War for America,* 108.
4 John F. Luzader, *Saratoga: A Military History of the Decisive Campaign of the American Revolution* (New York: Savas Beatie, 2008), 13–4.
5 Ibid., 17.
6 Jeremy Black, "British Military Strategy," in *Strategy in the American War of Independence: A Global Approach,* eds. Donald J. Stoker, Kenneth J. Hagan and Michael T. McMaster (London: Routledge, 2010), 64; Luzader, *Saratoga,* 18; On the various conflicts prior to the War of Independence, see Douglas Edward Leach, *Arms for Empire: A Military History of the British Colonies in North America* (New York: Macmillan and Company, 1973), 44–7, 244–6.
7 Burgoyne, quoted in Luzader, *Saratoga,* 18.
8 Paul David Nelson, *General Sir Guy Carleton, Lord Dorchester: Soldier Statesman of Early British Canada* (London: Associated University Presses, 2000).
9 On Native American warfare in general, see Patrick M. Malone, *The Skulking Way of War: Technology and Tactics among the New England Indians* (Baltimore, MD: John Hopkins University Press, 1993).
10 Luzader, *Saratoga,* 24–5.
11 Gavin K. Watt, *Rebellion in the Mohawk Valley: The St. Leger Expedition of 1777* (Toronto: The Dundurn Group, 2002), 27–30.
12 Mintz, *Generals,* 80–2. See also, Watt, *Rebellion in the Mohawk,* 29–30.
13 Mintz, *Generals,* 134.
14 John Burgoyne, General Orders. June 20, 1777, in *Orderly Book of Lieutenant General John Burgoyne,* ed. E. B. O'Callaghan (Albany, NY: J. Munsell, 1850), 2.
15 Ibid., 17.
16 Ibid.
17 Burgoyne, General Orders for 3 July 1777, quoted in Burgoyne, *Orderly Book,* 25–6.
18 Luzader, *Saratoga,* 55; Dean Snow, *1777: Turning Point at Saratoga* (New York: Oxford University Press, 2016), 18.
19 Later became the state of Vermont-contested between New York and New Hampshire.
20 Burgoyne, General Orders for July 7, 1777, quoted in Burgoyne, *Orderly Book,* 30.
21 Mackesy, *War for America,* 133.
22 Ibid.
23 Robert K. Wright, "A Crisis of Faith: Three Defeats that Cost a Reputation," in *The Hessians: Journal of the Johannes Schwalm Historical Association* 21 (2018): 52.
24 Snow, *1777,* 37–8.
25 Samuel Adams to Samuel Cooper, Philadelphia, July 15, 1777, quoted in Paul H. Smith, ed., *Letters of the Delegates of the Continental Congress,* vol. 7, May 1–September 18, 1777 (Washington, DC: Library of Congress, 1981): 343. Hereafter, *LDC.*
26 Mark Edward Lender, *Cabal! The Plot against General Washington* (Yardley, PA: Westholme Press, 2019), 3–4.
27 Luzader, *Saratoga,* 86–91; Snow, *1777,* 52–3.
28 Mackesy, *War for America,* 137.
29 John S. Pancake, *1777, the Year of the Hangman* (Tuscaloosa, AL: University of Alabama Press, 1977), 140.
30 Watt, *Rebellion in the Mohawk Valley,* 61.
31 Ibid., 154–75, 243–9.
32 Mackesy, *War for America,* 134.
33 Wright, "Crisis of Faith," 55.

34  Ibid., 54, 58.
35  Mackesy, *War for America*, 135.
36  Ibid., 137.
37  Luzader, *Saratoga*, 264–5.
38  Snow, 1777, 267–7.
39  Burgoyne, *Orderly Book*, 145.
40  Committee on Foreign Affairs to the Commissioners at Paris, October 31, 1777, quoted in *LDC*, vol. 8, 215.
41  Mohawk, Oneida, Onondaga, Seneca, Cayuga and later Tuscarora.
42  Sun Tzu, *Art of War*, 78.
43  Calloway, *Indian Country*, 26–64.
44  Michael I. Handel, *Masters of War: Classics of Strategic Thought* (London: Frank Cass, 2001), 182.

# 5

# SHIFT TO THE MIDDLE

While Burgoyne made his way southward from Canada, another force sailed from New York to seize Philadelphia. The political capital of the colonial insurgency, and the most populous city in the colonies, capturing the city held its own appeal.[1] Howe submitted the first draft of his plan for the 1777 campaign in November 1776. At that time, British military fortunes in North America rode high. He planned an ambitious campaign designed to end the war in a year. Much of the plan's internal logic was contingent on the idea that any British advance from Canada would be slow. In this initial iteration, the plan called for a reinforcement of some 15,000 troops. Howe would utilize 10,000 of these reinforcements to invade Rhode Island. They could then move toward Boston if all went well. Another force would move up the Hudson and rendezvous with the invasion force advancing from Canada. The plan demonstrates that Howe, at least initially, planned on supporting the invasion from Canada. Five thousand troops would remain to garrison New York City. A third force composed of 8,000 men would engage in New Jersey operations designed to hold Washington in check while the other campaigns played out.[2] Holding Washington and his main army in position constituted support for Burgoyne preventing the Continental Army from shifting troops north.[3] As Andrew O'Shaughnessy observed: "Howe had delayed his departure from New York until he was confident that Burgoyne's expedition was well under way."[4]

## Center of Gravity

If the northern campaign proved successful, Howe planned a thrust against Philadelphia in autumn, 1777. If he should take the American capital and the rebels continued resistance, he intended to fight a winter campaign in South Carolina and Georgia. In his ambitious design for operations in 1777, Howe's objective appears as the capture and occupation of various regions and, in doing so, suppress the

DOI: 10.4324/9781003041276-8

rebellion one region at a time. In essence, he sought to break the rebellion by seizing territory. Likewise, a major aspect was the move through disaffected areas with overwhelming force to disrupt communications between the main centers of rebellion. Howe's proposal arrived in England on the last day of 1776. Germain refused to provide the requested reinforcements. The Secretary reduced the number of men dispatched to Howe from the requested 15,000 down to only 4,000. In one of the great mathematical subterfuges of eighteenth-century warfare, he managed to end up at the same final number of 30,000 effectives Howe initially requested. To accomplish this feat, Germain counted all of the troops sent to North America the previous year, not allowing for erosion of forces through sickness, combat casualties, and desertions. The desire to keep war costs minimized stood as the main reason behind Germain's creative mathematics.[5]

The disparity between Howe and Germain and their differing perspectives on troop needs demonstrate the competing perceptions as to how to conduct the war. For Howe, the correct approach meant defeating rebel forces and occupying the country colony by colony. As Howe later observed in testimony before Parliament:

> [A]s my opinion has always been that the defeat of the rebel army is the surest road to peace, I invariably pursued the most probable means of forcing its Commander to action, under circumstances the least hazardous to the royal army.

Germain, according to this interpretation, did not see the necessity for occupation; merely defeat the Continental Army and the local populace would rejoin the happy fold of loyal subjects. Howe went on to contend thus: "If the British commander was to have a force large enough to garrison every conquered district, caution in the field was the best policy so long as enough was done to expand steadily the area of British occupation." Thus, for Howe, the Continental Army represented the essential Center of Gravity. Washington, as well, appreciated that the Continental Army served as the embodiment of the revolt. If destroyed in a field engagement, then the goal of independence might die with it.[6] Securing Philadelphia while retaining New York would return another urban area and major port to Crown control. At the same time, Howe's remark belies a certain conservatism. Some attribute this attitude to the casualties incurred in the Bunker Hill assault of 17 June 1775, which Howe planned. Others attribute this attitude to a general risk-averse streak in his nature. The general's conservative streak is supported by the next line of his testimony: "for even a victory, attended by a heavy loss of men on our part, would have given a fatal check to the progress of the war, and might have proved irreparable."[7] Clearly, Howe sought a victory over Washington on terms least hazardous to his own forces. At the same time, manpower shortages represented a major concern when operating 3,000 miles from the Home Islands.

Still, before Howe's letter even reached England, the general altered the proposal as the strategic situation in North America developed. His first revision, dated 20 December 1776, deferred the planned attack on Boston until further reinforcements arrived. In addition, it had the virtue, at least in so far as Germain was concerned, of calling for only about half the troops requested in Howe's original concept. Howe altered parts of his original operational assessment as well, noting that the northern army invading from Canada was unlikely to reach Albany before the middle of September with further progress based on the prevailing situation.[8] To some extent, Howe himself seemed uncertain of just what his next move should be. The first revision seemed a fallback on what he might accomplish on a more limited scale. It rested on the notion of greater support from Philadelphia area Loyalists. Some actually fled Philadelphia for New York and gained direct access to Howe. Chief among these was Joseph Galloway, who, some historians assert, convinced Howe that Philadelphia constituted an appealing target.[9]

For his part, when Germain received Howe's November letter, he neither dismissed nor approved it. In response, the minister conceived the idea of raids along the New England coast and concluded that only about 2,500 fresh troops would be available for the next year's operations, reducing the number of reinforcements Howe could count on for the ensuing campaign.[10] In this interaction, the ill of conflicting strategic concepts between the civilian authority in London and the commander in the field is seen, a dynamic that continuously undercut any hope of a coordinated and successful Crown strategy for suppressing the rebellion and pacifying the colonies.

Howe submitted his next iteration on 2 April 1777. He first acknowledged the receipt of Germain's reply to his November letter. He then went on to state that he had given up on any offensive plans concerning Rhode Island, at least for the time being. In essence, British strategic thinking shifted away from any significant thrust at New England, the "heart of the rebellion," and toward isolating those colonies from the middle (i.e., the Hudson Valley Campaign), along with increased military and political efforts directed at the Middle Colonies, Pennsylvania, in particular. Howe's revised plan called for some 11,000 troops to invade Pennsylvania, leaving not quite 5,000 allocated to the defense of New York and with an additional 2,400 for Rhode Island operations, and 3,000 provincials for New York. This plan no longer called for any actions along the Hudson River. The new plan called for the invasion of Pennsylvania by sea, rather than by land, another significant difference.[11] Here one sees the genesis of the unhinging of the Hudson Valley divide and conquer concept months before Burgoyne's force stepped off from Canada. Howe's letter crossed one from Germain in transit. The minister's letter, a response to Howe's of 20 December 1776, granted approval. Howe's letter communicating his latest revision did not reach Whitehall until 8 May and lay unanswered until 18 May. Thus, this most recent iteration reached Germain so late that it essentially presented the secretary with a *fait accompli*.[12]

Two developments significantly altered Howe's campaign concept over the course of his correspondence with the Secretary. First was the knowledge that he would not receive the requested reinforcements.[13] Second, Washington's surprise and brilliantly executed turnabout in the Trenton-Princeton actions demonstrated that the Continental Army still had life, stamina, and capability. The Trenton and

Princeton raids, though small in size, exerted a significant effect on both sides' morale. The attitude of many of the Crown forces is captured by the Hessian *Jäger* Captain Johann Ewald:

> Thus had the times changed! The Americans had constantly run before us. Four weeks ago we had expected to end the war with the capture of Philadelphia, and now we had to render Washington the honor of thinking about our defense.[14]

Howe spent much of spring 1777 attempting to bait his adversary into a pitched battle in northern New Jersey. The ploy supports Piers Mackesy's contention that for the commander of British forces in North America: "Only the destruction of the enemy's army in battle would end the war."[15] Tactically, Howe displayed an adversity to direct confrontations and instead preferred to outflank his opponent as demonstrated at Long Island. Likewise, while the Patriot capital remained his overall objective, Washington's presence on his flank ruled out a direct advance. Such an approach meant a march of 90 miles through hostile territory with a long, exposed line of communications and logistics in his rear. To keep that line open, he would have to weaken his strike force by leaving detachments in his rear. It seemed much more sensible to make an amphibious descent on the city, which boasted fine port facilities. Likewise, it would take advantage of the mobility and surprise his brother's fleet afforded as well as maintain communications with New York. In this one sees the traditional expeditionary strategic culture that had dominated Britain since at least the Elizabethan Era. The ability to use naval power to transport, land, and support the ground troops gave British forces an immense operational advantage over a purely land opponent, a feature that still dominates UK military concepts in the twenty-first century. Howe set down his latest conception in a letter to Germain on 2 April 1777. This draft included the revision that his advance would be by sea as opposed to overland.[16]

Howe hoped that if he could engage the Continental Army in a set-piece battle, he could annihilate it and thus break the back of the rebellion, or at least crush one of its essential Centers of Gravity. Washington, for his part, maintained his adherence to the Fabian strategy he adopted the preceding fall. The CinC used much of the late winter and early spring to build up a new army safely ensconced behind the Watchung Mountains in Morristown, New Jersey. He did take advantage of Howe's forays to give his men combat experience. At the same time, he refused to be lured into a major engagement. The largest engagement from this game of move and counter-move came on 26 June 1777 known as the Battle of Short Hills.[17] On 9 June, Howe moved a sizeable force of 11,000 British and German troops from Staten Island to Perth Amboy, New Jersey. On 11 June, they moved forward to New Brunswick. Washington's spies informed him that Howe had left the equipment necessary for a major river crossing in New York, so Philadelphia was not threatened. Still, he did call up elements of the New Jersey militia. This episode nicely illustrates a feature that while not always apparent to contemporaries, poor intelligence continuously plagued Crown operations and aided the Patriots. Washington benefitted from a far more robust intelligence gathering apparatus such as the Cowper spy ring on Long Island. Recent scholarly research shows that Washington and his officers developed and operated a vigorous intelligence apparatus supplying valuable situational information on Crown movements. Conversely, Crown authorities lacked such a network.

## The City of Brotherly Love

On 26 June, Howe's troops moved out in two columns. Crown forces engaged with Continentals under William Alexander in the area known as Scotch Plains north of Brunswick. Washington, seeing that his subordinate was seriously outnumbered and in danger of being overrun, moved down from the Watchung Mountains. Still, he fell back rather than commit to a full-out battle with Howe. In the end, casualties on both sides were minimal.[18] The military successes of early 1777 had hopes rising in the Continental Congress, as well as among Whigs more generally, that victory was near to hand. When this proved not to be the case later in the year, it contributed to criticisms of Washington as military commander.[19] But in early 1777, all of this remained in the future. For the moment, Washington continued to ride high on a wave of both congressional and popular support, significant in that it allowed him to implement reforms initiated in the dark period of late 1776. These reforms resulted in a more professional and long-service Continental Army, a regular fighting force resembling more its British adversary than the colonial militia. Here again, Washington's view on the force structure necessary to win the war differed from many in Congress, but with a continuing string of military successes, the opposition found it difficult to challenge the commander's judgment. The problem was that Washington's stature hinged on his continued military successes. The fighting in New Jersey seemed to bolster his military reputation as after all, the British had, as of 30 June, evacuated the state.[20]

The attempt to lure Washington into a decisive field engagement in northern New Jersey having failed, Howe implemented the campaign plan he had sketched out in his correspondence with Germain. Washington, for his part, continued adhering to his Fabian strategy; Howe's attempts resulted in minor engagements but no general battle. These clashes insured that any attempt to march overland for Philadelphia would meet stiff resistance. It was not until 5 July that the troops and stores were all loaded, and the British armada cleared Sandy Hook destined for the Delaware Bay. Once out in the Atlantic, the wind died. Men and horses suffered horribly under the oppressive heat and humidity of a late east coast summer. Provisions ran short.

The frigate HMS *Roebuck* had engaged in patrol duties for some time at the mouth of the Delaware and clashed with the Pennsylvania Navy that patrolled the river up to Philadelphia. Thus, *Roebuck* possessed critical information on the defenses, including obstacles in the river. In essence, a direct river approach to Philadelphia was not feasible, given the defense in depth the Patriots had constructed. The choice of the Chesapeake for the landing over the Delaware indicated that the British still enjoyed uncontested control of the sea lines of communication. They could still move troops and naval assets with impunity. With the change in landing site, the ships reached Head of Elk, Maryland (modern Elkton), on 25 August. After dispersing some local militia, the landing commenced in two waves. Crown troops encountered only minimal and temporary resistance. Regardless of the initial successes, several of Howe's subordinates doubted the wisdom of the campaign. Writing to Prince Frederick Wilhelm of Prussia, Colonel Count Carl Emil von Donop noted thus: "If I dared to tell you what I think of the present situation, I should say outright that our expedition into these parts of the south is not to my liking."[21]

After regaining physical health, the men moved northward. On 3 September, near modern Christiana, Delaware, the lead elements engaged in a running skirmish with Continental Light Infantry. The clashes only served as delaying actions as Crown forces made their way inexorably toward Pennsylvania. For his part, Ewald was astounded that the Americans did not utilize the terrain to greater effect and more thoroughly contest the advance:

> The army marched past Newark [Delaware] and toward morning on the 8th [September] crossed the White Clay Creek, which was surrounded on both sides by steep, rocky heights that formed a most frightful defile half an hour in length . . . where a hundred riflemen could have held up the army a whole day and killed many men.[22]

While only marginally effective against the conventional Crown forces, skirmishes supported the strategy of attrition, a hallmark of a Fabian strategy. As the war developed, these small-scale encounters grew in occurrence and effectiveness, particularly after French and Spanish intervention. Crown commanders could ill afford the losses in men and material.

On 11 September, the advance elements of both armies clashed just south of Brandywine Creek in southeastern Pennsylvania, resulting in the largest and longest (11 hours) single-day battle of the war, the Battle of Brandywine.[23] Continental light infantry conducted a fighting withdrawal as the Hessian forces closed with them. The Hessians drove them back as the lights retired in a staged retreat to the north side of the Brandywine.

An American physician, Dr. Ebenezer Elmer, noted that "a very severe Cannonading at Random was kept upon both side [sic] for some time."[24] This encounter engagement erupted into a full-scale engagement as Howe executed a flawless flanking maneuver that drove the Continentals from the field. The Hessian assault constituted a feint, however. Howe used his German units to lock the Continentals in place. Then, he personally led the main force in a swing around and rolled up of the Patriot right flank, a maneuver he employed previously on Long Island

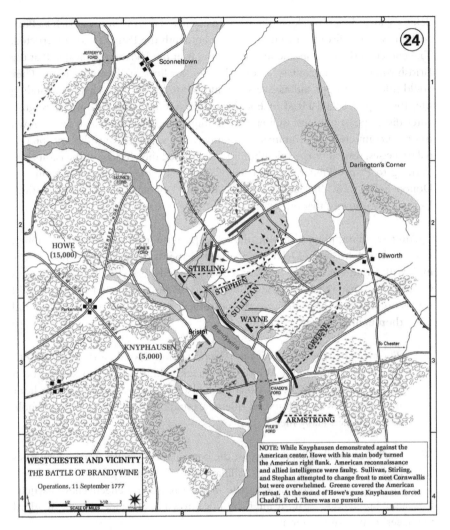

NOTE: While Knyphausen demonstrated against the American center, Howe with his main body turned the American right flank. American reconnaissance and allied intelligence were faulty. Sullivan, Stirling, and Stephan attempted to change front to meet Cornwallis but were overwhelmed. Greene covered the American retreat. At the sound of Howe's guns Knyphausen forced Chadd's Ford. There was no pursuit.

WESTCHESTER AND VICINITY

THE BATTLE OF BRANDYWINE

Operations, 11 September 1777

**MAP 5.1**   Battle of Brandywine

*Source:* Map Courtesy of the United States Military Academy Department of History, West Point, New York

to great effect. Though bested in the field again, Washington's Continental Army gained tremendous combat experience. At Brandywine, the Continentals did not break and run. Instead, they countered the British flanking movement. Greene commanded a rear guard action that put up a dogged defense, in turn allowing the majority of Continentals to disengage and retreat in good order. The Patriot withdrawal demonstrated the growing proficiency of the soldiery as they conducted a successful disengagement under fire. British officers noted the growing ability of their foes in this encounter.[25]

Following the battle at Brandywine, Washington initially fell back on Chester to regroup. The British pursuit followed only as far as Aston, Pennsylvania. Howe's army sustained considerable damage and spent the following days reorganizing. After drawing in stragglers, Washington set his troops in motion. They marched north through Darby, crossed the floating bridge at the Middle Ferry (modern Market-Street Bridge), and entered the outskirts of Philadelphia. On the one hand, this movement placed Washington behind the natural barrier of Schuylkill River, a strong defensive position. On the other hand, it placed the army on a peninsula with numerous crossing points that Howe might use. The only factor that prevented Patriot forces from being caught on death ground lay in the fact that Admiral Howe could not bring the bulk of his shipping up the river due to a series of rebel maritime defenses consisting of several forts, various sunken obstructions, and elements of the Pennsylvania state and Continental Navies. The Patriots had constructed a powerful attritional defense in depth that could potentially sap a great deal of British strength as they moved up the river.[26]

While the river defenses addressed one potential threat to the Continentals, another loomed in the peninsula's geography. Numerous crossings of the Schuylkill had to be guarded lest Howe repeat his recent flanking attempt at Brandywine. Compounding this problem, the various crossings were spread across a greater

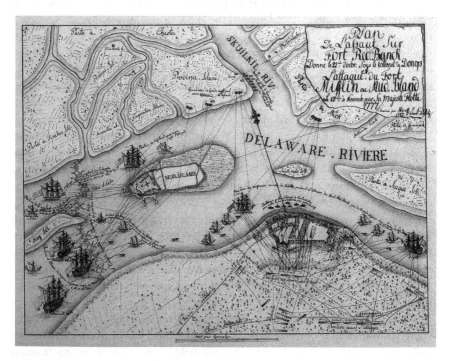

**MAP 5.2**  The Delaware River Defenses

*Source:* Map Courtesy of the Hessisches Staatsarchiv Marburg, Germany

distance than those at Brandywine, making defense and surveillance an even greater challenge.[27] Added to this, Washington felt compelled to cover the army's depots at Reading, Lancaster, and Bethlehem. Ultimately, the defense of logistics proved paramount and Washington moved out of the city once again. With simply too much to defend with under 11,000 troops to hold the city, the hinterland depots, and the river line simultaneously, priorities had to be set and choices made. On 14 September, Washington moved out of Germantown and marched toward Chester County.

Howe remained idle. Historians have ascribed numerous reasons for his inertia. One common theme is the general's innate conservatism. Another is the dual role played by Sir William and his brother as commanders of the land and sea forces respectively as well as peace commissioners. Their dual appointment as peace commissioners and military commanders was the only way to convince the brothers, both considered military innovators and highly respected by the troops, to serve in North America. Whatever the reason, Howe did not move. At this juncture, had Howe been more aggressive, he could have defeated, and possibly even dispersed the Continentals.[28]

Washington's movement to Chester County assured that that region would become the locus of operations for the following weeks. If the Continental commander did not have enough troubles to contend with, he even manufactured some of his own. For example, serious problems in the civil-military relationship erupted. A major issue revolved around the appointment of Philippe du Coudray, recruited in France by John Jay and promised the command of the Continental Artillery. Congress initially supported him in this rank, which enraged a number of Washington's senior officers, including Greene and Knox, and led them to challenge Congress' authority. Caught in the midst of this controversy, Washington maneuvered adroitly between the political Scylla and Charybdis. Initially, he asked Congress not to accept the resignations of his chief subordinates. At the same time, he reminded them of the supremacy of the civil authority. Eventually, Washington made du Coudray Inspector General of Ordnance. Unfortunately, in this role, the French engineer made erroneous assessments of the Delaware River defenses and wasted precious time and effort in altering them.[29] The river defenses became crucial during the latter stages of the campaign. Washington's decision in placing the French engineer in charge proved a poor one. He ultimately removed himself as an issue when he drowned while attempting to cross the Schuylkill River in a heavy rain. Nonetheless, the du Coudray episode indicated that the lines of demarcation between the civil authority and the military hierarchy of the nascent republic had yet to be clearly established. There would be additional issues between the two sides in the coming months.

At the moment, however, the key issue was Howe's next move, or more accurately, his overall lack of movement. At the same time, Washington attempted to make good his losses from Brandywine and field a force capable of confronting Howe. He called for additional troops from points as diverse as William Smallwood's Maryland militia, 2nd Rhode Island Regiment, and 2nd Connecticut Brigade.

The former consisted of roughly "1,400 poorly armed and barely trained men with no artillery, little ammunition, and almost no supplies."[30] If this formation even made it to camp, it would likely pose more of a burden than an asset, siphoning off vital supplies and adding little in terms of combat capability or effectiveness. The other formations were at least on the Continental establishment and could be counted on to remain with Washington through the campaign. Nevertheless, the move illustrates the desperate manpower situation now faced by Washington.

As Washington drew in additional manpower, he ordered southeastern Pennsylvania stripped of anything of military use.[31] Chester County contained pockets of Loyalists. It, therefore, made sense to remove any materials useful to Howe as offered by the local Loyalists. Meanwhile, Howe, dispatching troops off to Wilmington, including the wounded from Brandywine, led the main body past Dilworth and Turk's Head Tavern (modern West Chester, Pennsylvania) moving to a junction with the column under Cornwallis at the Goshen Friends Meeting House. These movements placed the two armies on a collision course.

Washington continued to maneuver as Howe and Cornwallis rendezvoused. He took up a position on South Valley Hill. Observing the enemy's movements and deployment, Howe ordered an advance. Just then, as often occurs in the Philadelphia area in late summer, a severe thunderstorm erupted, drenching the footsore men on both sides. Under normal circumstances, such an event would be greeted with pleasure for its relief from the heat. For the Patriots, however, it was damning. Due to a defect in their manufacture, the American cartridge boxes were not waterproof. Thus, the sudden storm destroyed much of the Continentals' ammunition. Simultaneously, Howe's forces could move forward with the bayonet, a preferred tactic. On the rebel side, many troops lacked this vital piece of military equipment. Those who did have a bayonet were certainly not as proficient in its use as their British adversaries. Washington thus ordered his men to disengage and retreat. There followed some skirmishing but Howe did not press the attack. Washington moved off toward Yellow Springs (modern Chester Springs), ten miles distant. The British camped on and around the battlefield that night. The tactical defeat in this aptly named Battle of the Clouds had significant strategic implications. The following day, it became clear that the road to Philadelphia now lay open and undefended. It also meant that the initiative in the campaign now rested with Howe. The Clouds event illustrates how, particularly in pre-Industrial Age warfare, physical elements such as terrain and weather often exert an extraordinary influence on events.

The Continental Army moved into Yellow Springs, a critical supply depot, in the early hours of 17 September and pressed on toward Warwick Furnace. A detachment of the Pennsylvania Continental Line under Brigadier General Anthony Wayne remained to guard the depot and harass any British advance.[32] The Patriot supply situation worsened when the British light infantry moved into Valley Forge and in a night raid destroyed substantial stores. Losses such as at Valley Forge, where only desultory resistance occurred, exacerbated the already failing state of the Continental finances, a factor that continuously hampered military operations.

The Continental Congress resolved on 22 May on an issuance of 5 million dollars in new currency.[33] But, as simple economics so amply illustrates, when a government turns the currency printing presses, inflation inevitably follows. That inflation further exacerbated the army's logistical woes. Farmers, husbanders, victualers, and goods suppliers of all kinds became less and less willing to accept the inflated and increasingly worthless scrip.

Given the number of area Loyalists, Wayne had barely taken up his new position when Howe became aware of the Pennsylvanian's presence.[34] That intelligence precipitated the next clash. Howe once again divided his force with Cornwallis leading down the Lancaster Road. Howe, with Knyphausen's Germans, marched east along the Swedes Ford Road. Meanwhile, the Continental Congress evacuated Philadelphia and fled to York as did many rebel supporters. Military supplies stored in the capital were removed from the warehouses and shipped across the Delaware into New Jersey, eventually relocating at Trenton, making Continental Army logistics far more problematic. With both armies in motion, Washington ordered Wayne to change locations. Washington planned to cross north of the Schuylkill River and catch Howe in a pincer between his and Wayne's forces. Thanks to an intercepted communique from Washington to Wayne, the British general was well aware of his opponent's intentions.[35] The interception of an opponent's communications, a fundamental aspect of warfare at all levels and in all eras, proved particularly common in the eighteenth century. Roving patrols intercepted riders, horses gave out, ships and packet boats were captured or lost at sea, and so on. As with the physical features, many a battle plan has been compromised by unreliable communications. Washington now fell victim to this dynamic. To make matters worse for the Patriots, the two columns' maneuvering actually pushed them further apart, leaving Wayne without support from the main Continental Army. As a result, the Pennsylvanians went from being the hammer to Washington's anvil to hanging out as a tempting bait for Howe. The British commander was not long in taking it and took full advantage of his position to move into Philadelphia and to attack Wayne's force. The move certainly kept with Howe's conservativism. An enemy force in one's rear constituted a potential threat to future operations and should be dealt with before initiating those operations.

Wayne apparently received some indication of his danger. At least two credible informants entered his camp bringing warnings. Despite this fact, the Pennsylvanian failed to heighten security.[36] Howe chose Major-General Charles Grey, a skilled and veteran officer, to command the counterattack. He ordered Grey to strike Wayne's camp in the night. When the British broke into the camp, they found the Pennsylvanians silhouetted clearly before their campfires. The attackers cheered, certainly a terrifying sound in the night for the surprised rebels, and charged with the bayonet. To maintain silence and surprise, flints had been removed from the muskets. Discipline broke down among the rebels, though some did rally and attempted to resist the assault, their numbers too few and efforts too little to resist the red tide that swept through the camp. Wayne reacted quickly and got his men into column to extricate them from the danger. Wagons and artillery had to be moved complicating the retreat. Despite the surprise, and the aggressive night assault, Wayne managed to withdraw most of his division, including artillery.[37] Grey did not pursue the retreating Continentals. So far, his night attack had been very successful and he declined to risk anything going awry. Still, Wayne's division was too scattered and beat up to fight. There would be no pincer movement. The affair came to be called the "Paoli Massacre." This moniker constituted a useful interpretation of the event by the Patriot leadership. It supported the depiction of the British as not following legitimate practices in warfare. In reality, it stood as something quite different. For his success in the assault, Grey received the *nomme de guerre* "No Flint" Grey. He ordered flints removed from the muskets prior to the march so that no one would accidentally discharge their weapon during the approach and give away the enterprise. In an age when night attacks were generally considered too risky due to the ease with which men could get lost, get detected by sentries or picquets, and compounded by the lack of accurate maps, the attack constituted a resounding tactical success. With Wayne dispensed with, Howe could take advantage of the maneuvering that placed him between the main Continental Army and Philadelphia. While the Paoli affair seemed a huge Crown victory, the resultant impact on colonial public opinion proved devastating in the long run as the war churned on and on and serves as an excellent illustration of the civil and cultural aspects of societies in conflict, dynamics that often determine outcomes far away from the actual battlefield. Depictions of British brutality and inhumanity increasingly undercut success on the actual battlefield. The dire warning of Henry Clinton as to winning the "hearts and minds" became increasingly haunting.[38]

## Occupation

On 26 September, Cornwallis led the British vanguard as it moved into Phila-delphia with the Loyalist Joseph Galloway at his side, who first became the city's military administrator during the British occupation, then one of Howe's most virulent critics following the withdrawal the following year. Howe managed to take the enemy's capital; however, this Pyrrhic victory did not amount to check-mate. Following close on the heels of Brandywine, the Continental Congress sim-ply abandoned the city for the inland town of York, Pennsylvania. While smaller and certainly poorer in urban refinements than Philadelphia, Congress could still organize the war effort from the town. Likewise, while Howe had defeated Wash-ington's main army at Brandywine and administered a clear check to one of its detachments at Paoli, he failed to cripple the force. Two of the Patriot Centers of Gravity remained intact. On the British side of the ledger, they managed to occupy a city located on an isthmus, in essence, a geographical dead end that invited a siege as had Boston previously and Charleston and Yorktown to come. Furthermore, the Pennsylvania authorities, with the occasional aid of the Continental Congress, had erected a potent defense in depth, which stretched from the Delaware Bay up to just below the confluence of the Delaware and Schuylkill Rivers. Washing-ton understood the potential in the Delaware River defenses. He wrote to John

Hancock, President of the Continental Congress: "I am not yet without hope that the acquisition of Philadelphia may, instead of his good fortune, prove his Ruin."[39] Since 1775, local authorities with irregular assistance from Congress developed a defense in depth centered on the Delaware River. These efforts bore fruit in the form of several rows of sunken obstacles, known as *chevaux de frise*, three forts, and a state navy to interdict any hostile forces coming up the river. These defenses now took on a renewed importance since to hold Philadelphia, Admiral Howe would have to bring his fleet with the vital victualling ships up the river. General Howe initiated the first steps in clearing the river defenses and opening the Delaware to traffic on 29 September, sending a force to assault the southernmost fortification at Billingsport, New Jersey. The Patriots abandoned the post in the face of superior numbers with the garrison evacuated by the Pennsylvania Navy and brought to Fort Mifflin further up the river.[40]

Washington launched an attack on the British outer defenses at Germantown on 4 October as Howe sent detachments to occupy Chester, Pennsylvania, and Wilmington, Delaware, as well as to seize the works at Billingsport. Washington sensed an opportunity to strike at a portion of his adversary's weakened force. With the remaining British force divided between Philadelphia proper and an outlying village known as Germantown, he hoped to inflict a defeat on Howe and perhaps even force him to abandon the city. The plan called for four columns to march along widely separated routes the night before the battle and rendezvous early on the morning of 4 October. Some units had to march upward of 20 miles to reach their jumping-off points on time. A column under Greene had to march a greater distance than the troops under John Sullivan, yet still be in a position to launch a simultaneous attack with the latter.[41] Likewise, the forces were of uneven quality. Some Continental units had a fair amount of experience, while others were newly raised militia formations.[42] A night march in the period, always fraught with hazards due to desertions, units becoming disorganized or disoriented, and a lack of real-time communications between columns and elements represented a hugely problematic dynamic, especially with poorly trained troops. Surprise represented a crucial element in the plan. However, this element was lost before the first volleys were loosed. Ewald stated:

> Toward evening Professor Smith from Philadelphia came to me, who owned a country seat close to the *Jäger* post for which I had provided protection. He asked me to take a little walk with him, which I was quite willing to do since we had enjoyed several days' rest. He led me behind the camp, and when he thought no one would discover us, he addressed me with the following words: "My friend, I confess to you that I am a friend of the States and no friend of the English government, but you have rendered me a friendly turn. You have shown me humanity which each soldier should not lose sight of. You have protected my property. I will show you that I am grateful. You stand in a corps which is hourly threatened by the danger of the first attack when the enemy approaches. Friend, God bless your person! The success of

your arms I cannot wish.—Friend! General Washington has marched up to Norriton today!—Adieu! Adieu!"[43]

Ewald noted that his first reaction: "I stood for a while as if turned to stone." Recovering his composure, he duly reported this intelligence. According to his account, Howe disregarded the information. However, Knyphausen initiated defensive measures at once.[44] This report was not the only warning the troops stationed in Germantown received of the pending attack. Lieutenant Martin Hunter recalled that at about one in the morning:

> [W]e had information from a deserter, as he said he was, but I rather think he had lost his way. He was brought in by one of our patrols, and positively said that he had left General Washington and his whole army on their march to Chestnut Hill.[45]

The Patriot attack jumped off in the early dawn of 4 October, with much of the area shrouded in a heavy fog. Patriot forces enjoyed some initial success driving in the pickets and forcing the Light Battalion to retreat. Numerous factors combined to bring about a tactical culminating point of attack. First, the Patriots had marched through the night, and the battlefield itself remained shrouded in a morning fog. Stiff resistance by a composite force from several regiments at the house of local justice Benjamin Chew blunted the assault. Their use of the house as a defensive position further exacerbated this literal fog of war.[46] British troops fled into the residence to find shelter from the swarming rebels. They barricaded the doors, closed all the shutters, and managed to resist all attempts by the attackers to break in. Furthermore, they rejected all appeals to surrender. Their stout defense derailed the rebel initiative. Not only did some Patriot troops balk at the sounds of cannon and small arms fire in their rear, many of the Continentals were low on ammunition and fresh troops with full cartridge boxes were increasingly siphoned into the assaults on the Chew House.

The fighting around Chew House provided Crown forces with a much-needed respite, a breathing space in which reinforcements could be brought up from Philadelphia. These fresh troops came into contact with Patriots who had marched through the night, many of whom were low or out of ammunition. Patriot forces crumbled, then buckled, then retreated, forcing Washington to order a general withdrawal. Among the American officers most effected by the reverse at Germantown was Sullivan. Blamed for his role in the Brandywine defeat, now, his column, which had kicked off the assault on Germantown, was among those retreating. As one historian noted, "The American officers, devastated by how close they had come to victory, were frustrated by the series of events that had turned their success into a chaotic defeat—none more so than John Sullivan."[47]

Breaking off a fight and returning back from whence they came without the retreat degenerating into a thorough route was evidence of growing technical proficiency of the Continentals even prior to the intervention of Baron von Steuben at Valley Forge the following winter. That said, at this point in the conflict, while Crown forces without much difficulty executed night attacks, multi-column advances, and other tactical movements, the Continental Army still had many lessons to learn. That they performed better with each engagement represented a bad harbinger that Crown commanders would have been well-advised to note. The longer the conflict protracted in accordance with a successful Fabian strategy, the more efficient Patriot forces became. Simultaneously, the longer the protraction drew out, the worse the attrition became for Crown resources and manpower.

While Washington reported to John Hancock news of yet another Patriot reverse, he at least drew some solace from the fact that many of his men perceived themselves as robbed of victory by the elements. In a balanced critique of the plan and its implementation, John Buchanan observes that while the plan for Germantown was certainly overly complex, that the Continentals could implement it as well as they did testifies to their growing level of professionalism. Still, the plan for the attack was Washington's, and its repulse exacerbated criticism of his leadership among both Continental Congress members and some subordinate officers.[48] While Washington's leadership produced nothing but reverses, Gates was winning his contest against Burgoyne in New York.

Following Germantown, both sides focused on the Delaware River. British efforts at reducing these obstacles became a joint operation between the army and navy.[49] Howe's first attempt at opening the river to maritime traffic began on 1 October, when he dispatched troops to cross the Delaware, south of Philadelphia at Chester. Their objective consisted of reducing Billingsport, which consisted of little more than a redoubt with the guns overlooking the lower row of *chevaux de fries*. Once either occupied or reduced, the Royal Navy could remove the sunken obstructions. Outnumbered and defenseless on the landward side, the garrison defenders could not stand. British troops occupied the fort and spiked the guns before withdrawing back across the river. Had the British commander been more aggressive, he could have ended the struggle for control of the river.[50] At this time, Fort Mercer had no garrison. That post might have been seized as well. The Royal Navy cleared the lower row of obstructions. Opening the river to British supply and merchant shipping enabled Howe to maintain his prize. Still, it cost him time and manpower. As long as the Royal Navy and Crown troops engaged in opening the Delaware, none could be detached to reinforce Clinton and allow him to support Burgoyne in the Hudson Valley. Thus, there existed a cascading effect that soon led to British defeat along the Hudson and ultimately made the war far more than a simple colonial revolt. The events of September and October 1777 in Pennsylvania and New York transformed the war from a revolt suppression to yet another Anglo-French global confrontation.

The emphasis now fell on reducing the remaining Delaware River forts with the first target as Fort Mercer in New Jersey. When word that the British commander contemplated an expedition leaked out, Colonel von Donop of the Hessian contingent sought the command. In late 1776, von Donop commanded New Jersey Crown forces, which included Trenton. The defeat of Colonel von Rall stood as a prominent blemish on the Hessian contingent overall. Von Donop sought to clear the blemish by leading the assault on Fort Mercer. The plan called for the Hessians to attack the fort on 23 October while simultaneously the Royal Navy bombarded Fort Mifflin, thus preventing either post from supporting the other. Key shortcomings emerged from the outset. When von Donop sought heavier artillery to bombard the site, Howe turned down the request, stating that if they required British guns, the British would take the post. In addition, the expedition possessed no scaling ladders. While von Donop rounded up Whig sympathizers whose names were provided to him by local Loyalists, some did manage to escape and bring advanced warning to Fort Mercer.

Von Donop launched his troops at Fort Mercer in the late afternoon of 22 October, a day ahead of the planned attack. Launching the assault prematurely threw the entire plan into confusion. Hearing the sounds of battle, some Royal Navy ships began bombarding Fort Mifflin. Von Donop's troops were soundly repulsed, the colonel himself lying among the wounded. Meanwhile, later that same day the British third-rate ship-of-the-line HMS *Augusta* ran aground becoming mired in the mud. Seeing the ship's predicament, the Fort Mifflin gunners singled out the warship for special attention. About 10 the following morning, the ship caught fire. Flames quickly spread to the powder magazine, which exploded. The *Augusta*, as well as the frigate *Merlin*, which came to the aid of the former, were lost. All in all, the assaults represented an embarrassing disaster for the Howes and for the British and Hessian reputations. Members of the Continental Congress understood the importance of these events. In a letter from the Committee on Foreign Affairs to the Commissioners then working in Paris, they noted not only Burgoyne's surrender but the successful defense of Fort Mercer and the destruction of the *Augusta* and *Merlin*. Following their report on the preceding events, they enjoined the Commissioners, "We rely on your wisdom and care to make the best and most immediate use of this intelligence to depress our enemies and produce essential aid to our cause in Europe."[51]

Crown efforts settled on the reduction of Fort Mifflin by a siege conducted by ships in the Delaware as well as land batteries. The siege lasted through most of October and into November. Washington learned that the British had found a way to transport supplies into Philadelphia along a backchannel waterway. The discovery generated some consternation since the reason for dedicating scant Continental Army resources to the forts and the Pennsylvania Navy was to prevent supplies from getting through to the city so as to make it untenable for the British occupiers. If Crown forces found a hole in the cordon, then the whole campaign failed. This reverse, combined with recent battlefield defeats, led to significant political repercussions. Following an especially heavy bombardment on 15 November of roughly 350 guns aimed at Fort Mifflin, the post was deemed untenable. During the night, the last defenders abandoned the battered fortification, leaving the flag still flying as a decoy.

Finally, on 5 December Howe marched a large column out of Philadelphia to the then outlying area of Chestnut Hill. Over the course of several days of skirmishing, he attempted to draw Washington into an open fight and outflank him. The Virginian maintained his Fabian approach and Howe returned to the city on 8 December going into winter quarters. For some time, the Continentals remained outside Philadelphia in a shadowing position but refused to be drawn into a major engagement. Finally, on 19 December, the Continental Army marched into Valley Forge along the Schuylkill River and into winter quarters. The site offered a vantage point from which the army could keep the British under surveillance and protect against any sudden forays into the Pennsylvania interior. The position guarded the Patriot depots at Reading and Lancaster as well.[52]

## Stalemate in the Middle

The 1777 campaign against Philadelphia demonstrated growing proficiency of the Continental Army, if not its leader. While Washington had been outflanked at Brandywine in essentially the same manner as in the previous year on Long Island, this time the troops did not panic and run. Likewise, they came close to succeeding in a very complex attack on Germantown, and finally, the Rhode Island regiments at Fort Mercer succeeded in repulsing a major Hessian assault. Granted, von Donop bears significant responsibility for the defeat, still, the Patriots held the post unlike the failed defense of Fort Washington the previous year.

The belief that the British would find significant support in the Philadelphia area proved only partially true. While many Loyalists came out and welcomed the Crown forces, few men joined either British regular units or any of the various Provincial formations. While some new Loyalist units did form, they in no way made up for the 15,000 reinforcements Howe had requested. The phenomenon of known Loyalists refusing to participate actively on behalf of the Crown should have been a clarion call to British strategists and policy decision-makers. The illusion of a vast Loyalist outpouring persisted and soon precipitated the ultimately catastrophic Southern Campaign.

In the final analysis, the fighting in the Delaware truly unhinged any thoughts of cooperation between Howe and Burgoyne. Howe, his reputation coming under increasing criticism in Westminster, submitted his resignation in October 1777. In resigning his command, he claimed that he had received insufficient support from the Germain ministry. He would make this case again in the parliamentary inquiry into his command in 1779. Howe departed Philadelphia on 18 May 1778 after his officers held an ostentatious celebration organized by Major John Andre and known as the *Meschianza*, a play on the Italian term for medley, as a farewell token of their esteem.

## Notes

1 There are a number of useful works on the Philadelphia campaign of 1777. Among those are: Thomas J. McGuire, *The Philadelphia Campaign*, 2 vols. (Mechanicsburg, PA: Stackpole Books; 2006); John F. Reed, *Campaign to Valley Forge, July 1, 1777-December 19, 1777* (Philadelphia, PA: University of Pennsylvania Press, 1965); Stephen R. Taaffe, *The Philadelphia Campaign, 1777–1778* (Lawrence, KS: University of Kansas Press, 2003);

Michael C. Harris has contributed two battle narratives: *Brandywine: A Military History of the Battle That Lost Philadelphia But Saved America, September 11, 1775* (El Dorado Hills, CA: Savas Beatie, 2014) and *Germantown: A Military History of the Battle for Philadelphia, October 4, 1777* (El Dorado Hills, CA: Savas Beatie, 2020).

2  On William Howe's plans for the 1777 campaign, see Gruber, *Howe Brothers*), 174.

3  Lender, *Cabal!*, 11.

4  O'Shaughnessy, *Men Who Lost America*, 107.

5  Ibid., Gruber, *Howe Brothers*, 175, 179–81.

6  William Howe, *The Narrative of Lt. Gen. Sir William Howe to a Committee in the House of Commons on the 29th of April, 1779* (London: H. Baldwin, 1779), 19; Troyer Steele Anderson, *The Command of the Howe Brothers during the American Revolution* (New York: Oxford University Press, 1936), 218. On the concept of center of gravity, see Clausewitz, *On War*, 595–6.

7  Anderson, *Command of the Howe Brothers*, 218.

8  Gruber, *Howe Brothers*, 179–80.

9  Anderson, *Command of the Howe Brothers*, 219–20; John W. Jackson, *The Delaware Bay and River Defenses of Philadelphia, 1775–1777* (Philadelphia, PA: Philadelphia Maritime Museum, 1977), 1.

10  Anderson, *Command of the Howe Brothers*, 220.

11  Ibid., 221–3.

12  Ibid., 227–8; Gruber, *Howe Brothers*, 207–8; Harris, *Brandywine*, 18.

13  O'Shaughnessy, *Men Who Lost America*, 105–6.

14  Ewald, *Diary*, 44.

15  Mackesy, *War for America*, 121.

16  Ibid., 122.

17  The engagement is also referred to as Flat Hills, Metuchen Meetinghouse, or Westfield depending upon the source.

18  On the battle of Short Hills see Ward, *War of the Revolution*, 327–8.

19  Lender, *Cabal!*, 4–5.

20  Ibid., 5, 12.

21  Carl Emil von Donop, "Letters from a Hessian Mercenary." trans., and eds., C. V. Easum and Hans Huth, in *PMBH* 62, no. 4 (October 1938): 499.

22  Ewald, *Dairy*, 79–80.

23  Harris, *Brandywine*, viii.

24  Ebenezer Elmer, "Excerpts from the Journal of Surgeon Ebenezer Elmer of the New Jersey Continental Line, September 11–19, 1777," in *The Pennsylvania Magazine of History and Biography* 35, no. 1 (1911): 104.

25  Harris, *Brandywine*, 396–7.

26  On the river defenses, see Gregory M. Browne, "Fort Mercer and Fort Mifflin: The Battle for the Delaware River and the Importance of American Riverine Defenses during Washington's Siege of Philadelphia," (MA Thesis: Western Illinois University, 1996); Worthington C. Ford, ed., *Defenses of Philadelphia in 1777* (Brooklyn: Historical Printing Club, 1897. Reprint, De Capo Press, 1971); John W. Jackson, *The Pennsylvania Navy 1775–1781: The Defense of the Delaware* (New Brunswick, NJ: Rutgers University Press, 1974); John W. Jackson, *The Delaware Bay and River Defenses of Philadelphia 1775–1777* (Philadelphia, PA: Philadelphia Maritime Museum), 1977; Frank H. Stewart, *History of the Battle of Red Bank with Events Prior and Subsequent thereto* (Woodbury, NJ: Board of Freeholders of Gloucester County, 1927); William S. Stryker, *The Forts on the Delaware in the Revolutionary War* (Trenton, NJ: John L. Murphy Publishing Co.), 1901.

27  Harris, *Germantown*, 32.

28  Ibid., 35.

29  Concerning the controversy over du Coudray, see Thomas J. McGuire, *The Philadelphia Campaign, Vol. 1 Brandywine and the Fall of Philadelphia* (Mechanicsburg, PA: Stackpole Books, 2006), 282; See also, Harris, *Germantown*, 43, 49.

30 Harris, *Germantown*, 44.
31 Ibid., 47.
32 Ibid.
33 Ford, *Journals of the Continental Congress*, vol. 8, 377.
34 Ibid., 74.
35 Ibid., 66, 78.
36 Ibid., 86–7.
37 Ibid., 106.
38 Clinton asserted in 1776 that Britain must: "gain the hearts and subdue the minds of America." Report of conversation with L [Lord] D[James Drummond] and Tryon [William Tryon], 7 Feb. [1776]. *Clinton Papers*. William L. Clements Library, University of Michigan, Ann Arbor, MI, 13/36.
39 George Washington to John Hancock, September 23, 1777, in W. W. Abbot and Dorothy Twohig, eds., *The Papers of George Washington, Revolutionary War Series*, Vol. 11 (Charlottesville, VA: University of Virginia Press, 2001), 302.
40 Jackson, *Delaware Bay*, 5–7; Jackson, *Pennsylvania Navy*, 131–6.
41 Jackson, *Pennsylvania Navy*, 297.
42 McGuire, *Philadelphia Campaign, Vol. 2*, 49–50; Harris, *Germantown*, 431–3.
43 Ewald, *Diary*, 92.
44 Ibid.
45 Martin Hunter, *The Journal of Gen. Sir Martin Hunter and Some Letters of His Wife, Lady Hunter*, ed. A. Hunter (Edinburgh: Edinburgh Press, 1894), 33 as quoted in Harris, *Germantown*, 266.
46 Clausewitz, *On War*, 117–8.
47 Harris, *Germantown*, 370, 374.
48 John Buchanan, *The Road to Valley Forge: How Washington Built the Army that Won the Revolution* (New York: Barnes and Noble, 2007), 282; Lender, *Cabal!*, 24–5.
49 The British accrued significant experience at joint operations as seen in the previous conflict with the siege and capture of Havana, Cuba. For example, see Thomas More Molyneux, *Conjunct Expeditions, or Expeditions that have been Carried on Jointly by the Fleet and Army: With a Commentary on Littoral Warfare* (London: R. and J. Dodsley, 1759).
50 Jackson, *Pennsylvania Navy*, 134.
51 Committee for Foreign Affairs to the Commissioners at Paris, October 31, 1777, quoted in Paul H. Smith, ed., *Letters of the Delegates*, vol. 8, September 18, 1777–January 31, 1778 (Washington, DC: Library of Congress, 1981), 214–5.
52 Wayne Bodle, "Generals and 'Gentlemen': Pennsylvania Politics and the Decision for Valley Forge," in *Pennsylvania History* 62, no. 1 (January 1995): 59–89.

# 6

# A HARSH WINTER

Stephen R. Taaffe noted: "For the British, the Philadelphia campaign was their last chance to focus their undivided attention on suppressing the American revolt."[1] Burgoyne's defeat and his subsequent surrender at Saratoga held global implications. The Patriots quickly grasped the diplomatic opportunities in their ongoing negotiations with the court of Versailles. Still, all was not well in the Patriot camp. Gates rose to prominence as a national hero for stopping Burgoyne's drive down the Hudson Valley. Meanwhile, Washington's lackluster performance in the Philadelphia campaign, coupled with his advocacy of a regular army, established along British lines left many in Congress questioning his leadership.

## Cabal

In the waning days of the 1777 campaign, Washington faced a challenge from a different quarter, in this case, political—the Conway Cabal. Historians disagree as to the extent of the challenge to Washington's leadership or if one even existed. The most recent scholarship remains divided. John Buchanan supports the notion that some sort of conspiracy seemed to be going on and takes the challenge to Washington's authority quite seriously. Buchanan connects the criticism of Washington to the notion held by many Patriot leaders that the war would be a short one. When the conflict protracted, they sought a concrete reason for why, and placed the blame on Washington's military leadership.[2] Conversely, John Ferling interprets the cabal as the result of Washington's own insecurity and asserts: "In all likelihood, the supposed intrigue never amounted to more than a handful of disgruntled individuals who grumbled to one another about Washington's shortcomings."[3]

Mark Edward Lender, who studied the purported cabal in depth, notes that given the lack of successes in the Philadelphia campaign: "it would have been surprising if the Patriot general's record had not evoked censure, or at least serious

DOI: 10.4324/9781003041276-9

questions."[4] These issues came not just of Washington's military capability but concerning his view of the Continental Army as well. He sought to develop a more professional force along the lines of the British model. More radical Whigs in Congress found this concept odious. They placed their confidence in the pure citizen soldier as embodied in the local militia formations, disregarding that by this point in the conflict, the militia repeatedly demonstrated their unreliability.[5]

Lender divides the challenge to Washington's leadership into two stages. The first stage revolved around Brigadier General Thomas Conway. Born in Ireland to a Catholic family, he subsequently immigrated to France at age six. There he received an education and joined the French Army in 1747 as a *lieutenant en second*, experiencing his first combat during the War of the Austrian Succession (1740–48). In 1772, he rose to the rank of colonel. With fighting in the colonies, Conway sought and received royal permission to sail for America. The long-time professional soldier initially impressed Washington, who forwarded Conway to the Continental Congress with a commendatory letter. The body granted Conway the rank of brigadier general; he served with some distinction at the battles of Brandywine and Germantown. Soon, however, the relationship between the CinC and his subordinate soured. Historians have speculated on the reasons for the change. Some perceive Conway as the military professional looking with disdain on Washington the amateur, while others see him as believing replacing Washington with a more capable commander represented the only means of rescuing the Continental Army from its deteriorating fortunes. Conway often lobbied for higher rank, a sure way to ruffle feathers among peers. The spark that ignited the controversy within the army and between the army and Congress occurred following Saratoga. He wrote a congratulatory letter to Gates in which he supposedly included the line: "Heaven has been determined to save our Country or a weak General and bad Councellors would have ruined it." Since the original letter is lost, the account derives from hearsay as reported by a general's aide supposedly overheard in a tavern. In what Lender refers to as the "classic Cabal" narrative, the letter affair tipped the hand of a group of conspirators who sought to replace Washington as CinC with Gates. Once exposed, Washington responded to the conspirators, sending a message to Conway, including the quote just cited, thus exposing the faction, which included Gates.[6]

Concerns over Washington's leadership derived from profound worries over the success, or lack thereof of the Patriot war effort. Coupled with these concerns was a feeling that something dramatic had to be done to save the flagging war effort. Tensions reached a boiling point as the Philadelphia campaign closed; those who opposed Washington now had a replacement—Horatio Gates. Surely, Gates, a former British officer, military professional, and hero of Saratoga along with another respected European, Thomas Conway, and Quartermaster General Thomas Mifflin, a member of Congress with numerous political connections might represent the saviors of the Patriot cause. The group did not challenge Washington directly, rather proposed to sideline the commander through a reformed Board of War. Their efforts occurred during the army's stay at Valley Forge; it is, therefore, apropos to discuss the efforts of the Board in the context of the encampment.

## Valley Forge Winter

On 19 December, the Continental Army went into winter encampment at Valley Forge located on the upper reaches of the Schuylkill River some 18 miles from Philadelphia. Nestled amid rolling hills, it formed a solid, defensible location for Washington to interpose his army between the British in Philadelphia and Continental supply depots further west. The army stood in an ideal position to block any sudden British thrust into the countryside. Still, if Howe decided on a winter campaign, an unlikely event given the general's past predilections, it was unlikely that the Continentals could stop his advance. Of the 11,000 troops that shuffled into Valley Forge, a full 2,000 were without shoes.[7] Others lacked clothing articles and equipment. The popular memory of Valley Forge is one of determination in the face of unmitigated suffering. Certainly, there is merit to this perception. By February 1778, for instance, roughly 4,000 troops were unfit for duty due to lack of shoes, clothing, blankets, soap, medicines, and other basic necessities.[8] A number of factors contributed to the supply shortfalls at Valley Forge. Among the most basic was the terrain, which served as both a boon and a bane to the Continentals. While the hilly countryside of eastern Pennsylvania provided strong natural defenses, it simultaneously made camp access difficult in a time of dirt roads turned to sodden swamps by winter rains and snowfall, making the encampment cut off from the outside world. Wagons bearing provisions had to travel long distances along poor roads in inclement weather. Simple human greed, corruption, and mismanagement of the Commissary and Quartermaster Generals Departments exacerbated the problems, a plague on military services for time immemorial. Minimal preservation added to the problem. Often, waggoneers, to lighten their loads and spare their animals, dumped the brine from salted provisions, leading to spoilage. In the end, all the factors rendered a cost in human lives. Between December 1777 and June 1778, 2,500 Continentals succumbed to exposure, malnutrition, and various camp diseases. Desertion, the perennial gauge of morale, increased. Discipline reached a precarious nadir as soldiers chanted "no bread, no soldier."[9]

Writing to the president of the Continental Congress, Washington sought to make the delegates aware of the full gravity of the supply situation. He stated bluntly concerning the army's lack of provisions:

> I am now convinced beyond a doubt that unless some great and capital change suddenly takes place in that line this Army must inevitably be reduced to one or the other of these three things. Starve—dissolve—or disperse, in order to obtain subsistence in the best manner they can.

Driving home his point, he added: "Rest assured, Sir, this is not an exaggerated picture, and that I have abundant reason to support what I say." Washington's forthright assessment achieved the desired goal. It woke the delegates from their torpor, forcing them to take positive action. By this point in the conflict, they understood that the army constituted a vital Center of Gravity. No army, no independence.[10]

For a time, Washington acted as his own quartermaster and commissary general. As one commentator observed:

> Until a comprehensive reorganization of the military system as a whole could be effected in conjunction with Congress, a substantial part of the day-to-day business of administering the army consisted of making *ad hoc* adjustments aimed at coaxing whatever service could be gotten out of the existing mechanism.[11]

This approach could not be sustained. First and foremost, with Washington attending to the myriad details that fall under logistics management, little time remained to act as CinC. Second, while the *ad hoc* approach might work when the army remained stationary, once active campaigning resumed, the lack of any rational system guaranteed logistics breakdowns would return and jeopardize any renewed war effort.

Responding to Washington's dire warning, Congress appointed a delegation, the Committee at Camp, to come to Valley Forge and confer. Initially, the appointees were not much to the general's liking as they included Mifflin and Gates, also members of the newly formed Board of War. At the last moment, the Board of War representatives dropped out and additional delegates from Congress joined the committee. On learning of the committee, Washington demonstrated his political skill in that he who sets the agenda has the initiative in dictating the course of the proceedings.[12] He set his staff to work developing an agenda for the committee. They produced "[t]he Representation [that] provided the Committee, in the absence of a detailed specification of its mandate from Congress, a broad framework on which to base its inquiry."[13] The committee arrived on 24 January 1778. Their first task lay in addressing the supply situation, which the committeemen now saw in stark reality, witnessing the army's suffering first-hand. The revelation brought about a "subtle but important alteration" in the committee's role regarding the army's relationship with Congress.[14] It also brought the Committee at Camp into conflict with the reinvigorated Board of War.

The Board of War, originally created in 1776 to act as a support service for the Continental Army and to focus on supply issues, was revamped by Congress in late 1777. The reformed Board included several men critical of Washington's leadership, Mifflin and Gates among them. In the Board's plan for a reformed Quartermaster Department, much of the control over the army's supply would be removed from Washington's hands and placed with the body. Clearly, this action reduced the CinC's authority. Washington perceived the proposed reform as a direct threat to his authority and responded accordingly.[15] Meanwhile, with the Committee members more and more in his corner, the gulf between the Board of War and Congress widened considerably.[16] In the end, Congress went along with the recommendations presented by the Committee over those presented by the Board of War. In doing so, they indirectly sided with Washington. Likewise, the legislature rejected the plan put forward by the Board for an invasion of Canada. Thus, the political machinations of those who sought to reduce Washington's authority were defeated across a broad front.[17] Resultantly, he emerged from the challenge to his authority in a stronger position. By the same token, the general needed a battlefield victory to brace up his position as well as silence critics.

The supply situation improved when Jeremiah Wadsworth, a wealthy Connecticut merchant, took over the Commissary, and Nathanael Greene, albeit reluctantly, accepted the post of Quartermaster General. As a result of their efforts, along with those of local government throughout New England, food and clothing started arriving in Valley Forge.[18] These reforms, despite occasional logistics breakdowns, represented solid progress. Simultaneously, the struggle for control of the army leaned more and more in Washington's favor. The cabal and the Board of War challenge constituted a defining moment in civil-military relations for the fledgling republic. Washington successfully maintained the subordination of the military arm to the civil authority, while preserving enough power for army leaders to perform effectively their functions.

Washington contended with not only the suffering and privation of the rank and file but murmurings of discontent in the officer corps as well. These stemmed from several sources. First, the officers' self-image as gentlemen contributed. Like officers in European armies, many Continental officers perceived themselves as coming from the "better sort" in society.[19] They saw themselves as gentlemen and, therefore, took issues of rank and seniority quite seriously. In 1777, several instances of Congress promoting foreign officers over their American-born contemporaries occurred (e.g., Thomas Conway and Phillipe du Coudray). These episodes generated friction between the officers and Congress. At the same time, the civilian authority saw in the reaction of these men to their oversight as a threat to republicanism.

In addition to matters of honor, very real and concrete, economic hardship effected many in the officer corps. As the struggle continued, many of Washington's subordinates watched their private income shrivel. Some were forced to choose between loyalty to the cause and responsibility toward their families. Often, the latter won out. Meanwhile, they observed those who stayed in civilian life grow wealthy as wartime inflation drove up prices. In late 1777, a group of officers composed a memorial to Congress asking for a common prerequisite of European armies–half-pay for life at the war's conclusion. It was meant to provide a basis for reestablishing their fortunes at the end of service and give them the financial stability that allowed them to stay with the army.[20] At first, Washington remained aloof from this proposal as he rightly saw that it would rankle the more radical republicans in Congress. As the officer corps hemorrhaged talented leaders, however, Washington had no other choice but to support the measure. Many in Congress denounced the proposal as a further erosion of republican spirit. They could not see that the officers' altruism and dedication to the cause had limits. Likewise, some in Congress were among those growing rich while officers watched their fortunes dwindle. In the end, the body supported the measure, but the seeds of future ill-will were sown. The Committee at Camp took up this issue on their arrival. After a week of discussion, it remained unsettled. Eventually, Congress gave in on this issue to an extent. In May 1778, they approved pensions but only for seven years. Additionally, they approved a bonus of $80 for each enlisted soldier who extended his term for the war's duration.[21]

The failure to supply the army as well as the disputes over half-pay exerted lasting effects on both the officer corps and the rank and file. Officers felt betrayed by a Congress they perceived as not supportive. Martin and Lender note in their study of the Continental army: "The winter at Valley Forge had convinced both foot soldier and officer alike that they would get little more from republican society than they demanded—and quite often forcibly took for themselves." Overall, both officers and soldiers felt that the civilian population did not support them sufficiently with the basic necessities of survival—food, clothing, and pay. Officers were further annoyed by Congress over the pensions and felt betrayed by those who remained in civilian life profiteering off the war effort while they served. Martin and Lender go on to note that soldiers and officers never made common cause in their respective grievances with the civilian authorities. Certainly, the issues with Congress led many officers to support the Federalist Party in the years following the end of the war.[22]

The Valley Forge encampment encompassed more than just an extended period of physical suffering. Continentals regularly engaged in small, irregular-type operations or *petit guerre* in a precursor to what later occurred in the South on a much larger scale. They deployed on small patrols that interdicted supplies destined for Philadelphia. Likewise, they harassed enemy movements and protected the interior supply depots. To ensure that dispersed contingents functioned toward a clear strategic goal and did not descend into wanton pillage, headquarters maintained tight control.[23] Though the Valley Forge encampment is most remembered in the popular imagination as resilience in a time of privation, it represented a period of solid progress as well. A key change in the Continental Army came from the work of Wilhelm von Steuben. Known as "Baron von Steuben," the former Prussian officer standardized Continental Army drill based on the Prussian model. He established a model training company. With instruction in the morning, soldiers then returned to their parent units to pass on the new evolutions. In essence, von Steuben utilized a "train the trainer" method.[24] Resultantly, a battle-hardened force of veterans now possessed a coherent and standardized doctrinal and tactical approach.

Coming out of the Valley Forge encampment, Washington received another asset in the return of Charles Lee from British captivity. Captured in Basking Ridge, New Jersey, in December 1776 while maneuvering in the rear of the forces pursuing Washington's main army, Lee spent the next several months on parole in New York City. Certainly, the most experienced senior officer in the Continental Army, Lee's loss was perceived as a major blow to the cause. At the same time, Lee's personality was essentially defined as eccentric.[25] On his return, he quickly alienated other top officers as he maintained that the Continentals were incapable of fighting the British on even terms.

By April 1778, things had improved at Valley Forge. Steuben's training built not only proficiency among the troops but *esprit de corps* as well. As convalescents from the various military hospitals and reinforcements arrived along with fresh supplies of clothing, more troops became fit for duty. As the weather warmed at Valley Forge, the army demonstrated a new confidence born of their growing professionalism. They received a morale boost as well. News of the French Alliance reached Valley Forge in May. In celebration, Washington held a grand troop review. Simultaneously, the event showcased the Continentals' new military capacity. Among the consequences of the military pact was a decline in Continental Army recruitment. The relief brought about by French support combined with a general war weariness promoted a decrease in the number of young men volunteering for military service. More and more, new recruits came through conscription and hailed from the lower echelons of American society.[26]

## Alliance

The French alliance marked a transformation in the war from one of liberation to an international great power conflict. Congress had sought international recognition and aid from early 1776 to undergird the independence declaration. French motives for entering the conflict stemmed from their defeat and loss of national prestige in the Seven Years' War. In this regard, their motive supported Clausewitz's observation that even the ultimate outcome of a war is not always to be regarded as final. Able diplomacy by American negotiators, in general, and Benjamin Franklin, in particular, paved the way to securing these treaties. With the negotiations far from secret, William Bancroft, the Secretary to the American Commissioners, even operated as a British spy. The North Ministry remained informed as to the activities. When Lord North dispatched a representative, Paul Wentworth, to meet with the Americans in Paris, they were more than willing to do so. The ministry only authorized Wentworth to offer the Americans concessions that constituted their demands from the First Continental Congress before military operations started. While the American commissioners had no desire to accept these terms, they were more than willing to use their meetings with Wentworth to influence the French foreign minister, Charles Gravier, Comte de Vergennes.[27] Franklin and his compatriots made no secret of the meetings with the British representative. Vergennes then utilized the intelligence to influence his sovereign, Louis XVI, to open formal negotiations with the American representatives. These duly began in January 1778 and resulted in the treaties being signed the following month. The diplomatic machinations were clear–both Britain and France courted the Americans. In this instance, the French monarchy won the race to gain America as an ally.[28]

All these factors helped push the French into a Treaty of Amity and Friendship with the American rebels. The agreement set France on a clear course for open conflict with Britain. The Franco-American alliance altered the war's political objectives, thus altering the military commitment as well.[29] French entry meant a change in the overall strategic dynamic. Britain had focused its formidable military and economic power against her rebellious colonies. French participation made this an impossibility. It forced the Crown and the ministry to make a strategic reappraisal and prioritize force commitments accordingly. First and foremost, some forces had to remain in reserve for Home Islands' defense from invasion. New manpower needed raising. Caribbean and Indian interests had to be guarded. The West Indies Island colonies possessed great economic importance and required defense, especially against a foe with a powerful navy.

The French Navy posed a real threat to British maritime dominance. As Piers Mackesy noted: "This was the only war of the eighteenth century in which England failed to win ascendancy at sea."[30] The French navy had undergone a renaissance of sorts following its collapse during the Seven Years' War.[31] Its resurrection constituted a truly national effort. The new French naval minister, Étienne François duc de Choiseul, set in motion the first stages of this effort. He formed the Corps of Seaman Gunners, gunnery specialists to improve that weak aspect of French naval skill. By 1778, the navy boasted 52 ships-of-the-line to Britain's 66. The naval imbalance generated concern in Parliament. Addressing the body in March 1778, Tempel Lutterell presented a gloomy assessment of the Royal Navy's condition. Near the end of his two-hour remarks, he observed: "I do not think the ships of our fleet, in general so conditioned, with their reduced establishments, as to fight at odds against those of France."[32] The following year, British naval superiority disappeared with Spain's joining in the war as a French ally.

In Britain, French entry led to a stiffening of resolve. Where many were reluctant to engage in what they perceived as a fratricidal war against the colonists whom they perceived as fellow subjects of the Crown, France stood as the perennial enemy. One response to the French alliance was the Carlisle Commission, which was developed out of a major shift in direction by Lord North. In the view of John Ferling, North "took a long step toward what ultimately would become Britain's commonwealth system."[33] The Prime Minister remained vague concerning the plan's specifics; he preferred to provide secret guidance to the commissioners and kept his plans close to the vest as he still had not determined on what his final concessions would be.[34] Parliament authorized the commission in February 1778 to negotiate a settlement with the Continental Congress. The peace mission was organized and led by William Eden, Earl of Carlisle, a young and ambitious politician. Horace Walpole commented that Carlisle was "very fit to make a treaty that will not be made."[35] His comment is apropos. While the concessions may have appeared appealing early in the conflict, with the coming of the French alliance, it no longer possessed much attraction. Congress had secured a powerful ally with a navy that could contend with the Royal Navy. Likewise, Willcox noted: "to offer to repeal statutes and pardon offenders was to offer too little too late."[36] The commission included George Johnstone and the commanders of the army and navy in North America. It thus fused civil and military authority. Parliament authorized the negotiators to concede everything to the Americans short of actual independence.

After embarking for America, the commissioners learned that Clinton, Howe's replacement as CinC, had orders to evacuate Philadelphia (see Figure 6.1). Rightly sensing that the move would strengthen Congress' resolve while simultaneously undercutting their own negotiating position, Carlisle asked Clinton to delay the move.

Clinton refused stating that his orders called on him to act without delay. The evacuation further undermined the commission's position. Still, on 13 June, they submitted peace proposals to the Continental Congress at York. Congress responded by insisting that either the British government recognize American Independence or that all British forces withdraw. The commission lacked the authority to grant either of these demands. There followed some political jockeying between commission members and Congress, none of which changed Congress' position. In fact, their efforts further reinforced the determination to continue the fight until gaining full independence. The last Carlisle Commission members left for England in November 1778.

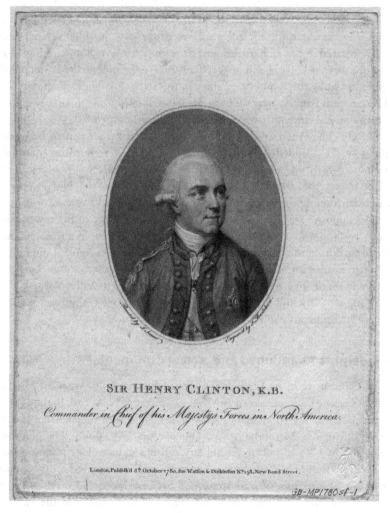

**FIGURE 6.1**  Lieutenant-General Sir Henry Clinton

*Source:* Courtesy of the Anne S.K. Brown Military Collection, Brown University Library, Providence, Rhode Island

Concerning Howe, many perceived his campaign in Pennsylvania as a failure. While he did take the Patriot capital, he had not captured the Continental Congress or rendered the Continental Army combat incapable. Sir William, sensing the ministry's diminishing support for his leadership and increasing criticism for his failure to assist Burgoyne, wrote Germain on 22 October 1777 and tendered his resignation.[37] Following his resignation there transpired a series of private parties and balls. The former commander, not one to shun an evening of revelry, happily attended the festivities, hosting several balls at his own headquarters. The most ostentatious of these gatherings, the *Meschianza*, occurred on 18 May 1778, shortly before the general's departure. The event was the brainchild of Major John André and paid for by a subscription taken up from the various officers in Philadelphia.[38] When the invited officers and their female companions assembled at one of the wharves along the Philadelphia waterfront, they boarded several sumptuously decorated sloops and cruised along the river for several miles. Houses along the route were decorated and at specified intervals, cannons fired salutes, which were returned by the Royal Navy ships in the river. The guests then debarked at old Association Battery (near Old Swedes Church in Philadelphia). The assembled company passed through two arches decorated in honor of the navy and army, respectively. They then entered a field where a mock tournament between the Knights of the Blended Rose battled the Knights of the Burning Mountain to determine which side possessed the fairest escorts. There followed a ball inside Walnut Grove, the mansion of Joseph Wharton, a successful Philadelphia merchant, with a sumptuous feast served at midnight. The total cost for the affair came to 3,312 guineas. The affair was not without critics. Many of these were among Howe's rivals. Some critics were quick to point out that Sir William's conduct of operations during the last campaign did not merit such an opulent display.[39] The gala affair exuded an aura of fancifulness and lack of reality; a reinvigorated and unbowed Continental Army was about to emerge from its Valley Forge lair at the same time that Britain's military capability now had to accommodate a vengeful and highly dangerous traditional rival—Bourbon France.

## Philadelphia Abandoned and a New Continental Army

Henry Clinton, born in 1730, spent part of his youth in America. His father, Admiral George Clinton, served as Royal Governor of New York in the 1740s. He gained his first military experience serving in a New York Independent Company in 1745 during the War of the Austrian Succession (1740–1748). He then traveled to England in 1749 to pursue his military career and gained a commission in the 2nd Regiment of Foot Guards (Coldstream Guards). He served on the continent during the Seven Years' War and returned to America in 1775. He served with Howe during the 1776 campaign, and while relations between the two began cordially enough, Clinton often offered military advice to his superior, even when not asked. By the end of the 1776 campaign, the two men did not speak directly. In January 1777, Clinton took leave to travel back to England but returned and commanded the New York garrison during Howe's Philadelphia campaign where he made some efforts to reinforce Burgoyne's invasion as it bogged down.[40]

O'Shaughnessy notes: "As commander in chief, Clinton was a gifted strategist who grasped the realities of the war, and understood the precarious military situation of the British."[41] Following French intervention, he received orders to evacuate Philadelphia and dispatch substantial troops for the West Indies. Given the conflict's new global parameters, Clinton explored new strategic options, thus giving rise to the Southern Strategy. At the same time, given his reduced manpower, he shortened the British lines, which meant giving up Philadelphia. As Clinton prepared to abandon the City of Brotherly Love, he realized that numerous Loyalists who had come out to openly support the British would now be in grave danger. He, therefore, decided to evacuate as many as possible by ship. The decision created its own ripple effect—there would not be enough space to transport troops as well. Clinton, therefore, determined to march the bulk of his troops overland to New York.

Washington received intelligence of British intentions from a unit operating to block Crown foraging efforts and suppress Loyalists in New Jersey. He reinforced these troops and gave orders to coordinate their actions with the New Jersey militia under Major General Philemon Dixon and to gather intelligence on British movements. Indications clarified that the British intended to abandon Philadelphia as their first elements crossed the Delaware River into New Jersey on 15 June. The rear guard crossed three days later as the British concentrated around Haddonfield. There, Clinton divided the army into two divisions. The first comprised some 10,470 under Cornwallis. The second of 9,000 men commanded by Knyphausen included the German auxiliaries and most of the Loyalist provincial troops. The baggage train of 1,500 wagons accompanied the second division. The same day that Howe enjoyed the *Meschianza*, Washington dispatched Gilbert du Motier, Marquis de Lafayette, with 2,100 Continentals and five guns to reconnoiter and interdict British foraging (see Figure 6.2). With the young major general's first independent command, Lafayette crossed over the Schuylkill and moved off to the south, taking up a blocking position. The British quickly discovered the Patriot's presence and determined to attack. Major-General James Grant with a force of 5,000 men and 15 guns maneuvered a part of his force along a circuitous route to cut off Lafayette's retreat. In effect, Grant planned to surround the Americans on three sides and attack at dawn. Here again the British proficiency at maneuvering in the night was on display. Light skirmishing resulted in few casualties. Unable to draw the Continentals into a major engagement, Clinton continued evacuation preparations.[42]

The marches were conducted in short increments as the heat often soared into the 90s during an early summer heat wave. The slow pace did not bother Clinton as he sought to conserve the troops under his command. The two columns marched along parallel routes for mutual support with flankers and advanced guard deployed. Even with these precautions, frequent skirmishes occurred with Patriot regular and militia forces as the columns advanced northward. Skirmishes could be quite intense if fairly short in duration. For instance, just outside of Mount Holly,

**FIGURE 6.2** Major General Gilbert du Motier, Marquis de Lafayette

*Source:* Courtesy of the Anne S.K. Brown Military Collection, Brown University Library, Providence, Rhode Island

New Jersey, a British detail labored to repair a damaged bridge. As they completed the work, a rebel militia detachment fired from a nearby house. Covering forces attacked the house, and the militia fled.[43] Such actions, while irritating, did not inflict many casualties, yet they gave further indication of the frustrating irregular, hybrid warfare to come.

On 25 June, Clinton moved ahead of the army to Sandy Hook to prepare for embarking onto Royal Navy vessels to ferry them to New York. The following day, the two columns combined, thus creating a single column 12 miles in length, an appetizing target for the pursuers. The 26th witnessed nearly constant skirmishing. Knyphausen reached Monmouth Courthouse in Freehold County that morning; Crown forces concentrated in that area. Troops arrived exhausted by the successive marches in the extreme heat—the army needed rest.

On the Patriot side, when Washington learned of the British withdrawal, he convened a council of war at which all save two of the 17 generals present believed that the Continentals were still incapable of standing against the British in an open field engagement. Lee, never one to hold back on his opinions, went so far as to assert that it would be criminal to attempt such a confrontation. Nonetheless, Washington determined to pursue the British and seek any opportunities that might present. He divided his army into two divisions under Lee and William Alexander. The Continentals marched out of Valley Forge on 18 June with Lee's division in the lead.

Washington reached Hopewell on 23 June and sent Daniel Morgan ahead with light infantry to harass the British columns. The following day, on receiving intelligence that Clinton lingered in New Jersey in hopes of provoking a general action, he convened another council of war. Again, Lee was the most vociferous in arguing against an attack. He asserted that it would be best to allow the British to return to New York unmolested. Anthony Wayne of Pennsylvania took the most aggressive stance, arguing that a force of Continentals be sent forward to make an "impression in force" on the British. In the end, the council reached a compromise—a picked force of 1,500 would be sent forward to reinforce the Continental vanguard. Initially, Lee refused to command any force sent against Clinton. However, when he learned that Lafayette would then get the command, he changed his mind citing seniority and requested the command.[44] At the last moment wrote a long missive to Washington:

> When I first assented to the Marquis of Fayette's taking the command of the present detachment, I confess I viewed it in a very different light than I do at present. I considered it as a more proper busyness of a Young Volunteering General than of the Second in command in the Army—but I find that it is considered in a different manner; They say that a Corps consisting of six thousand Men, the greater part chosen, is undoubtedly the most honourable command next to the Commander in Chief, that my ceding it would of course have an odd appearance. I must entreat therefore, (after making a thousand apologies for the trouble my rash assent has occasion'd to you) that if this detachment does march that I may have the command of it.[45]

Many officers ardently supported seniority: Lee's invocation of the concept found willing listeners. More practically, having Lee assume command of the advance force placed the general officer with the most combat experience in charge of the troops most likely to cross steel with the Crown forces. By the same token, Lee had been sidelined for well over a year and had not had time to know the soldiers or their officers. The Continental Army of 1778 was far different from the force of 1776. If he led the force into combat, it would be imperative to have some understanding of his subordinates and their capabilities.[46] The injunction of Sun Tzu applies: "Know the enemy and know yourself; in a hundred battles you will never be in peril."[47] Instead, Lee was more likely to be ignorant both of his enemy and of himself, a reality that placed him in great peril. By 27 June, Lee stood in position to attack. The following day, as the British began their march out of Monmouth, Lee moved to engage the rear guard. Poorly coordinated, the Continentals were quickly overwhelmed. Some Patriot units retreated as Lee lost control of his force.

As soldiers streamed from the field, many in panic, Washington arrived with the main body, began restoring order, and deployed his force for battle. When he encountered Lee, the men exchanged harsh words. Washington demanded to know why Lee's troops retreated. Lee, who expected praise for his success at disengaging, was initially dumbstruck. When he replied, he blamed subordinates and faulty intelligence. Washington replied that where this might true, Lee was in command and the attack was his responsibility.[48] Washington then turned to

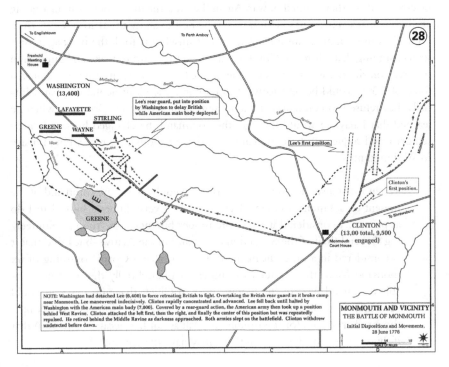

**MAP 6.1** Battle of Monmouth Courthouse

Source: Map Courtesy of the United States Military Academy Department of History, West Point, New York

rally the Continental vanguard with Lee trailing at some distance, believing he had been relieved of command. Washington ordered Wayne to take three battalions and set up a rear guard to delay the British. He detached Pennsylvania and New Jersey regiments to act as a rallying point for the disorganized vanguard as Washington stabilized the line. At this juncture, he offered Lee the chance to assume command of the rear guard or fall back and organize the main army. Lee opted to remain with the rear guard, vowing that he would be the last to leave the field. He established his position on the crest of a hill to the right of Wayne with four guns and two infantry battalions. Soon, the British advance moved on their positions. Continentals fired volleys at their oncoming foes and inflicted significant casualties. The British responded with an infantry charge supported by cavalry, driving the Patriots back. As Wayne and Lee fell back, Washington deployed his main line.

The rearguard action only lasted half an hour. Still, it bought precious time for Washington to complete his deployments. He used the time well, establishing a strong defensive position anchored above the main road and extending about a mile to a substantial hill. There followed a break in the infantry action as both sides battered their opponents across the brook separating them with artillery. The cannonade occurred through the hottest portion of the day; more men succumbed to the heat on both sides than did to enemy fire. At this point Clinton, seeing nothing to be gained from continuing the fight save for more casualties, decided to break off. This decision meant he would have to disengage his forces while in contact with the enemy, something Washington had successfully executed the previous October at Germantown. Washington, while unclear on British intentions, sensed an opportunity as he heard renewed fighting from the direction of an orchard and the silence of the British batteries. He, therefore, ordered Wayne to move forward with additional troops. He collided with retreating grenadiers inflicting heavy casualties; they had no time to deploy to receive the attack. Throughout the day, Knyphausen continued his march with the baggage. Clinton rejoined him the following day having successfully retired from the field and, by his earlier counterattack, allowed the baggage train to proceed out of danger.

While Monmouth was, in essence, a drawn battle, both sides claimed victory. Washington, in need of a tactical success to reinforce his control of the army, claimed the victory as he prepared to fight the following day. In reality, despite who actually won or lost at Monmouth Courthouse, a sea change had become obvious. The Continental Army that fought at Monmouth constituted a significantly improved force from the one at Germantown. Whether seen as a Patriot victory or merely a draw, the engagement was far from decisive.[49] Monmouth changed nothing concerning the relative positions of the British and Patriot forces in the northern theater, thus ensuring a continuous stalemate in the Middle Colonies. Clinton still succeeded in moving the bulk of his force overland to New York. Likewise, Washington brought on an engagement that showcased his improving army and silenced any lingering political detractors. The Monmouth episode revealed an army much more technically proficient, especially in battlefield maneuver. But, following the battle with the inevitable standoff, the force quality quickly degenerated. Many long service veterans, unable to remain in the ranks as their domestic economy collapsed, resigned their commissions or declined to re-enlist.[50]

Clinton, for his part, could claim some success. Tactically, his troops remained on the field at the end of the day. Under the rules of eighteenth-century warfare, he won a tactical victory. More importantly, he succeeded operationally in moving his army across hostile territory and returning it to New York intact, including an amphibious withdrawal at Sandy Hook, no mean accomplishment. Strategically, abandoning Philadelphia remained a setback. After spending much of a campaign season taking the city in an operation that essentially ensured Burgoyne's failure, to give it up without a fight was a clear concession of defeat. Likewise, the withdrawal exerted its own effect on British morale at home. When the king made his opening speech to Parliament the following year, there were strong clamors from the opposition to end the conflict.[51]

While Monmouth heralded the last major engagement in the North and Middle in 1778, the small-scale war of raids and reprisals continued in the vicinity of New York. The year further witnessed the first actions of the Franco-American alliance—the failed attempt to drive the British from Rhode Island.[52] More importantly, British decision-makers in London and in New York now faced a strategic conundrum—what next? Faced with the need to defend the Home Islands against an expected Franco-Spanish invasion attempt and possible interference in Ireland as well as Allied offensives against the West Indies and Gibraltar, a new strategic plan had to emerge. This need produced the Southern or Loyalist Strategy that kicked off in autumn of 1778. That strategic choice ultimately led to the disastrous surrender at a small hamlet along the south shore of the York River in Tidewater Virginia in October 1781.

## Notes

1 Taaffe, Philadelphia Campaign, 2.
2 Buchanan, *Valley Forge*, 292–3. Robert Middlekauff discusses the perceived threat in very hesitant terms. See Robert Middlekauff, *Washington's Revolution: The Making of America's First Leader* (New York: Alfred A. Knopf, 2015), 176–7. The most recent and thorough examination of the cabal is Mark Edward Lender, *Cabal! The Plot against General Washington*, which makes the case that there indeed was some threat to Washington's authority at this time.
3 Ferling, *Almost a Miracle*, 282.
4 Mark Edward Lender and Gary Wheeler Stone, *Fatal Sunday: George Washington, the Monmouth Campaign and the Politics of Battle* (Norman, OK: University of Oklahoma Press, 2016), 25.
5 Charles Royster, *A Revolutionary People at War The Continental Army and American Character, 1775–1783* (Chapel Hill: University of North Carolina Press, 1979), 35–43, 63–9.
6 Ferling, *Almost a Miracle*, 282–3; Conway to Gates, date unknown, original lost, quoted in Lender, *Cabal!*, 85.
7 James Kirby Martin and Mark Edward Lender, *A Respectable Army: The Military Origins of the Republic, 1763–1789* (Woodridge, IL: Harlan-Davidson, Inc., 1982), 100.

8  Ibid., 101.

9  Wayne W. Bodle and Jacqueline Thibaut, *Valley Forge Historical Research Report*, vol. 1 (Valley Forge, PA: United States Department of the Interior, National Park Service, 1980), 79; A standard history of the Continental Army's supply situation is E. Wayne Carp, *To Starve the Army at Pleasure: Continental Army Administration and American Political Culture, 1775–1783* (Chapel Hill, NC: University of North Carolina Press, 1984), 33–51; Martin and Lender, *Respectable Army*, 101.

10 Washington to Laurens, 23 December 1777, quoted in Abbot and Twohig, *Papers of George Washington, Revolutionary War Series*, 12:683.

11 Bodle and Thibaut, *Valley Forge*, 139.

12 Lender, *Cabal!* 146.

13 Bodle and Thibaut, *Valley Forge*, 206.

14 Ibid., 214.

15 Lender, *Cabal!*, 110–11.

16 Bodle and Thibaut, *Valley Forge*, 214.

17 Ibid., 243–4.

18 Lender, *Cabal!*, 147.

19 Royster, *Revolutionary People*, 200–4; Martin and Lender, *Respectable Army*, 103.

20 Royster, *Revolutionary People*, 204.

21 Martin and Lender, *Respectable Army*, 107–10; Bodle and Thibaut, *Valley Forge*, 208.

22 Ibid., 126–7; Richard H. Kohn, *Eagle and Sword: The Beginnings of the Military Establishment in America* (New York: The Free Press, 1975), 10–3. See also, Timothy Leech, "Crossing the Rubicon: The Establishment of the Continental Army and American State Formation, 1774–1776," (PhD Diss.: Ohio State University, 2017).

23 Ibid., 86.

24 Paul Lockhart, *The Drillmaster of Valley Forge: The Baron de Steuben and the Making of the American Army* (New York: Harper Collins, 2008), 95–116.

25 Ibid., 109–10.

26 Royster, *Revolutionary People*, 268–71.

27 On Vergennes, the standard biography in English is Orville T. Murphy, *Charles Gravier, Comte de Vergennes: French Diplomacy in the Age of Revolution, 1719–1787* (Albany, NY: State University of New York Press, 1982). A more recent study is J. F. Labourdette, *Vergennes, Ministre principal de Louis XVI* (Paris: Editions Desjonquières, 1990).

28 James Prichard, "French Strategy and the American Revolution: A Reappraisal," in *Strategy in the American War of Independence: A Global Approach*, eds. Donald Stoker, Kenneth J. Hagan and Michael T. McMaster (London: Routledge, 2010), 142; Clausewitz, *On War*, 80; Mackesy, *War for America*, 160; Ferling, *Almost a Miracle*, 262–3.

29 On the connection between the political objective and the military commitment in war, see Clausewitz, *On War*, 81.

30 Mackesy, *War for America*, 166.

31 These efforts are covered in Jonathan R. Dull, *The French Navy and American Independence: A Study of Arms and Diplomacy, 1774–1787* (Princeton, NJ: Princeton University Press, 1975).

32 Tempel Lutterell, 11 March 1778 quoted in John Stockdale, ed., *The Parliamentary Register; or, History of the Proceedings and Debates of the House of Commons: Containing an Account of the Most Interesting Speeches and Motions; Accurate Copies of the Most Honourable Letters and Papers; of the Most Material Evidence, Petitions &c Laid before and Offered to the House, during the Fifth Session of the Fourteenth Parliament of Great Britain*, Vol. 8, (London: Wilson and Co., 1802), 119.

33 Ferling, *Almost a Miracle*, 264.

34 Ibid.

35 Quoted in Mackesy, *War for America*, 159.

36 William B. Willcox, "British Strategy in America, 1778," *Journal of Modern History* 19, no. 2 (June 1947): 103.

37 Gruber, *Howe Brothers*, 252.
38 The *Meschianza* description derives from John W. Jackson, *With the British Army in Philadelphia* (San Rafael, CA: Presidio Press, 1979), 239–54.
39 Ibid., 249.
40 O'Shaughnessy, *Men Who Lost America*, 207–46.
41 Ibid., 220.
42 Jim Stempel, *Valley Forge to Monmouth: Six Transformative Months of the American Revolution* (Jefferson, NC: MacFarland and Company, Publishers, Inc., 2021), 97–106.
43 Lender and Stone, *Fatal Sunday*, 130.
44 Ibid., 171–7.
45 Charles Lee to Washington, 25 June 1778, in Abbot and Twohig, *Papers of George Washington*, 15: 541–2.
46 Lender and Stone, *Fatal Sunday*, 189–90.
47 Sun Tzu, *Art of War*, 84.
48 Lender and Stone, *Fatal Sunday*, 289.
49 Ferling, *Almost a Miracle*, 306; Lender and Stone, *Fatal Sunday*, 382–3.
50 Lender and Stone, *Fatal Sunday*, 419.
51 Stockdale, *Parliamentary Register,* vol. 10, 1–50.
52 On the Battle of Rhode Island, see Christian M. McBurney, *The Rhode Island Campaign: The First Franco-American Operation in the Revolutionary War* (Yardley, PA: Westholme Press, 2011). Dated but very useful is Paul F. Dearden, *The Rhode Island Campaign of 1778* (Providence, RI: Rhode Island Bicentennial Federation, 1980).

# PART III

# Southern Gambit

# 7

# "A WANT OF DISCRIMINATION"

With the war stalemated in the Northern and Middle colonies, Britain needed a new military and political strategy, particularly after French intervention turned the colonial affair into a global, great power, maritime conflict. From this new security, dynamic emerged the Southern or Loyalist Strategy. Relying on a massive outpouring of Loyalist support in the Carolinas, Georgia, and the Floridas (East and West, British colonies since 1763), Britain launched the Southern Campaign aimed at pacifying and re-establishing rule one colony at a time from Georgia northward. But the grandiose plan and subsequent Southern Campaign of 1778–1781 ended in disaster at Yorktown, Virginia, three years later.

The strategic concept called for retaking each colony in turn from the south to the north while establishing the conditions whereby local Loyalists could restore Crown authority and civil government. Though Continental Army forces consistently lost major conventional engagements, Patriot partisans and irregulars successfully continued the resistance. By engaging in hit-and-run guerilla-style insurgency warfare characterized by small unit actions, ambushes, rapid movements and escapes, and Loyalist intimidation, rebel bands prevented the implementation of such a pacification strategy. Cornwallis viewed the key to victory as the destruction of regular Continental forces, an attitude that led to two separate invasions of North Carolina, the chase of Nathanael Greene's army into southern Virginia, and major engagements at Camden, South Carolina, and Guilford Courthouse, North Carolina. In a tactical sense, he won both engagements; in the overall strategic sense, suffering devastating losses, especially at Guilford Courthouse, he ultimately lost the strategic initiative to Greene. Finally, with the backing of Germain and in direct opposition to Clinton's strategic desires, he advanced into Virginia, an act that precipitated the collapse. The British concept for victory proved a thin reed. The framework upon which it rested—the Loyalist Strategy—proved unreliable and flawed.

DOI: 10.4324/9781003041276-11

As Crown forces prepared for the new campaign season in southern climes, the Continental Army took up winter quarters surrounding New York. Despite the arrival of great stores of uniforms and supplies from France, the army remained ill-shod, ill-clad, and poorly fed. But, like a nautical "fleet in being" whose very presence represents an existential threat to a more powerful naval force, Washington's Continentals consumed the thoughts and heightened Clinton's anxiety for New York's safety. More importantly, that threat, especially when combined with the arrival of French land forces in 1780, drove his strategic thinking in a direction completely counter to what might have been a war-winning strategy.

## The Strategy Unfolds

The amphibious landings and subsequent siege of Charleston in spring 1780 represented the main southern initial offensive; however, precursor operations supported the overall strategy. Two cities in northeastern Georgia–Savannah on the coast and Augusta up the Savannah River—represented endpoints in a critical line of demarcation that, if controlled, isolated Georgia from South Carolina. Beyond Augusta to the north and west lay frontier with little colonial settlement. Savannah provided an excellent port for seaborne operations. Control of these two endpoints allowed Crown forces to dominate the border, inhibiting Patriot supply or reinforcement movement into Georgia. The geography combined with the relatively small population gave Clinton an ideal starting point.

Another element played into the equation—the Floridas. Obtained from Spain in the 1763 Treaty, they provided a safe haven for displaced Loyalists. With both East and West Florida firmly under Crown control and populated by an overwhelmingly Loyalist citizenry, Crown forces stationed in St. Augustine and Pensacola stood well-positioned to impede any French or Spanish interference. To bolster the strategic thinking, both Patrick Tonyn, Royal Governor of East Florida, and his military commander, Major-General Augustin Prevost, forecast that the South would not be difficult to conquer: "I am certain the four southern provinces are incapable of making any formidable resistance; they are not prepared for a scene of war."[1]

Commanded by Lieutenant-Colonel Archibald Campbell and Commodore Hyde Parker, a Crown assault force composed of British regulars, German auxiliaries, and Loyalist Provincial troops sailed for Georgia on 27 November 1778. The plan anticipated a large outpouring of Georgia, Florida, and South Carolina Loyalists, as well as local Indian allies. Based on reports, large numbers of ardent Loyalists could be anticipated who would restore Crown authority, thus freeing the regulars for offensive operations. Lord Jeffrey Amherst, newly appointed Army CinC, argued that the army's failure to hold ground allowed Patriot government entities to maintain effective control, thus failing to protect Loyalists and their interests. The Southern Campaign concept called for aggressive, offensive actions against Patriot forces but required holding conquered territory by Loyalists backfilling the forces to restore royal governance and tamp down Patriot activity.[2]

Indian allies might prevent Patriot reinforcement from the north and, in theory, provide a bulwark.[3] However, the Indian association with the Crown and the problems incurred should have been obvious to British authorities. For many frontier settlers, the Indian threat far outdistanced any concern over Crown authority or perceived oppression. The two Cherokee Wars of 1761 and 1776 in the Carolinas demonstrated that faulty assumption.[4] The 1776 Cherokee War not only united Carolinians in common cause, but the Indian association with the Crown swayed many neutrals toward the Patriot camp.

## Savannah

The Savannah operation illustrated the dominant strategic culture of Britain based on sea power, command of the sea, and expeditionary operations since the rise of the Royal Navy in Henry VIII's reign (1509–1547). Britain had used that capability in the assault on New York in 1776 and again employed it in the Southern Campaign. Major General Robert Howe, with less than 1,000 Continentals and roughly 100 Georgia militiamen, commanded at Savannah. A North Carolina planter, he had significant military experience.[5] But constant disputes and poor relations with Georgia state authorities compromised his military situation and ability to defend the state. To add to his difficulties, the constant drain of troops and resources for operations into East Florida and the repulse of multiple incursions from St. Augustine, as well as dealing with Indian raids from the west, undercut his manpower. Added to the usual strain of disease and desertion, Howe now faced a much larger and highly experienced invasion force.

The Savannah defense unraveled from the outset. In a weakly opposed landing on 28 December 1778, Campbell captured a small militia band and moved his force ashore with little difficulty. Howe planned to defend the city along the approach road flanked by swamps, rice fields, and a river. Despite warnings from subordinates that the position lay vulnerable to flank attack, he declined to flood the rice fields or post blocking forces at the trails and approaches to his main position south of the city. Recognizing the vulnerability in Howe's defensive arrangement, Campbell used the deception device of drawing into battle line apparently for a frontal assault when in reality the main attack came in the Patriot rear and right flank. Campbell discovered an unguarded path through the swamp and careened into Howe's flank while the main force pressed the front. The Patriot defenders dissolved into chaos and retreated across a causeway into South Carolina. Not only did Savannah fall, but Crown forces captured almost 500 Continentals and militia, numerous field pieces and mortars, massive amounts of gunpowder, and all the shipping at the Savannah wharfs.[6] Howe's destruction and Savannah's loss laid bare the entire Patriot southern flank. Prevost, advancing from North Florida, captured Sunbury Fort on 16 January 1779, eliminating the last organized Patriot opposition on the Georgia coast. From the strategic perspective, the Southern Strategy began with a stunning Crown victory. Campbell boldly announced: "[T]he rebel army was beat, and hurried out of the province in six days after the landing . . . shoals flock to the royal standard daily; and I have got the country in arms against the Congress."[7]

With the successful capture of St. Lucia in the West Indies earlier in the year, Clinton anticipated the return of that expeditionary force to New York, giving him additional troops to pacify South Carolina. However, neither a firm plan to reinforce Georgia nor specific commander's intentions from Clinton materialized, thus leaving the local field commanders to their own initiative. Faced with no organized opposition, Campbell and Prevost initiated operations that ultimately undid the success at Savannah. Crown efforts suffered from poor planning and a lack of clear operational direction from the key decision-makers, both in New York and in London. Well before Cornwallis arrived, the pattern of British strategic incoherence emerged characterized by operations and engagements that, while successful in destroying enemy forces in battle, failed to undo Patriot opposition or pacify territory.

With Howe's defeat, Congress turned to a New Englander, Major General Benjamin Lincoln, a prominent former Massachusetts militia leader, as the new commander of the Southern Department. Highly regarded as an expert in such key military areas as supply and logistics, recruitment, and training, he had extensive military experience from the French and Indian War and the northern engagements. A patient, diplomatic, and meticulous man who could organize and rationalize a deteriorating military situation, he seemed the perfect fit to master the evolving whirlwind of chaos and disaster. As with the appointment of the Virginian Washington to command the army in New England, sending Lincoln, a northerner, to command southern forces, fostered a sense of unity and brought recent operational experience.[8]

With the threat to South Carolina now imminent, the issue of blacks serving the Patriot cause again rose with some momentum. The success of the 1st Rhode Island Regiment won over Colonel John Laurens of South Carolina, who proposed raising a light infantry corps of 5,000 slaves, who for their service, would be freed at the war's end. The plan earlier in 1778 went nowhere, but with the loss of Savannah, suddenly re-emerged winning over Alexander Hamilton: "I have not the least doubt that the negroes will make very excellent soldiers . . . if we do not make use of them in this way, the enemy probably will."[9] Without Washington's support, who feared the loss of the southern states should slaves be embodied as combatants, the measure failed.

## Augusta

In late January, Campbell initiated the next operation. Augusta inhibited the movement of Patriot supplies and manpower and added to the security of Loyalist enclaves and Crown outposts in the South Carolina backcountry. With the support of the Loyalist Rangers, Campbell and Prevost set out from Savannah in January 1779. From the start, the expedition broke down. Campbell expected an outpouring of Indian and Loyalist support—neither materialized. Recent history should have demonstrated the folly of relying on Indian allies. Burgoyne learned this harsh lesson in New York. With an entirely different strategic and social culture than white Europeans, those Indian allies that did join Crown expeditions tended to become restless and simply walk away in frustration. Campbell and Prevost should also have noted the 1776 Cherokee War experience. Few things were more likely to arouse the backcountry frontier population, both Patriot and Loyalist, than the threat of British-allied Indians rampaging through the countryside. Fortunately for Campbell, few Indian allies actually joined the force making its way up the Savannah River. A more problematic issue lay in Loyalist turnout. Initially, support appeared promising as British arms prevailed. Occupying Augusta took little effort and cost few casualties. Holding it became a different matter. Two seminal events turned against Campbell, the engagements at Kettle Creek and Brier Creek.

John Boyd, a prominent South Carolina Loyalist, accompanied the expedition to Georgia; he departed Savannah in mid-January 1779 to recruit South Carolina Loyalists. Promoted to colonel on the Provincial Establishment based on the British scheme of commission and rank for recruitment numbers, a process that did not always guarantee effective military leadership, Boyd was optimistic for success. Having embodied a strong force of Loyalists, he made camp at Kettle Creek near Augusta. However, a crucial flaw emerged in the operation that repeatedly flummoxed practically every Crown commander—lack of reliable intelligence. Boyd did not realize that the bulk of the Crown troops occupying Augusta had departed for Savannah leaving his forces isolated and vulnerable. Campbell in Augusta never received word of Boyd's approach. Meanwhile, South Carolina and Georgia Patriot militia prepared to attack the unsuspecting Loyalist camp. As might be expected, the action soon degenerated into a chaotic melee. As often happened in the clash of irregulars, a key leader went down and the troops panicked. Boyd collapsed, mortally wounded. The undisciplined, untrained Loyalists panicked, fleeing the battle as it disintegrated into chaos. Though casualties were relatively light, the consequences for Crown success were immense.[10]

Kettle Creek represented the struggle at the local level between American colonists on both sides. Often, no Continental Army or Crown regulars participated except for a few senior officers. These affairs tended to be disorganized melees that typically turned into routs once one side or the other broke and ran. While seemingly insignificant compared to the greater conventional battles, these small struggles effectively tamped down Loyalist enthusiasm and simultaneously inspired Patriot hopes; most of the victories belonged to the Patriots. Kettle Creek set a trend that should have been noted by Crown authorities in New York and London, who placed such high hopes both in the willingness of Loyalists to turn out for service and on their fighting ability. The fact that Boyd raised only 600 volunteers, despite the relative ease with which Savannah and Augusta fell, should have given pause in British strategic decision-making circles. On the "knife's edge" of the struggle, the Kettle Creek disaster certainly convinced Prevost of the bankruptcy of reliance on Loyalist enthusiasm: "[L]aws formed by the most rebellious provinces [that] are so severe and awful in execution . . . the most zealous amongst them [the Loyalists] are deterred. . . . Our success . . . must depend on the exertions of the King's troops."[11]

Kettle Creek established a pattern of Loyalist failure that plagued Cornwallis and all other Crown commanders throughout the campaign and ultimately destroyed the strategy's very foundation. In short, this type of "hybrid warfare" (a combination of regular linear and unconventional irregular warfare) doomed Crown efforts to restore the South to allegiance and pacification.

The second significant event resulted in a Crown victory—the Battle of Brier Creek. Faced with growing enemy activity, Campbell evacuated Augusta on 14 February. Major General of Militia John Ashe, a prominent North Carolina planter and politician, commanded 200 Georgia Continental Army regulars and over 1,000 North Carolina militia. Raw, inexperienced, and untrained, they arrived near Augusta to form a blocking force against Crown incursions across the Savannah River into South Carolina. As Campbell withdrew, Ashe received orders to engage leading to a Patriot disaster. With desertions already running high and enlistments expiring, attacking an experienced, well-trained, and disciplined British force represented folly of the highest order. Nonetheless, he persisted; the Battle of Brier Creek resulted in a disastrous Patriot defeat.

The battle lasted only a few minutes. Surprised and unready, the North Carolina militia fled, carrying Ashe along with them. British "cold steel" prevailed causing stunning Patriot casualties. Brier Creek illustrated several essential dynamics of the coming campaign in the South. When British regulars came up against Patriot militia, the results were often devastating. Continentals by this late stage in the war generally could stand toe to toe with their British and Provincial counterparts, but with the destruction of large Continental Army forces at Charleston and Camden in 1780, regular army commanders never had enough troops to seriously challenge Cornwallis and other Crown commanders in the field until the British defeat at Cowpens in January 1781. However, as the campaign progressed, regular troop engagements did not ultimately win the war in the South. While a conventional engagement—a traditional siege—characterized the Franco-American Yorktown victory, the antecedents for the British disaster lay in the many small engagements throughout the South leading up to October 1781. Despite a few victories, the Loyalist Strategy foundered, driven by continuous defeats at Patriot hands in one small engagement after another. Irregular actions ultimately undercut an essential leg of the British strategy—active Loyalist support. Thus, British strategic and operational planners and decision-makers suffered not only from a profound strategic incoherence and a breakdown of command and control in the field but also in a devastating misunderstanding of the nature of the war in the South and especially the enthusiasm and willingness of local Loyalists to volunteer for military service and to provide political and logistical aid.

## Prevost's Invasion

Despite the Brier Creek debacle, Patriot enthusiasm in Georgia and South Carolina swelled. By early April, nearly 5,000 Patriots had embodied in South Carolina, giving Lincoln a numerical if not qualitative advantage. He decided to go on the offensive. The operational plan called for a march along the Savannah River threatening the Georgia backcountry. Prevost, however, illustrating the dictum that in war, the enemy always has a vote at your strategic table, flummoxed the Continental Army commander. Rather than defend Georgia, Prevost launched an offensive thrust toward Charleston. Crossing the Savannah River, he quick-marched for Charleston hoping to draw Lincoln away from Georgia. A chase ensued. From time memorial, in warfare, swiftness and rapidity of movement have always given an advantage to the offensive force. So it was with Prevost.

In Charleston and stunned by Prevost's rapid advance on the city, Governor John Rutledge proposed a flag of truce and a parley assuming that in accordance with the Articles of War, soldiers paroled and disarmed could return to their homes and with civilians and property unmolested. Prevost reacted coolly and insisted that all inhabitants must declare their allegiance to the Crown; all who did not would be refused parole and regarded as prisoners of war. Although senior officers attempted to convince the governor that their forces roughly equaled Prevost's and Patriots held the defensive advantage, the civilians buckled. The Privy Council declared South Carolina neutral, its status guaranteed by a future treaty with Britain. Prevost refused the deal and Colonel William Moultrie declared that the garrison would defend the city. The delay allowed Lincoln to close, forcing Prevost's retreat. The offensive, despite the failure to take Charleston, had tremendous strategic and operational implications. Not only did it ensure the Crown hold on Georgia, but it established Charleston as a prime target for the next British assault. Like falling dominoes, the affairs of late 1778 and early 1779 set in motion a chain of events that culminated in the tiny village of Yorktown over two years distant.

While the struggle for the South unfolded, events in the North failed to alter the military status quo. Clinton initiated several coastal raids, including William Tryon's Connecticut raids against New Haven, Fairfield, and Norwalk. In reaction, Continental forces under Anthony Wayne captured Stony Point, New York, on 15 July. The Patriot assault against Verplanck's Point failed. Unwilling to commit to a major action, Washington abandoned Stony Point.[12] The British post at Castine, Massachusetts (now Maine), came under an amphibious assault in late July, but the resultant siege came to naught; Castine and Penobscot Bay remained in Crown hands. With the stalemate, Patriot and French attention turned toward recovering Savannah.

## "Carrying War into Theirs"

With Washington in a defensive posture based in the Hudson Highlands and northern New Jersey awaiting French support, he decided to deal with the threat of the British Indian allies, the Iroquois Confederation. At Oriskany, Oneidas had fought for the Patriots, which resulted in a revenge raid by Joseph Brant's Volunteers. Retribution raids followed setting the northwest frontier aflame, most notably the Loyalist-Indian raids on Wyoming Valley, Pennsylvania, and Cherry Valley, New York. The response meant taking the struggle to the enemy's territory to relieve pressure on the frontier settlements: "Nothing can so Effectively draw the Indians out of your country, as Carrying the War into theirs."[13]

Accordingly, Washington initiated a multi-pronged offensive into Seneca and Iroquois territory with over 4,000 troops, a significant percentage of the army, coordinated with a diversionary feint toward Canada. Major General John Sullivan drove deep into Indian country destroying village after village and, more importantly, foodstuffs. Having fallen for the diversion against Canada, British regulars had withdrawn north, leaving the Indians and Loyalists vulnerable to the onslaught. At least 40 villages and tens of thousands of corn bushels were destroyed. Despite the punishment, terror and revenge raids continued along the frontier for several more years.

## The French Counterattack

By mid-1779, the British achieved the initial objective of obtaining a critical southern port and securing the flank from attacks from Georgia. Realizing the danger in the loss of Savannah, a combined Franco-American operation to recover the city under the French Admiral Charles-Henri-Theodat, *comte* d'Estaing, came to naught. With a force of nearly 4,000 French regulars and Patriot troops, including over 600 Volunteers of San Domingo, the first free black unit in the French forces, d'Estaing sailed from Haiti on 16 August, initiating an assault against Savannah on 9 October 1779. The landing alerted British defenders of the pending invasion, a factor that weighed heavily in the ultimate outcome.

The *comte* held both a vice-admiralcy and lieutenant general's commission; therefore, he served as the overall commander of land and sea forces, perhaps a fatal flaw. D'Estaing, a veteran naval officer, lacked an understanding of the vital importance of speed, surprise, and mass/concentration in a land campaign. Prevost took advantage to upend all Franco-American efforts. Resultantly, the initial landing force essentially sat in place, alerting the defenders and allowing Prevost time to prepare defenses. In landing what was essentially a scouting force at Tybee Island, the French squandered the initial advantage of surprise.

Between 12 and 14 September, d'Estaing landed the bulk of the force 12 miles south of the city. As is so often the case in early-modern warfare, the troops embarked upon a campaign of pillage and looting, confiscating farm animals, horses, cattle, wagons, and alcohol stores. d'Estaing called on Prevost to surrender based on the overwhelming array of land and naval forces. Such a gentlemanly act, normal in traditional European siege warfare, further undercut d'Estaing's position. Prevost requested a temporary truce to consider the surrender proposition; the *comte* agreed and the second critical error further sealed the expedition's defeat To be fair to d'Estaing, he simply followed the prevailing rules of siege warfare. Under this rubric, once a siege commenced and there appeared little hope for imminent relief, if the garrison surrendered after initially offering some form of resistance and particularly if the defenses had been breached, the besiegers were obligated to afford the Honors of War. The surrendering defenders could then march out of the castle or town under arms with music and colors. While the Honors of War might seem comical to the modern reader, the positive effect on the loss of life represented a practical reason for the mercy. However, if the doomed garrison resisted beyond the degree deemed reasonable to satisfy honor, then all civilities vanished. Once the garrison had fallen, rape, pillage, burning, looting, and murder of survivors inevitably followed.

While Prevost considered and d'Estaing waited, reinforcements arrived having made their way into the city without opposition. Sappers (engineers) constructed stout fortifications and positioned artillery. Almost immediately, the plan went awry for the invaders. Clausewitz cautions that war is the realm of chaos and probability. Few examples in the American War better illustrate this dynamic than the badly mismanaged Savannah campaign. With Lincoln covering the northern approaches and the French to the south, Prevost would be isolated and helpless. No one accounted for the British force that found its way through the swamps, woods, and backcountry into Savannah unmolested. Lincoln badly underappreciated the strength of British defensive works and the state of Prevost's defenders. Coordination suffered. Delays plagued Lincoln in assembling his forces, giving the British added time to fortify. Relations between Lincoln and d'Estaing became frosty and uncooperative. Poorly executed, badly coordinated, lacking swiftness, and failing to concentrate forces, the attack faltered despite a considerable allied numerical advantage. The French abandoned the operation, re-embarked, and returned to Newport. Lincoln could only retreat to Charleston to await the eventual onslaught.[14]

The initial capture and subsequent defense of Savannah seemingly validated the British Southern Strategy. Events in Georgia created the illusion that battlefield victories through conventional operations represented the key to victory and the ultimate restoration of southern allegiance. It negated French sea power as well and in no way undercut the Royal Navy's ability to conduct traditional British expeditionary strategy. French naval presence did not compromise the ability to transport land forces across great swaths of ocean, land them successfully on the periphery of a defended site, and sustain and reinforce those forces logistically from the sea. Had Crown military officials been more reflective, they would have noticed the disappointing Loyalist turnout. But, flush with confidence in the Southern Strategy, Sir Henry in New York laid plans to press ahead with the next target of the Southern Campaign—Charleston.[15] In preparation, Stony Point, Verplanck's Point, and Newport were abandoned as Clinton consolidated forces. Of the repulse of the allied force at Savannah, Clinton commented: "I think this is the greatest event that has happened the whole war. . . . I need not say what will be our operations in consequence."[16]

The string of Crown battlefield victories continued into mid-1780. Beneath the surface, however, the seeds of destruction lay germinating in the South Carolina backcountry. At this juncture—victorious, encouraged, and emboldened—British authorities failed to understand the ultimate nature of the war in the South and the fatal strategic and operational flaw in the Southern Strategy—Loyalist support and turnout. The lessons of the Georgia undertaking that launched the southern gambit proved simply the wrong ones. Nonetheless, the colonial economy had collapsed, the Continental Army hardly existed as a fighting force, French land forces had not arrived in great strength, the Franco-Spanish invasion attempt was thwarted, and the Southern Strategy started with victories. All events indicated significant progress. Despite the apparent successes of 1779, doubt and frustration prevailed in Clinton's mind. The naturally cautious and pessimistic Clinton later summed up the Crown frustration as the New Year opened with plans to press ahead with the Southern Strategy: "Another year's expense of this destructive war was now going to be added to the four which had so unprofitably preceded, without a probability of its producing a single event to better or brighten our prospects."[17]

As Clinton fretted in New York, America's new minister plenipotentiary for peace arrived in Paris, having previously served for several months in France representing the new United States. John Adams believed that the war must be won in America. Accordingly, he vowed to convince his French allies that the pathway to victory required a greater commitment of French naval support and a larger land contingent. He argued that Britain was weak everywhere. By cooperating in combined and joint operations, he forecast that French and Patriot forces had the opportunity and ability "for conducting this War to a Speedy, successful and glorious Conclusion."[18] Vergennes remained reluctant. Relations with the Bourbon Spanish ally did not go smoothly following the Ushant naval defeat. Spain single-mindedly focused on recovering Gibraltar and another invasion attempt while Vergennes sought Britain's humiliation, not destruction. He also pointed out that if the Bourbon alliance did crush the British, thus upsetting the delicate continental balance of power, other kingdoms might come to Britain's assistance. Spain reluctantly backed down and concentrated on Gibraltar, leaving the road clear for France to focus naval power on the West Indies and ultimately to send the deciding factor to America—a potent land force under the *compte* de Rochambeau. Adams, thus, won the argument.

For Britain, with the threat of home invasion diminished, the Cabinet became bolder. Sir George Rodney convoyed relief and reinforcements to Gibraltar, then proceeded to the West Indies to bolster defenses, especially Jamaica, and commence offensive operations. Additionally, Rear-Admiral Sir Thomas Graves sortied with five ships-of-the line for North America. In Paris, Vergennes fretted over French lack of success, as exemplified by the Savannah debacle. He put forth his new plan—*Expédition Particuliére*—calling for sending a substantial force to America. Approved by the king and the council with an additional cash subsidy for the Patriots, it was hoped that the aid would speedily end the conflict as France went heavier and heavier into debt. On 15 July 1780, Rochambeau and 6,500 French troops landed at Newport. With that event, Washington, still hankering for a combined and joint assault on New York, now had the requisite forces to go on the offensive.

## "Courage and Toil"

Clinton saw the capture of Charleston as the tipping point to destroy the rebellion or at least recover the more economically valuable southern colonies. In August 1779, he made a fateful decision—shift the main action southward. Attempts to lure Washington into a major battle came to naught. Patriot threats to northern Georgia also factored into his decision. Therefore, he decided to abandon the war in the north and focus on Charleston. In splitting the force leaving a defensive garrison in New York and mounting a southern offensive against Charleston, Clinton took a great gamble that violated one of the most fundamental principles of war—concentration. A risky gambit; success or disaster relied on the Royal Navy maintaining command of the sea.

Congress ordered reinforcement of the Charleston garrison, sending over 3,500 men of the Virginia and North Carolina Continental Line and three frigates under Commodore Abraham Whipple, along with substantial powder and other military supplies. Washington detached Maryland and Delaware Continentals under Major General Johann de Kalb. Washington sent stores and troops reluctantly. It had been a harsh winter in the New Jersey hinterland. With a collapsing economy, an unsure ally, and ill-nourished troops, he now faced a reinvigorated, aggressive opposition.

On 9 February, the first British forces landed at Simmons Island, initiating the greatest British siege operation of the war. Charleston, the economic dynamo of the South, had long been a target. Clinton's 1776 expedition failed to overcome the defenses and the sand bars outside the harbor. The British would not repeat those dynamics. The invasion force of nearly 9,000 troops and 400 horses sailed from New York on Boxing Day 1779 (26 December) to launch the main Southern Campaign operation. The force included regular British units, substantial Loyalist Provincials such as the British Legion, and a company of black pioneers from New York with a further 200 black troops from Georgia.

Vice-Admiral Marriott Arbuthnot commanded naval forces. Clinton personally embarked to lead the invasion army for the next crucial step in the Southern Campaign. Arbuthnot, known as crotchety, frequently obstreperous, prone to vacillation and to changing decisions willy nilly once made, and Clinton, prickly, overly concerned with criticism and often personally unsociable, simply did not get on with each other. While the admiral spent the campaign in his sea cabin with Clinton ashore, very little coordination occurred. In truth, the lack of cordiality and more importantly, joint army to navy cooperation did not affect seriously operations once the army went ashore; however, the lack of coordination was symptomatic of the strategic incoherence that plagued British efforts in the final years of the war. More importantly, the frostiness between Clinton and senior subordinates, most critically, Lord Cornwallis, second-in-command of the expeditionary force, plagued command unity. Though each officer respected the other, relations had been curt and strained due to an earlier 1776 incident when Clinton, on a rant against Howe, made indiscreet remarks that Cornwallis passed on to their commander. Paranoid about personal criticism, Clinton regarded the incident as a personal betrayal. The increasing ill will roiled relations and exploded in a disastrous series of miscommunications, muddled orders, and confused strategic intent.

Relations between the CinC and Whitehall impacted cohesion as well. Clinton resented civil authority interference in his war management and strategic decision-making. Moreover, he chaffed at the reduction of forces in New York for what he viewed as ill-conceived peripheral operations in the West Indies. He feared that any failure would be blamed on him when he had little input into the actual decisions.

Over the lack of strategic and operational control, he fairly shouted to Germain his frustration:

> For God's sake . . . if you wish that I should do anything leave me to myself, and let me adapt my efforts to the hourly change of circumstance. If not tie me down and take the risk of my want of success.[19]

Foul weather caused a difficult passage, but by February, Clinton arrived off Charleston. The British plan called for approaching the city landward and initiating a classic siege cutting off the city by siege works on the narrow Charleston Neck and controlling the waterways. Charleston's position made an indirect approach possible by land and invulnerable to defenses set to repel a seaborne attack. Lincoln frequently suffered from interference from local and state political authorities, including Governor Rutledge. Civil authorities defied sound military recommendations, insisting on defending the city in the face of an unwinnable situation and refusing to allow the Continental Army to withdraw.

From a standpoint of operational planning, Charleston presented an easy target. Surrounded on three sides by water (Ashley and Cooper Rivers and Charleston Harbor), the narrow isthmus meant that a besieging force need only control the strip of land leading inland. Clinton enjoyed mobility and the flexibility to strike at any point and at any time. In eighteenth-century warfare, so long as the besieger had superior or equal numbers and adequate artillery, particularly heavy siege mortars, the result generally favored the attacker unless the beleaguered garrison received reinforcements. With Crown forces controlling the waterways, Lincoln and the Charleston defenders had little hope. He recognized his dilemma, but civil authorities nullified any escape plan. Even with reinforcements of North Carolina and Virginia Continentals and substantial improvement in the fortified line, the situation worsened each day (see Figure 7.1).

From the base on James Island, on 29 March, Clinton struck. Moving by flatboats across the Ashley River, he conducted an amphibious landing several miles northwest of the city. Meanwhile, Arbuthnot's warships blockaded the harbor, prevented reinforcement by sea, and, perhaps most importantly, attracted attention, thus masking landward movements. As the British parties toiled by night digging the first parallel trench, the last of the Continental reinforcements arrived. Church bells rang out in celebration and troops fired a *feu de joie*, an ultimately useless gesture and waste of gunpowder. Reinforcements only added to the tally of prisoners of war weeks later. By 8 April, the stranglehold tightened with the completion of the first parallel stretching across the isthmus. Fortified artillery batteries came into action two days later. Work progressed inexorably. With the bombardment batteries fully operational, Clinton sent in a surrender summons. Lincoln demurred, thus sealing the fate of Charleston and over 5,000 defenders. Arbuthnot sent his frigates past Fort Moultrie on Sullivan's Island in a dash for the inner harbor, thus rendering it unavailable for either escape or reinforcement. Only the Cooper River remained open as Lincoln's window for escape gradually closed.

**FIGURE 7.1**   Siege of Charleston

*Source:* Courtesy of the Anne S.K. Brown Military Collection, Brown University Library, Providence, Rhode Island

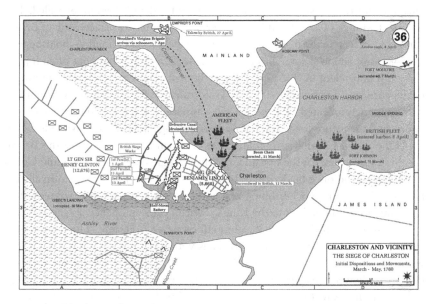

**MAP 7.1**   Charleston Campaign

*Source:* Map Courtesy of the United States Military Academy Department of History, West Point, New York

## Green Dragoon

For Clinton, the imperative lay in cutting off Lincoln's line of retreat and in intercepting incoming reinforcements. Accordingly, he dispatched troops under the command of two of the most notable and controversial officers of the campaign, Major (promoted to Lieutenant-Colonel on the American establishment) Banastre Tarleton and Major Patrick Ferguson. In previous actions, the 26-year-old dragoon commander demonstrated the skills and leadership that soon made him feared and respected but also hated by Carolina Patriots. He exhibited the bold, aggressive, sometimes impetuous, but supremely confident air and attitude that won him the loyalty and admiration of his troopers and gained him field promotion to a lieutenant-colonelcy on the Provincial Establishment. Clinton had the perfect officer for the rapid movements and bold action needed to slam shut any hope of escape from the city or succor from the north.

Brigadier General Isaac Huger and several hundred Continentals maintained a critical supply depot at Monck's Corner crossroads on the Cooper River. Approaching before dawn, Tarleton and Ferguson overran the ill-prepared and poorly guarded positions. Huger's dragoons and infantry, some of the best in the Continental Army, could not overcome the sudden assault; the defense collapsed. By early May, several Monck's Corner refugees along with local militia had reassembled north of the Santee River. Attacking and capturing a foraging party, they attracted Tarleton's attention. At Lenud's Ferry, in characteristic fashion, Tarleton charged through and past the picket guard and smashed into the main body. Ill-prepared for battle and surprised, the Continentals had no chance. Tarleton, soon dubbed "The Green Dragoon" for the forest green uniforms worn by his British Legion, prevailed. The actions at Monck's Corner and Lenud's Ferry represented a characteristic of British commanders seen in the many struggles over the next several months—bold, aggressive, offensive action led by officers of the same ilk and mentality but often injudicious and imprudent in risk-taking and in the willingness to attack without proper intelligence or "situational awareness." Unfortunately for Crown arms, the otherwise supremely talented officers typically dismissed or ignored the imperative to understand the nature of the conflict, battle, or engagement about to be undertaken.

As the fall of Charleston unfolded, the command team that drove the British Southern Campaign for the remainder of the struggle emerged. In granting Cornwallis a free hand once he departed back to New York in June, stating: "In all this, however, I rely on your Lordship's zeal and knowledge to act in every respect in the manner most beneficial to the King's service," Clinton opened a Pandora's Box of evils from which British pacification efforts never overcame. The determined, aggressive, and often headstrong Cornwallis with strategic concepts often at odds with his superior, increasingly chafed at any direction from Clinton. But in 1780, the orders allowed the aggressive Cornwallis free rein, and he took full advantage.[20]

In an ironic way, the easy victory in the Monck's Corner and Lenud's Ferry ultimately became a strategic disaster for the Crown. The events validated Cornwallis' concept that bold, aggressive, offensive action against seemingly ill-prepared opposition would win the day and crush the rebellion. Less apparent was that in destroying conventional enemy forces in such actions, enemy interaction and adaptation would inevitably occur. Faced with few strategic alternatives, South Carolina Patriots turned to insurgency warfare in the following months. Despite their best efforts to rouse the Loyalists and tamp down the insurgents using regular forces, Cornwallis and his subordinate officers never implemented an effective counterinsurgency strategy. For Cornwallis, as he marched inland in pursuit of the conventional victory, his task became harder and harder as the underlying British lack of strategic cohesion and breakdown in command and control charged to the fore. Indicative of the coming shattering of the strategic cohesion between Cornwallis and his commander are Clinton's words of 26 April: "He will play me false, I fear."[21]

## Charleston Falls

Using classic siege techniques, British diggers advanced the siege trenches forward. Most of the digging occurred at night. With the canal breached by the 30 April, British engineers drained the last great barrier between the lines in preparation for the inevitable infantry assault. By 8 May, the British works had advanced to within a few yards of the defensive breastworks. To add to the Patriot difficulties, the Fort Moultrie garrison surrendered on 6 May to a Royal Navy landing party allowing unhindered British passage into the harbor.

Clinton sought to avoid unnecessary civilian casualties. British warships periodically closed the range and opened fire. Whipple's few ships remained powerless to oppose Arbuthnot's periodic attacks. In Charleston, besieged from land and sea, Lincoln proposed that all militia should be demobilized and sent home, rather than become prisoners of war; he insisted that the Continentals be allowed to march out of the city with regimental colors and martial music. Civilian leaders refused to allow an honorable surrender. A frustrated Clinton remarked: "I begin to think these people will be blockheads enough to await the assault."[22] Johann Ewald described the action thus:

> [O]rders were given to fire on the city with red-hot shot, which set fire to several houses and made the sight more terrible and melancholy, whereupon the enemy fire weakened somewhat. The Commander in Chief, who pitied the city being reduced to ashes, issued orders about ten o'clock to stop the firing of red-hot shot, and granted the besieged time to reconsider.[23]

The threat of British "hot shot" so unnerved the civil authority that on 11 May, the Council advised Lincoln to seek the best possible terms. His rage at this decision to capitulate must have been sublime. Had the civilian leadership not been insistent on defending the city, Lincoln did have some alternatives. By moving his forces northwest of Charleston and allowing Clinton to occupy the city, he might have become the besieger. With the British in Charleston, French forces could initiate a siege, while the French Navy challenged the Royal Navy's command of the sea. By

11 May, that chance disappeared. In early afternoon, a white flag appeared above the Patriot defenses. On 12 May, Lincoln surrendered Charleston and his army unconditionally. By the surrender terms, militiamen received a parole to return home but without arms and ammunition. Ten regiments of Continentals became prisoners of war. Losing only 76 and less than 300 hundred wounded, Clinton inflicted the worst defeat of the war on the American Patriots.

Charleston represented the apex of British effort to regain the South. British arms had crushed Continental Army resistance by conventional operations and secured a key geographic position. Charleston then served as the keystone for the pacification efforts in the hinterland by force of arms, allowing Loyalists to turn out and re-establish royal government and security. Ironically, the fall of Charleston by a classic siege, land and sea operational cooperation, trapping of the opponent in a fixed and vulnerable site where the loss of command of the sea negated reinforcement or escape, mirrored precisely the Yorktown dynamic 17 months later.

Within weeks, British hopes for restoring the South to allegiance started to fray. Based upon the self-serving reports of prominent southerners, the Southern Strategy based on Loyalist support and massive turnout offered the possibility of ending the rebellion in the South. But, the plan foundered on one central, pivotal dynamic-winning popular support. In the hybrid warfare that quickly developed in the South, without public support, even a weak, irregular force has a chance for victory. Without it, even the most capable, resolute, and powerful conventional force can be defeated. The British Southern Strategy relied not only on the goodwill of Southern Loyalists but also on their active military and logistic support. Loyalists would not only reinforce and support the regular operating forces but would provide security, maintain royal control once the main army had moved on, suppress rebel activity, and encourage and protect Loyalists and neutrals. Within weeks, three separate events undermined the Southern Strategy—the proclamations of 22 May to 3 June 1780, the Waxhaws Massacre of 29 May 1780, and the Battle of Ramsour's Mill in Lincoln County, North Carolina, 19 June 1780.

## "A Want of Discrimination"

Clinton departed for New York on 5 June, leaving Cornwallis in overall command for seemingly simple mopping up operations combined with embodying, training, and equipping the Loyalists. Although neither officer nor any other senior officer recognized it at the time, Clinton's issuance of the 3 June proclamation became a tipping point in favor of the Patriots. While the proclamations issued on 22 May, 1 and 3 June generally granted lenient paroles to captured soldiers and promised harsh treatment for anyone guilty of harassing or attacking Loyalists, a provision of the 3 June decree stipulated that all citizens who failed to take the oath of allegiance stood in rebellion. A captured and released Continental Army or militia soldier could not be on parole and remain neutral. While many neutrals might have simply ignored events in hopes of staying above the fray, the proclamation ensured that no one could legally remain neutral.[24]

The 1st of June proclamation, issued by Clinton and Arbuthnot serving as joint peace commissioners charged with civil government and the restoration of tranquility, promised that former rebels would have all of their property restored, guaranteed, and protected and not subject to parliamentary taxation. Additionally, it offered a full pardon to all prisoners of war as well as any other rebels still fighting if they laid down their arms and swore the oath, having full rights as Britons restored. Colonists still in rebellion faced two starkly opposing alternatives—either take the loyalty oath and return home peaceably or suffer dreadful consequences.

The 1st of June proclamation astounded and alarmed Loyalists. Anticipating harsh punishment for treason and rebellion ranging from property sequestration to death by hanging, Loyalists expected Crown authorities to exact strict punishment for the oppression suffered at Patriot hands. Instead, the proclamation granted rebels all the rights and protections for which Loyalists had fought, suffered, and died. To Clinton, the proclamations seemed a legitimate measure to restore tranquility and assure a gradual, stable transition to royal governance. Clinton's 3 June measure further divided the Americans by warning the colonists that they must actively support the British effort or be treated as rebels. Ultimately, most neutrals went over to the Patriot camp. Additionally, many of the paroled militia and Continentals, faced with a hard choice of swearing a false allegiance or breaking parole, chose the latter.

The proclamations created uncertainty and disillusionment. The proclamations undercut the ability to protect, nurture, or exploit Loyalists who openly embraced the royal cause. Clinton and Arbuthnot perhaps felt that the proclamations would be successful based on the New York/New Jersey precedent. Following the 1776 campaign, the Howes issued a similar joint proclamation leading to an upsurge in volunteers for Loyalist Provincial units. Cornwallis found the proclamations a hindrance and eventually repudiated most of the terms. They galvanized opposition, which gained strength and momentum through the summer of 1780 just as Cornwallis moved inland. They created the impression that the British acted in bad faith and alienated Loyalists who expected better treatment than former rebels. Patriots and Loyalists soon engaged in violent, irregular, low-intensity, and vendetta struggles that escalated into a terrible internecine civil war and political disorder. Lieutenant-Colonel Francis, Lord Rawdon, wrote with discouragement on the almost immediate detrimental effect of the proclamations:

> That unfortunate Proclamation of the 3d of June has had very unfavorable consequences. The majority of the Inhabitants in the Frontier Districts, tho' ill-disposed to us, from the circumstances were not actually in arms against us . . . and nine out of ten of them are now embodied on the part of the Rebels.[25]

Cornwallis also realized the devastating effect of the proclamations. In a letter to Arbuthnot, he stated succinctly:

> I hope you will not be offended when I assure you that the Proclamation of the Commissioners, of the 1st [June], and that of the General [Clinton] of

the 3rd, did not at all contribute to the success of my operations. Nothing can in my opinion be so prejudicial to the affairs of Great Britain as a want of discrimination. You will certainly lose your friends by it, and as certainly not gain over your enemies. There is but one way of inducing the violent rebels to become our friends, and that is by convincing them it is in their interest to be so.[26]

## Tarleton's Quarter

Within days of the first proclamation's issuance and Cornwallis' opening moves, an incident occurred that epitomized the struggle's coming brutality. Colonel Abraham Buford's 3rd Virginia Regiment, along with some Continental dragoons and local militia, had been on the march to reinforce Charleston. Hearing of the surrender, they retreated toward North Carolina by way of the Waxhaws settlement just south of the North Carolina line. Buford's 400 men represented the only organized Patriot military force in South Carolina. Clinton, seeing an opportunity to catch the refugees with a fast-moving "flying column," detached Cornwallis with 2,500 troops accompanied by Tarleton's British Legion and several field pieces. By 26 May, Cornwallis had only reached Nelson's Ferry on the Santee River. At this juncture, the earl, in an action that characterized his *modus operandi* throughout the war, defied the normal doctrinal commandment to concentrate forces; he detached Tarleton on 27 May with 270 dragoons and mounted infantry to give chase. Tarleton moved swiftly to engage Buford's bedraggled command in a two-day forced march in the intense, humid early-summer air and overtook the Virginians on 29 May at the Waxhaws Settlement.[27]

With Buford's men strung out in a ragged line along the road and the artillery too far ahead of the column to provide effective support, Tarleton attacked. Buford formed a single line through a lightly wooded, flat area, ideal terrain for cavalry deployment, a critical tactical error. The worst possible formation to receive charging cavalry is an extended line. Meanwhile, the Continental baggage wagons and artillery pressed on in flight, another grave tactical error. Tarleton retorted with a three-pronged attack on the left and center while simultaneously hitting the line's rear. According to Tarleton's account, Buford ordered the line to hold fire until the approaching enemy reached ten paces, yet another grievous tactical error.[28] With few casualties inflicted and the charging dragoons full upon them, carnage ensued as troopers slashed at the hapless infantry with cavalry sabers and broadswords. The sudden, violent charge collapsed the rebel line.[29] A junior officer on the Continental right flank attempted to parley by mounting a white cloth on his sword and walking forward. However, Continentals on the far side of the line, either refusing to surrender or not understanding the parley attempt, kept on fighting. At roughly the same time, Tarleton's horse went down trapping the commander under the saddle. Thus, on both sides, command and control collapsed for a crucial few minutes as troopers freed Tarleton from under the wounded mount. Other dragoons, enraged and believing that their commander had been killed or wounded, made no distinction between surrendering enemy troops and those still resisting. A slaughter ensued as individuals and groups of soldiers attempted to surrender. Legion troopers slashed with heavy sabers and thrust with bayonets at stunned victims in the blistering late afternoon sun.

Patriot accounts of the engagement claimed that Buford had raised a surrender flag, yet Tarleton drove his men on to the attack. According to these accounts, Crown troops kept up their assault for a full quarter hour. Tarleton reported that he had been dismounted and his horse killed and that the word spread among his men that he had been slain. By the time he remounted and took positive control of events, the massacre had been done (see Figure 7.2). The entire engagement lasted for only a half hour, but the damage to the Crown cause proved immense. Jim Piecuch explodes the Waxhaws mythology through a systemic evaluation of the accounts from participants and commentators. He concludes thus:

> The evidence does indicate that some British troops killed Americans who tried to surrender because the British believed these men had killed their commander. These killings clearly occurred on a small scale, both in absolute numbers and relative to similar incidents perpetrated later in the war. An objective analysis shatters the myth of the Waxhaws "Massacre."[30]

**FIGURE 7.2**  The Waxhaws "Massacre"

*Source:* Courtesy of the Anne S.K. Brown Military Collection, Brown University Library, Providence, Rhode Island

Whatever the truth of the matter, it became irrelevant in terms of public perception. As word of the catastrophe spread, the event came to be called the "Waxhaws Massacre" and the rallying cry of "Tarleton's Quarter" became a symbol of resistance. While British commanders viewed the Waxhaws as a complete victory, the incident symbolized British cruelty and brutality and accelerated the slide of neutral southerners toward the cause of independence. Thus, in the battle for the loyalty, and perhaps more importantly, the outright physical support from the southern Loyalists, British commanders squandered public goodwill through actual or perceived egregious actions that violated popularly held concepts of the civilized conduct of war. Ironically, Lord Germain wrote to Clinton:

> Convey to Major Tarleton His Majesty's Approbation of His Conduct, and of the Behaviour of the Corps he commanded in the affair at Wacsaw, The celerity of the March, and the Vigor of the Attack, do them equal Honor, and merited the complete Victory with which they were crowned.[31]

## "This Unlucky Business"

Events in North Carolina spiraled out of control. Despite Cornwallis' orders to await his arrival in the fall, western North Carolina Loyalists gathered at Ramsour's Mill along the Little Catawba River west of Charlotte. Lieutenant-Colonel John Moore arrived from Charleston on 7 June to raise the western North Carolina Loyalist militia. A Lincoln County native, he had served with Crown forces through the South Carolina campaign and wore a colonel's uniform, thus giving some credibility to his mission. Moore announced Cornwallis' intent to invade North Carolina and free the Loyalists from the oppression of their Patriot neighbors. His enthusiasm and apparent authority had the necessary effect. By 20 June, 1,200 Loyalists had gathered at the mill. Although nearly a quarter lacked proper weapons, many were veterans of the 1776 Cherokee War and had served for years in the North Carolina royal militia. Patriots quickly responded. Brigadier General Griffith Rutherford called out the North Carolina militia on 3 June. Within two weeks, rebel forces in the state included nearly a thousand militia infantry under Rutherford, several troops of horse, and roughly 300 Continental light infantry. A further 400 militiamen, drawn from local counties, gathered under Lieutenant-Colonel Francis Locke. Rutherford ordered Locke to attack and disperse the Loyalists mustered at the mill.

A local Patriot briefed Locke on the enemy's position. In the early morning of 20 June, Locke's force advanced in the heavy fog, undetected. Surprised by the approaching Patriots using concealment and cover to approach the unwary sentries, the pickets loosed several random, ineffective shots. Although alerted to the enemy's presence, chaos spread through the Loyalist force. Several fled without taking any part in the ensuing action. Locke's mounted troopers, though few in number, only increased the panic. Once Moore and his company commanders restored order, a counterattack threw the horsemen back but ultimately failed to drive off the Patriots. More Patriot infantry arrived and essentially surrounded the Loyalists. With the exception of some senior officers, few men had formal uniforms. Loyalists attached green leaf twigs to their hats, while Patriots pinned on white papers. Inevitably, these identifiers fell off; enemy identification became practically impossible. Hand-to-hand combat erupted with a mixture of crude weapons. Muskets and rifles became cudgels. Unarmed men fought with rocks and branches or simply with fisticuffs, often neighbor against neighbor. Despite superior numbers, tactical deception, and simple boldness determined the outcome. As the battle disintegrated into a melee, Moore requested a truce to recover the dead and wounded. Realizing the hopeless situation, he ordered as many as could to slip away. Few Loyalists remained once Locke re-formed his line for another assault. Casualties on each side appear equal; however, Loyalist senior leadership had been decimated. In the absence of an effective organizing element, the western North Carolina Loyalists became a non-factor for the war's remainder.

A significant feature of the Ramsour's Mill event previously missing in the Southern Campaign in 1780 was the element of engagements involving only irregular forces on both sides. Hitherto, the actions had been generally between regular troops or a mixture of regulars and militia. At Ramsour's Mill, neighbor fought neighbor. Crown authorities in South Carolina regarded the Ramsour's Mill episode as "this unlucky business [that] will not materially affect the general Plan, or occasion any commotions on the frontiers of this Province."[32] In reality, the seemingly little affair in western North Carolina heralded a disaster for British plans. Combined with the proclamations and the Waxhaws, the three events of 22 May to 20 June 1780 set in motion a chain of events that ultimately doomed any hope of restoring the South to the royal fold. The proclamations placed citizens on "death ground" forcing them to either swear allegiance that violated their conscience or be regarded as treasonous. The Waxhaws incident created a firestorm of bad public perception that not only caused neutrals to lean away from the Crown but further motivated rebels. Ramsour's Mill removed a substantial Loyalist force that would have been useful in light infantry operations such as foraging, scouting, reconnaissance, intelligence gathering, and suppression of irregular enemy forces. Additionally, the Loyalist defeat set in motion the cycle of violence that roiled the Carolinas for months. It led to the inhibition of North Carolina Loyalists to actively either join Cornwallis for his North Carolina operations or provide the necessary logistical support to maintain his fast-moving offensive in a lightly populated and rugged frontier environment. While no one in the British high command fully understood the implications of these events in the early summer of 1780, clearly, a pattern had been established that made Cornwallis' quest simply unachievable.

## Notes

1 Tonyn to Amherst, St. Augustine, East Florida, 19 January 1778, WO34/144/42; Tonyn to Amherst, St. Augustine, East Florida, 14 November 1778, WO34/111/184.

2 WO34/110, 144–6. (hereafter cited as WO34/vol, pages).

3 See Louis De Vorsey, Jr., *The Indian Boundary in the Southern Colonies, 1763–1775* (Chapel Hill, NC: The University of North Carolina Press, 1961) for details of the various agreements and treaties that established the boundary lines.

4 For details of the Cherokee Wars of 1761 and 1776, see John R. Alden, *John Stuart and the Southern Colonial Frontier: A Study of Indian Relations, War, Trade, and Land Problems in the Southern Wilderness, 1754–1775*. (University of Michigan Publications, History and Political Science, Vol. XV. Ann Arbor, MI: University of Michigan Press, 1944); Jim Piecuch, *Three Peoples, One King: Loyalists, Indians, and Slaves in the Revolutionary South, 1775–1782* (Columbia, SC: University of South Carolina Press, 2008).

5 Following his defeat at Savannah, Howe was court-martialed and acquitted but still relieved of command in the South. He joined Washington in May 1779 and failed in the attempt to capture Verplank's Point on the Hudson River. Howe sat on the court-martial of Major John Andre. He saw no further significant action and, following the war, returned to his New Hanover County plantation near Wilmington, North Carolina.

6 For details of the fight at Savannah and Campbell's report, see Archibald Campbell, *Journal of an Expedition against the Rebels of Georgia in North America*, ed. Colin Campbell (Darien, GA: Ashantilly Press, 1981); Robert S. Davis, "The British Invasion of Georgia in 1778," *Atlanta Historical Journal* 24 (1980): 5–25; Alexander Lawrence, "General Robert Howe and the British Capture of Savannah in 1778," *Georgia Historical Quarterly* 36 (1952): 303–27.

7 NA WO34/112/3–4.

8 For a comprehensive study of Benjamin Lincoln, see David B. Mattern, *Benjamin Lincoln and the American Revolution* (Columbia, SC: University of South Carolina Press, 1995); and, Carl P. Borick, *A Gallant Defense: The Siege of Charleston, 1780* (Columbia, SC: University of South Carolina Press, 2003).

9 Hamilton to John Jay, President of the Continental Congress, 14 March 1779, *Papers of Alexander Hamilton*, eds. Harold C. Syrett and Jacob E. Cooke (New York: Columbia University Press, 1961–1979), 2:17–9.

10 Details of the Battle of Kettle Creek can be found in Robert Scott Davis, Jr., *Georgians in the Revolution: At Kettle Creek (Wilkes Co.) and Burke County* (Easley, SC: Southern Historical Press, 1986); *Kettle Creek: The Battle of the Cane Brakes, Wilkes County*. (Atlanta, GA: State of Georgia, Dept. of Natural Resources, Office of Planning and Research, Historic Preservation Section, 1975).

11 Prevost to Germain, 5 March and 10 June 1779, K. G. Davies, ed., *Documents of the American Revolution, 1770–1783*. 20 Vols. (Shannon: Irish Universities Press, 1976).

12 WO 34/115/63–7; WO34/118/171–2.

13 John Sullivan to Colonel Samuel Hunter, 30 July 1779, Otis G. Hammond, ed., *The Letters and Papers of Major-General John Sullivan, Continental Army*, 3 vols. (Concord, NH: New Hampshire Historical Society, 1930–9), 3:89.

14 For details of the Siege of Savannah, see Franklin B. Hough, *The Siege of Savannah by the Combined American and French Forces under the Command of Gen. Lincoln and the Count D'Estaing in the Autumn of 1779*. 1866. Reprint (New York: Da Capo Press, 1974).

15 Clinton to Germain, New York, 23 December 1779, NA CO5/99 pt. 1/29.

16 Clinton to Eden, New York, 19 November 1779, Benjamin F. Stevens, ed., *Facsimiles of Manuscripts in European Archives Relating to America, 1773–1783*, 10:1032 (London, 1889–95).

17 Clinton, *American Rebellion*, 277.

18 Adams to Lafayette, 21 February 1779 and Adams to Leray de Chaumont, 5 October 1779, *The Papers of John Adams*, eds. Robert J. Taylor et al. (Cambridge, MA: Harvard University Press, 1977), 7:421 and 8:191.

19 Clinton to Germain, New York, 22 May 1779, NA CO5/97/679.

20 Clinton to Cornwallis, Head Quarters, near Charleston, 23 April 1780, NA PRO CC 30/11/2/9.

21  Clinton to Phillips, New York, 26 April 1781; Benjamin Franklin Stevens, ed., *The Campaign in Virginia 1781: Clinton-Cornwallis Controversy.* 2 Vols. 1888. Reprint, (Charleston, SC: Nabu, 2010) hereafter indicated as C-CC, 1:435–40.
22  Clinton to Cornwallis, Charleston, South Carolina, 6 May 1780, NA PRO CC 30/11/2/28.
23  Ewald, *Diary*, 237.
24  Proclamations of 22 May and 3 June 1780, NA CO5/99 pt. 2/300; NA CO 5/99 pt. 2/302.
25  Rawdon to Cornwallis, Camden, 7 July 1780, NA CC PRO 30/11/2/252; NA CO5/99 pt. 2/300; NA CO5/99 pt. 1/102.
26  Cornwallis to Arbuthnot, Charlestown, South Carolina, 29 June 1780, NA PRO CC 30/11/77/18.
27  Tarleton to Cornwallis, Wacsaw, South Carolina, 30 May 1780, NA HQ PRO 30/55/23/2784.
28  NA CO5/99 pt. 2/308.
29  Clausewitz, *On War*, 85.
30  Jim Piecuch, *The Blood Be upon Your Head: Tarleton and the Myth of Buford's Massacre, The Battle of the Waxhaws: May 29, 1780* (Lugoff, SC: Woodward Corporation, 2010), 40.
31  Germain to Clinton, Whitehall, London, 5 July 1780, C-CC, vol. 1:229; NA CO5/99 pt. 2/280; NA CO5/100/1.
32  Cornwallis to Clinton, Charleston, South Carolina, 30 June 1780, C-CC, vol. I, p. 224; NA CC 30/11/72/18; NA CO5/100/105.

# 8

# CAMPAIGN IN THE CAROLINA BACKCOUNTRY

By mid-summer, British authorities looked out over a seemingly tranquil South Carolina. With Charleston in hand, Lincoln defeated, and posts established throughout the backcountry, the strategy appeared to work. The Ramsour's Mill affair, while troubling, had not yet had the eventual devastating effect of suppressing North Carolina Loyalist enthusiasm. No Continental Army force operated in the South except for the small contingent under DeKalb; only scattered Patriot militia groups represented any armed opposition. Georgia had been pacified, the Floridas secured, and South Carolina seemingly so. It was an illusion. As summer passed, Loyalists became increasingly anxious and angry over the proclamations. Parolees and neutrals flocked to the Patriot side as partisan bands formed throughout June and July. The Waxhaws Massacre reverberated through the backcountry with talk of "Bloody Ban" Tarleton and British barbarism. The observation of Major James Wemyss should have added to Cornwallis' worries over backcountry opposition (see Figure 8.1): "It is impossible for me to give your Lordship an idea of the disaffection of this country. Every inhabitant has been or is concerned in the rebellion and most of them very deeply."[1]

## "In Arms Against Us"

Through the summer of 1780, Patriot partisan bands formed and conducted raids and ambushes on British logistics and communications while simultaneously inhibiting Loyalists from turning out. Occasionally, partisans engaged in larger-scale actions that undercut Crown troop strength. Not only did these actions inflict casualties on an already woefully undermanned force but caused Cornwallis to detach troops to chase down the rebel bands and to garrison or defend vital posts. Through their actions and activities, partisans successfully attacked both the British strategy and, by intimidation, the Loyalist alliance. Despite several battlefield

DOI: 10.4324/9781003041276-12

**FIGURE 8.1**    Lord Charles Cornwallis

*Source:* Courtesy of the Anne S.K. Brown Military Collection, Brown University Library, Providence, Rhode Island

victories against these irregular and Continental Army regular forces, Cornwallis never pacified the backcountry. Whenever Crown forces defeated or drove off a partisan force, it simply popped up elsewhere. Combined with the losses at King's Mountain in October and Cowpens in January 1781, Cornwallis never successfully cleared or held South Carolina with the exception of a few defended posts. Frustrated with the inability to control South Carolina, he launched an invasion into North Carolina that ended in disaster at King's Mountain in October. In January 1781 in a futile attempt to destroy yet another Continental force under Daniel Morgan, he lost another thousand troops in the disastrous Cowpens defeat.

Crown forces garrisoned key sites such as Camden, South Carolina, where they established a forward-operating base and an extensive magazine. At Ninety Six, west of Charleston near the Georgia border, another significant post guarded the main trading trails into Georgia. These posts represented "targets of opportunity" for the Patriots. Thus, as the summer and autumn unfolded in the backcountry, Cornwallis and subordinate commanders sought to ferret out and destroy Francis Marion, Thomas Sumter, Andrew Pickens, and other shadowy enemies so as to establish Loyalist control as the main regular force moved north in search of a conventional battlefield victory. In this endeavor, they failed. In truth, the chances of cowing the backcountry by proclamations, Crown battlefield victories, or fire and sword declarations were minimal. These events were more likely to prompt frontiersmen and backcountry residents to greater resistance. These settlers, scrapping out a frontier existence or in small, subsistence upland farms exhibited a fierce independence and willingness to do violence when wronged. Such hardy people are typically far less likely to break or bend under strain. Loyalty oaths and charges of treason bore no more weight with them than did Ferguson's threat of "Fire and Sword" issued in October 1780. John Buchanan captures the tenor of the backcountry folk:

> These were the people who buried Buford's dead soldiers where they died, nursed the wounded at the Waxhaws Presbyterian Church, and plotted dark deeds of revenge. These were the people who in the blackest time for the cause would bend but never break. They were hard men and women, accustomed to privation, travail their normal lot, mercy to an enemy never uppermost in their thoughts.[2]

Largely Scots-Irish in origin and Presbyterian in theology, their Calvinist outlook held that government, whether monarchy or republican, had the duty to enforce the law, rather than being the source of law; that remained only God's prerogative. These religious beliefs produced political views that naturally led to opposition and an unwillingness to be dictated to by a faraway government. The Fincastle Resolves from Virginia of early 1775 capture the tenor of the backcountry folk and express a common sentiment throughout the rural South:

> Many of us . . . left our native land . . . we crossed the *Atlantic*, and explored this then uncultivated wilderness, bordering on many nations of Savages . . . who have incessantly been committing barbarities and depredations on us. . . . These fatigues and dangers we patiently encountered, supported by the pleasing hope of enjoying those rights and liberties which had been granted to

*Virginians* . . . and of transmitting them inviolate to our posterity; but even to these remote regions the hand of unlimited and unconstitutional power hath pursued us, to strip us of that liberty and property with which *God*, nature, and the rights of humanity have vested us. We are ready and willing to contribute . . . for the support of his Majesty's Government, if applied to constitutionally, and when the grants are made by our own Representatives, but cannot think of submitting our liberty or property to the power of a venal *British* Parliament, or to the will of a corrupt Ministry.[3]

## Huck's Defeat

Despite the apparent operational success of Crown arms, a series of small actions typically fought between the rising partisan bands and Loyalist units, often augmented by Continental, British, and Provincial regulars, continued throughout the backcountry. At Williamson's Plantation, a significant milestone further hampered Cornwallis' efforts to subdue the interior and promote Loyalist domination. Philadelphia Loyalist Captain Christian Huck of the British Legion had been given an independent command composed primarily of British regulars to suppress rebel activity along the North Carolina border and intimidate the local population into signing the loyalty oath. Despite Cornwallis' explicit instructions to avoid plunder and other depredations, Huck's troops committed acts designed to instill terror.[4] Throughout June and early July, Huck charged about upstate South Carolina disrupting Patriot attempts to muster forces. On 12 July, at Williamson's Plantation, a large Patriot force assaulted his encampment at dawn. Some three hundred militiamen approached the house at dawn and struck the unwary Loyalist camp. Huck, roused from his sleep, rode out to rally his men only to be shot out of the saddle in the first volleys. His routed forces fled.[5] Huck's defeat represented a further breakdown in Crown control of the South Carolina backcountry. Cornwallis sensed it: "This little blow will, I fear, much encourage the enemy and greatly increase the difficulty of protecting our borders. I see no safety for this province but in moving forward as soon as possible."[6]

Throughout the summer, partisans made significant inroads in British control over the backcountry. Thomas Sumter, a former Continental Army officer and plantation owner whose home had been looted and burned by Tarleton's dragoons, emerged as one of the primary insurgents. Known as "The Gamecock," Sumter proved especially effective at interdicting British supply and logistics lines. On 1 August, Sumter struck. Rocky Mount along the Catawba River, an outlying advance post for Camden, provided a tempting target. He possessed two advantages—mobility and firepower. With most of his troops mounted and outnumbering the defenders by a more than 3 to 1, Sumter could strike at any point. Additionally, many of the backcountry men possessed rifled weapons, more common along the frontier than in the lowlands. Increasingly, frontiersmen from the Carolina and Virginia hills and Appalachian Mountain regions played an important role in events such as King's Mountain, Cowpens, and Guilford Courthouse. In a conventional linear battle, rifled weapons were of little use except for initial snip-ing at an advancing enemy line. However, in the small, irregular warfare actions in the rural South, rifled troops held a keen advantage. At Rocky Mount, stout walls and well-delivered musket volleys overcame Patriot numbers, mobility, and rifle firepower, but the pattern of irregular warfare and partisan assaults on Crown posts and logistic trains had been set.

An even more devastating event occurred two days earlier. At Thicketty Fort on 30 July, Colonel Isaac Shelby's rebels captured a Loyalist party of nearly 100 men without firing a shot. At Hanging Rock on 1 August, North Carolina Patri-ots assaulted an encampment and routed the garrison. Chastened by the defeat, the British sent reinforcements. Sumter mounted a renewed attack on 6 August. Formed into three assault columns, the militia moved to the attack. Despite effec-tive volleys from the defenders, the Patriots captured the post. The attack might have been more complete except that the Patriots fell into looting the British camp with the rum ration as the primary booty. More arms, ammunition, and horses fell into Patriot hands. Another significant Loyalist force, in this case well-trained and equipped Provincial units, had been defeated and another strongpoint lost. Other partisans such as Colonel Francis Marion, a prominent planter and former Con-tinental Army officer, whose irregular, guerilla-type operations along the Santee and Pee Dee Rivers, continually frustrated and complicated British operations. Marion's first significant action occurred on 12 August at Port's Ferry as he crossed the Pee Dee River and defeated a Loyalist detachment, the first of many successes that not only fired up the spirit and enthusiasm of local Patriots but further inhib-ited and suppressed Loyalist support.

As such engagements flared up throughout the backcountry, Cornwallis expressed his growing disenchantment with the local Loyalist militia. From Ram-sour's Mill, through the demise of Huck and several other small affairs, Loyalist and regular Crown forces suffered debilitating casualties. More importantly, as Corn-wallis contemplated an advance into North Carolina, he left behind an unsettled backcountry where Patriot irregulars dominated the region. A frustrated and per-plexed Cornwallis reported:

> [T]he Whole Country between Pedee [sic] and Santee has ever since been in an absolute State of Rebellion; every friend of Government has been carried off, and his Plantation destroyed; & detachments of the enemy have appeared on the Santee, and threatened our stores and Convoys on that river.[7]

To overcome the chaos in South Carolina, Cornwallis believed that the path to success lay in advancing north, key to his plans to crush the rebellion. His warfare concept embraced bold, risky, aggressive, offensive action at which he proved a master of war, tactically and operationally. These actions proved completely coun-ter to a war-winning strategy in the South. Destroying the rebel's political will by destruction of his war-making ability and the elimination of regular, conventional forces proved a false concept. But for the earl, that concept meant invading North

Carolina forthwith. Thus, by early autumn 1780, he committed to an attrition campaign by a strategic offensive that carried him eventually to the final calamity at Yorktown. Patriots handed him the very justification for launching his offensive—the arrival of a new southern Continental Army force under the Saratoga victor, Major General Horatio Gates, who led a newly reconstituted Continental force into South Carolina leading to the clash at Camden, an overwhelming British battlefield victory that for the earl, validated his strategic concept of aggressive, bold offensive action.

## "Cool Intrepidity"

DeKalb's forces arrived too late to relieve Charleston but provided the core of a new Southern Department army, which contained significant North Carolina militia of dubious quality. Additionally, Virginia militia soon rendezvoused with the Continentals. While more than doubling the numbers, the militia's poor fighting quality played a major factor at Camden. Leadership represented another qualitative factor. Appointed by Congress to replace the captured Lincoln, Gates arrived to take command in July near Hillsborough, North Carolina, where he found roughly 1,400 ragged, ill-nourished, and destitute troops. Despite all the burdens, he ordered an immediate march toward Camden, a woefully ill-considered move, given the troops' physical state. Basing his decision on the erroneous report that Cornwallis had departed for Savannah, he sought a quick strike. Gates marched directly through the North Carolina Sand Hills rather than a longer route westerly through Salisbury and Charlotte, both Patriot strongholds likely to provide fodder and food. On the march, the men subsisted on green corn and unripe fruit, which caused considerable gastrointestinal distress, especially dysentery. Despite promises of food and spirits just ahead, none materialized as the weary and starving Patriots trudged through the oppressively hot and humid Carolina summer.

From Cornwallis' perspective, intelligence reports indicated parolees joining Sumter along with estimates of DeKalb as having over 2,000 Continentals and militia. He concluded that the enemy intended not only to defend the Carolinas vigorously but to initiate offensive operations. Accordingly, he moved provisions, ammunition, and arms to Camden roughly 100 miles north of Charleston. Lord Rawdon, commanding at Camden, reported that he had no intelligence of Gates' movements even though he had many "emissaries abroad."[8] Throughout the first days of August, Rawdon attempted to ascertain Gates' whereabouts with little luck. However, he felt confident that the Patriot commander meant to assault Camden and perhaps get between himself and Charleston. The young Irish lord remained supremely confident in his men's ability to withstand any assault. While rumors put Gates' forces at over 5,000, Rawdon believed it to be much less. He fretted over the number of "Sick Present," particularly in the 71st Fraser's Highlanders, hardest hit by malaria and other illnesses. Summer campaigning in the South brought disease and illness, especially dysentery and malaria.[9] While a preventive assault against the advancing force might have accrued some advantage, Rawdon demurred: "No opportunity offered of attacking him consistent with the safety of our magazines, tho' I thought my force fully equal to the attempt."[10] Cornwallis departed Charleston on 10 August. Despite an apparent numerical disadvantage, he resolved to initiate battle, a decision certainly in keeping with his nature in "having left Charlestown sufficiently garrisoned and provided for a siege, and seeing little to lose by a defeat and much to gain by a victory, I resolved to take the first good opportunity to attack the rebel army."[11]

Arriving north of the town, Gates ordered a night advance, a difficult maneuver for well-trained troops and harder still for the militia. The march evolved into a disaster. The area alternated between wooded areas and a single road bordered by swampy marshland. Exhausted, hungry, and undisciplined troops fell out of formation. Stragglers wandered all about the countryside. Men fell ill to stomach disorders. Discipline collapsed among the militia. Despite all, Gates initiated the action and made two ultimately fateful command decisions.

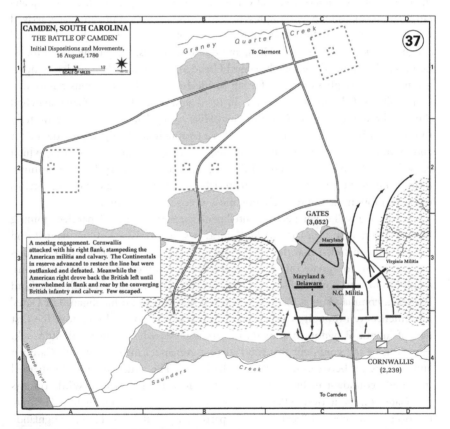

**MAP 8.1**   The Battle of Camden

*Source:* Map Courtesy of the United States Military Academy Department of History, West Point, New York

To ambush Cornwallis moving up from Charleston, Gates detached a company of Maryland Continentals, some artillery, as well as North Carolina militia to join Sumter on the Camden to Charleston Road, which deprived him of some of his most effective and reliable soldiers. Meanwhile, Cornwallis arranged his line of battle. Tarleton's dragoons and other light infantrymen formed the lead element, the first to make contact with the enemy. Unlike the desperate and struggling Patriot force, well-rested and fed Crown troops demonstrated the value of discipline, training, morale, and experience as their night march proceeded up the post road with little trouble. In the humid heat of a Carolina summer night, the two armies marched in the dark toward each other. More critically, Cornwallis had three of the most veteran, battle-hardened, disciplined, and capable of all the line regiments in America, all supported by the best and most experienced of the Provincials. Against this force, Gates could only rely upon the Delaware and Maryland infantry. The qualitative odds stood starkly against him.

Gates made his second critical error in the early morning. He made no overall battle plan, and, therefore, individual commanders fought separate engagements, rather than a coordinated, unified effort. Moreover, he placed the militia on his left and center facing the British regular regiments. The Continentals formed the right and reserve facing the Loyalist Provincials. Cornwallis struck first. Immediately, Patriot cohesion crumbled. Advancing with parade-ground precision, British regulars commenced volley firing before coming to the "Charge Bayonet." In a single motion, hundreds of bayonets came to the ready as the line emerged from the dense smoke created by their volley fire, made thicker by the damp summer air. The sight of advancing redcoats compounded by the sound of their "huzzahs" with each forward step to the rhythmic beating of drums, unnerved the militiamen. Many threw down their arms and fled. All cohesion in the Patriot line dissipated. Only a single unit of North Carolina militia held firm. Attempts to staunch the hemorrhaging line with the Maryland Continentals in reserve had little positive effect, as they were driven back by the advancing red line. Gates' left crumbled in only minutes. Cornwallis, in his post-action report, stated:

> Our line continued to advance in good order, and with the cool intrepidity of experienced British Soldiers, keeping up a constant fire or making use of bayonets as opportunities offered, and after an obstinate resistance during three quarters of an hour threw the enemy into total Confusion, & forced them to give way in all quarters.[12]

Events went better for the Patriots on the right. The Continentals stood their ground and even advanced against heavy volley fire. However, with the Patriot left flank gone, the British executed a wheel maneuver on the Continental's left flank, pouring in volley after volley of enfilading fire. Despite their courage and steadfastness, the Continentals could not stay long in this cascade of bullets and withdrew in good order. DeKalb received multiple mortal wounds while desperately attempting to rally his men. In an act that will forever disgrace his reputation, Gates mounted his horse "Fear Naught" and fled the battlefield, reportedly not stopping until he reached Charlotte some 65 miles distant.[13] As the refugees streamed into North Carolina, leaving the wreckage of a battle lost over miles of country road—dead and dying, wounded men, baggage, wagons, and supplies—to the British, North Carolina now seemed ripe for conquest (see Figure 8.2).

Camden represented a stunning and complete victory of British arms. It demonstrated the competency and superb field leadership of Cornwallis and subordinate officers. In a single day, Cornwallis removed from the field a substantial enemy force of any consequence in the South. While Camden represented a stunning tactical victory, it also sprang a strategic trap for Cornwallis. Flush with victory, he moved further inland into the backcountry and away from his base of support and maritime sustenance at Charleston, which complicated his already tenuous supply and reinforcement situation. The move made the partisan attacks more deleterious while simultaneously providing many more potential targets for Marion and his peers. The Charleston and Camden defeats removed the regular Continental forces, thus forcing partisan bands to emerge, who owed little allegiance to either civil or military chains of command or authority, thus creating a nightmare scenario for the conventional warfare-minded British forces. The earl became a victim of his own success.

Camden validated Cornwallis' concept of victory that by smashing every regular Continental Army force, he would overawe and intimidate the rebels into submission. But, an increasingly debilitating factor set in-force attrition. Though Crown

BATTLE OF CAMDEN – DEATH OF DE KALB.

**FIGURE 8.2** Battle of Camden, Death of Baron DeKalb

*Source:* Courtesy of the Anne S.K. Brown Military Collection, Brown University Library, Providence, Rhode Island

casualties at Camden numbered barely over 300, it represented a 20 percent casualty rate among the regular line regiments, an increasingly critical factor. Finally, Gates' defeat and humiliation brought into the fray perhaps the most strategically adept general officer in the Continental Army, Nathanael Greene. But, to Cornwallis, the Battle of Camden validated his operational and strategic concepts; he resolved to carry forward the invasion of North Carolina.[14]

## A Season of Discord

Cornwallis consistently advocated a diversionary action in the Chesapeake in support of his march into North Carolina. He understood that such an action would block any southerly movement by the Continental Army. Just after Camden, he again suggested the idea to Clinton and advised that the success of his proposed North Carolina campaign depended on the "operations which your Excellency may think proper to pursue in the Chesapeak[sic], which appears to me, next to the security of New York, to be one of the most important objects of the war."[15] Despite the unsettled status of South Carolina and so as to strike home again his concept, he reminded Clinton:

> If we succeed at present and are able to penetrate into North Carolina, without which it is impossible to hold this province [South Carolina], your Excellency will see the absolute necessity of a diversion in the Chesapeake, and that it must be made early.[16]

In late summer, the debate over a Chesapeake operation erupted, roiled command relations, and flummoxed any attempt at a cohesive British strategy. Pushing the issue, Cornwallis wrote:

> An early diversion in my favour in Chesapeak [sic] Bay will be of the greatest and most important advantage to my operations. I most earnestly hope that the Admiral [Arbuthnot] will be able to spare a convoy for that purpose.[17]

In New York, Clinton dithered. Not only did he worry about New York's safety, but potential French activities complicated plans for a robust two-pronged campaign in the South. In a growing pattern of caution and resistance to taking aggressive action, Clinton hinted at possible French moves that threatened New York:

> [A] second [possible French move] is talked of to Chesapeak [sic], which may possibly frustrate our views in that quarter. Indeed, without I am reinforced considerably, I dare not go there in force, and, without I do, nothing can be expected.[18]

One can imagine Cornwallis' reaction to those words. The pattern of strategic disintegration between the CinC and his main field commander marched steadily toward disaster. The Chesapeake concept had actually been in Clinton's mind from the start of the Charleston operation. However, he cautioned Cornwallis that the highest priority was to defend the posts in South Carolina, especially Charleston. Further, operations into North Carolina should be along the Cape Fear River basin to maintain water communications with the coast; Chesapeake operations could commence in due course. One of the major waypoints along the road to Yorktown occurred as Clinton ordered 2,500 troops to the Chesapeake under Major-General Alexander Leslie in October to establish a defensive post in Hampton Roads and conduct raids inland. In December, he detached Brigadier-General Benedict Arnold with a further 2,000 troops to Portsmouth, Virginia, to conduct raids. But such raiding did not represent the sort of pincer offensive advocated by the earl. Clearly, a differing strategic concept set in, one that increasingly debilitated southern pacification efforts. Cornwallis reminded his superior of the absolute need to commence simultaneous actions in support of his, or in lieu of a diversionary expedition, at least a substantial reinforcement of his own dwindling command:

> I most sincerely hope that Nothing can happen to prevent your Excellency's intended diversion in the Chesapeake. If unfortunately any unforeseen Cause should make it impossible, I should hope that you will see the absolute Necessity of adding some Force to the Carolinas.[19]

Following Camden, the partisan war intensified. The collapse of all Continental Army military power in the Carolinas did not deter the partisans. Rather, it had the opposite effect. Taking advantage of the Camden victory, Cornwallis vowed to pursue and destroy the irritating partisans and deployed his best instrument-Tarleton and the British Legion. A series of small-scale engagements occurred in the late summer and autumn that undid all the victories of Charleston and Camden despite some Crown victories that gave the impression of strategic success. Cornwallis expected the colony to calm, stating: "[T]he rebel forces at present being dispersed, the internal commotions and insurrections in the province will now subside."[20] Here is seen a fundamental flaw in the entire British strategic concept. This rebellion was not like any other in these men's experiences and certainly not like previous rebellions that had been crushed by brute military force.

Meanwhile, the north remained stalemated. The arrival of Admiral Sir George Rodney, commanding the Leeward Islands Station, gave Clinton strategic mobility, and he considered an expedition against the French occupying Newport. However, the West Point affair in late September where its commander, Benedict Arnold, sought to betray the post and defect to the royal cause collapsed with Clinton's adjutant-general, Major John André, captured and executed for espionage. Control of West Point jeopardized Patriot control of the Hudson Highlands and threatened Washington's position. But the failure of Arnold's treason meant that Clinton rejected a joint operation against Newport as proposed by Rodney.

From Washington's perspective, the French arrival at Newport proved frustrating. Insisting on keeping their naval and land forces together at Newport, the French allies refused to cooperate in an attempt on New York or Canada. Stalemate continued in the North.

## "Fire and Sword"

With resolve to press ahead despite the obstacles, Cornwallis implemented his campaign plan in September. He commenced the movement on 22 September with the ultimate objective of Hillsborough to re-establish royal authority and create a magnet for Loyalist support. While the move into North Carolina represented the next natural action, others viewed the move with trepidation. Charles Stedman, Commissary General to Cornwallis' army, commented that the earl's decision seemed "to confound human wisdom . . . [and] derange the best concerted schemes [of men]."[21]

To cover his western flank, he detached Ferguson to operate west of Charlotte. Ferguson had raised nearly 1,000 recruits in western South Carolina since his appointment as Inspector of Militia. The Scot arrived in North Carolina on 7 September and promptly initiated action. At this point, the earl had some trepidation about the willingness of the North Carolina Loyalists to rise again, perhaps due to the Ramsour's Mill affair. He wrote to Colonel Nesbit Balfour, commanding at Charleston:

> Ferguson is going to advance with some militia. . . . I think it rather hazardous, but he says he cannot positively get them to stay longer where they are; and to be sure, this is a favorable time for advancing, and if ever those people will fight, it is when they attack and not when they are attacked.[22]

Arriving at Gilbert Town, about 50 miles west of Charlotte, Ferguson released a prisoner to carry his threat to the colony's western region stating that if the residents did not desist in their support of the rebel cause, he promised to lay waste to the countryside. The threat of retribution rang loud: "if they did not desist from their opposition to the British arms, he would march his army over the mountains, hang their leaders, and lay their country waste with fire and sword."[23] The infamous threat message had profound results. Within days, militia leaders throughout western North Carolina and Virginia collected their forces for a general rendezvous. Predominately mounted and armed with hunting rifles, these frontiersmen or Over-Mountain Men came from the western side of the Blue Ridge Mountains. By late September, the assembled force headed south. Ferguson retreated and sent urgent messages requesting reinforcement and eventually established a camp on the plateau of King's Mountain just across the border into South Carolina.

Marching in a soaking rain, the rebel forces proceeded toward the mountain. They covered the locks of their weapons with blankets and shirts to keep them dry.

Late on 7 October, they formed multiple columns and conducted a multi-pronged coordinated assault. North and South Carolina Loyalists waited on the summit along with elements of several Provincial units. Capped by a flat plateau, King's Mountain provided ideal ground for linear tactics. But, the terrain gave the Patriots the tactical advantages of cover and concealment. The Provincials delivered three bayonet charges, but the attackers returned to the plateau each time and delivered murderous fire. The battle lasted about an hour by which time the Loyalists, suffering heavy casualties, fell into confusion and disorder. Several white flags came out as men attempted to surrender. Meanwhile, Ferguson sought to create a tipping point by a mounted charge with what few volunteers he could muster. As the men mounted up, riflemen shot them out of the saddle. Ferguson frantically rode across the battlefield to rally the men, charged the enemy, and received at least seven rifle ball wounds. Dragged into the tree line by his dead foot still in the stirrup, the only native Briton at King's Mountain perished (see Figure 8.3).[24]

King's Mountain further complicated the British difficulty. Not only had Cornwallis lost his left flank covering force, but the damage to the Loyalist Strategy proved substantial. In a process begun earlier in the year at Ramsour's Mill, Ferguson's destruction accelerated the decline in both Loyalist recruitment and a willingness to actively support Crown forces. After King's Mountain, Lord Rawdon

**FIGURE 8.3** Death of Major Ferguson at King's Mountain

*Source:* Courtesy of the Anne S.K. Brown Military Collection, Brown University Library, Providence, Rhode Island

expressed the dismay of senior British officers at the lack of enthusiasm among the North Carolina Loyalists:

> [W]e have a powerful body of friends in North Carolina, and indeed we have cause to be convinced, that many of the inhabitants wish well to His Majesty's arms; but they have not given evidence enough either of their number or their activity, to justify the stake of this province, for the uncertain advantages that might attend immediate junction with them.[25]

Cornwallis discovered just how powerful this enthusiasm gap had become as he trudged through the North Carolina wilderness in the following winter and spring. In frustration, Cornwallis wrote:

> We receive the strongest professions of friendship from North Carolina. Our friends, however, do not seem inclined to rise until they see our army in motion. The severity of the rebel government was so terrible and totally subdued the minds of the people, that it is very difficult to rouse them to any exertions.[26]

Though forced to retreat back into winter quarters at Winnsborough, South Carolina, following King's Mountain, Cornwallis resolved to carry on with his intentions. True to his aggressive nature, he embarked in January 1781 upon a bold and risky move to regain the strategic initiative, the elimination of Greene's re-constituted Southern Department army, a decision that led to the destruction of Tarleton's command at the Cowpens, the chase to the Dan River in Virginia, and the costly pyrrhic victory at Guilford Courthouse.

## "Rise, and Fight Again"

Shortly after King's Mountain, Congress made a momentous decision and replaced Gates with Nathanael Greene as commander of the Southern Department. His appointment represented a sea change in Patriot leadership quality, strategic thinking, and operational ability in the South. Greene and Washington had developed a special bond of respect and confidence that had tremendous consequences for the cause of independence and to Cornwallis' detriment. He soon proved his genius at organization, logistical management, and an ability to play the consummate diplomat between divergent interests and personalities.[27]

Despite the King's Mountain victory and the destructiveness of the Carolina partisans, 1781 opened badly for Washington and the army at Morristown. A mutiny in the Pennsylvania Line regiments erupted on New Year's Day. Unpaid for over a year, deprived of basic rations, and living in miserable conditions, the men had had enough when despite their three-year enlistments expiring, the army refused to discharge them. Congress interpreted the enlistment as three years or the war's duration. Roughly 15 percent of the army rebelled, demanded their pay or a cash bounty for a further enlistment, and many marched on Philadelphia. Eventually, terms were reached, and the mutiny settled down with half the mutineers choosing to re-enlist for a substantial bounty despite the economy's desperate state. Indeed, Congress requested a further loan from France, an amount double that of 1776. Nonetheless, the point had been made; the country and the very struggle for independence teetered on the edge of collapse. Washington understood this dynamic as did his British opponents. Clearly, the decisive battle to finally determine the issue had to be near at hand or all was lost or gained depending on one's side. Through all this miasma and chaos emerged the bright light of superior leadership that saved the war of independence—the emergence of Nathanael Greene and Daniel Morgan in the Southern theater.

Greene headed south with orders to continue the ongoing irregular warfare. Arriving at Charlotte in December, he found a motley and gravely discouraged force: "literally naked, and a great part totally unfit for any kind of duty."[28] Despite the difficulties, the sad little army represented the only force of any consequence between the South and Washington's army near New York. If Greene failed, then Cornwallis might sweep up through North Carolina, Virginia, and Maryland and threaten Washington with a two-pronged attack. As events unfolded, Greene's strategic genius manifested in one of the most amazing and effective defensive campaigns in the history of warfare. He established a commissariat to address the chronic supply difficulties and corresponded with the partisans. Although he mistrusted militia, he realized that he must incorporate them into his overall strategy of attrition: "I see but little prospect of getting a force to contend with the enemy upon equal grounds . . . and therefore must make the most of a kind of partizan war."[29] While he certainly believed in the value of irregular and militia as force multipliers, he also understood that the final, culminating victory required regular troops in conventional battle. In this regard, his views mirrored those of Washington and Cornwallis:

> Partisan strokes in war are like garnishings on a table, they give splendor to the army and reputation to the officers; but they afford no substantial national security. . . . You may strike a hundred strokes, and reap little benefit from them, unless you have a good army to take advantage of them.[30]

He understood that Cornwallis' critical weakness lay in supply and logistics. Partisans could interdict and complicate Crown command, control, communications, and logistics. He recognized the criticality of the southern water systems as barriers having scouted river crossings, fords, and ferries and gathered boats and watercraft at key locations for river crossings. Closely following the key tenet of the Fabian Strategy to maintain one's force in being and only give battle when the potential rewards exceed the risk, Greene played a game of hide-and-seek until the decisive, culminating battle. While it occurred in Virginia, the Yorktown victory was ultimately Greene's doing in North Carolina. He conceived of his forces as a "flying army" in that mobility, speed, sanctuary, and partisan attacks would frustrate and harass Crown forces. As Cornwallis advanced into North Carolina in pursuit,

Greene executed a brilliant retreat to draw the earl evermore further from his supply line. He: "denied the enemy resources, limited their mobility while increasing his own and constantly wore down Cornwallis' forces to lead the British general into making mistakes."[31]

Unbeknownst to Cornwallis, another harbinger of ill fortune arrived. Brigadier General Daniel Morgan did great service with his riflemen in the Saratoga Campaign. Although he had retired from the army, Greene convinced Morgan to command the Virginia Continentals. With this reinforcement, he committed what most military theorists insist is an error in dividing one's force in the face of a numerically and qualitatively superior enemy.[32] In Greene's plan, once each force reached the intended operating area, they stood over a hundred miles apart with no chance of mutual support. In dividing his force, Greene opened up the possibility of Cornwallis defeating him in detail. He detached Morgan with a substantial force into western South Carolina to "spirit up the people," interdict British logistics, and conduct attacks on the British left flank or rear should the enemy advance into North Carolina. Meanwhile, the remainder of the force moved east into South Carolina hill country. Cornwallis could launch forces against one or the other. Or, he could use his usual device—Tarleton and the British Legion. He chose the latter and disaster ensued. In justifying his decision to split the force, Greene explained that the action: "makes the most of my inferior force, for it compels my adversary to divide his."[33]

## "The Late Affair Has Almost Broke My Heart"

Moving southwest to operate on the British left flank and threaten Ninety Six, Morgan initiated his harassment operation actions forcing Cornwallis to respond. Cornwallis faced an agonizing decision. He had to support Ninety Six, but Greene had to be confronted. He resolved to mass as much strength as possible against Greene while simultaneously detaching Tarleton to protect Ninety Six and hunt down Morgan. On New Year's Day, Tarleton moved toward the Broad River with a potent strike force setting the stage for the affair at Hiram Saunders' cow pens.[34]

Forced back against the Broad River, Morgan decided to stand at the Cowpens. The open ground bereft of undergrowth from cattle grazing and generally flat and open represented excellent terrain for Tarleton's horsemen. Morgan understood his opponent's tactical concepts of a fast-moving cavalry assault to break down a formation, then follow-up with infantry. Morgan took a calculated risk in placing his force with their backs to the river but reasoned that this feature would stiffen the militia's resolve to stand and fight with little hope of flight. He admonished his militiamen to give a few sharp volleys and then retire, hoping that their fire would unhinge Tarleton's initial assault to the point that the better-disciplined Continental Line could withstand the attack.

As dawn broke on 17 January, Morgan arrayed his men in three lines. Tarleton advanced hastily in his usual manner. Mobility and speed characterized his tactical concepts. Tarleton made several critical decisions that determined the battle's outcome. He engaged a well-rested enemy situated in a firm defensive position, with a tired and hungry force. He ordered a general advance well before all his forces were in place. He failed to conduct a proper reconnaissance of enemy strength and dispositions. Finally, he assumed that the enemy militia would withdraw in panic, thus, he ordered a hasty cavalry charge. The attack became disjointed and confused. In one of those rare moments when militia carry out their assignment perfectly, their volleys mauled the British with numerous casualties among the officers and senior ranks. The British line halted in stunned amazement, but hours and hours of drill and training prevailed; the line reformed and advanced again with fixed bayonets.

Through a mistaken order, the Continentals started to retire, but Morgan halted the retreating line and ordered an about face and a volley. Simultaneously, militia that had re-formed on the British left and rear delivered devastating fire into the now disorganized mass. On the British right flank, Continental cavalry poured into Tarleton's disorganized dragoons. The battle unraveled as British troops now engaged in the front, rear, and left, crumbled into a disorganized mob; many fled. Tarleton had lost control of his force. He attempted to rally his troops and save the guns to no avail as a rout ensued. With what few forces he could muster, the "Green Dragoon" fled the field. Morgan inflicted a devastating blow on the royal cause (see Figure 8.4). Cornwallis confided: "The late affair has almost broke my heart."[35]

**FIGURE 8.4**   Battle of Cowpens

*Source:* Courtesy of the Anne S.K. Brown Military Collection, Brown University Library, Providence, Rhode Island

## "Striking Blows in the Air"

Following the King's Mountain and Cowpens debacles, Cornwallis faced an increasingly confident and growing rebel presence. King's Mountain compounded the negative public reaction to the Charleston proclamations and the Waxhaws affair. Cowpens destroyed the British Legion and two regular line battalions. Perhaps more importantly, the Continental Army and local militia team had finally defeated a skilled Crown force in an open, linear, conventional engagement, albeit not against Cornwallis himself. Bereft of much of his light infantry, Cornwallis suffered a debilitating loss of reconnaissance, scouting, skirmishing, and fast strike force capability. Making matters worse, he moved a hundred miles inland away from reliable seaborne supply. Although several bastions such as Camden and Ninety Six remained, the difficulty of moving supplies and reinforcements in the face of the marauding partisan bands proved increasingly dicey. With winter, foraging became equally problematic. Throughout the campaign, he seemingly disregarded the problem of logistical support once he moved inland and abandoned his seaborne connection. He pursued opponents in spite of difficult water crossings, lack of logistical support, and foul weather. William Willcox strikes true in his assessment of Cornwallis' failings:

> The Earl does not seem to have understood the two underlying necessities for British success in the South, sea power and loyalist support; and he certainly did not understand the connection between them. They were linked by logistics. An army that was out of touch with the sea was an army chronically short of supplies; it had to move in search of them or starve. Because it could not stay long in one area, it could not call out, protect, and organize the loyalists; therefore it could not hold territory. An army that held nothing, but merely marched through the countryside, would never force the Americans to battle; they might fight it on their own terms and in their own good time, or leave it to strike blows in the air.[36]

Disregarding the geographic factor, Cornwallis re-entered North Carolina. From the strategic viewpoint, the Cowpens disaster forced Cornwallis into a rash action in chasing Greene into North Carolina despite leaving substantial enemy forces in his rear. Given the earl's risk-taking nature, however, he could have hardly done anything else. Cornwallis had focused on a North Carolina invasion since before Camden:

> It may be doubted by some whether the invasion of North Carolina may be a prudent measure, but I am convinced it is a necessary one and that, if we do not attack that province, we must give up both South Carolina and Georgia and retire within the walls of Charlestown.[37]

Despite the increasingly perilous Crown position in the Carolinas, 1781 began with some optimism. The Franco-American alliance had not yet yielded any positive results for the Patriot cause. The North ministry remained in place, thanks to parliamentary election victory largely fueled by the anti-Catholic Gordon Riots and anti-Bourbon sentiment fired by the Franco-Spanish alliance. Despite the addition of the Dutch in late 1780 and the League of Armed Neutrality dynamic, British finances remained sound. Gates' Camden defeat meant that the best the partisans could do was snipe at the earl. By January, Continental Army morale collapsed. Shortages in rations, arms, uniforms, and ammunition all flummoxed Washington's ability to maintain a viable field force. Given those dynamics, the advance into North Carolina in early 1781 seemingly made strategic and political sense; following the Camden and Charleston news along with the 1780 election victory, support for the war in Britain actually rose.

## "A Chain of Evils"

As an indication of Clinton's ultimate strategic intent to undertake peripheral operations in Virginia and the Chesapeake, he expected Cornwallis to first subdue North Carolina and maintain control of South Carolina before any movement into the Old Dominion. Herein lies the seed of the disastrous strategic incoherence that erupted in late spring 1781.[38] Clinton made clear his intentions that Cornwallis should operate in North Carolina and establish an operating base in Virginia to: "carry on desultory expeditions in Chesapeak [sic] till more solid operations can take place." Clinton clearly intended for his field commander to operate in Virginia and even suggested the possibility of taking up winter quarters at Portsmouth. For Cornwallis, his strategic assumptions revolved around a practical concept; if he could control North Carolina, he could shut down supplies and reinforcements from the northern and middle colonies, thus starving the South Carolina partisans into irrelevancy. While the partisans could readily obtain basic supplies from locals, they could not obtain gunpowder and weapons. Supply from the north had to remain relatively free from Crown interference for the partisans to remain active.[39] Even so, as Cornwallis' troops stepped off into the tan-brown bleakness of a North Carolina winter, the situation remained tenuous:

> [T]he perpetual risings in different parts of this province, the invariable successes of all these parties against our militia, keep the whole country in continual alarm and render the assistance of regular troops every where necessary.[40]

Despite the hazards, Cornwallis expressed optimism: "O'Hara's brigade . . . sets the example of rigid discipline and perfect good will on all occasions. Our men are healthy and full of zeal. If opportunity offers, I trust I shall send you good news."[41] Following the King's Mountain debacle, Cornwallis had severe doubts about the efficacy of the Loyalist Strategy. Nonetheless, he declared:

> We will then give our friends in North Carolina a fair trial. If they behave like men it may be of the greatest advantage to the affairs of Britain. If they

are as dastardly and pusillanimous as our friends to the southward, we must leave them to their fate and secure what we have got.[42]

What doubts must have been running through the earl's mind as he contemplated charging into the North Carolina hornet's nest unsure of Loyalist support. Subordinate commanders also expressed misgivings regarding the level of Loyalist enthusiasm. A frustrated Lord Rawdon stated shortly after King's Mountain of the North Carolina Loyalists: "Not a single man attempted to improve the favourable moment or obeyed that summons for which they had been so impatient."[43]

British officers seemingly did not grasp the dynamics retarding Loyalist turnout, particularly the effectiveness of Patriot militia engaged in intimidation actions. A second dynamic was how many enthusiastic Loyalists remained in North Carolina by late 1780. Many had already taken the King's Shilling and, indeed, provided excellent military service. After years of abuse, harassment, and condemnation by their Patriot neighbors, could one have expected a large Loyalist turnout unless the regular army showed that Crown forces could indeed stay in place? Cornwallis made the two forays into North Carolina, but there existed no credible military presence capable of supporting and sustaining the pacification strategy once he hastily departed back to South Carolina and again into Tidewater Virginia. Cornwallis, the traditional and conventional military man faced with the collapse of his irregular and unreliable allies, now reverted to his core strategic, operational, and tactical beliefs. If the Carolina Loyalists could not maintain or accomplish their role in the Southern Strategy, then the formally trained and conventional military man would carry out the mission with his own reliable and trusted troops—the regulars of the British Army and the increasingly skilled and veteran Provincial units. Essentially, he now rejected the foundational principle of the Southern Strategy and opted for a purely conventional military solution. As modern observers have learned, in an ideological or religious-based internecine struggle, such solutions are rarely successful. They must be combined with the elements of psychological warfare, as well as an opponent's physical destruction. In hybrid warfare, a purely conventional military solution had little chance for success.

The fragility of British logistics, breakdown in command and control, and, ultimately as Cornwallis abandoned North Carolina for the Virginia adventure, an increasing strategic incoherence between Cornwallis, Clinton, and Lord Germain, and most importantly, the loss of active Loyalist support following the King's Mountain affair, all combined to doom the earl's valiant little force as they struck out across the Carolina winter landscape. As Clinton later remarked of King's Mountain, it "proved to be the first link in a chain of evils that followed each other in regular succession until they at last ended in the total loss of America."[44] Like a row of falling dominoes, the "chain of evils" followed Lord Cornwallis into the North Carolina backcountry.

## "Infinite Danger"

Cornwallis commenced his march north on 19 January 1781 after securing a seaborne logistics base. Colonel Nesbit Balfour, in Charleston, detached a force to take Wilmington, North Carolina, some miles up the Cape Fear River from the sea and an excellent port facility. Major James Craig took the city as well as collected boats to bring supplies up the Cape Fear. Craig found the city and supporting defenses practically nil and occupied it after dispersing a militia force.[45] While operating near the coast, Crown forces could expect reasonable if not wholly satisfactory supplies, especially rations and animal fodder. Once a force moved inland as Burgoyne learned in 1777, British logistics failed with disastrous results, a lesson in military science that Cornwallis should have absorbed. With Wilmington, he had a secure operations base in North Carolina, albeit 300 miles away. With the difficulty of transportation over an undeveloped infrastructure combined with the Patriot interdiction operations, Wilmington represented a useless asset so long as the army operated at a distance. Similarly, the depot and magazine at Camden proved no more valuable. Although much closer than Wilmington, with the partisan problem, even that shorter distance proved tenuous. Thrashing about in the North Carolina backcountry, Cornwallis had little hope for supplies and, as he learned bitterly, the intimidated local Loyalists had little to offer his hungry and footsore troops. The earl realized that factor too late to help the royal cause in North Carolina: "the want of navigation rendering it impossible to maintain a sufficient army in either of those provinces [North and South Carolina], at a considerable distance from the coast."[46] Greene, in contrast, displayed a genius for logistics. His business background and time as Washington's Quartermaster General taught him the criticality of reliable and constant logistical support. He comprehended the nature of the coming campaign; Cornwallis did not. The evil results of the earl's misunderstanding of the nature of the southern logistical dynamic soon played out in the red clay mud and raging rivers of North Carolina.

With his left flank now exposed by the Cowpens disaster, Cornwallis faced the first of his great decision points as he advanced northward, assuring Clinton that:

> It is impossible to foresee all the consequences that this unexpected and extraordinary event may produce, but your Excellency may be assured that nothing but the most absolute necessity shall induce me to give up the important object of the winter's campaign.[47]

Already, the difference between the two became apparent with Cornwallis charging off in pursuit of the elusive Greene while the more cautious, risk-averse, and pessimistic Clinton feared for the safety of New York. Despite his caution and concern, Clinton assured his subordinate of continued support in that the:

> experiment [advance into North Carolina] will . . . be fairly tried . . . if it succeeds and we hold the entrance to the Cheasapeak [sic], I think the rebels will never attempt either of those provinces [North Carolina and Virginia].[48]

Morgan presented a problem. The earl took decisive action to cut off Morgan's retreat. If he could get between Morgan and his line of retreat and destroy the Old Wagoner's force, he could make up for the losses at Cowpens. A two-day delay while awaiting reinforcements under Leslie gave Morgan the chance to escape. Ultimately, Cornwallis turned the army west toward the Little Broad River on the hunt for the Cowpens victor. In actuality, Morgan headed in the opposite direction. On discovering Morgan's moves, the army raced north into western North Carolina in pursuit. Burdened by the heavy equipment and wagons of a conventional army on the march and slowed by poor roads in an undeveloped wilderness, the army advanced methodically, but slowly.

Reaching Ramsour's Mill on 25 January, the army had only marched 72 miles in seven days, hardly adequate to catch the nimbler Morgan, still a two-day march and two difficult river crossings ahead. Cornwallis resolved to lighten the burden; at Ramsour's Mill, the army burned its baggage. Setting the example, Cornwallis threw in his own possessions, leaving only a few wagons to transport sick or wounded, food, ammunition, salt, and medical supplies. The army would advance with what the individual troops could carry in their haversacks and knapsacks. Tentage went into the blaze as well, a bold step in the midst of winter. Cornwallis said of the decision to burn the baggage:

> As the loss of my light troops could only be remedied by the activity of the whole corps, I employed a halt of two days in collecting some flour, and in destroying superfluous baggage and all my wagons, except those loaded with hospital stores, salt, and ammunition and four reserved . . . for sick and wounded . . . tho' at the expense of a great deal of officers' baggage, and of all prospects in future of rum, and even a regular supply of provisions to the soldiers, I must in justice to this army, say that there was the most general and cheerful acquiescence.[49]

Stedman, a Loyalist serving as Cornwallis' Commissary, summed up the baggage burning and the men's reaction:

> And such was the ardour both of officers and soldiers, and their willingness to submit to any hardship for the promotion of the service; that this arrangement, which deprived them of all future prospect of spirituous liquors, and even hazarded a regular supply of provisions, was acquiesced in without a murmur.[50]

Some deserted, but surprisingly few considering the general rate of eighteenth-century military desertion. Brigadier Charles O'Hara, commanding the Brigade of Foot Guards, captured the attitude of the army on that cold winter's day as they set out in pursuit:

> In this situation, without baggage, necessaries, or provisions of any sort for officer or soldier, in the most barren, inhospitable, unhealthy part of North

America, opposed to the most savage, inveterate, perfidious, cruel enemy, with zeal and with bayonets only, it was resolved to follow Greene's army to the end of the world.[51]

Sergeant Lamb commented on the egalitarianism displayed by Cornwallis in discarding his own camp gear, tentage, and personal belongings: "in all this his lordship participated, nor did he indulge himself even in the distinction of a tent; but in all things partook our sufferings, and seemed much more to feel for us than for himself."[52] As the men stepped off from the encampments on 28 January, they had every reason to believe that Greene's Continentals would be the next victim of British arms. Cornwallis cannot be faulted for assuming that this former Quaker would be easy prey as had Lincoln and Gates before. He did not yet realize that Greene, the militia private in 1774 and the brigadier in 1775, had become perhaps the most talented and astute strategic and operational field commander in the Continental Army by early 1781.

## Notes

1  Wemyss to Cornwallis, Cheraw Court House, South Carolina, 20 September 1780, NA CC PRO 30/11/3/80.
2  John Buchanan, *The Road to Guilford Court House: The American Revolution in the Carolinas* (New York: John Wiley and Sons, 1999), 89.
3  Freeholders of Fincastle County, Virginia, Committee of Safety, *Address of the People of Fincastle County, Virginia, to the Delegates from that Colony, who attended the Continental Congress* (Chicago, IL: University of Chicago American Archives Documents of the American Revolution); *The Virginia Gazette*, No. 2 (10 February 1775).
4  Proclamation Issued by Lieutenant-Colonel Innes, Broad River, South Carolina, 14 June 1780, NA CC PRO 30/11/2/157; Cornwallis to Wemyss, Charlestown, South Carolina, NA CC PRO 30/11/78/52.
5  Cornwallis to Clinton, Charlestown, South Carolina, 15 July 1780, NA CC PRO 30/11/72/30.
6  Ibid.
7  Cornwallis to Clinton, Charlestown, South Carolina, 6 August 1780, NA CC PRO 30/11/72/36; NA HQ PRO 30/55/25/2949; NA CO 5/100/115.
8  Rawdon to Cornwallis, Camden, South Carolina, 3 August 1780, NA CC PRO 30/11/63/9.
9  See Elizabeth A. Fenn, *Pox Americana: The Great Smallpox Epidemic of 1775–82* (Boston, MA: Hill and Wang, 2002).
10  Rawdon to Cornwallis, Camden, South Carolina, 11 August 1780, NA CC PRO 30/11/63/34.
11  Cornwallis to Germain, Camden, South Carolina, 21 August 1780, NA CC PRO 30/11/76/9; C-CC, vol. I, 249–56.
12  Ibid.
13  According to General Otho Holland Williams' report of the battle.
14  An excellent primary source for all the major engagements from the British perspective in the Southern Campaign is Roger Lamb, *An Original and Authentic Journal of Occurrences During the Late American War* (Dublin: Wilkinson and Courtney, 1809). A sergeant in the 23rd (Royal Welch Fusiliers), Lamb wrote an articulate and detailed account of the campaign from the soldier's perspective based on his diary.

15 Cornwallis to Clinton, Camden, South Carolina, 23 August 1780, C-CC, 1:259; NA CC PRO 30/11/72/42.

16 Cornwallis to Clinton, Charlestown, South Carolina, 10 August 1780, NA CC PRO 30/11/72/40.

17 Ibid.

18 Clinton to Cornwallis, Head Quarters, Philipsburg, New York, 14 July 1780, NA CC PRO 30/11/2/296.

19 Cornwallis to Clinton, Camden, South Carolina, 29 August 1780, C-CC, 1:261–64; NA CC PRO 30/11/72/47.

20 Cornwallis to Germain, Camden, South Carolina, 21 August 1780, NA CC PRO 30/11/76/9.

21 Charles Stedman, *The History of the Origin, Progress, and Termination of the American War*, vol. 2 (1794, reprint, Charleston, SC: Nabu, 2010), 15.

22 Cornwallis to Clinton, Charlestown, South Carolina, 6 August 1780, NA CC PRO 30/11/72/36; NA HQ PRO 30/55/25/2949; NA CO 5/100/115; Cornwallis to Balfour, Camden, South Carolina, 29 August 1780, NA CC PRO 30/11/79/45.

23 Quoted in Lyman C. Draper, *King's Mountain and Its Heroes: History of the Battle of King's Mountain, October 7th, 1780, and the Events Which Led to It* (1881, reprint, Charleston, SC: Nabu, 2010), 169.

24 For details of the Battle of King's Mountain, see: Hank Messick, *King's Mountain: The Epic of the Blue Ridge "Mountain Men" in the American Revolution* (Boston, MA: Little, Brown, 1976).

25 Rawdon to Clinton, Camp between Broad River and Catawba, South Carolina, 29 October 1780, C-CC 1:277–80; NA CO 5/101/43.

26 Cornwallis to Clinton, Camden, South Carolina, 29 August 1780, NA CC PRO 30/11/72/47.

27 For Greene's biography, see Terry Golway, *Washington's General: Nathanael Greene and the Triumph of the American Revolution* (New York: Henry Holt and Company, 2005).

28 Greene to Washington, Charlotte, North Carolina, 7 December 1780, *The Papers of General Nathanael Greene, Vol. VI, 1 June 1780–25 December 1780*, eds. Richard K. Showman et al. (Chapel Hill, NC: University of North Carolina Press, 1991), 6:543.

29 Quoted in Golway, *Greene*, 232.

30 Greene to Sumter, Camp on the Pedee [sic], South Carolina, 8 January 1781, *Greene*, 7:74–5.

31 For a thorough discussion of Washington's Fabian Strategy, see Stoker, *Strategy in the American War*.

32 Clausewitz, *On War*, 204; Sun Tzu, *Art of War*, 139.

33 Greene to an Unidentified Person, Camp on the Pee Dee River, South Carolina, undated.

34 Cornwallis to Clinton, Camp on Turkey Creek, Broad River, South Carolina, 18 January 1781, NA CO5/101/214. The more common name is Hannah's Cowpens. The best study of the Battle of Cowpens is Lawrence E. Babits, *A Devil of a Whipping: The Battle of Cowpens* (Chapel Hill, NC: University of North Carolina Press, 1998).

35 Cornwallis to Rawdon, Buffalo Creek, North Carolina, 21 January 1781, NA CC PRO 30/11/84/78.

36 William Willcox, *Portrait of a General: Sir Henry Clinton in the War of Independence* (New York: Knopf, 1962), 353.

37 Cornwallis to Clinton, Charlestown, South Carolina, 6 August 1780, NA CC PRO 30/11/72/36; NA HQ PRO 30/55/25/2949; NA CO 5/100/115.

38 Clinton to Cornwallis, New York, 13 December 1780, NA CC PRO 30/11/4/316.

39 For a fuller examination of Cornwallis' concept that to control South Carolina, he must control North Carolina, see Paul H. Smith, *Loyalists and Redcoats: A Study in British Revolutionary Policy* (Chapel Hill, NC: University of North Carolina Press, 1964).

40  Cornwallis to Clinton, Wynnesborough, South Carolina, 6 January 1781, NA CC PRO 11/30/72/75.

41  Cornwallis to Lord Rawdon, Ramsour's Mill, North Carolina, 25 January 1781, NA CC PRO 30/11/84/83.

42  Cornwallis to Leslie, Wynnsborough, South Carolina, 12 November 1780, NA CC PRO 30/11/82/32.

43  Rawdon to Clinton, Camp Between the Broad River and the Catawba, South Carolina, 29 October 1780, NA CC PRO 30/11/3/297.

44  Clinton, *American Rebellion,* 261.

45  Craig to Balfour, Wilmington, North Carolina, 4 February 1781, NA CC PRO 30/11/5/67; Cornwallis to Clinton, Wynnesborough, South Carolina, 6 January 1781, NA CC PRO 30/11/72/75.

46  Cornwallis to Clinton, Williamsburgh, Virginia, 30 June 1781, NA CC PRO 30/11/74/18.

47  Cornwallis to Clinton, Camp at Turkey Creek, Broad River, North Carolina, 18 January 1781, NA CC PRO 30/11/5/47.

48  Clinton to Cornwallis, New York, 13 December 1780, NA CC PRO 30/11/4/316.

49  Cornwallis to Germain, Guildford, North Carolina, 17 March 1781, NA CC PRO 30/11/5/281.

50  Stedman, *American War,* 2:326.

51  O'Hara to the Duke of Grafton, Wilmington, North Carolina, 20 April 1781, *Grafton Papers,* Suffolk Record Office, Acc. 423/191.

52  Lamb, *Journal,* 381.

# 9
# THE NORTH CAROLINA AND VIRGINIA INVASIONS

By most tactical considerations barring the logistics issue, Cornwallis held the advantage. He had created an essentially all-light infantry and battle-hardened veteran force capable of rapid movement even over the undeveloped Piedmont North Carolina backcountry. Despite the lack of infrastructure, a winter campaign meant that on many days British troops could rely on either frozen or at least hard-packed roads. Cornwallis counted on catching Greene well before travel became muddy and difficult. Rivers flowed south by southeast out of the Appalachians. Greene understood that the key to outrunning the aggressive Briton lay in rapid river crossing and denying the opponent the same opportunity. Accordingly, he ordered the construction of large *batteaus* suitable for river crossing and staged them along the probable route of retreat. To Greene's advantage, every mile north moved the Continentals closer to their supply sources in Virginia, while Cornwallis moved ever further away from his. As the combatants moved toward Virginia, four large rivers made for a challenging journey. All had potentially fordable shallows. However, the heavy winter rains meant that most areas now approached flood stage; until they crested, fording by men and horses proved difficult, deadly, and highly problematic. Speed, rapidity of movement, and maneuver became the guiding imperative for both forces in the "Race to the Dan" (Dan River in southern Virginia). In the critical arena of logistics, Greene far outperformed his British counterpart. By prepositioning supplies along the route of march, Greene enjoyed continuous supply. Cornwallis, conversely, did not. Greene retreated toward, not away from, reliable logistics support while for every mile travelled, the earl's force slogged deeper into the North Carolina winter wilderness (see Figure 9.1).

DOI: 10.4324/9781003041276-13

GEN. NATHANIEL GREENE.

**FIGURE 9.1** Major General Nathanael Greene

*Source:* Courtesy of the Anne S.K. Brown Military Collection, Brown University Library, Providence, Rhode Island

## Cowan's Ford

Departing Ramsour's Mill on 28 January, Cornwallis moved to cross the rain-swollen Catawba River at one of three passable fords. To impede the British advance at all potential fords, Greene posted North Carolina militia, orders that led to one of the campaign's more dramatic episodes. On 1 February, Cornwallis' main force broke camp and marched for the Catawba. He employed a deception. By making moves toward each possible ford, he forced the militia to spread the defense. The main body headed for Cowan's Ford as Lieutenant-Colonel Webster marched to Beattie's Ford and began an artillery barrage to play out the deception. Arriving at the ford, the earl realized that though the river was fordable by infantry and horse, it would be a dangerous undertaking. At 500 yards wide and rapidly moving, any man or animal that stumbled on the slippery stone bottom might be washed away. With the continuous pelting rain, he realized that the water, even then up to the average soldier's waist and chest, would soon make the crossings impassible. Cornwallis ordered the advance. No one was to fire until they reached the opposite bank. Soldiers held their cartridge boxes and muskets as high over their heads as possible or secured the leather boxes about their necks. Covering the ford with militia and some cavalry, Brigadier General William Davidson hoped to delay the crossing. Advancing four abreast, the soldiers struggled through the swift-moving, waist-deep, frigid water. As the lead elements reached midstream, random, unco-ordinated fire came from the opposite bank. Some casualties fell from the fire. Men slipped and fell as they stumbled over mossy rocks. The swift current swept men downstream, particularly the wounded. Horses lost their footing, dumping riders into the murky, dark, roaring water. Despite the current and enemy fire, the men pressed ahead and reached the bank in good order where they formed ranks and drove off the enemy militia.[1] With Davidson killed, the unsteady militia hastily retreated up the Salisbury Road with Tarleton in hot pursuit. Although casualties on both sides remained light, the Battle at Cowan's Ford gave a hint of the nature of the emerging campaign. The men's steadfastness in crossing a rapid-moving river under heavy fire maintaining disciplined unit cohesion with the general officers in the lead illustrated to all that the coming campaign would be hard fought, rapidly moving, and aggressive. It also indicated that geography would play a pivotal role in the outcome. With impassable roads and an exhausted force, Cornwallis knew that he had won only a temporary victory. The quarry lay miles away and out of reach.[2]

## Race to the Dan River

Cornwallis hoped to trap the Continentals between the Catawba and the Yadkin Rivers. Destroying more wagons, he drove his force forward, but weather and sheer exhaustion conspired to ruin the chances—that and Greene's careful advance battlefield preparations. Battling rain, darkness, and bad roads, Tarleton's troopers did not arrive at the Yadkin until about midnight, where they captured some abandoned wagons and drove off the militia. Patriot forces made the north bank in safety, leaving Tarleton and Cornwallis frustrated across the roaring Yadkin. With boats previously gathered at the river crossings, Greene's troops consistently crossed just ahead of the frustrated British. On more than one occasion, Crown advance forces arrived at riverbanks only to find Greene's rearguard already safely across. With no boats to be had and the enemy on the opposite shore, all the earl could do was fire a few artillery rounds with no effect. Logistics woes dogged the Crown advance, causing periodic stops to feed the men and horses and forage for whatever stores might be found.

For Greene, to the north lay the Dan River and safety. There were essentially two imperatives—speed and misdirection. He detached a small force to mislead Cornwallis into heading in the wrong direction. The ruse worked causing Cornwallis to march temporarily off in a wrong direction. Greene soon consolidated his entire force across the Dan just ahead of the pursuers. The Rhode Islander knew full well the movements and location of his opponent and while on the defensive, he lured Cornwallis further and further away from his logistical support while simultaneously building his own numerical strength of both regulars and local militia. Here was seen Greene at his strategic best, and, for the royal cause, Cornwallis at his worst in terms of bold risk-taking and aggressiveness without the necessary prudence. This failing would soon cost him.

British advance scouts reached the Dan River on 16 February and could only stare across the impassable river at the Patriots on the other side with all the available boats. Greene had reached the Old Dominion. The diversion force also reached safety just ahead of Tarleton: "All our troops are over and the stage is clear. . . . I am ready to receive you and give you a hearty welcome."[3] Tarleton complimented his foe: "Every measure of the Americans, during their march from the Catawba to Virginia, was judiciously designed and vigorously executed."[4]

In one of the most extraordinary occurrences in military history, the cold, exhausted, hungry men of the British and Continental Armies, many without proper shoes or boots, accomplished incredible feats. They had force-marched 230 miles in eight days, averaging 28 miles per day. Without boats to cross and faced with a trek upstream for a ford, Cornwallis reluctantly admitted that he had been bested. He wrote to Rawdon expressing his frustration: "I tried by a most rapid march to strike a blow either at Greene or Morgan before they got over the Dan but could not effect it." He turned toward Hillsborough 60 miles to the south.[5]

Within weeks, the Southern Campaign suffered more debilitating blows. The British tactical victory at Guilford Courthouse on 15 March, coupled with the loss of Pensacola to a Spanish force, dramatically altered the strategic situation in the Patriot's favor.[6] Ultimately, Greene knew that he had to defeat or somehow disable Cornwallis; to do so meant re-engaging in North Carolina. He sent a force back across the Dan to harass Cornwallis and suppress Loyalist activity. This crossing represented the opening phase of the British month of discontent, March 1781. With Cornwallis' departure, Greene now had the strategic initiative. Reinforced by ever-increasing North Carolina and Virginia militia, he marched back into The Old North State to bring the exhausted British force to battle, but on his terms. Greene expressed his optimistic attitude to North Carolina Governor Abner Nash: "The moment the enemy moves towards Hillsborough I shall fall into their rear."[7] Cornwallis' retirement to Hillsborough and Greene's crossing into North Carolina ultimately determined the course of the War of American Independence. Having driven Greene out of the Carolinas, Cornwallis had technically won the

Southern Campaign. On his departure for Hillsborough, he lost the War of American Independence.

Despite no significant Continental force in the Carolinas and Georgia, the specter of the proclamations and the disasters at Ramsour's Mill, King's Mountain, and Cowpens, all played their role. At Hillsborough, Cornwallis expected an outpouring of Loyalist support and recruits. They failed to show. In response to his proclamation inviting Loyalists to muster at Hillsborough under arms and with ten days' rations, few men came forward except in idle curiosity to see the army and then departed. O'Hara commented:

> I am certain that in our march of near a thousand miles, almost in as many directions, thro' every part of North Carolina, tho' every means possible was taken to persuade our friends as they are called and indeed as they call themselves to join us, we never had with us at any one time one hundred men in arms. Without the experiment had been made, it would have been impossible to conceive that government could in so important a matter have been so grossly deceived. Fatal infatuation![8]

The earl understood the strategic imperative to defeat Greene so as to rally the North Carolina Loyalists and tamp down Patriot support. Greene gave him the opening. Despite the woeful turnout of Loyalist support, he vowed to catch the elusive Rhode Islander. But, in late February, an event illustrated the frustration of reliance on the North Carolina Loyalists and likely eliminated any hope of raising substantial forces from the local population. Known variously as Pyle's Massacre or Pyle's Hacking Match, the incident illustrated the increasingly barbaric nature of the Southern Campaign. Henry ("Light Horse Harry") Lee's Legion struck a death blow to British hopes of a general Loyalist uprising in central Piedmont in devastating a large Loyalist force under Colonel John Pyle as it approached the British position near Hillsborough. Surprised and unprepared, the Loyalists mistook the green-coated Continental dragoons for Tarleton's green-coated British Legion; carnage ensued. Thus, as Cornwallis and Greene committed to battle at Guilford Courthouse on the Ides of March 1781, the earl did so without the hoped-for Loyalist contingent.

## "Another Such Victory"

Greene sought to keep in close contact with his adversary and marched toward Hillsborough. Despite his numerical superiority bolstered by Virginia and North Carolina militia, Greene never fully trusted the militia. He expressed this sentiment to Thomas Jefferson, Governor of Virginia: "[militia] soon get tired out with difficulties and go and come in such irregular Bodies that I can make no calculations on the strength of my army."[9] Despite his concern, he resolved to face the earl in a conventional battle. Accordingly, on 14 March, he positioned his force near Guilford Courthouse; he regarded the site as good defensible ground and awaited his nemesis' arrival. The terrain south of the courthouse undulated with pine trees and the occasional hardwood. In the field to the south, a split rail fence provided some cover for defending troops. More importantly, the corn fields, open and cleared, provided an excellent field of fire for the front-line militia. If Greene could replicate the militia's success at Cowpens, he gained a singular advantage. The long sloping ground allowed for militia in the front line to move off to the flanks and rear without interfering with the fire and movements of subsequent lines. Taking Morgan's example from Cowpens, Greene placed the least experienced militia in the first line astride the road roughly a half mile south of the courthouse. Unlike Morgan's deployment at Cowpens, Greene placed his three lines several hundred yards apart, thus they could not support each other. Additionally, the wooded terrain further isolated one from another. In essence, then, there were three separate engagements, all with different dynamics as the Crown force advanced. Some 300 yards to the rear of the first line, he positioned the Virginia militia. A further 500 yards back stood the Continentals in front of the courthouse.

The 15th broke with an early spring frost as Tarleton advanced up the road. Flanked on both sides by heavy woods, the gently rolling terrain provided excellent ground for cavalry and linear infantry formations. Cornwallis ordered a general advance toward the enemy's first line. At double quick time, bayonets leveled at "Charge Bayonet," the redcoats hurled themselves toward the North Carolinians. At nearly point-blank range, the militiamen fired off the first volley doing great devastation among the British ranks. A return volley plowed through the Patriot line. The second and third rebel volleys did even greater devastation, but the British regulars pressed forward. Panic ensued among the militia as men raced for the woods. Cornwallis had won the engagement of the first line, but with significant casualties. The Patriot second line soon crumbled, but with the same heavy British casualties. Faced with the loss of his first and second line and pressed by the still advancing British force against the steadfast Maryland and Delaware Continentals, Greene ordered a retreat. Cornwallis attempted a pursuit, but his men, marching and fighting since before dawn with no food or rest, could not answer the order. Greene collected his forces and stragglers and made his way out of danger, and out of British reach. Cornwallis' casualties were horrendous—25 percent.

By the tenets of eighteenth-century warfare, Cornwallis had won the laurels. The enemy retreated. He held the field. The Patriot total casualties of killed, wounded, and missing (mostly from local militiamen simply heading home rather than reporting for further duty) from a purely statistical viewpoint seemed devastating. While perhaps a tactical victory, from the strategic viewpoint, Guilford Courthouse represented yet another costly Crown victory. With nearly a quarter of his force killed or wounded, the earl had spent his power. He failed to destroy Greene as he had Gates at Camden. Many of his best troops lay dead or dying on that early spring Carolina evening. In London, when reports of the battle arrived in early June, the opposition leader Charles James Fox is reputed to have stated: "Another such victory will ruin the British Army."[10]

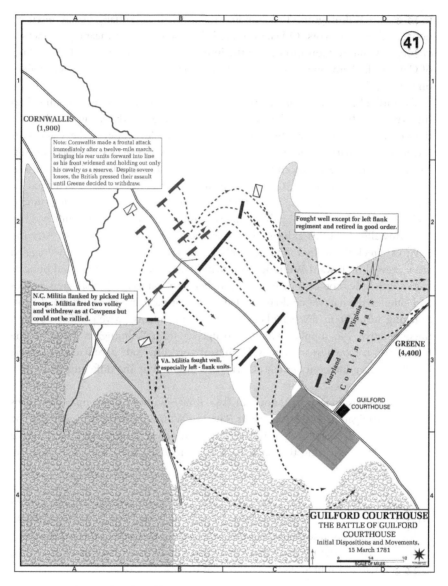

**MAP 9.1**   The Battle of Guilford Courthouse

*Source:* Map Courtesy of the United States Military Academy Department of History, West Point, New York

## "Sad and Fatal Effects"

Faced with the inability to destroy Greene, Cornwallis now confronted a sad choice. With the dead and dying all about him, with no rations and little chance for foraging to gather anything of value in the face of roving Patriot bands, and with no prospect of re-engaging the enemy, Cornwallis made his fateful decision to retreat to Wilmington. Two hundred miles across potentially hostile territory now faced the survivors. O'Hara captured the essence of the meaningless tactical victory at Guilford Courthouse and the inordinate British casualties. To the Duke of Grafton, he bemoaned the "sad and fatal effects" of the loss of British casualties on that day.[11]

Accordingly, on 18 March, leaving behind the most seriously wounded to the care of a British medical staff and Greene's surgeons, the army marched for the safety of the Scottish Highland settlements at Cross Creek, the Cape Fear River, and ultimately Wilmington in search of rations, relief, and reinforcement. Meanwhile, Greene advanced into South Carolina to confront Lord Rawdon and threaten Charleston to force Cornwallis to abandon North Carolina and defend his posts in the lower Carolina. The Rhode Islander pointed out to Washington that such a move "is warranted by the soundest reasons both political and military."[12]

Cornwallis drove his exhausted army across the Carolina Piedmont. Arriving at Cross Creek the army found little relief. Few joined the force. The bedraggled army pressed on toward Wilmington arriving a week later, exhausted and hungry. Faced with little food or time to forage, soldiers broke into local inhabitants' homes and plundered whatever could be hauled away, sparing neither Loyalist nor Patriot. Foraging brought in few supplies. The local inhabitants proved unfriendly and uncooperative. No supplies had arrived upriver from Wilmington owing to the Cape Fear's narrowness and rapids. High banks on either side gave Patriot harassers excellent cover and concealment. Cornwallis summed up the difficulties:

> Provisions were scarce, not four days' forage within twenty miles-and to us the navigation of the Cape Fear River to Wilmington impracticable, for the distance by water is upwards of a hundred miles, the breadth seldom above one hundred yards, the banks high, and the inhabitants on each side generally hostile.[13]

Arriving at Wilmington, Cornwallis attended to administrative matters such as arranging for prisoner exchanges while the army recovered its fighting strength and healed wounds. By mid-April, the growing dispute between Clinton and Cornwallis over where the main combat operations should occur became apparent. To Germain, Clinton hinted, however subtly, at the festering discord:

> I cannot agree to the Opinion given me by Lord Cornwallis . . . that the Chesapeak [sic] should become the Seat of War even if necessary at the expense of abandoning New York: as I must ever regard this post to be of the utmost Consequence.[14]

The earl's next move—the march into Virginia—broke open the simmering disagreement between the CinC and his field commander. By early summer, the differences over the next strategic moves created a rift that threatened not only the Southern Campaign's objectives but the entire British dominion of the North American colonies.

## "In Quest of Adventures"

Cornwallis faced a monumental decision. He had essentially three options. He could wait at Wilmington, restore his spent force to good health, and then evacuate by sea. He could travel overland. Wilmington is only a few days' march from Camden or Charleston. Once recovered, he could unite with Rawdon for operations against Greene and the South Carolina partisans. Alternately, he could travel by sea negating any confrontation with Greene. The third option lay in a march into Virginia and in combination with Crown forces already present, wreak destruction on that vital colony. If Virginia fell, the Crown would be in a position to negotiate a settlement with the remaining colonies. While he might have chaffed at abandoning North Carolina, he proposed:

> [A] serious attempt upon Virginia would be the most solid plan, because successfull [sic] operations might not only be attended with important consequences there but would tend to the security of South Carolina and ultimately the submission of North Carolina.[15]

Departing Wilmington on 25 April, he made Virginia the Seat of War. In so doing, the earl set in motion the last great act of the War of American Independence and unleashed the gremlin of profound strategic incoherence. In a moment of candor as he departed Wilmington, Cornwallis stated:

> [O]ur experience has shown that their [Loyalists] numbers are not so great as had been represented and that their friendship was only passive: For we have received little assistance from them since our arrival . . . and altho' I gave the strongest and most publick assurances that. . . . I should return to the upper Country [Piedmont and Hillsborough areas], not above two hundred have been prevailed upon to follow us either as Provincials or Militia.[16]

Cornwallis expressed his frustration to Major-General William Phillips, sent by Clinton into Virginia in anticipation of some operation aimed at the Chesapeake region:

> Now, my dear friend, what is our plan? Without one we cannot succeed. . . . If we mean an offensive war in America, we must abandon New York and bring our whole force into Virginia; we then have a state to fight for, and a successful battle may give us America. If our plan is defensive, mixed with desultory expeditions, let us quit the Carolinas . . . and stick to our salt pork at New York, sending now and then a detachment to steal tobacco.[17]

Cornwallis chided Clinton with:

> I am very anxious to receive your Excellency's commands, being as yet totally in the dark as to the intended operations of the summer. I cannot help expressing my wishes that the Chesapeak [sic] may become the Seat of War, even (if necessary) at the expense of abandoning New York. Until Virginia is in a manner subdued, our hold of the Carolinas must be difficult, if not precarious.[18]

On his own accord, Cornwallis two weeks later led his troops north and like it or not for Clinton, the subordinate made Virginia the Seat of War, an action that soon brought ruin to British North America.

While Cornwallis made for Wilmington, Greene marched to South Carolina with 2,600 men, almost two-thirds of them Continentals. His plan called for cooperation with local partisans. Correspondence went out to the major leaders. Close, coordinated operations characterized the war in South Carolina in 1781 and 1782. Greene lost a close engagement with Rawdon at Hobkirk's Hill near Camden on 25 April, but the engagement resulted in Rawdon evacuating the post, deeming the position unsustainable, and retreating to Charleston. Once again, Greene had lost the tactical field but forced the strategic advantage to his side. By late May, only Charleston, Augusta, Savannah, and Ninety Six remained in British hands. On 5 June, Augusta fell to a siege. Ninety Six held out for 27 days until a relieving force under Rawdon induced Greene to lift the siege. Nevertheless, Rawdon abandoned the fortress town as an untenable position; in losing a tactical engagement, Greene again won a stunning strategic victory. What should have been an overwhelming battlefield victory for Greene turned into a disappointment at Eutaw Springs on the Santee River on 8 September. A stout British defense and the loss of discipline among the troops in the looting of the overrun British camp forced Greene to withdraw. But the cumulative effect of these engagements in South Carolina and Georgia by the time of the Yorktown siege was the almost complete loss of all British control over the South with the exception of Savannah and Charleston.

The British dilemma burgeoned as the controversy over the advance into Virginia further poisoned relations between Cornwallis and Clinton. An exasperated earl declared: "I am tired of marching about the country in quest of adventures."[19] More specifically, Greene's successful Fabian Strategy undid the earl's North Carolina invasion and set him on the road to Virginia and disaster. On 25 April 1781, Cornwallis and the army turned north toward Tidewater Virginia, crossing the Roanoke River on 13 May. British major military operations moved to the Chesapeake, the final Seat of War. In abandoning North Carolina, Cornwallis, like another highly aggressive, bold, and risk-taking commander, Gaius Julius Caesar, two thousand years earlier, crossed his own Rubicon.

## A New Seat of War

With Cornwallis headed north, events elsewhere that soon shaped a new and independent nation coalesced. In March, Maryland finally ratified the Articles of Confederation, the first attempt at a national constitution. While the Articles struggled with issues of states' rights, taxation, and commerce regulation, they represented the recognition that the new nation required a national unity and foundational structure. Though the Articles eventually failed due to weak tax and commerce regulations, they nonetheless set the stage for the eventual US Constitution. Now, the allies required that final decisive, culminating battle, a key element of a Fabian Strategy to convince the stronger opponent to end the conflict. Cornwallis supplied the possibility of just such an event. But, in the background, Vergennes increasingly doubted Patriot resolve and more importantly, capability for victory. America had created a financial horror house for French royal finances, a monster that would growl loudly by 1789. The minister resolved that if the war was not won by years' end, France likely would negotiate and withdraw. Although he remained coy regarding actual French intentions, clearly Adams and the other representatives in Paris could "read the tea leaves." Militarily, Washington had to act soon and win that decisive culminating victory.

As Cornwallis entered Virginia, Clinton, in New York had his own command problems as Germain in March put pressure on him to mount offensive operations southward:

> I doubt not that you will avail yourself of his [Washington's] weakness, and your own great superiority, to send a considerable force to the head of the Chesapeak [sic]. . . , I flatter myself the southern provinces will be recovered to his Majesty's obedience before the long-promised succours . . . can arrive from France.[20]

Germain made the point even more forcefully in May:

> [I]t was a great mortification to me to find . . . your ideas of the importance of recovering that province [Virginia] to be so different from mine. . . . I am commanded by his Majesty to acquaint you that the recovery of the Southern Provinces and the prosecution, by pushing our Conquests from South to North, is to be considered the chief and principal Object for the Employment of all the Forces under your command.[21]

In a single stroke, Germain, normally given to broad platitudes and sweeping strategic conceptual thoughts, roiled the already shaky command relationships. In invoking the king's opinion, the Secretary implied that for Clinton, he had no choice but to prosecute the war in Virginia.

With the situation in constant flux, a more or less uncontrollable field commander, and faced with the threat of Washington and the French, Clinton, ever cautious, decided not to commit further forces to the southern effort despite pressure from Whitehall. Indeed, the senior commander hinted that he did not intend to move the Seat of War to the Chesapeake.[22] To Clinton, the Chesapeake meant establishing a presence that could control the narrow land space between the bay and mountains (the Delaware Neck) to interdict supplies and reinforcements flowing from the north and establish a safe haven for Loyalists from which to conduct operations against Patriot interests. Clearly, Clinton did not mean to move the main action from New York to Virginia, yet Cornwallis' taking the commander's intent to the ultimate interpretation of his operational prerogatives did exactly that. From Clinton's perspective, the operational execution called for a slow, methodical, and deliberate advance northward along the coast with naval support assured.

Strategic incohesion emanated from the top. The Cabinet debated for months as to who would replace Arbuthnot and on what reinforcements to send Clinton. Germain, loathe to issue definitive orders, shied away from such commands. Rather, he issued vague suggestions about the preferred strategy and resultant operations. Instead of either sending definitive orders or establishing broad strategic objectives, the role of the civil authority in a properly functioning civil-military relationship, he split the middle, never directly ordering Clinton to conduct specific operations or providing his commander with realistic, achievable strategic guidance. Decisions more properly determined at the field level were made in Whitehall and transmitted through vague messages. Indecisiveness reigned.

A critical step in Clinton's Chesapeake plan included sending forces into Virginia to conduct raids and establish an initial operating post on the Chesapeake, most likely at Portsmouth. In response, Washington detached Lafayette in late February with 1,200 Continentals. In early February, a small flotilla of French warships departed Newport for operations in Hampton Roads. Additionally, Washington and General Jean Baptiste de Donatien de Vimeur, the *compte* de Rochambeau, initiated consultations that led to the combined Franco-American operation against Cornwallis (see Figure 9.2). In response, Clinton dispatched 2,000 British troops under Phillips to the Chesapeake. His orders carried the germ of the coming disaster. In addition to supporting Cornwallis, he was to harass rebel positions, interdict supplies, and establish a defensible post on the Chesapeake from which ships-of-the-line could operate.

With the lack of faith in future positive results from strong offensive operations in Virginia, the CinC strongly suggested to Cornwallis:

> I beg leave to recommend it to you, as soon as you have finished your active operations you may now be engaged in, to take a defensive station in any healthy situation you chuse [sic] be it at Williamsburg or York Town.[23]

**FIGURE 9.2**  Washington and Rochambeau

*Source:* Courtesy of the Anne S.K. Brown Military Collection, Brown University Library, Providence, Rhode Island

Clearly, by early June, Clinton intended to withdraw into a defensive mode, react to enemy movements, and conduct harassment operations in the Chesapeake using the naval station as the operating base. He never directly ordered Cornwallis to fortify Yorktown specifically despite the earl's later claims. The CinC, did, however, direct the field commander to establish a suitable defensive post capable of supporting a Chesapeake naval station.

## Virginia Campaign

By early summer, Cornwallis now had his largest force of the campaign at 7,200 effectives against Lafayette with half as many. If the situation looked positive for Cornwallis in early June 1781, the perception was brittle. Already, the forces against him started in motion. Rochambeau sat at Newport with thousands of excellent, well-trained, and equipped French troops and had begun negotiations with Washington for a combined Allied offensive. In March, French Admiral Francois

Joseph Paul de Grasse, the *comte* de Grasse, departed Brest with 20 ships-of-the-line bound for the West Indies. Added to the Newport squadron, France had a numerical superiority over Royal Navy forces in North American waters. Whitehall responded meekly. Rear-Admiral Robert Digby, Arbuthnot's designated relief, departed Britain with only three ships-of-the-line. In June, Pennsylvania Continental Line troops under Wayne rendezvoused with Lafayette allowing the Frenchman to commence more active operations.

In May, Washington and Rochambeau met in Wethersfield, Connecticut to coordinate operations. Washington advocated a combined attack on New York, while the French argued for supporting Lafayette in Virginia. Rochambeau, under orders to allow Washington to determine the overall plan, demurred to the New York operation but did not inform Washington of de Grasse's intention to make for the Chesapeake. Upon learning that de Grasse had agreed to come north and operate at least until early November, Washington finally relented. He agreed to conduct the combined operation with the French squadron wherever it arrived in North America. With agreement in hand, Rochambeau secretly ordered the admiral to sail the squadron for the Chesapeake.

Germain advised Clinton that de Grasse had sailed from Brest earlier but could not say whether the squadron headed to the West Indies or Virginia. This uncertainty caused Clinton to recall troops from Cornwallis and to prepare for a defensive struggle.[24] Cornwallis, though disappointed and in disagreement, nevertheless prepared to strip his forces, but he would not retire without a fight. He lured the impetuous Wayne into a trap near Green Spring Farm on 6 July. Only the Pennsylvanian's courage in action and darkness saved the Continentals from destruction. Upon hearing of the engagement, Greene cautioned Wayne to "be a little careful and tread softly, for, depend upon it, you have a modern Hannibal to deal with in the person of Lord Cornwallis."[25]

Cornwallis received several letters in quick succession. The first, dated 29 May, informed the earl of Clinton's displeasure with the move into Virginia. The second and third letters, dated 8 and 12 June, instructed Cornwallis to send forces to reinforce New York and prepare for an assault on Philadelphia. Cornwallis complied with the orders and readied a force to move toward Pennsylvania. Then, on 20 July, he received the countermand order. Clinton once again altered the plan; he instructed Cornwallis to recall any troops still under his control and to fortify Old Point Comfort. Hastily debarking his forces, Cornwallis sent engineers to assess the designated locale, which proved unsuitable for supporting large warships; proper defensive works could not be constructed owing to the unsuitable soil conditions. A further order dated 11 July arrived in the midst of these movements ordering Cornwallis to establish a post on the York River.[26] The grand plan to overawe the South by British military might and secure the peace and allegiance through the rising of the majority Loyalist population had withered away in the heat of a southern summer.

Confused, defensive, desultory, and lacking in any sort of war-winning strategic vision, Britain's problem compounded itself repeatedly. In London, Germain, still expected the massive rising of Loyalists. In New York, Clinton waffled between a highly offensive conventional effort to destroy the enemy's war-making capability or a purely defensive enclave strategy that relied upon occupying key cities. In Clinton's defense, the shifting New York situation caused largely by the unknown French naval intentions confounded his decision-making. Meanwhile, Cornwallis viewed his superior as meandering and indecisive; he resolved to follow orders as best he could. Finally, Clinton chose the defensive, informing Cornwallis that: "until the season for recommencing operations in the Chesapeak [sic] shall return, your Lordship . . . must, I fear, be content with a strict defensive."[27] Slogging through the Tidewater Virginia countryside toward the hamlet on the York River, Cornwallis must have felt neutered, abandoned, and betrayed by his senior officer. On 2 August 1781, the earl tied himself irrevocably to the defense of Yorktown. In so doing, he lost any chance of conducting effective Chesapeake operations.

On 9 June, Rochambeau marched out of Newport toward New York. When word arrived that de Grasse had sailed for the Chesapeake, Washington made one of the most crucial decisions of his career:

> Matters having now come to a crisis and a decisive plan to be determined on, I was obliged, from the shortness of Count de Grasse's promised stay on this coast, the apparent disinclination of their Naval Officers to force the harbor of New York and the feeble compliance of the states to my requisition for men . . . to give up all idea of attacking New York; and instead to remove the French Troops and a detachment from the American Army . . . to Virginia.[28]

Eventually, Clinton recognized the enemy movement and reacted. Writing to Cornwallis on 2 September, he warned that:

> Mr Washington is moving an army to the southward with an appearance of haste; and gives out that he expects the cooperation of a considerable French armament. Your Lordship, however, may be assured that if this should be the case, I shall either endeavor to reinforce your command by all means within the compass of my power; or, make every possible diversion in your favor.[29]

## "A Measure of the Utmost Importance"

A prosperous town dealing in the tobacco trade, Yorktown had once been a principal port but by 1781 had been eclipsed by other locations. To fortify the site, Cornwallis erected a series of inner and outer works forming a crescent around the town and port area. Several creeks and ravines cut through the area between the two sets of works provided an additional defensive protection. As strong points to anchor the line, redoubts 9 and 10 dominated the British left. Light field pieces and 18-pounders drawn from the frigates anchored in the river moved into batteries to supplement the field artillery. Across the river at Gloucester Point, the defenders constructed a triangular palisade-style fort and a series of earthworks along the bluff. Suffering from the heat, meager rations of poor quality, brackish water, and periodic desertions, especially among the German units, the army pressed ahead with construction through the dog days of August. Much of the labor was performed by blacks, mainly former slaves who escaped to the British lines in search of the promised freedom. Unbeknownst to Cornwallis busy digging in, de Grasse sortied from Havana, Cuba on 2 August with 29 ships-of-the-line, four frigates, and over 3,000 troops bound for Chesapeake Bay.

The first week of September brought unkind news. Cornwallis received warning that Washington had departed from New York and would likely move toward Virginia.[30] In a curt and alarming letter, he informed Clinton of de Grasse's arrival in strength: "Comte de Grasse's fleet is within the Capes of the Chesapeak [sic]. Forty boats with troops went up the James River yesterday and four ships lie at the entrance of this river [York]."[31] The distant cannonade heard on 5 September gave evidence that the Royal Navy had arrived in force, but the return of the French to the Chesapeake several days later squashed any chance of immediate relief. Rarely has a Royal Navy force lost to either the French or Spanish, but in the running sea Battle of the Virginia Capes between 5 and 9 September, Rear-Admiral Thomas Graves did just that (see Figure 9.3). As the chase continued down the North Carolina Outer Banks, a French squadron carrying the siege guns and mortars from Newport slipped into the bay unchallenged and unmolested. The defeat of Graves' squadron not only doomed Cornwallis but made possible the conditions whereby the Franco-American allies forced his surrender in October, thus effectively ending the War of American Independence.[32]

**FIGURE 9.3** Battle of the Virginia Capes

*Source:* Courtesy of the Naval History and Heritage Command, Washington Navy Yard, Washington, DC

## "Mortification to Inform"

Finally realizing the deception that had anchored him to his New York post for days while the opponent marched and sailed south, Clinton resolved to rescue his field force. He informed Cornwallis: "As . . . I can have no doubt that Washington is moving with at least, 6,000 French & Rebel Troops against you, I think the best way to relieve you, is to join you . . . with all the Force that can be spared from [New York], which is about 4,000 men."[33] He advised Lord Germain:

> We are therefore no longer to compare Forces with the Enemy, but to endeavor to act in the best Manner we can against them. . . . With what I have, inadequate as it is, I will exert myself to the utmost to save Lord Cornwallis . . . [and would assure] his Lordship that I would either reinforce him by every possible means in my Power, or make the best diversion I could in his favor.[34]

While Cornwallis awaited the promised relief, Washington acted. He posted forces to impede any British escape attempt either up the York River or across to Gloucester Point. By 21 September, the Allied army arrived safely. On 27 September, Washington initiated the siege of Yorktown. The following day before dawn in the dry and still warm early Virginia autumn, the Allied army marched out of Williamsburg toward Yorktown with Continentals in the lead. By late afternoon, British pickets reported French troops on the Williamsburg Road and exchanged shots before retiring inside the breastworks. By evening, Allied forces took up their positions and began entrenching. Successively closer trenches and artillery batteries eventually forced the British to abandon the outer defensive works. As the Allied army fanned out into the encircling positions, for Cornwallis, the contradictory orders had changed his actions from an aggressive offensive to a passive enclave defensive and cost him the opportunity to defeat the enemy in detail.

In Yorktown, in a sign of the growing desperation, the lack of fodder caused the British to kill over 600 horses and dump their carcasses into the river. The horrible stench must have added to the dismal atmosphere inside the beleaguered garrison. In the first week of October, little fighting occurred as troops dug entrenchments, filled sandbags, built *gabions, fascines, abatis,* and stakes-material of a standard siege. On the night of 6 October, the Allies completed and opened the first parallel. Supported by a French diversionary attack and the lighting of large campfires, the men filled the *gabions* with dirt and sand. The British neither spotted nor heard the work and at dawn, the astonished defenders realized that the enemy had entrenched only a few hundred yards distant. By 9 October, with batteries finally in place, French artillery opened fire. One by one, the Allied barrage beat down the British works and, more critically, silenced British artillery.

Word of further delay in New York reached Cornwallis advising that the relief force could not sail until at least 12 October. Cornwallis realized the virtual

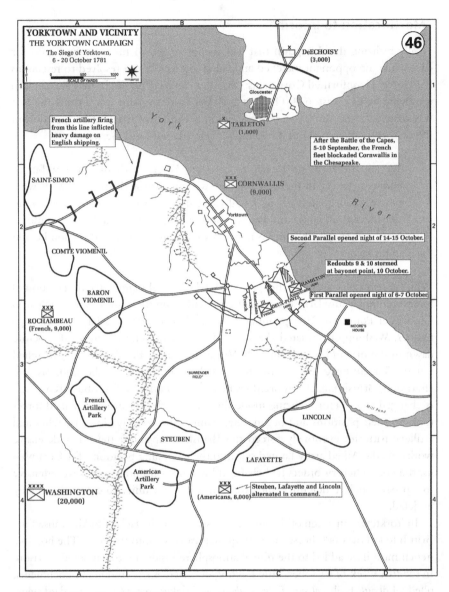

**MAP 9.2** The Siege of Yorktown

*Source:* Map Courtesy of the United States Military Academy Department of History, West Point, New York

hopelessness of the situation. Over 50 enemy guns lobbed rounds and hot shot into the town and defensive works. Cornwallis informed his commander thus: "[W]e cannot hope to make a very long resistance." In a poignant postscript appended later that afternoon, he added: "Since my last letter was written, we have lost 30 men."

Two hours later, he added: "Last night the enemy made their second parallel at the distance of 300 yards. We continue to lose men very fast."[35]

As days passed, the relief force sailing date moved ever farther out and only by 19 October made its way toward the Virginia Capes. By then, the garrison had capitulated. With the completion of the second parallel, redoubts 9 and 10 came into prominence. To advance further toward the town, the Allies had to neutralize these two fortified positions anchoring the British left. Accordingly, on the night of the 12 October, two storming parties took the two redoubts. Within hours, the Allies moved batteries into the captured redoubts; the second parallel now extended the entire length of the front. In a last gamble, Cornwallis attempted to escape through Gloucester, but a sudden squall blew up making any crossing impossible. On the morning of 17 October, Cornwallis and O'Hara assessed the grim situation. With only a single gun left firing and that with just a few rounds left, he called a council of war. With ammunition nearly exhausted and the dead and wounded increasing by the hour, the senior officers realized that all hope had drained away. They had fought a courageous fight and by the laws of war in such a hopeless situation, an honorable surrender was acceptable. All agreed. Cornwallis dictated a letter to Washington: "Sir, I propose a cessation of hostilities for twenty-four hours, and that two officers may be appointed by each side to meet at Mr Moore's house to settle terms for the surrender of the posts at York and Gloucester."[36] At ten in the morning, a lone drummer appeared on the parapet and beat the *en chamade*, a request to parley. A British officer waving a white handkerchief descended the works. Firing ceased as an American officer blindfolded the Briton and escorted him to Washington. The Virginian replied that a negotiation would be acceptable. During the night, the British destroyed as much hardware, arms, and ammunition as possible. The defenders either scuttled or burned the last remaining ships in the harbor and blew up the powder magazine. Early on 18 October, Washington delivered the terms, which included that all soldiers and sailors would be regarded as prisoners of war. The commissioners for each side met in the afternoon at the Moore house behind the allied lines. By midnight, they worked out all details for a formal surrender to occur on the afternoon of 19 October.

In accordance with the surrender terms, the Allies formed lines in a field down the Williamsburg Road from Yorktown. The roll of drums and shrill pitch of fifes and bagpipes was heard from the town as the British forces marched out of their breastworks. O'Hara led the column, carrying the earl's sword. Cornwallis, as had many in the army, had three separate bouts of malaria during the campaign and remained at his quarters with dysentery. Believing that the French general commanded the Allied forces, O'Hara attempted to surrender his sword to Rochambeau, who directed him to Washington, indicating that the Virginian commanded the allied army. Swinging his mount over to Washington, O'Hara again offered the sword, which Washington refused. O'Hara apologized for Cornwallis's absence. At this point, Washington indicated that his second-in-command, Benjamin Lincoln, would conduct the surrender. Of the British garrison, only 3,500 soldiers, marines, and sailors emerged from the town to "Ground Arms" that October afternoon, so devastating were illness and casualties. In acts of last defiance, angry veterans of the brutal struggle that had consumed them since the landing at Simmon's Island near Charleston with such high expectations months earlier expressed their passionate feelings. Continental Army Surgeon James Thacher captured the surrender event's somber mood, commenting in his *Journal*:

> At about twelve o'clock, the combined army was arranged and drawn up in two lines extending more than a mile in length. The French troops, in complete uniform, displayed a martial and noble appearance. . . . The Americans though not all in uniform nor their dress so neat, yet exhibited an erect and soldierly air, every countenance beamed with satisfaction and joy. The concourse of spectators from the country was prodigious, in point of numbers was probably equal to the military, but universal silence and order prevailed.[37]

## Notes

1 Cornwallis to Rawdon, Salisbury, North Carolina, 4 February 1781, NA CC PRO 30/11/85/1; O'Hara, *Grafton Papers,* Acc. 423/191.
2 For a complete description of the Crossing of the Catawba, see Carpenter, *Southern Gambit.*
3 Greene to Williams, Irwin's Ferry, Virginia, 14 February 1781, *Greene,* 1:287.
4 Banastre Tarleton, *A History of the Campaigns of 1780 and 1781 in the Southern Provinces of North America* (1787, Reprint, New York: Arno Press, 1968), 229.
5 Cornwallis to Rawdon, Hillsborough, North Carolina, 21 February 1781, NA CC PRO 30/11/85/9.
6 For detailed analysis of Florida's role in the War of American Independence: see Martha C. Searcy, *The Georgia-Florida Contest in the American Revolution, 1776–1778* (Tuscaloosa, AL: University of Alabama Press, 1985); Barton Starr, *Tories, Dons, and Rebels: The American Revolution in British West Florida* (Gainesville, FL: University of Florida Press, 1976); J. Leitch Wright, Jr., *Florida in the American Revolution* (Gainesville, FL: University of Florida Press, 1975).
7 Greene to Nash, Halifax County, Virginia, 17 February 1781, *Greene,* 1:302.
8 O'Hara, *Grafton Papers,* Acc. 423/191.
9 Greene to Jefferson, Near the High Rock Ford, North Carolina, 10 March 1781, *Greene,* 7:419.
10 Quoted in Franklin and Mary Wickwire, *Cornwallis: The American Adventure* (Boston, MA: Houghton Mifflin, 1970), 311.
11 O'Hara, *Grafton Papers,* Acc. 423/191.
12 Greene to Washington, Head Quarters at Col. Ramsay's on Deep River, North Carolina, 29 March 1781, *Greene,* 7:481.
13 Cornwallis to Germain, Wilmington, North Carolina, 18 April 1781, NA CC PRO 30/11/5/254.
14 Clinton to Germain, New York, 23 April 1781, NA CO5/102/42.
15 Cornwallis to Germain, Wilmington, North Carolina, 18 April 1781, NA CC PRO 30/11/5/270.
16 Ibid.
17 Cornwallis to Phillips, Wilmington, North Carolina, 10 April 1781, NA CC PRO 30/11/85/31.
18 Cornwallis to Clinton, Wilmington, North Carolina, 10 April 1781, NA CC PRO 30/11/5/209.

19  Cornwallis to Phillips, Wilmington, North Carolina, 10 April 1781, NA CC PRO 30/11/85/31.
20  Germain to Clinton, Whitehall, London, 7 March 1781, NA CO5/101/156.
21  Germain to Clinton, Whitehall, London, 2 May 1781, NA CO5/101/311.
22  Clinton to Cornwallis, New York, 13 April 1781, NA HQ PRO 30/55/29/3446; NA CC PRO 30/11/5/303.
23  Ibid.
24  Clinton to Germain, New York, 18 May 1781, NA CO5/102/109.
25  From "Life and Letters of General Anthony Wayne" By His Son (Philadelphia: Casket, 1829) quoted in Henry P. Johnston, *The Yorktown Campaign and the Surrender of Cornwallis, 1781* (New York: Harper & Brothers, 1881), 68.
26  Clinton to Cornwallis, New York, 11 July 1781, NA CC PRO 30/1/68/43.
27  Ibid.
28  George Washington diary entry for 14 July 1781, Sparks, *Writings of George Washington,* vol. VIII, 134.
29  Clinton to Cornwallis, New York, 2 September 1781, C-CC, 2:149–50; NA CO 5/103/124; NA CC PRO 30/11/68/77.
30  Ibid.
31  Cornwallis to Clinton, York Town, Virginia, 2 September 1781, NA CC PRO 30/11/74/82.
32  Details of the Battle of the Virginia Capes, 5–9 September 1781 will be provided in Part IV.
33  Clinton to Cornwallis, New York, 6 September 1781. NA/CC/PRO 30/11/68/81.
34  Clinton to Germain, New York, 7 September 1781, NA CO5/103/124.
35  Cornwallis to Clinton, York Town, Virginia, 11 October 1781, C-CC, 2:176–77; NA CC PRO 30/11/74/103.
36  Cornwallis to Washington, York in Virginia, 17 October 1781, C-CC, 2:189; NA CO5/103/275; NA CC PRO 30/11/74/118.
37  James Thacher, M.D. Late Surgeon of the American Army, *A Military Journal During the American Revolutionary War, from 1775 to 1783, Describing Interesting Events and Transactions of This Period with Numerous Historical Facts and Anecdotes* (Boston, MA: Richardson and Lloyd, 1823, reprint, Cranbury, NJ: The Scholar's Bookshelf, 2005), 346.

**PART IV**

# A Measure of the Utmost Importance

# 10

# SEA POWER AND THE AMERICAN WAR

Sea power played a crucial role in the North American theater, as well as in the wider global struggle. One of the most important facets of the War of American Independence was naval power in a conflict where the initial belligerents were separated by over 3,000 miles of ocean. Largely a maritime theater, it consisted of over 1,000 miles of coastline, protected bays and ports, inlets, rivers, and lakes. With the war's expansion in 1778 from a regional, colonial rebellion to a global war, conflict arose in the West Indies, Mediterranean, Indian Ocean, and the English Channel. From small canoes to ships-of-the-line, utilizing naval forces appropriately was essential for victory. Proper execution of naval power led to important operational victories and conversely, poor execution doomed otherwise successful ventures. Strategically, naval power helped dictate the ebb and flow of the war by radically altering priorities due to maritime threats.

## Mahan and Corbett

It is fitting to begin this analysis with the venerable father of naval theory, Rear Admiral Alfred Thayer Mahan, US Navy, who specifically addressed naval power in the American War in his most famous work: *The Influence of Seapower Upon History 1660–1783*.[1] Mahan spent six out of the 14 chapters examining the American War, almost exclusively interested in the maritime war between 1778 and 1783. Mahan's objective was to provide examples and instruction on the proper way to develop and utilize a navy. During war, this strategic dynamic meant concentrating the fleet and seeking out the enemy for decisive battle. Essentially, he argued that a state should win command of the sea through decisive battle between great battle fleets. Mahan's narrative was highly critical of the Royal Navy's performance, similarly harsh toward the French and Spanish navies, and largely dismissive of the rebellious colonies' contributions to the maritime domain. Mahan's argument is simple but

DOI: 10.4324/9781003041276-15

effective: in trying to defend their entire empire by spreading out their naval forces, the British almost lost everything. Certainly, the war in North America was lost due to British failures in concentration. The only reason the other European powers did not achieve more success was because they too committed naval strategic and operational sins.

While Mahan's naval theory is still actively debated and taught in the world's service colleges, his history of the war has not aged as gracefully as he might have hoped. When he published *The Influence of Seapower* in 1890, his intent was to convince the United States to become a strong sea power. Unsurprisingly because of this purpose, Mahan ascribes too much importance to the North American colonies from 1778 onward. The entirety of the British Empire was threatened once France and Spain entered into the conflict, yet Mahan assumed retention of the rebellious colonies was still the primary Crown objective. Furthermore, Mahan was mostly dismissive of American naval efforts and especially sour toward commerce raiding despite the privateers' deleterious effect on British commercial and public sentiment. Despite these flaws, Mahan is still a good origin point for analyzing the American War maritime dimension. He emphasizes how vital naval forces were for all the belligerents, especially the American rebels. They needed allied warships to isolate the British so that Washington could transition to the offensive. Furthermore, Mahan's global naval war description sets the stage for comprehending how the war fundamentally changed in 1778 (see Figure 10.1).

To understand the importance of navies and sea power, it is useful to first define the terms. As Sam Willis argues, navies are often conflated with formalized institutions but in this war, *ad hoc* navies were formed by almost all the colonies, and sea power exerted by the rebels before Congress created a formal Continental Navy. Furthermore, there were privateers-individual vessels invested in and kitted out to raid enemy commerce-wobbling back and forth between state-sponsored actors and pirates.[2] Broadening the definitional horizon of navy serves to give a more complete picture. Likewise, the term "sea power" or "command of the sea" needs refinement. Often, command of the sea delineates between saltwater and freshwater control (rivers, lakes, etc.), but that line is also blurred. Often it is interpreted in a Mahanian sense and imparts a binary aura; a belligerent either does or does not have command of the sea. There is some value in this simplicity when understanding the maritime domain. For example, the British lost command of the sea in North America, and therefore the Americans and the French were able to achieve a victory at Yorktown.

Yet, this definition of command of the sea is more limiting than helpful. A better conceptualization is found in the theories of Mahan's contemporary, Sir Julian Stafford Corbett.[3] He argued that unlike land, which can be controlled and held by whichever belligerent occupies it, water's natural state is in flux. It is always neutral and can only be held or "commanded" temporarily. Control by naval forces is, therefore, on a gradient and shifts back and forth during the course of a war. This definition best describes the American War, particularly in the North American theater. The amount and breadth of the waterways ensured that command of an

**FIGURE 10.1**   The "Wooden Wall," Royal Navy Officer Caricature

*Source:* Courtesy of the Anne S.K. Brown Military Collection, Brown University Library, Providence, Rhode Island

area was temporary at best, and more often in active contention. It also explains how difficult it was for the British to stop smuggling and privateering by the rebellious colonies, but at the same time use their naval forces, in conjunction with the army, fairly effectively during the early years of the conflict.

It is important to understand the strategic dilemmas facing both the American rebels and the British. Some problems were unique. For the rebellious colonies, was it wise to build a navy at all, and if so, what was the make-up and purpose of that force? The British already had an established, dominant navy, and its enemy did not even have a naval force at the start of the conflict. However, questions of mobilization, logistics, and strategic application plagued the Royal Navy. Uniting the strategic landscape of both sides was the French question: would they intervene, when, and in what capacity? By understanding these problems, the naval forces' early operations are placed in proper strategic context, as is the decision to intervene by the French.

During the Seven Years' War (1754–1763), the British Empire was severely tested on both land and sea. Early naval defeats and embarrassments, culminating in the execution of Admiral John Byng for his lack of aggression in the Mediterranean, potentially put the entire empire at risk. However, these failures eventually gave way to success. Perhaps the most important victory was off the coast of France at the Battle of Quiberon Bay (1759). British Admiral Edward Hawke risked gale-force winds in unfamiliar waters to chase down a French fleet. His victory, combined with similar success against the French at the Battle of Lagos (Portugal), ensured the Home Islands remained safe.[4] From a naval perspective, the war went exceptionally well for the British, and incredibly poorly for its enemies.

Shipbuilding and shipping ramped up during the conflict. The fleet blossomed from 80 ships-of-the-line in 1754 to 120 by 1763, an incredibly large force designed to protect the empire from the combined French and Spanish fleets. It also protected the empire's seaborne shipping, of over 8,000 commercial vessels.[5] However, the fleet size was in no way sustainable during peacetime. Maintaining the navy at wartime levels was an impossible task, both fiscally and materially. The fiscal tools and acumen of the British state ensured that the debt incurred was not going to ruin the country, but the fleet still needed to be reduced significantly.

Many ships built or repaired during the war were constructed with green instead of seasoned wood for expediency. This practice ensured rapid deterioration, leading to disparities between ships available and ships operationally capable. The overall navy budget shrank precipitously during the 1760s. In 1762, the Royal Navy budget stood at £7,000,000 but by 1769 shrank to just £1,500,000. Materials needed to sustain ships and the manpower to crew them were always in need, but after most of the North American colonies rebelled in 1775, Britain lost access to a key producer of both.[6] Perhaps as many as a quarter of the seamen in the fleet in 1775 were American colonists. It was understandable why the naval reductions occurred; wartime mobilizations are not the same as peacetime fleets. Nonetheless, this reduction held significant consequences for the war. Perhaps no one understood this dynamic better than the First Lord of the Admiralty, John Montagu, 4th Earl of Sandwich (1718–1792).

Sandwich, First Lord of the Admiralty in 1771, inherited a whole host of problems. Fortunately, he was familiar with the situation being the third time he had served as First Lord. His government service career went back almost 30 years. Sandwich understood the complexities of maintaining the fleet and undertook a series of reforms. An advocate for maintaining a large fleet in a state of permanent readiness, he understood the difficulty of mobilizing a navy on short notice.[7] Quick mobilization meant reliance on new wood and rushed construction, which hurt the longevity of ships and led to increased costs for fleet repair. Sandwich's solution to this systemic problem was to build more ships during peacetime, slower, and with seasoned wood. He diversified timber acquisition with the ultimate goal of having three years' worth of seasoned timber in reserve. Finally, Sandwich sought to reform labor practices and productivity in the royal dockyards. He pushed to change worker pay from a "days worked" to "tasks completed" system to increase production.[8] Combined, these reforms represented a significant increase in peacetime expenditures, but they theoretically ensured a long-term fleet, and therefore British security.

The First Lord often found himself in conflict with other cabinet members, both before and during the war.[9] When he pushed to increase the size of the fleet, the king's chief minister, Lord Frederick North, advocated reducing the fleet even further. Few in government wanted to spend the money on the navy during peacetime. When the colonies rebelled in 1775, Sandwich requested permission to fully mobilize the fleet. The cabinet disagreed, arguing that suppressing the colonial dissidents was possible without expanding the navy. There was also a diplomatic argument against mobilization—the risk of goading France into war if Britain expanded the navy.[10] Consequently, when the North American colonies revolted, Sandwich's vision for the fleet was not yet in place. Some things were ready, like the seasoned timber and other expanded naval stores. But without the order to fully mobilize the fleet, the Admiralty could only do so much; full mobilization did not occur until August 1777. With his hope for careful, slow ship construction, he looked beyond the royal facilities and contracted out to private shipyards at extra expense. The new task system of labor was not universally accepted, and crucially, dockyard workers at both Portsmouth and Plymouth protested via strike in 1775.[11]

Full mobilization mattered the most if France and Spain entered the war. If the British suppressed the rebellion quickly, foreign intervention was less likely. The North American theater proved very different from the previous French and Indian War. The army, bolstered by hired German auxiliaries, now fought against rather than with the colonies against an outside enemy. This dynamic meant access to local fodder, food, and other supplies was limited at best, and at worst, the local population was actively hostile. Supplies that could not be locally foraged needed to be shipped from elsewhere, usually the Home Islands, a 3,000-mile trip across the Atlantic. Transporting supplies was not an unfamiliar logistical challenge, but the scope and scale were unprecedented.

A large share of this burden fell upon the Admiralty via the Navy and Victualling Boards. Transporting troops, armaments, camp supplies, and so forth all fell under the navy's purview. In addition to ensuring their own ships were properly manned and furnished, the navy also had to hire out substantial numbers of seaworthy transports, crews, and agents. When the rebels officially declared independence in July 1776, the Navy and Victualling Boards had already sent over 146,000 tons of transports. To contrast, the maximum shipped by the same two Boards during the Seven Years' War was 100,000 tons.[12] However, the logistics system was not fully centralized. Both the Treasury and Ordnance Board contracted out and sent their own transports to North America. Crucial to the war effort, the Treasury was tasked with supplying the army provisions. They operated outside of naval jurisdiction with minimal interaction unless they requested an escort. In part, this dynamic resulted because the Admiralty initially refused to provision the Army.[13] It was also due to the friction between Sandwich and Germain.

Strategic incoherence plagued British leaders, affecting their ability to recognize the true nature of the war and craft successful strategies. An example of inter-personal friction contributing to the incoherence was the animosity between Sandwich and Germain. It was not just that they disliked each other, though that was certainly true, but Germain's actions at times directly hindered the navy. For example, Germain purposely outbid the navy on supplies that then went to the army. Naval troop transports sailed via convoy, but the contracted shipping company that Ordnance and Treasury used chose to sail unescorted at greater risk for privateers. Lord North as the king's chief minister, ideally the person to mediate and direct the two other ministers, failed as a wartime leader in bringing together all the war-making entities into a cohesive union. The transport system was only centralized in 1779 when Treasury successfully negotiated a deal with Admiralty to assume provisioning the Army over Germain's objections.[14]

The Admiralty had responsibility for more than just hiring transports and providing warships to ferry troops and supplies. Warships were also required to conduct joint operations with the army, blockade the North American coast, and protect British commerce from privateers. Often, these goals were unrealistic; it was hard enough to blockade a single port like Boston, let alone interdict all contraband traffic up and down the American coast. Use of transports and warships jointly with the army proved effective during the early years of the war, but that prevented ships from being tasked to blockade or protecting commerce.

The Royal Navy had on the lists 199 major warships in 1775, which on paper seemed impressive.[15] However, those lists included ships being refit, obsolete, held in ordinary (reserve), being built, or in need of major repair. Warships ready to crew and send to sea were never near the total on the lists.[16] Furthermore, seaworthy ships were spread out across the empire and not necessarily available for service elsewhere. For example, out of fear that the French would take advantage of a weakened home fleet, Sandwich refused to release any ships-of-the-line for duty in North America during the first two years of the war. Realistically, early on, the Royal Navy lacked sufficient ships to accomplish all their strategic or operational goals. Though the British were in a relatively weaker position during the first few years of the war, the balance of maritime power overwhelmingly favored the Royal Navy. A significant gulf existed in both numbers and quality of British sea power and that of the American rebels, who needed to build a navy from scratch.

## American Naval Forces

Patriot sea power fought a biblical David and Goliath struggle but with no chance for David to win a decisive victory or attain local control of the seas. Still, in a Corbettian sense, the Patriot naval effort still influenced the command of the sea and sea lines of communication (SLOCs) dynamics accomplished through a wide variety of vessels and approaches. Small, *ad hoc* naval vessels made up the bulk of rebel sea power, especially early on. New England Patriots used whaleboats to conduct small-scale raids and attacks on British targets. Double-ended, oar powered, and easy to maneuver, this style of boat was used in North American warfare since the late seventeenth century. A different type of small boat, the *bateaux*, found its origins in the northern fur trade. *Bateaux* were heavily utilized as transport during the failed rebel invasion of Canada in 1776. Ultimately, no matter what the style, if it floated, the rebels utilized it to move men and material along the coastline, inlets, rivers, and lakes.[17]

Small boats were useful for logistics and attacks on weak or unaware British targets, but they could not strike out against large warships or British commerce. To accomplish that, a traditional navy, or at least a fleet of privateers, was needed. Like most facets of the war, initially there was little consensus on what a naval component looked like. A July 1775 order from the Continental Congress instructed each colony to defend its own waterways and coastline as it saw fit. Many took to the order with relish, steering their shipbuilding capability to create their own navies. Fireships, blocking vessels, floating batteries, and armed sloops made up the bulk of the forces. Some colonies built larger and more complex ships to defend ports and river entrances: Pennsylvania and Virginia built war galleys with one or two cannons at the bow. A type of warship more familiar to the sixteenth-century Mediterranean than North America in 1775, these galleys showed the resolve to find a stopgap to the naval imbalance.

It was each colony's navy for itself; initially with no central direction to guide policy. The fleet make-ups were also defensive in nature. They could try and stop the British from completely dominating the coastline but not much else. To achieve a loftier objective such as attacking commerce or taking on a larger vessel, the rebels needed a centralized naval administration. Congress needed to act, but significant political and economic factors interfered. Creating a centrally controlled navy meant moving further toward full separation from Britain, a significant step. Moreover, navies were incredibly expensive to build and maintain. For a fledgling pseudo-government with limited access to specie and no real ability to levy taxes or raise revenue for ship construction and maintenance, it was a daunting prospect.

Despite these considerable challenges, many rebel leaders understood the strategic value, even necessity, of a centralized naval force. Essential to the establishment of what ultimately become the Continental Navy were key members of the Second Continental Congress and George Washington. Both parties were acutely aware of the rebellion's precarious position without any maritime force. Pressing the individual colonies to pursue naval defense could only go so far. Framing the debate were two objectives: achieving the capability to strike at British naval power in some way, and arguably more importantly, opening American ports to all foreign trade. There was considerable anxiety toward these ideas, and naturally there were several Congressional representatives who resisted creating a navy. If the colonies were to do such a thing, it would further hurt any chance of reconciliation.

Furthermore, how could the colonies ever hope to resist Royal Navy dominance? Countering the negativity were the proponents of naval power led by the representatives of Rhode Island. Concerned by the vulnerability of coastal populations and towns, they proposed to build and equip a fleet as fast as possible. This vague, expensive, and politically hazardous "Rhode Island proposal" met with considerable resistance and was tabled multiple times in 1775.[18] However, Rhode Island and other proponents of a Continental Navy were aided by two important catalysts in the latter half of 1775.

The first such event was in early October when information reached Congress about two unescorted and unarmed resupply brigs en-route from England to Quebec. A committee was soon formed to decide the best way to capture the ships and their cargoes. The three committeemen—John Adams, Silas Dean, and John Langdon, all New Englanders and avid supporters of a Continental Navy—initially suggested asking individual colonies to "loan" ships for the mission at Congress' direction and expense. They then proposed a new plan: purchase and outfit two ships under complete Congressional control.[19] It represented a true possibility for a new navy, a movement given even more momentum in mid-October when Congress received surprising news from Massachusetts; Congress already was paying for naval vessels and had been doing so since August 1775.

Washington in Massachusetts had leeway to act as he saw fit; his commission allowed him "full power and authority to act as you shall think for the good and Welfare of the service."[20] Though the order was broad, he stretched the limits of his charge when he officially commissioned naval vessels. During his tenure in New England, he came into contact with Colonel John Glover, commander of the 21st Massachusetts Regiment. Glover owned a small fleet of trading and fishing vessels; Washington came to him about outfitting one as an armed cruiser. Glover had just such a boat: a Marblehead schooner named *Hannah*. In August, he entered into a contract with Washington to arm *Hannah* and enter into Continental service. They did not realize it yet, but Congress now had the beginnings of a navy. Washington purposefully did not mention that fact in his correspondence. It was possible that he thought commissioning a ship into service of the Continental Congress surpassed his authority. It is also possible that he wanted the endeavor to bring results before informing Congress. He recognized that the action was not just a tactical or operational change. Leasing the *Hannah* was a strategic shift, one that came with economic and diplomatic consequences. Congress did not learn about Washington's naval endeavors until October when they received his letter informing them about the *Hannah*, and two other vessels subsequently contracted. Ultimately, Washington hired eight ships in similar fashion. His letter was read to the governing body while they were in the midst of debating Adams, Deane, and Langdon's proposals. His actions altered the discussion. Those Congressional members who outright opposed the creation of a navy were stuck; the issue was a *fait accompli*. Now it was time to decide how large and expensive a navy the American rebels were willing to fund.[21]

The Naval Committee presented to Congress a plan to convert existing merchant ships to wartime use. They proposed ten ships of varying sizes, all outfitted for a little over $166,000, an ambitious goal. However, Congress knew that naval funding primarily relied on the largess of individual colonies. Approval was given to acquire four ships, and $100,000 appropriated for outfitting. The Naval Committee was expanded and given oversight of the project.[22] Two months later, the Rhode Island proposal once again came up for debate. Not shunted aside as before, there was much support for naval expansion. Unlike *ad hoc* and often suboptimal merchant ship conversions, these were intended to be state-of-the-art frigates, warships capable of standing up to their Royal Navy equivalent. Over $750,000 in funds were appropriated to build, equip, and man the ships. Their construction was to be spread out among seven colonies. Congress created an administrative wing dubbed the Marine Committee to manage the Gordian knot of logistics, supply, and manning.

In December 1775, the Continental Navy finally existed on paper with a fair amount of enthusiasm for what the rebellious colonies could accomplish. As often happens with naval building programs, a significant gulf between perceptions and reality remained. Sometimes funding fell through, and planned ships never constructed. Those that did make it past the planning phase were expensive to outfit. During the war, 47 ships ultimately served in the Continental Navy. Crew numbers varied from year to year with 1777 the largest at approximately 4,000 sailors, a fraction when compared to the Continental Army.[23]

## Letters of Marque and Reprisal

The Continental Navy experienced some success but never large enough to seriously challenge the Royal Navy. Not until the rebellion entered into an alliance with France was there potential for naval parity in North America. Yet there was a third homegrown aspect of Patriot sea power capable of harassing the British naval presence: privateers. Privateering was by far the largest and most volatile component of rebel sea power, and undoubtedly its most successful facet. Privateer vessels were privately funded and owned commerce raiders. Crews signed on to converted merchant ships hoping to take prizes. Investors risked funds to outfit, equip, and hire crews in hopes of a substantial return. A privateer's ideal objective was a fully laden British unescorted merchant vessel. Most privateers were fast and agile but lightly armed. If they encountered even the smallest warship (such as a brig, sloop, or schooner), the odds were not in their favor. Still, the tantalizing convergence of rebellious, patriotic zeal, and prize money drew many moths to the flame. It created competition with the Continental Navy. A privateer crew split the proceeds (according to shares) among the captain, crew, and investors. A Continental Navy ship only kept one-third the profit (one-half if it was a warship); the rest went to paying the considerable expenses of maintaining the navy.[24]

Balancing the potential for fame and fortune was the fact that only a piece of paper prevented them from being considered (patriotic) pirates. Privateers were issued Letters of Marque and Reprisal, documents that stated the holder could legally seize the vessels and cargo of a specified enemy nation. These commissions were issued both by the individual colonies and by Congress, neither of which were internationally recognized as legitimate. Depending on the port of call or the capturing ship, a privateer crew could be treated as pirates. The British position held that they were committing both piracy and treason, but they were not alone in their condemnation. French, Spanish, and Dutch officials at one time or another arrested American privateers on charges of piracy. The danger from non-British enforcement waned post-1778, but a privateer's legitimacy was never fully assured.[25]

Privateering proved very hard for the British to counter. That it vexed them should not be surprising; the English themselves used privateers to great effect in the sixteenth and seventeenth centuries, especially against Spain before they became a dominant naval power. It was the oceanic counterpart to the guerilla warfare waged in the Southern Campaign; the British simply did not have enough warships to counter the privateers. British merchant ships and even military supply ships were often unescorted, especially early in the war. Later, the Royal Navy was too concerned with the combined French and Spanish fleets to devote much attention to the problem. The attack on commerce riled both British merchants and the general public to the point where it affected their will to continue the war against the colonies, especially following the Yorktown surrender.

The development of American naval power was in many ways extraordinary. For over a century and a half, the colonies were regulated by the British mercantilist system and protected by the Royal Navy. In just a few short years, they built their own naval force and a large fleet of privateers, albeit motivated by varying levels of profit and patriotism. Moreover, it was important at tactical, operational, and strategic levels. Both the Continental Navy and the privateer fleet contributed to the rebellion's legitimacy. Building a navy represented a significant step toward independence over half a year before the official declaration of July 1776. Issuing Letters of Marque to privateers was even one step further along the spectrum to independence. With those commissions, state actors (colonies or Congress) declared not only were they legitimate, but they had the power to approve non-state violence against their enemies.

The influence and effectiveness of American sea power should not be overstated. From a tactical and operational level, American naval power was a mixed bag. The Royal Navy was simply too large, established, and competent to be toppled by a fledgling competitor, at least not without foreign help. Britain sought ways to use the Royal Navy to end the insurrection before that help arrived. Similarly, the American rebels used their new naval power to gain legitimacy and hold out in hopes of foreign recognition and aid. The possibility of France entering into the war defined the early years of the naval conflict.

## The Neutrality of Water

The North American theater, particularly the inland waterways, was too large, and British naval forces too spread out to ever assert full control. Nonetheless, even temporary command of the sea or waterways imparted important operational and strategic results and had important consequences for the war during the early years. Temporary control was particularly important for transport and logistics. The ability to use waterways to move troops and supplies represented a vital aspect in the early fighting. For the Patriots, amphibious operations proved essential to survival. Perhaps the most mythologized operation was Washington's famous crossings of the Delaware River in December 1776. These amphibious operations enabled attacks on British/Hessian forces in Trenton and later Princeton, New Jersey, delivering much-needed tactical victories to a beaten and downtrodden Continental Army. However, there was an even more important crossing that occurred earlier in the year, one that if not successful, likely meant the end of the Continental Army.

In late August 1776, Washington's forces found themselves pinned down in Brooklyn, the East River on one side and a numerically and qualitatively superior British force on the other. It was a terrible situation and one that could have been catastrophic if not for the fact that the British naval forces did not have full command of the sea. Though present and dominant, the Royal Navy could not achieve full sea control because of American coastal batteries, galleys, and often poor winds. This factor gave Washington an opportunity to execute an escape by an amphibious withdrawal to Manhattan via the East River. Colonel Glover commanded the operation. Utilizing as many flat-bottomed boats and small transports as they could find, the Continental forces ferried troops across the river in the early evening of 29 August. Despite the operation lasting until sunrise the next day, the evacuation remained undetected by the British.[26] Nighttime, poor winds, employment of intelligence, and early morning fog all contributed to the British failure to stop the rebels, but it was the American ability to carve out temporary command of the sea that framed the operation.

American amphibious operations also experienced significant failure to balance out their moments of success. Perhaps the most ruinous occurred during the attempted 1775 Canadian invasion. The primary military objective was to seize Quebec City, essentially hoping to repeat the success the British found against the French during the Seven Years' War. To accomplish this goal, two avenues of approach were attempted. The goal was to transit Lake Champlain, take Montreal, and then move eastward to Quebec City. A secondary group, led by Benedict Arnold, intended to use the Kennebec, Chaudière, and St. Lawrence Rivers to ferry troops and supplies for a Quebec City siege. Both groups needed naval power for transport and to neutralize British maritime power. Consisting primarily of two very lightly armed transports (capable of holding 250 men each), a schooner, and a sloop, this small flotilla faced a hostile fort at St. Johns, a heavily armed schooner, and the garrison at Montreal. Still, it was enough to progress, slowly and painfully, north.[27]

Arnold's expedition faced different challenges getting to Quebec City. His roughly 1,100 men would not face any serious British resistance until they reached the city, but to get there, they traversed dangerous rivers and untamed wilderness. For that effort, Arnold built two hundred *bateaux* as transports.[28] Constructed hastily out of green wood, these boats leaked and fell apart almost immediately becoming a weak link in an already treacherous journey. The more *bateaux* lost, the more men had to walk along flooded, overgrown shoreline. Rough waters and rapids caused some boats to overturn, losing the expedition's food, ammunition, and powder. Not risking the vessels on the rapids and over low water meant all needed to portage the sodden, shoddy *bateaux*, which further dampened morale. Men first died of disease, then as supplies ran low, hunger and exposure set in creating an altogether miserable experience.[29] The expedition force lost hundreds of men to death and desertion, and the 600 who remained were demoralized and emaciated. The assault on Quebec City failed. Montgomery lost his life in the process, and Arnold faced a British counterattack down Lake Champlain. The attempt to forcefully bring Canada into the rebellious fold failed, in large part because of sub-par amphibious operations.

When it came to directly contesting British naval power, Patriot forces were generally outmatched with few exceptions. Whaleboat raids on unsuspecting or lightly defended British vessels found some success, especially along the New England and Long Island coasts. The British, not fully mobilized, did not have nearly enough warships to defend everywhere. Still, the Continental Navy envisioned by Congress largely foundered in the face of British naval power.

When those early warships budgeted for, built, and outfitted by Congress came to fruition, their performance often lacked. The first frigate to launch, the *Randolph*, lost both masts (rotten wood) early in its maiden voyage. Other ships were scuttled in the face of oncoming British forces or trapped in harbor by blockade. The *Trumble* was too big for the river where it was built and drew too much water to actually make it out to sea. Even when the warships successfully operated such as the frigates *Hancock* and *Boston*, their success was fleeting. In 1777 they put out to sea when the majority of Royal Navy forces were supporting the attack on Philadelphia. They temporarily seized control of New England waters and captured a British frigate. However, once Royal Navy leaders realized the attacks, they assigned a squadron to nullify the threat and successfully retook the captured ship.[30]

Patriots fared a bit better when on the defensive, but even then, it served to delay, rather than stop, the British naval threat. Arnold's Lake Champlain defense represented one such incident. Following the failed invasion into Canada, the Patriots worried (rightfully so) about a possible counterattack via Lake Champlain. They built a small fleet of warships, mostly galleys, to defend against the British. On 6 October 1776, at the Battle of Valcour Island, the British decisively defeated the Patriots causing Arnold to retreat back to Fort Ticonderoga.[31] The next year the

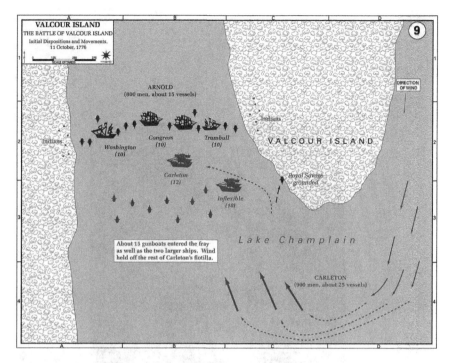

**MAP 10.1**   Battle of Valcour Island

*Source:* Map Courtesy of the United States Military Academy Department of History, West Point, New York

Patriots utilized galleys, converted warships, and coastal fortifications to slow down the Royal Navy's advance in Pennsylvania. It was a spirited defense; the HMS *Augusta*, a third-rate ship of the line, exploded and sank while under fire, though the cause was disputed.[32] But like at Lake Champlain the previous year, ultimately the American defense crumbled in the face of the Royal Navy. Philadelphia fell and British sea lines of communication were secured via the Delaware River.

The most successful aspect of American naval power was its *guerre de course* against British shipping. Though there were Continental Navy participants (most notably John Paul Jones' *Ranger* and *Bonhomme Richard*), many participants were privateers, risking death for the promise of substantial rewards. The attack on British shipping began early on in the war but continued to ramp up and become more effective as the years continued. Rebel naval power was at its most successful when they utilized temporary command of the sea to protract the war out and survive to fight another day. When they undertook offensive operations, the results were routinely disappointing. The American rebels were quite fortunate that the British never converted their naval advantages for decisive effect during the early years of the war (see Figure 10.2).

**FIGURE 10.2**   John Paul Jones, Father of the United States Navy

*Source:* Courtesy of the Anne S.K. Brown Military Collection, Brown University Library, Providence, Rhode Island

## British Operations

Similar to the Americans, the first years of the conflict brought mixed results for British amphibious and naval operations. Even more so than the rebels, the British took advantage of the temporary command of the sea to transport forces around the theater. While not without flaws, the larger, professional navy used its experience in joint operations to good effect. However, outside of transport, matters were more difficult. The ability to translate naval strength was hindered by a number of factors: the overall number of ships available, the tension between operating a 3,000-mile sea line of communication while also devoting enough attention to in-theater operations, and finally the inability to convert skill and experience into a winning strategy.

The British Army had occupied Boston, Massachusetts, since May 1774, a result of the Boston Tea Party and subsequent implementation of the Intolerable Acts. It became a hub of military activity in 1775, as both the perceived center of the rebellion and a base from which the Royal Navy operated along the New England coast. But the British had neither enough troops nor ships to fully accomplish their goals. Armed whaling ships attacked and harassed supply vessels. Warships could not strike at the small coastal harbors they operated from because of coastal fortifications. Ideally, army troops could be used in coordination with the Royal Navy to jointly assault these areas, but there were not enough troops in the theater. There were brief instances where the British demonstrated the potential consequences of a powerful naval force, including the attack on the small coastal village of Falmouth, Massachusetts (now Portland, Maine). Part of a reprisal operation for the capture of an armed schooner, Royal Navy forces spent eight hours bombarding the town. It sent a shockwave through the rebel leadership and emphasized the coastal vulnerability to British sea power.[33] However, these attacks were the exception rather than the rule. Generally speaking, the British were unprepared for the level of resistance they faced in New England, and they eventually transitioned the campaign to New York.

Before that campaign occurred, the British needed to extricate themselves from Boston. Washington's occupation of the Dorchester Heights in early March 1776 gave Continental forces the ability to shell both the city and Boston harbor. Complicating the dilemma, due to the elevation of Dorchester Heights, warships could not elevate guns high enough for counter-battery return fire. The new British commander, William Howe, had two choices: attack the Continentals and retake the Heights or extract his troops with as little bloodshed as possible. Howe chose the latter option and negotiated a peaceful removal of British forces by threatening to destroy Boston via naval bombardment.[34] The forced evacuation of Boston illustrated how British naval power was effective enough to avoid disaster but not able to achieve victory.

Once in New York, British naval fortunes somewhat improved due to an increase in available ships and troops but also due to the arrival of Vice-Admiral Howe. An exceptional and experienced commander, he understood what would be required of the Royal Navy to fight in North America. What he could not do was solve the problem of being in multiple places at once. The operational concept as envisioned by the Howe brothers involved swift army operations supported by the navy and a strong blockade of the North American coast. Howe barely had enough ships to accomplish the first goal and never enough to achieve the second. A complete blockade was not possible. Even if the entirety of the Royal Navy was set to the task, the area of operations was simply too large. Conversely, a more focused blockade targeted primarily at preventing rebel smugglers from bringing in armaments, powder, and other materiel was potentially viable but usually out of grasp: the majority of ships were always needed for joint operations with the army.

In 1776, Howe's naval strength numbered close to 70 ships of varying sizes and types. In August, only 24 were tasked with blockading the entire North American coast; every other ship was assigned to supporting operations in New York or Canada. Two months later, the situation had not improved much, and large coastal areas remained unpatrolled. The year 1777 was similarly lopsided in apportionment due to the campaign to capture Philadelphia.[35] The *Hancock* and *Boston* exploits were only possible because the blockade had been removed out of operational necessity. To make matters worse, heavy fighting to control the Delaware River defenses resulted in the loss of two ships. The whole endeavor frustrated the British, particularly because there was the potential with the blockade to severely hurt the rebel war effort. Patriot forces relied on smuggled goods and trade to keep the army supplied. Foreign assistance was vital, and the French were especially willing to aid surreptitiously. For the Royal Navy to stop or at least significantly control the sea lines of communication could have made a palpable difference in the Patriot ability to remain a cohesive fighting force. Compounding the numbers problem was the British inability to repair and refit ships in theater. Blockading vessels operated along a hostile coast for significant periods. Even if a ship escaped battle damage, natural wear and tear was an inevitability. Some minor repairs could be made in the cities they controlled, such as New York, but additional ships were needed to defend those bases contributing to the overall shortage. Most repairs, including careening, meant a ship was forced to go to the Royal Navy station at Halifax, Nova Scotia, or the West Indies. Any major work typically required a trip back to the Home Island dockyards.[36] These unavoidable requirements further strained the ability to blockade the coast.

## Notes

1  Alfred Thayer Mahan. *The Influence of Sea Power Upon History 1660–1783* (New York: Dover, 1987).
2  Sam Willis, *The Struggle for Sea Power: A Naval History of the American Revolution* (New York: W. W. Norton, 2016), 6–8; Chapter 12—War Termination discusses the dynamics of the privateers in depth.
3  Sir Julian Corbett, *The Principles of Sea Power* (London: Longman and Green, 1911).
4  Daniel Baugh, *The Global Seven Years' War 1754–1763* (New York: Pearson Education, 2011), 431–46.
5  Paul M. Kennedy, *The Rise and Fall of British Naval Mastery* (London: A. Lane, 1976), 105–6.
6  Ibid., 109–10.
7  O'Shaughnessy, *Men Who Lost America*, 326–8.
8  Rodger, *Command of the Ocean*, 369–73.
9  Thirty years in government/politics also meant Sandwich had developed a healthy list of detractors.
10 O'Shaughnessy, *Men Who Lost America*, 326–8.

11 Rodger, *Command of the Ocean*, 372–3.
12 Ibid., 333.
13 Syrett, *Shipping and the American War*, 129.
14 Rodger, *Command of the Ocean*, 332–5; Syrett, *Shipping and the American War*, 136–9.
15 In this case, major ships is defined as either ships-of-the-line (1st Rate—4th Rate) or Frigates (5th-6th Rate)
16 Rodger, *Command of the Ocean*, 606–8.
17 Willis, *Struggle*, 74–6.
18 William M. Fowler Jr., *Rebels Under Sail: The American Navy during the Revolution* (New York: Charles Scribner's Sons, 1974), 47–50.
19 Ibid., 50–1, 53–4.
20 Continental Congress to George Washington, June 19, 1775, Commission as Commander in Chief. *George Washington Papers at the Library of Congress, 1741–1799*: Series 8b, Manuscript Division. Library of Congress, Washington, DC.
21 James L. Nelson, *George Washington's Secret Navy, How the American Revolution Went to Sea* (New York: McGraw Hill, 2008), 81–4, 86.
22 Fowler, *Rebels*, 55–7.
23 James M. Volo, *Blue Water Patriots: The American Revolution Afloat* (Westport, CT: Praeger, 2007), 43–4.
24 Ibid., 44–5; Willis, *Struggle*, 94–5.
25 Volo, *Blue Water Patriots*, 45–6.
26 Ibid., 190–2.
27 James L. Nelson, *Benedict Arnold's Navy: The Ragtag Fleet That Lost the Battle of Lake Champlain But Won the American Revolution* (New York: McGraw Hill, 2006), 91–2.
28 Type of canoe used in Eastern North America.
29 Nelson, *Benedict Arnold's Navy*, 80, 93–104.
30 Willis, *Struggle*, 194–5.
31 There is an argument to be made that despite losing to the British, the defense of Lake Champlain delayed the British long enough that they could not advance southward until the next year.
32 Willis, *Struggle*, 171–2.
33 John Ferling, *Whirlwind* (New York: Bloomsbury, 2015), 137.
34 Ibid., 148–9.
35 David Syrett, *Admiral Lord Howe* (Annapolis: Naval Institute Press, 2006), 62–3, 69–73.
36 Ibid.

# 11

# A GLOBAL WAR

The War of American Independence can be framed in a number of different, equally valid ways. Viewed from one perspective, it is a story of internal revolution, one where polities grew enough apart that violent revolution arose from the chasm between them. The revolution also created a civil war, pitting the citizens of each colony against each other in a contest of loyalties. Once the French entered the war, the scope blossomed. The fight was no longer solely centered on North America but expanded across the entire British Empire. Modern strategists use a "boxes of war" characterization as a clear method to describe wars within wars. Divided by scope and type, these wars fit within one another as boxes or nesting dolls, each containing something differently sized but contributing to the whole. The largest box in the War of American Independence was a global war, a primarily maritime fight that engulfed every part of the British Empire. When King George III argued that British territories around the world were threatened by the North American rebellion, it was a largely speculative menace. When France entered the war on the side of the rebels, the global threat changed from mostly theoretical to worryingly existential. The whole of the British Empire needed to be protected. At the forefront of this defense stood the Royal Navy, already overextended by operations in North America.

This type of maritime contest, pitting the British against its longtime continental foe France, had occurred multiple times over the past century. Global war helped define Britain's "long" eighteenth century, from the Glorious Revolution in 1688–1689 to the end of the Napoleonic Wars in 1815. Be it islands in the Caribbean, influence in India, or land in North America, it was during these conflicts that the British expanded and solidified their overseas empire. In that regard, the expansion of the American rebellion was a familiar, but by no means welcome, transition.

There were multiple reasons as to why the French, Spanish, and Dutch intervention was a worrying development. The Royal Navy's capability in North

DOI: 10.4324/9781003041276-16

American waters was already stretched thin. A potential hostile fleet of equivalent power added yet another point of responsibility. Sandwich anticipated a potential French entrance into the war and put in place shipbuilding/mobilization programs even before 1775. However, these programs took time to ramp up, and, more importantly, the Royal Navy defended more than just North America. Every other part of the empire, including the Home Islands, was threatened by this transition into global war.

Compounding woes was Britain's acute strategic isolation. Apart from the Hessian auxiliaries in North America, Britain was bereft of any significant allies; this lack of alliances caused the most concern for British political and military leaders. To understand why this was potentially catastrophic, it is necessary to look back to the previous global fight, a conflict during which Britain found resounding success, winning Canada and Florida in the peace settlement. Protection of Britain's colonial possessions, the capture of enemy colonies, and financial support for continental allies became essential for British success. The British were so successful at the end of the Seven Years' War that it created problems after the peace. Once global war became a reality during the War for American Independence, most major European powers either wanted vengeance or to see the British at the very least humbled. Britain found itself bereft of any significant continental allies with no European war to split the attention of France and Spain. Britain faced foes purely focused on the maritime dimension. To compound the problem, the French prepared for this specific confrontation. The French Navy, broken and demoralized at the end of the Seven Years' War, had rebuilt with a specific purpose in mind: redemption.

## French Intervention

For France to achieve redemption, several stars needed to align. It was not enough that Britain's North American colonies were rebelling. For France to turn the situation in its favor, there needed to be both the political will to adopt an aggressive policy and the military capability to follow through. Louis XVI held absolute decision-making authority, but his policy goals were developed in concert with handpicked advisors. These counselors were not unanimous in their support for intervention. The loudest voice against intervention was Anne-Robert-Jacques Turgot, controller-general of finances. He argued that France's financial health needed to take precedence over any perceived benefit from either covertly or overtly supporting the American rebels. He favored placing domestic reforms first and did not think that France's tax revenue system could support a major war. Internal stability should be prioritized over external opportunity. Moreover, he argued that if Britain held onto the North American colonies, they would continue to act as a security and a drain on resources, which would eventually allow France to secure gains elsewhere.[1] In hindsight, Turgot's arguments seem overwhelmingly apropos, but in 1776 their value was less clear, especially when the French monarch was presented with pro-intervention arguments.

Secretary of State for Foreign Affairs, the *comte* de Vergennes understood that the best strategy was to weaken but not destroy Britain through intervention in North America. He argued that by supporting the American rebels, France's overall diplomatic position was strengthened while achieving *revanche* (revenge), a simplified sobriquet for a more complex set of French policy objectives. Vergennes wanted to see Britain's power reduced, but a weakened Britain was important for reasons beyond simple *schadenfreude*. France's reasons for entering such a war were also tied to continental matters. The primary goal was to regain the French position as a political arbiter in Europe. The humiliating peace upended the balance of power upon which rested France's diplomatic power. By taking part in the American War, France could both regain lost prestige and potentially attempt an accord with a deteriorated Britain. France's continental diplomatic position was also such that an assault on Britain's overseas possessions represented a viable way to regain position. The king was ultimately persuaded by Vergennes and Turgot dismissed from office.

Vergennes' plans initially centered on indirect involvement with the American rebels, primarily through the shipment of arms, powder, and funds. Beginning in 1776, vitally needed support went covertly to the Americans.[2] The chance for direct French involvement was a possibility, and it became more of an inevitability as frictions between the two powers developed from 1776 onward. If there was to be direct conflict, Vergennes envisioned a maritime war centered on North America and the West Indies. It was, therefore, incumbent upon the French Navy to shoulder much of the burden of a potential war. The French Navy was almost destroyed during the Seven Years' War. The decade that followed saw some improvements to France's naval fortunes, but it was at best measured and at worst counter-productive, such as when the entire leadership system of the dockyards was upended. This event put the dockyards into disarray and hurt France's ability to refit and rearm the navy. It took potential war with Britain to accelerate and refine the reform process. Thus, the most consequential period of improvement began in 1774 with the ascension of Antoine de Sartine to naval minister. Despite no previous experience in naval affairs, Sartine enthusiastically took to his new job, a near Sisyphean task. Even if direct intervention was the preferred policy in 1776, rather than indirect aid, the French Navy was not capable of supporting such a mission.[3]

Sartine prepared France's maritime capabilities by reversing the changes made to the dockyards. He faced significant challenges beyond leadership tweaks: the French Navy was routinely low on funds, short on essential supplies, and while there were several warships laid up in dockyards, very few were seaworthy. Masts, general construction timber, and hemp were all vital to the navy's maintenance and expansion and almost always in short supply. Timber and masts needed to be purchased from foreign sources. Sartine did not initially have the budget to purchase wood for basic ship maintenance, let alone any type of expansion program.[4] To rectify the situation, he petitioned the king for an expanded budget using events in North America and rising tension with Britain as justification. Eventually, Vergennes' political vision and Sartine's naval reforms became mutually reinforcing. As the king adopted a more aggressive foreign policy toward Britain, Sartine received funding beyond the initial budget. Much of the extra appropriations took effect in 1776; the money went toward both refitting existing vessels and building new warships, giving the navy almost two years of preparation. Sartine doubled the number of operational ready ships-of-the-line in 1778 over two years earlier (52 vs. 24).[5]

French naval expansion did not go unnoticed and resulted in a significant escalation of tensions with Britain. The British defeat at Saratoga in autumn 1777 increased tensions, even further showing France that the Americans were potentially capable of winning a significant battle. The final catalyst was an alliance treaty between France and the Second Continental Congress. That the French recognized the American rebels as legitimate forced Britain to declare war on France as Vergennes desired. Since France did not initiate the conflict, Britain's defensive continental alliances did not trigger. France was now free to use its newly rebuilt navy against Britain in both North America and the West Indies. Despite the French Navy's advancements, they were still at a numerical disadvantage compared to Britain. To overcome the Royal Navy's quantitative advantage, other maritime partners needed to join with France. Understanding this problem, Vergennes pushed hard to convince Spain, another loser of the Seven Years' War, to join in the fight.

## The Family Pact

The Bourbon family line ruled both France and Spain and in 1761 the two countries implemented a diplomatic alliance known as the "Family Pact," which allowed for an easier alliance in a war against Britain. Furthermore, Spain's short-term reasons for fighting Britain were very similar to France: they too suffered humiliation and defeat during the previous war. In particular, the capture of Havana by British forces in 1762 shocked Spain. Longer-term grievances also contributed. British-controlled Gibraltar and Minorca, both territories gained during the War of Spanish Succession, were particular Spanish fixations. Minorca was captured and then given back to the British at the end of the war, but Gibraltar had not changed hands for over three-quarters of a century. Spain's monarch, Charles III (Carlos III), wanted both back.

Portugal was also a factor. A traditional British ally, significant tensions in 1775–1776 between Spain and Portugal in South America erupted. A Spanish fleet and troops conducted raids against Portuguese targets in Brazil. Vergennes, nervous that Spain would launch a preemptive invasion of Portugal proper, also worried that Britain would support Portugal and create a defensive chain reaction. Spanish aggression risked creating a crisis the French actively worked to avoid: a war on the continent. The solution, evident to Vergennes, was to keep Britain distracted in North America so they were not inclined to intervene in a dispute with Portugal. Though skeptical at first, Spain's prime-ministers, first Jeronimo Grimaldi and then in 1776, Jose Floridablanca, were eventually convinced that supporting the American rebels was the correct strategy.[6] Spain's initial involvement, generally in coordination with the French, meant providing covert support to the American rebels while remaining officially neutral. The money and supplies sent by either made it to the Continental Army via France as an intermediary or sent via Spanish-owned New Orleans and shipped up the Mississippi and Ohio River systems. Thus, Americans received aid from not just the coastal regions but also the interior.[7]

Key to both Spanish and French aid was Caron de Beaumarchais, a French inventor, watchmaker, playwright, and satirist. Close friends with Sartine, he parlayed his popularity into influence with both Louis XV and Louis XVI's courts, acting at times as a special agent for the Crown. Crucially for the Americans, Beaumarchais became an avid supporter of the rebellion and formed connections with American agents in London and Paris. Using those contacts, Beaumarchais convinced Vergennes that he should be the primary conduit. To that end, he formed Rodrigue Hortalez and Company, a shell company through which France and Spain funneled aid to the American rebels.[8] Soon ships loaded at Le Havre with all manner of war goods transited to North America often via the West Indies. Aid was considerable: in one month in 1777, Rodrigue Hortalez & Co. cost Louis XVI's government over one million *livres*.[9] Numerous other smaller ventures, individual smugglers, and direct American purchases from the Dutch Caribbean island St. Eustasius also contributed to Continental Army sustainment. Covert aid from France and Spain represented a key factor in the American rebellion remaining intact and operationally viable in the conflict's early years.

Still, there was a big difference between sustaining the effort and achieving independence. Material and financial assistance from France and Spain was both welcome and vital, but if the rebels were to achieve eventual victory, they needed direct military assistance, primarily in the form of warships. Furthermore, if France hoped to achieve success against Britain, Spain's naval power needed to be combined with their own. While the Family Pact had "greased the wheels" for covert aid, Vergennes and Floridablanca (alongside their respective monarchs) were not in agreement as to whether a direct alliance and military intervention was the correct strategy to pursue. Vergennes, in a difficult position, needed to convince Spain to directly participate in the fight against Britain. Floridablanca and Charles III were both angry at France for not telling them beforehand about formal recognition of the American colonists and the alliance that led to Britain's declaration of war. They worried that the Spanish Navy, despite doing well against Portuguese forces, was no match for the British Royal Navy. Finally, Spain was concerned about setting a potential precedent for supporting colonial rebellions. All these factors combined to make Spain reluctant to officially join in the war.[10]

France's options relative to Spain remained limited. When Britain declared war against France in 1778, Vergennes promulgated the useful fiction that Britain was the aggressor and France the aggrieved party, thus decreasing the risk of a general war on the continent and setting up a potential invocation of the Family Pact with Spain. The alliance dictated that an attack on one member of the Bourbon ruling family represented an attack on all members. Floridablanca rejected that argument, telling Vergennes that if the Pact was invoked, Spain would provide ancillary help at most; the Spanish fleet would not be used. Further complicating matters, Britain and Spain remained in diplomatic talks on a deal that would guarantee Spanish neutrality in return for Gibraltar returning to Spain.[11]

For Vergennes to secure Spain's help (and their fleet), strategic flexibility was required. Two of France's primary objectives were to support and ensure the independence of the American colonies and weaken Britain through military strikes in North America and the West Indies. Both priorities were compromised in service of attracting Spain. While the alliance between the American rebels and France was strong, Spain objected to guaranteeing American independence; the precedence represented risk to their own colonial possessions. Far more importantly, Spain's operational objectives were different.

Above all else, Spain wanted Gibraltar and Minorca, their top operational priorities. They insisted France go along with plans for their campaigns. Floridablanca also pushed for a combined invasion of England, France agreed but disagreed on scope. Vergennes advocated a punitive raid while Floridablanca pushed for a complete invasion resulting in regime change.[12] Regardless of the eventual plan, by agreeing to Spain's demands, France expanded the strategic scope and cost of the war. France needed to secure Spain's fleet, so compromises were made, and the Spanish strategic objectives incorporated into France's planning. Among the most important: France agreed to not make peace or a truce with Britain until Spain captured Gibraltar. With concessions agreed upon, Spain formally entered the war with the Treaty of Aranjuez in April 1779.[13] The combined Franco-Spanish fleet now outnumbered the British Royal Navy and threatened the entirety of the British Empire. Even those in Europe who had traditionally been British allies were not opposed to seeing Albion lose a little face. The war was fought without the counterbalance of continental conflict.

## Not a Friend in the World

The Royal Navy's capture of neutral shipping to interdict supplies sent to the American colonies created another troublesome issue. In 1780, Catherine the Great of Russia declared a practice of armed neutrality. If Great Britain searched Russian vessels, the Russians reserved the right to respond with force. Soon other countries joined Russia in forming the League of Armed Neutrality.[14] Otherwise neutral, they imparted significant diplomatic pressure on the British government. The tension brought on by the League induced the third European belligerent, the Dutch Republic, to join the war in 1780. The Dutch held a deserved reputation for trading with the American rebels. St. Eustatius in the Caribbean, a known hub of trade between American agents, smugglers, and Dutch merchants, willingly supplied the rebels so long as they could pay. Britain declared war against the Dutch in December 1780 upon receiving intelligence they considered joining the League. The Dutch, unlike the French and Spanish, did not join the conflict willingly but were forced into the war by the British.

Within three years, Britain went from suppressing an internal colonial insurrection to fighting a global war against France, Spain, and the Dutch. More importantly, with Spain and France's naval power now joined, the Royal Navy was outnumbered. In 1779, Britain expected to reasonably put to sea 90 ships-of-the-line. Facing them were France's 66 ships-of-the-line combined with Spain's 50. In terms of overall naval balance of power disparity, by 1780 the Bourbon alliance was 44 percent stronger than the British. The Royal Navy was also delayed in ramping up preparedness. Sandwich implemented a naval building program and fit out more warships early in the conflict (1774–1777) but was stopped by those who feared the potential political ramifications and cost of an expanded navy. Lord North was particularly opposed to naval expansion; in an ironic twist, he worried about naval mobilization enflaming tensions with France and potentially leading to larger war. Full naval mobilization was also expensive. With the war in North America already ballooning in cost, Parliament avoided committing more funds unless absolutely necessary. Sandwich only fully mobilized the Navy in January 1778, just as France entered the war.[15]

The enemy's numerical superiority created a problem, but full mobilization and additional shipbuilding eventually closed the gap. Furthermore, the quality and preparedness of Royal Navy sailors was higher than that of their opponents. But nothing could ameliorate the problem of distance: Britain's navy was already stretched thin. Full mobilization might have helped against the American rebels, but those ships were now needed to defend the empire.

From 1778 on, the entirety of the British Empire came under threat; choices had to be made for allocating resources. Germain pushed to send more ships to North America. Disagreeing, Sandwich wanted to switch to the defensive in North America while bolstering home forces in anticipation of an invasion and/or action on the European side of the Atlantic. George III, perhaps the most pragmatic in his strategic thought, preferred to risk a potential invasion of Britain in favor of defending the British West Indies. He argued that without the revenue from the sugar islands, there would not be enough money to continue the war.[16] Much like his policy toward suppressing the rebellion, the king advocated aggressive measures in the maritime war against the Bourbon powers, emphasizing that: "it is by bold and manly efforts Nations have been preserved not pursueing [sic] along the line of home defence."[17]

These competing views on how best to defend the empire from European enemies and win the war against the American rebels led to a diffusion of naval resources. North American commanders, given the option to withdraw to safer ports, also sent naval reinforcements to home waters and the Caribbean. The Channel and home forces were strengthened, but at the same time offensive operations in the West Indies initiated. A decision to send ships to one part of the globe meant another region was left wanting. The strategic incoherence that led to disasters like Saratoga now infected the global war.

## North American Operations

For the British, the French, and the Americans, maritime operations in North America were largely characterized by missed opportunities and unsatisfying results.

The most significant naval engagement in North America occurred between 5 and 9 September 1781 off the coast of Virginia. Known as the Battle of the Virginia Capes, it ultimately enabled a combined Franco-American force to defeat the British at Yorktown, which in turn served as a catalyst for war termination.

Operations in 1778 could have been decisive for the French and Americans. France signed two treaties with the Continental Congress in February 1778, the first a diplomatic and economic alliance and the second a military alliance. A month later Britain declared war on France, and a month after that France sent a fleet of 16 warships and troop/supply transports to North America. Admiral d'Estaing was charged with harassing the British and aiding the American rebels. With Spain not yet involved in the war, French strategic objectives remained limited to North America and the Caribbean. Unbeknownst to the French, the British were prepared to reduce efforts to subdue the rebellious North American colonies in favor of fighting France elsewhere. Orders went out to the Howe brothers to withdraw from Philadelphia, send forces to take the French island of St. Lucia in the Caribbean, reinforce Florida and Halifax, and be prepared to withdraw from New York and Rhode Island completely if militarily necessary. The pacification strategy in the northern and middle colonies was, for all intents and purposes, ended. General Howe was ordered back to London and Admiral Howe given permission to leave for health reasons.[18] Before France reached North America, it had already become a theater of secondary importance for the British. Admiral Howe stayed to assist the withdrawal of Philadelphia and reinforce New York alongside his brother's replacement, Clinton. Howe, however, outnumbered in ships-of-the-line despite reinforcements en route from Britain, was also handicapped with many smaller vessels strung out along the coast on blockade duty. The initial French/American objective was New York. If d'Estaing gained access to the waters off New York, there was a high chance that Britain would be forced to capitulate the epicenter of their command and control in the theater.[19]

Howe, in coordination with Clinton, chose to mount the defense of New York at the Sandy Hook barrier spit that controlled access to and from the Atlantic. Outnumbered and weakened, Howe showed considerable skill in his defensive planning. He pushed the rapid fortification and garrisoning of Sandy Hook by ground troops, ensuring the position could not be taken without a costly fight. More importantly, he skillfully positioned his ships such that French warships could only pass through the channel while under constant fire from a line of anchored British warships. The French ships arrived at Sandy Hook on 11 July. D'Estaing, overly cautious, failed to fully apply his strength resulting in 11 days of tense stalemate. On 22 July, the French sailed back into the Atlantic to try elsewhere.[20]

D'Estaing's next target, again in coordination with the Americans, was Newport. After New York, it was the next largest British center of command and not as heavily defended. Dividing his warships into three groups to cover the three avenues of approach to Newport, he effectively blockaded the port as well as covering American troops crossing over from the mainland into Portsmouth on the northern part of the island. Admiral Howe, having received word that Newport was the next likely target, sailed to contest the French. Reinforcements delayed, he was still outnumbered and outgunned, but here d'Estaing failed again to properly use his advantages. Instead of defensively mimicking the British at Sandy Hook, the French admiral lifted the blockade and concentrated most of his ships.[21] Howe successfully drew d'Estaing from his more defensible position to a fight in open water. Howe's forces sailed back toward New York, hoping to find the right time to turn and engage a chasing d'Estaing. Then, on the night of 11–12 August, a hurricane struck resulting in chaos, broken masts, and both sides limping away from one another. Howe returned to Sandy Hook; d'Estaing ultimately went to Boston, declining to help the Americans finish taking Newport out of fear for his weakened fleet.[22] A month later, Clinton urged Howe to take an amphibious force and destroy d'Estaing while he sat in Boston harbor. Tired and probably wary of the risk such an operation would bring, Howe declined and passed his command to his relief, Admiral John Byron.[23]

Byron took tentative steps toward attacking d'Estaing in Boston but was stymied by bad weather and the fog of war. By the end of 1778, both British and French naval forces sailed from North America toward different objectives in the Caribbean. Neither side basked in glory, particularly not the French. D'Estaing's biggest accomplishment was arguably that he succeeded in not losing his fleet. Forcing past Sandy Hook to New York, defeating Howe's fleet, or taking Newport were all potentially consequential objectives that would have struck at a time when Britain was already undergoing a reprioritization and reassessment of the war in North America.

For the next two years, while there were successes and failures on both sides, the maritime war was as indecisive as 1778. American naval forces experienced their worst single defeat of the entire conflict in July 1779 when the Commonwealth of Massachusetts sent a maritime force of 17 warships and as many transports to take the British outpost of Castine, Massachusetts (Maine since 1820). Royal Navy forces stopped them on the Penobscot River. The only two Patriot ships not destroyed were captured. The same year, d'Estaing failed to capture Savannah, Georgia, with a joint and combined French–American force, and was wounded in the attempt. Spain, more successful along the Gulf Coast under Bernardo de Galvez, Spanish governor of New Orleans, easily seized Mobile (1780) and Pensacola (1781) in West Florida.[24]

British offensive maritime operations reached a high point when a joint navy and army forces took Charleston in May 1780. Despite successfully holding onto Newport, they abandoned the port a year later to concentrate forces in New York. The French immediately saw the potential for a deep-water base in North America, from which they could attack all manner of British targets up and down the coast. Working in coordination with Washington and Lafayette, France occupied Newport in July 1780 and thereafter used it as a base for naval operations and a command center for French ground forces.[25]

The Newport occupation threatened all Crown operations in North America. Clinton advocated an assault to retake the port. To that end, he planned on an ambitious amphibious assault combined with a naval attack. To put his plan into action, he needed Royal Navy cooperation, but Clinton did not work well with Arbuthnot. The new overall commander of Royal Navy forces in North America ultimately refused to accede to the plan and offered no alternative of his own.[26] Nor did Arbuthnot work well with Admiral Sir George Rodney, who arrived in late 1780 with reinforcements and higher rank. Instead of cooperating, they traded barbs at one another. Rodney soon left to return to the Caribbean. Strategic incoherence, so emblematic of British wartime leadership in North America, allowed the French to operate out of Newport relatively uncontested. Ultimately this dynamic led to dire circumstances in September 1781, when the French and Patriot forces moved against Cornwallis in Yorktown.

## British Channel Operations

During wartime, control and defense of the English Channel are always of vital importance to Britain. It represents both the easiest point of access for any belligerent wishing to invade and a primary passage area for merchant traffic. In the eighteenth century, responsibility for protecting the channel lay with the Western Squadron, its primary purpose to maintain sea control in the channel. Sandwich, typically wary of weakening that force in favor of reinforcing other theaters, retained most ships-of-the-line in the home fleet, a policy arguably justified; a number of naval engagements occurred in the theater during the war. Western Squadron typical duties included taking station in or near the Channel, protecting British commerce, watching or blockading French ports, and seeking out and engaging an enemy fleet. In May 1778, Admiral Augustus Keppel took command. He first escorted a convoy out of the Channel, then proceeded to watch for any French activity from the Brest squadron. If the French attempted to exit the channel, he was to attack unless severely outnumbered. Keppel's task meant intercepting the French force leaving Brest and then defeating it in a decisive battle. He positioned his force off the island of Ushant (west of Brest), but in a difficult situation. Because full naval mobilization had been delayed, he lacked sufficient forces to ensure success. A detachment under Byron sent to North America to relieve Howe also reduced his available ships. Furthermore, many of the ships had inexperienced crews.

His counterpart in Brest, Lieutenant-General of the Navy (Vice-Admiral) Louis Guillouet, comte d'Orvilliers, also had untested crews and worried about numerical superiority. Both commanders vacillated between aggression and caution throughout June and July 1778. Keppel received intelligence that d'Orvilliers' had 27 ships-of-the-line ready to sail. Prudently, he sailed his 21 ships to Portsmouth and waited for the reinforcements that brought his total to 31. This move forced the French to be ever more wary of committing to battle. Finally, on 27 July, the two fleets engaged west of Ushant. Emblematic of a truism of naval battle in that they are rarely actually decisive, both admirals made mistakes and failed to press their advantage. While there were hundreds of casualties and significant damage to both, no vessels were sunk or captured. Both Keppel and d'Orvilliers returned to the safety of home ports to refit and recover. Keppel returned to sea but could not induce the French into another fight. Tension developed between Keppel and Admiral Sir Hugh Palliser, a subordinate at Ushant. Matters escalated. Palliser demanded that Admiralty court-marshal Keppel for neglect of duty. Unlike Vice-Admiral John Byng during the Seven Years' War, Keppel was acquitted, sparing both his life and career.[27] Still, from Britain's perspective, the Battle of Ushant remained problematic. The Royal Navy failed to stop the French at a crucial early point in the war as naval requirements to defend the empire rapidly expanded. For the French, d'Orvilliers may not have basked in glorious victory at Ushant but he kept the fleet intact. This result allowed France to both harass British shipping and trade in the region and formed the basis for what became the second failed operation in the English Channel: the French/Spanish Invasion of 1779.

A planned invasion of England, a requirement Spain placed upon France in exchange for entering the war, complicated alliance negotiations between Vergennes and Floridablanca as to the invasion's scope and location. Potentially invading Ireland and helping the Irish separatists was floated by Vergennes but rejected by the Spanish for not focusing enough on hurting Britain directly. The final plan called for a combined French and Spanish maritime force to first attack the Channel Fleet and either defeat or force its withdrawal to homeport. French troops would take the Isle of Wight. Once accomplished, the invasion force would move to capture Portsmouth. Franco-Spanish control of one of Britain's most important naval dockyards and stations would serve as a significant bargaining chip in any peace agreement. The invasion failed before a single soldier set foot on British territory. The combined fleet required warships from Brest, Toulon, Ferrol, and Cadiz to rendezvous; however, none arrived as planned. Delays occurred, expenses bloomed, and the timing increasingly pushed back. Illness struck d'Orvilliers' ships at Brest spreading viciously among the sailors. Spanish ships similarly suffered once they arrived. Poor weather, the bogeyman for potential invaders of England, became a factor. The combined fleet never brought the Royal Navy to battle; the invasion was called off in favor of focusing the fight elsewhere. The plan to invade England represented a severe strategic and operational blunder for France and Spain. The initial cost associated with the troop and ship buildup was immense; it tripled in size and scope between the planning and execution phases.[28] France's treasury, already severely strained, explained why Vergennes tried hard to convince Spain that a smaller, peripheral operation was preferable. Nor did the proposed operation's expense guarantee success. The plan required neutralization of Royal Navy forces, but the Channel fleet was strong enough to challenge even a combined Spanish and French force. Finally, even if the Isle of Wight and Portsmouth were both taken, the diplomatic repercussions were fuzzy. There were other kingdoms that wanted to see Britain humbled, but an invasion might have swayed otherwise neutral countries to intervene.[29] The sheer audacity of an attack also might have had the opposite reaction to the intention. Spain and France hoped Britain would sue for peace with Portsmouth as a negotiation lever. Instead, it might have stirred Britain's public to support a far longer and costlier war, a result Vergennes wanted to avoid.

Sporadic fighting occurred in and around the Channel for the rest of the war, but nothing reached the significance of Ushant and the failed invasion. The Admiralty felt secure enough to detach warships in support of other war theaters, including the West Indies and North America. Though ultimately ineffective in support of suppressing the rebellion in North America, for the West Indies and Mediterranean, the extra ships became vital for survival of British imperial territories.

## Mediterranean Operations

The Mediterranean theater was characterized by two dynamics. Spain made the capture of Gibraltar and to a lesser extent Minorca, their primary objectives upon joining in the war. The second was British obstinacy: they stubbornly held onto their base at the mouth of the Mediterranean when tactical and strategic considerations suggested easier alternative options. The result was a drain on the resources, time, and manpower for both sides. Much like the Channel ventures, the biggest strategic beneficiary from events in the Mediterranean were the American rebels. Minorca had a deep-water port (Mahon) but was harder to defend. Gibraltar, by contrast, never changed hands before the American War with the outpost always under British control. The "Rock" stuck out of southern Spain like a splinter— a constant, festering wound to Spanish psyche. In June 1779, just two months after France and Spain allied themselves, Spain initiated the siege and blockade of Gibraltar. Overland access to the rest of Spain was cut off, siege lines dug, and artillery sighted. Spanish warships established a close blockade to stymie any relief attempt.[30] Spain's diplomatic negotiations with Morocco ensured that Gibraltar could not source supplies from their southern neighbor. The strategy, as with most sieges, was to starve the British into surrender.

Lieutenant-General George Eliott whose military success during the Seven Years' War earned him a large amount of money, an estate, and multiple promotions, commanded the garrison.[31] Eliott understood Gibraltar's precarious position and prepared for a siege even before hostilities commenced. Five British regiments, three Hanoverian regiments, and a number of artillerymen, engineers, and naval personnel defended the outpost. Eliott collected as many working cannons, howitzers, and mortars as possible, positioning them to fire at any potential Spanish position on land or sea. By the end of the war, over 600 artillery pieces were employed by the British at Gibraltar.[32] But soldiers needed food and guns needed powder and shot. Eliott stockpiled supplies; once the blockade tightened, he relied on smugglers to bring in goods. This effort, though initially sufficient, allowed Gibraltar to survive long term, but it needed external aid and replenishment. This help came in the form of a relief convoy led by arguably the most consequential naval leader of the war, Admiral Sir George Brydges Rodney.

Rodney's importance was initially obfuscated by the fact that he spent most of the war's early years not aboard ship but hiding in Paris from creditors. Though a good naval officer and experienced in command, he was also an abuser of patronage, flouted Admiralty rules, and was bad with money. Sandwich rejected his appeals for a Royal Navy posting until he sorted out his finances and only by 1779 with the expansion to a global war did the First Lord negotiate for Rodney's return to active service. Sandwich needed an aggressive commander able to take the fight to France and Spain, especially in the West Indies. Rodney, having returned to London in 1778 but still drowning in debt, accepted Sandwich's offer of employment.[33]

Given a squadron of 20 ships-of-the-line to protect a troop and supply vessel convoy, Rodney was ordered to resupply Gibraltar and Minorca then sail to the West Indies and take command of that station. Setting sail on Christmas Day, he spotted and captured a Spanish convoy. Seven days later near the coast of Cape St. Vincent, Rodney's force engaged a smaller Spanish squadron under Admiral Don Juan de Langara. Known afterward as the "Moonlight Battle" since fighting continued throughout the night, it resulted in a clear victory for Rodney and the Royal Navy. One Spanish ship was destroyed and five captured. More importantly, with the blockade of Gibraltar temporarily broken, the resupply convoy easily delivered its cargo.[34]

Rodney's resupply of Gibraltar mission resulted in the first true British naval victory of the war. He both captured a Spanish convoy and defeated an enemy squadron in battle. More importantly, Gibraltar and Minorca received vital aid; Eliott actually had more supplies than at the siege's outset and enough to withstand another year of siege.[35] A second aid convoy in 1781 lacked the dramatic naval battle as preamble but successfully delivered supplies. A third convoy near the end of hostilities signified Britain's commitment to hold onto Gibraltar. Elliott's stalwart and stubborn defense became a symbol of hope for both British policymakers and the public. Whereas the war went badly in North America and unevenly in the Caribbean, Gibraltar's stubborn will to hold on in the face of Spanish obsession was notable.

Spain's preoccupation with Gibraltar altered the strategic landscape for France and the American Patriots. A large portion of the Spanish fleet remained at Cadiz in support of Gibraltar operations, unavailable for employment in other theaters. Money and manpower poured into the siege operations; by 1782 French forces worked in combination with the Spanish to bring about British capitulation. Starving out the garrison proved a hopeful, if not particularly feasible, strategy, given the multiple times Gibraltar was resupplied. Rather, Spanish/French forces decided to force capitulation through constant bombardment. Batteries on both land and warships at sea routinely poured shot into Gibraltar. This strategy culminated in September 1782 when ten floating batteries—ships purposely built for artillery bombardment—initiated what the Spanish and French assumed to be the dénouement of British Gibraltar. An impressive show of force, it ultimately resulted in a spectacular failure; several of the battery ships burned and sank. To make matters worse, the large, combined fleet assembled alongside the floating batteries failed to properly support the attack, dooming the last serious attempt to take Gibraltar.

Much like the Spanish insistence on an invasion of England, their almost singular focus on Gibraltar created strategic friction with France. Diffusion of focus combined with the considerable expense of maintaining the siege weakened the overall Franco-Spanish position. There was some success: Minorca ultimately fell to a combined French and Spanish force in 1782 and not returned to Britain during the peace. But ultimately, they failed to attain the prize they truly wanted. Gibraltar represented one of the longest formal sieges in history lasting three years, seven months, and 12 days. For the British, total casualties topped nearly 2,000.[36] Still, it represented one of the few bright spots in a very frustrating struggle. Eliott's steadfast obstinacy, combined with successful navy actions, ensured that the British Empire retained a strategic advantage at the mouth of the Mediterranean.

## Caribbean Operations

In 1778, the Caribbean financial pillar propped up the rest of the British imperial economy. Trade and money flowing from the British islands supported the Crown's ability to fund the ongoing war in North America. The islands also possessed outsized political influence; many major absentee landowners lived in Britain and held political office or seats in Parliament. The island colonies remained loyal despite the rebellion in North America. While politically stable, the British West Indies remained severely at risk of foreign invasion or capture. Once France entered the war, the risk became a reality. France had their own islands and financial interests in the region. Their most important colony, Saint-Domingue, outstripped even British Jamaica and Barbados in wealth and economic development.[37] Vergennes' initial strategy had two focal points: supporting the rebels in North America and taking as much territory in the Caribbean as possible. Whenever war erupted between Britain and France, the Caribbean islands became immediate targets. Even if any taken islands were not retained permanently, they made for good leverage during peace negotiations.

Once the war turned global, the Caribbean received the lion's share of Britain's strategic attention. France began the war with more troops in the theater, an advantage that allowed them to swiftly take the British island of Dominica. To prevent further losses, British authorities agreed to weaken the Channel Fleet to reinforce naval power in the West Indies.[38] They also reduced manpower elsewhere in favor of a Caribbean campaign. In October 1778, 5,000 troops transferred from North America and redeployed to the Caribbean, intended to capture French St. Lucia. Clinton chafed at the loss of such significant manpower believing that their lives were being squandered in an inhospitable and disease-ridden theater.[39] His concern was well-placed; troops sent to the Caribbean died of disease at a higher rate than in other theaters. Die they did, but not without military success. Those troops took St. Lucia in late 1778, the island near Martinique, France's primary theater naval base. For the rest of the war, St. Lucia operated as the staging point for British Caribbean operations. The next year, France retaliated by seizing St. Vincent and Grenada. Interspersed between these larger fights, minor naval battles and constant friction occurred between privateers, smugglers, and legitimate trading ships. A chaotic, violent theater, it had a palpable effect on the war and into which two new and ultimately significant players arrived—Rodney and French Admiral the *comte* de Grasse.

Following the relief of Gibraltar, Rodney sailed to the Caribbean, where he took overall command. Not only was the region a financial cornerstone of the empire, but the Caribbean was also the primary waystation through which the American rebels bought and sold illicit goods, typically via French-controlled islands. Beaumarchais, for example, routed many of his aid shipments via Martinique and Saint-Domingue. Not just the French facilitated trade with the Americans. Dutch St. Eustatius became an *entrepôt* for trade with the American rebels. Even some British island residents illegally sent goods to the rebellious colonies. When Britain declared war on the Dutch to prevent them from joining the League of Neutrality in 1780, St. Eustatius became a prime target. With 15 warships and 3,000 men, Rodney and his army counterpart Major-General John Vaughn captured an unsuspecting St. Eustatius in February 1781. The victory dealt a sharp blow to rebel efforts in America. Rodney thought that the island represented the primary reason that the rebels could sustain their war effort. Significantly, that line of thinking also combined with Rodney's propensity for self-enrichment, patronage, and likely, outstanding debts. He treated the island as a pirate haven, rather than a former part of the Dutch Republic, which allowed him and Vaughn to loot the residents at will. They spent three months taking prizes and confiscating goods, even going so far as to continue to fly the Dutch flag so unsuspecting ships would sail into the harbor to be captured.[40]

Rodney's actions at St. Eustatius troubled superiors back in London. But larger strategic issues beyond his willingness to flout rules and standards for self-enrichment proved more problematic. While at St. Eustatius, Rodney failed to send timely intelligence to Graves in New York about the whereabouts of the French fleet, which had sailed from France to Martinique. Rodney also positioned his ships to better protect his prizes, rather than watch the French fleet in Martinique. Finally, when it became clear that de Grasse had sailed for North America, he chose his second in command, Rear-Admiral Samuel Hood, to follow the French. Rodney himself sailed back to London intent on explaining his conduct at St. Eustatius and ensuring his share of the prizes. Thus, Hood, not Rodney, fought alongside Graves off the Virginia Capes in September 1781.[41]

With all the factors combined, it can be argued that Rodney's actions after the capture of St. Eustatius directly led to the defeat at Yorktown. Rodney escaped blame for the events, received a promotion, and retained his command, less a vindication of his actions and more a practical need to ensure someone with experience and a winning record commanded. Following success in North America, de Grasse sailed back to the Caribbean and captured St. Kitts, Montserrat, and Nevis. Jamaica, the most important British colony, became the next target. Rodney sailed back to the Caribbean with a fleet that outnumbered de Grasse' force as the Admiralty weakened the home fleet to protect Jamaica. With this force, Rodney saved

Jamaica and his reputation, and dealt a severe blow to France's policy objectives. In April 1782, de Grasse set sail from Martinique with 33 warships and transports filled with 10,000 troops. He intended to link up with Spanish forces in Santo Domingo and then assault Jamaica.[42] Watching near St. Lucia, Rodney followed the French with 37 warships and intent on intercepting the French before they could meet the Spanish. On 9 April, Rodney's force caught up with de Grasse, but with little wind, the French managed to retreat toward Guadeloupe. Three more days of chase and retreat followed, marked by collisions among the French ships, which slowed them down. On 12 April, Rodney finally engaged de Grasse in the Saintes passage near Dominica. The combatants fought a 12-hour running battle during which the Royal Navy broke through the French line at three places, crossing the French "T," and pouring destructive fire into the enemy from stem to stern. Although many French ships escaped the melee, de Grasse's flagship, the *Ville d'Paris* was encircled and captured. All told one French warship sank, four were captured (and thus soon added to the British Order of Battle as was the usual practice), and a French admiral made a prisoner of war.[43]

The Battle of the Saintes prevented the invasion of Jamaica. More importantly, it became the victory that the British public needed after Yorktown. It reinstated Royal Navy prestige and represented one of the few successes for British arms during the war. It also all but ended Franco-Spanish attempts to take the most important British islands. Rodney became a hero, but his embarrassing performance at St. Eustatius had not been forgotten. When Lord North's government collapsed in March, the new First Lord of the Admiralty immediately recalled Rodney. When news of his victory reached London, the ministry attempted and failed to recall the order before it reached the admiral. He lost his Caribbean command but gained public favor, a peerage, and a significant pension.[44]

## Reckoning

The final naval battle of the global war occurred after the peace agreements were signed, off the coast of Cuddalore, India, on 20 June 1783. It was the fifth time since early 1782 that the squadrons of Royal Navy Vice-Admiral Sir Edward Hughes and French Rear-Admiral Pierre André de Suffren engaged. Much like the previous four encounters, the fight was evenly matched, volatile, and ultimately indecisive.[45] The global war spread to India in 1780, where Hughes supported the East India Company's campaign against the Nabob of Mysore, who had French backing. The Dutch Republic's entrance meant their Indian territories became targets as well. However, the war in the sub-continent resulted in no change in the overall strategic picture. Events in India showed the scope of the war as a truly global conflict but had little impact on the resultant outcome.

Overall, France, Spain, and the Dutch Republic suffered from overly broad policy goals and non-complementary strategies. For Vergennes, this dynamic was a foreseen problem, but he was caught in a conundrum. Without Spain, France could not challenge the Royal Navy. But Spain's strategic priorities watered down the overall focus and effectiveness of the allies' strategy, putting even more strain on an already stressed French treasury. For Spain, had they repeated the Gulf Coast successes in the Mediterranean, their strategic priorities could have been met. The failure at Gibraltar ensured that much of their effort became an expensive mistake. The Dutch, drawn into the war unwillingly, made no significant war contribution once their trading posts were lost.

Britain's strategy incoherence transferred to the global war. Mahan argued that in trying to defend the whole empire, Britain came close to losing everything. From a naval perspective, he argues, it would have been better to concentrate the Royal Navy's power near the home waters, watching for the enemy fleet and attacking if it left the French coast.[46] Still, given the threats arrayed against them and the particular dangers of defeat in any of the theaters, it was understandable why the global war was prosecuted in such a diffuse fashion. Even with the loss of the rebellious colonies, Britain performed better in the global war and successfully fended off the dismantling of the empire.

## Notes

1 Dull, *French Navy*, 44–9.
2 Jessica M. Parr, "The Evolution of the Franco-American Alliance and France's Military Contribution," in *The Routledge Handbook of American Military and Diplomatic History: The Colonial Period to 1877*, eds. Christos G. Frentzos and Antonio S. Thompson (New York: Routledge, 2015), 114.
3 Ibid.
4 Ibid., 22–4.
5 Jonathan R. Dull, *The Age of the Ship of the Line: The British & French Navies, 1650–1815* (Lincoln, NE: University of Nebraska Press, 2009), 97.
6 Larrie D. Ferreiro, *Brother at Arms: American Independence and the Men of France & Spain Who Saved It* (New York: Alfred A. Knopf, 2016), 88–93.
7 Spain took control of New Orleans from France after the Seven Years' War.
8 Brian N. Morton and Donald C. Spinelli, *Beaumarchais and the American Revolution* (Lanham, MD: Lexington Books, 2003), 5–7, 41.
9 Ibid., 130.
10 Murphy, *Charles Gravier*, 261–3.
11 Neither side actually believed this deal would succeed, but Spain held out hope for Gibraltar. Britain knew the longer they kept Spain occupied, the more isolated it made France.
12 Murphy, *Charles Gravier*, 270–9.
13 Ibid.
14 Members of the League between 1780–83: Russia, Denmark-Norway, Sweden, Prussia, Austria, Kingdom of the Two Sicilies, Portugal, and the Ottoman Empire.
15 O'Shaughnessy, *Men Who Lost America*, 328–30.
16 Fortescue, *King George the Third*, 432–3.
17 Ibid., 435.
18 David Syrett, *The Royal Navy in American Waters 1775–1783* (Aldershot: Scholar Press, 1989), 93–4.
19 Dull, *French Navy*, 123.
20 David Syrett, *Admiral Lord Howe* (Annapolis: Naval Institute Press), 76–9.
21 Ibid., 83.
22 John B. Hattendorf, *Newport, The French Navy, and American Independence* (Newport, RI: The Redwood Press, 2005), 23–5.

23 Syrett, *Howe*, 87.
24 Syrett, *Royal Navy*, 126–8, 131; James W. Raab, *Spain, Britain, and the American Revolution in Florida, 1763–1783* (Jefferson, NC: McFarland, 2008), 135–6.
25 Hattendorf, *Newport*, 40–1, 49.
26 Ibid., 49–50.
27 David Syrett, *The Royal Navy in European Waters During the American Revolutionary War* (Columbia, SC: University of South Carolina Press, 1998), 42–6, 52, 54.
28 Dull, *French Navy*, 151–2.
29 John Hardman and Munro Price, eds., *Louis XVI and the comte de Vergennes: Correspondence 1774–1787* (Oxford: Voltaire Foundation, 1998), 79.
30 Blockades during the age of sail were not completely impenetrable, and the waters around Gibraltar made it particularly difficult to continually station ships to stop incoming and outgoing shipping.
31 T. H. McGuffie, *The Siege of Gibraltar 1779–1783* (Philadelphia, PA: Dufour Editions, 1965), 25.
32 Ibid., 33.
33 David Syrett, *The Rodney Papers Selections from the Correspondence of Admiral Lord Rodney Volume II 1763–1780* (Great Britain: Navy Records Society, 2007), 15–16, 234.
34 Ibid., 271–2.
35 James Falkner, *Fire Over the Rock, The Great Siege of Gibraltar, 1779–1783* (Barnsley: Pen and Sword Military, 2009), 53–8.
36 Ibid., 133.
37 Alan Forrest, *The Death of the French Atlantic: Trade, War, and Slavery in the Age of Revolution* (Oxford: Oxford University Press, 2021), 9.
38 Taylor, *American Revolutions*, 286–7.
39 O'Shaughnessy, *Men Who Lost America*, 222–3.
40 Andrew Jackson O'Shaughnessy, *An Empire Divided: The American Revolution and the British Caribbean* (Philadelphia, PA: University of Pennsylvania Press, 2000), 214–21.
41 O'Shaughnessy, *Men Who Lost America*, 308–10.
42 Taylor, *American Revolutions*, 297, 299.
43 Rodger, *Command of the Ocean*, 353–4.
44 O'Shaughnessy, *Men Who Lost America*, 316–7.
45 Rodger, *Command of the Ocean*, 356–7.
46 Mahan, *Influence of Sea Power Upon History*, 529–34.

# 12

# WAR TERMINATION

In theory, there is a logical point when a nation should end a war, as Clausewitz argues. If the time and effort of fighting the war exceed the value of the objective, the war needs to end.[1] Yet Clausewitz also understood that this situation represented an idealistic hope. Sunk costs, pride, differing perceptions, and greed are just some of the realities that postpone and alter the rational calculus of war termination. There is also rarely one singular event or battle that leads to war termination; it is more a cumulative process. These facets are key to understanding war termination in the War of American Independence; a series of catalysts made continuing the struggle and retention of the North American colonies impractical if not impossible.

The conflict was a nested war and should be perceived as three wars occurring simultaneously: revolutionary war, internecine civil war, and global war (primarily maritime, but not exclusively). The 1783 treaty codified Britain's defeat in the first two conflicts. The American colonies earned their independence and with it, those loyal to the Crown lost their civil war, an embarrassing defeat especially considering the British position after the Seven Years' War. However, the global war represented a different war termination dynamic. The imperial threat went beyond losing North American possessions. If Britain could not feasibly claim victory in the war, it was not clear that they were outright defeated.

## War Termination Catalyst: War on Commerce

Trade in the eighteenth century did not stop during wartime, but it did become more dangerous. Seaborne commerce was the lifeblood of the War of American Independence. Shipping became busier with more commercial vessels and military transports. Warships interdicted commercial vessels, a practice employed by all sides, often involving warships on blockade duty or smaller vessels on individual

DOI: 10.4324/9781003041276-17

cruises seeking out contraband. Capturing foreign trade represented an integral aspect of the Royal Navy's never-ending quest to stop supplies from reaching the North American rebels from France, Spain, and the Dutch Republic. Understandably, Britons proved unapologetically aggressive in capturing cargo since the rebel war effort could not be sustained without outside aid. But the zealous willingness of British captains to seize neutral shipping had negative consequences. Commerce raiding resulted in creation of the League of Armed Neutrality in 1780; the League's potential military power forced the British hand in declaring war against the Dutch. The League also put additional pressure on Britain to end the war as fast as possible.

For a small, weak force like the Continental Navy, attacking British trade emerged as the best, and often, the only way they could compete against the Royal Navy. At times it became an *ad hoc*, "make it up as you go along" process. Gustavus Conyngham, for example, an Irish-born seaman working in Philadelphia for a trading firm, traveled to Europe at the behest of the Continental Congress to procure war supplies. While in Paris, he approached Benjamin Franklin about the potential for commerce raiding. Franklin gave him an on-the-spot commission in the Continental Navy and arranged for him to surreptitiously purchase a ship in France. As captain of the *Surprise* (and later, the *Revenge*), Conyngham successfully plundered British shipping in European waters during the pre-Alliance years, concurrently increasing the diplomatic tension between Britain and France.[2]

The war's most famous Continental Navy captain—John Paul Jones—began his wartime career capturing commercial prizes but soon went beyond simple commerce raiding. In the sloop-of-war *Ranger*, Jones raided the British coastline, burning ships and towns, plundering, and generally causing havoc. Royal Navy ships mobilized and HMS *Drake*, a sloop of similar size, engaged *Ranger* off Northern Ireland. With *Drake*'s captain mortally wounded in an initial broadside, Jones proceeded to capture the ship, the first time a Royal Navy ship was taken by the Americans in British waters. Depending on the perspective, the event represented a propaganda boon or public relations disaster.[3]

Jones repeated the act when commanding the *Bon Homme Richard*, a converted French merchantman. Chasing a Baltic trade convoy, Jones was attacked by the British frigate HMS *Serapis*. In an intense four-hour battle, Jones emerged victorious, securing the surrender and capture of the *Serapis*. A pyrrhic victory resulted in that *Bon Homme Richard* ultimately sank and the Baltic convoy escaped unscathed. Jones wrote in his journal: "I saved only my signal flags. I lost all of my belongings, amounting to more than 50,000 *livres* . . . the officers and men of the ship also lost all their personal effects."[4] Still, taking the *Serapis* cemented his reputation and legacy as a Continental Navy officer (see Figure 12.1).

Jones' success in British waters represented an outlier. The standard story of Continental naval officers conducting commerce raiding proved far less dramatic. Abraham Whipple commanded the Rhode Island Navy: two small ships completely outgunned by most Royal Navy warships patrolling New England waters.

**FIGURE 12.1** *Bon Homme Richard* vs. HMS *Serapis*

Source: Courtesy of the Naval History and Heritage Command, Washington Navy Yard, Washington, DC

With his small force incorporated into the Continental Navy in late 1775, Whipple, promoted to captain and command of the new frigate *Providence*, operated in New England waters and the Caribbean, taking prizes, defending the coastline, and avoiding larger Royal Navy ships. Following the French alliance in 1778, he operated off the French coast. Whipple accomplished one of the most successful American commercial captures of the entire war when he took a British convoy off the coast of Newfoundland. Unfortunately, a year later, forced to surrender his force while defending Charleston, he spent the remainder of the conflict as a prisoner of war.

As adept as Whipple and others proved at commerce raiding, most failed to translate that success into direct competition with the Royal Navy. The Continental Navy's ability to seize British commerce remained its best and most successful operational trait.[5] For commerce raiding to have any significant effect, it needed conducting on a large scale. Neither the Continental Navy nor Royal Navy could provide that level of effort: the former due to its size and the latter because of its other strategic obligations. Therefore, for both belligerents, a public-private partnership made up the difference. Enterprising captains and ship owners could make good money not just in transporting goods but in the legal stealing of other nations' cargo. During peacetime, these actions constituted piracy and if caught, death or imprisonment represented the usual punishments. In wartime, the dynamic changed; privately owned warships gave a state-sponsored veneer of legitimacy to piracy. "Privateering" was officially sanctioned by governing bodies to strike at their enemies' commercial trade through the issuance of Letters of Marque and Reprisal, which legalized commerce raiding against an opponent's commercial vessels. For strong naval powers, this practice allowed them to attack an enemy's commerce without detaching warships. For weaker navies, privateering became their primary method of influencing the maritime domain. Two basic types of privateers emerged. The first were private men-of-war, ships converted specifically to hunt enemy commerce, funded, crewed, and commanded by private individuals. They were ships of similar size to those merchant ships they hunted, and with more cannon and crew. The other type were also converted merchant ships, but their primary objective was trade. Capable of and licensed for commerce raiding if the opportunity arose (due to a larger crew and potentially larger armament), raiding became a secondary consideration. Both types operated under a Letter of Marque and Reprisal. It gave them legitimacy and government backing as well as the difference between selling a prize in a friendly port instead of trial as a pirate.

British privateers, common in all the period major wars, emerged. When France joined the American rebels s in 1778, so too did British privateers. Over 35 percent of the entire British merchant fleet became privateers, the majority (70 percent) choosing to trade while holding a Letter of Marque, rather than converting to a private man-of-war. Once the war expanded globally with traditional enemies, it was business as usual for Great Britain.[6] For the Continental Congress, issuing Letters of Marque represented a bold new step, particularly since they began issuance in late 1775. The documents emphasized that they were a state actor approving non-state-sponsored violence, which implied autonomy even before the Declaration of Independence. More importantly, privateering was very popular to a point where it became an issue for the Continental Navy. A crewmember on a privateering vessel was typically paid more quickly for a capture than their Continental Navy counterparts. The share split was also more generous. Not only would a privateer get their money faster but there was more of it. Thus, a manning problem developed: sailors proved more likely to sign up for privateer service than serve in the Navy.[7] Privateering became a force multiplier for the American rebels, allowing them to wage *guerre de course* against Britain despite having a small, inexperienced navy.

The effects on commerce varied depending on perspective. The rebels used *guerre de course* primarily to strike at a superior foe in an oblique manner. These actions benefitted morale, allowed for vital supplies to be seized, and helped defray their own problems of accessing trade. It also ground down the opponent's morale and altered their strategic decisions. The American war on British trade cumulatively helped grind down the enemy. Continental Navy ships and privateers diffused the Royal Navy focus and ensured that trade still flowed. Conversely, the Royal Navy's attempts to blockade and stymie trade in North America were potentially ruinous to the cash-strapped and undersupplied rebellion. For Britons, attacks on commerce contributed to a feeling that the empire was being overwhelmed by the scope and severity of the war. Trade with the North American colonies all but completely stopped, further exacerbated by commerce raiders taking prizes in

North America and the Caribbean. Privateers forced merchant shipping insurance rates to double from pre-war values: convoyed vessels went from 2–2.5 percent to 4–5 percent, whereas a ship not sailing in convoy and therefore more vulnerable could pay up to 15 percent.[8]

These economic pressures on trade were palpable even before French and Spanish intervention. Competition between using vessels/sailors for merchant ventures versus military operations erupted, complicated by transport tonnage already stretched thin; global war severely exacerbated that problem. French and Spanish privateers joined the Americans in preying on British trade. Much closer to British home waters than the Americans, they further increased pressure on British merchants. On the opposite side of the coin, a surge in British privateer activity occurred. Liverpool, second only to London in terms of trade and economic power in late eighteenth-century Britain and hurt by the cessation of trade with North America, experienced a small economic rebound via privateering. Liverpool's wartime privateer fleet consisted of 390 vessels, one of the largest in the British Isles. While some American vessels were taken, most prizes brought in by Liverpool privateers were French. Indeed, the most damage done by British privateers during the war was to French, not American commerce, but overseas trade ultimately suffered. In previous eighteenth-century wars, British imports and exports expanded in scope but contracted between 1775 and 1783.[9]

Most importantly, America and its allies' attacks on British commerce also affected the Royal Navy's strategic choices. From 1778 onward, a good portion of Sandwich's focus was on the Channel and waters near the British Isles. The Royal Navy needed to protect overseas trade and the convoys flowing into and out of Britain as well as counter any seaborne invasion attempts. This focus meant more ships deployed closer to home and less available for other duties, be it service in a different theater or watching the French, Spanish, and Dutch along the European coast. This emphasis on protecting trade and the home islands from invasion allowed de Grasse to sail from France to the Caribbean unmolested and prevented significant naval reinforcements for North America.[10] It helped set the stage for an additional catalyst of war termination: the Battle of the Virginia Capes.

## War Termination Catalyst: Battle of the Virginia Capes

Despite a fair amount of blame for the disaster at Yorktown, British naval failure at the Battle of the Virginia Capes (5–9 September 1781, sometimes styled as The Battle of the Chesapeake Capes) determined the outcome. From a naval perspective, three primary points of failure/friction led to the loss of sea superiority at a critical moment. It began with the decision to not contest the establishment of a French base at Newport. Clinton understood the need to retake Newport, but incoherence and friction between him and the Royal Navy prevented any operation. More to the point: while Cornwallis prepared fortifications at Yorktown, Clinton still worked out a plan. Newport allowed the French a protected staging point for their ships and troops in the theater. It became a strategic concern for the New York-based British, who focused on the Southern Campaign after 1778 while also threatened from a hostile New England. French troops, supplies, and especially siege artillery dispatched from Newport, crucially supported Washington and Rochambeau's campaign against Cornwallis in Tidewater Virginia. Waiting for their arrival forced de Grasse to protect the Chesapeake Bay at the Battle of the Virginia Capes, and Newport-based French warships inhibited Royal Navy support for the trapped Cornwallis at Yorktown.[11]

A second point of failure was the inability of the Royal Navy to allocate sufficient warships to the North American theater, a dynamic experienced in every location due to the expanded naval responsibilities of global war. In this instance, Caribbean operations affected Chesapeake Bay. An uncharitable interpretation places blame on Rodney, who stayed in St. Eustatius for months after its capture, collecting loot and prizes for self-enrichment. When it was time to follow de Grasse northward, he chose to return with his prizes to London and to defend his actions, depriving the North American theater of warships and Rodney.[12] The more optimistic perspective argues that naval intelligence was often unreliable, Rodney was in ill health, and the ships he took with him were in disrepair.[13] No matter what the ultimate reasoning, the end result meant that the Battle of the Virginia Capes was fought with fewer British ships and without Rodney, an aggressive leader with a proven combat record.

The final point of failure was the inability of the Royal Navy commanders, Thomas Graves and Samuel Hood, to win the actual battle. The "fog of war" carries as much blame as any personal failings. Graves, newly in command of naval forces in New York, and Hood, were tasked by Rodney to follow de Grasse from the Caribbean. Rodney sent orders to Graves informing him of de Grasse' likely push northward and requiring him to link up with Hood near the Chesapeake. Unfortunately, the ship carrying those orders was captured by an American privateer. It eventually escaped, but the information carried was now both late and suspect. When Hood arrived at the mouth of the Chesapeake, Graves was not there, thus eliminating any possibility of a linked Graves/Hood force surprising de Grasse.[14]

Intelligence failures continued past the initial missed opportunity. Linking together off New York, Graves and Hood received intelligence that Commodore Jacques-Melchior Saint-Laurent, *Comte de Barras* was sailing from Newport with artillery and supplies for the Franco-American forces preparing to attack Cornwallis. On 1 September, the British sortied making for the Chesapeake with 19 ships-of-the-line, hoping to catch de Barras' much smaller force. Instead, on 5 September, Graves ran into de Grasse' larger and more heavily armed squadron. Lacking numerical parity, the fact that the North American and West Indies contingents had not trained or operated together caused additional friction. Nonetheless, Graves attacked hoping that a victory would restore local sea superiority. The fight itself, marred by several incorrect tactical decisions by Graves, proved anticlimactic given its ultimate strategic significance. Only one ship was scuttled after the battle, no ships sank outright, fighting lasted for a little over two hours followed by several days of inconclusive chase down the North Carolina Outer Banks, and tactically resulted in a draw.[15] Strategically, however, the result proved disastrous. Bereft of any chance for rescue, reinforcement, or evacuation, Cornwallis, reduced to few working cannon and artillery rounds and losing casualties by the hour, opted for an honorable surrender. Though not known at the time, that action precipitated a chain of political decisions that ultimately ended the conflict by 1783.[16]

At the Battle of the Virginia Capes, de Grasse prevented the Royal Navy from supporting Cornwallis at Yorktown, having lost local "command of the sea." It was a sharp loss but not entirely unpredictable, given the larger strategic outlook for Britain and the Royal Navy. The transition to a global war in 1778 meant that the North American theater was no longer the main priority for sending ships, if indeed it ever was. The overall ramifications of the Battle of the Virginia Capes and the Siege of Yorktown were palpable but not insurmountable. Naval superiority could be regained, and there were still a significant number of British troops in New York and South Carolina able to conduct operations. But battles and their effects do not occur in a vacuum. With six years of fighting in North America and little to show for it, there were significant domestic political consequences for those defeats.

## Catalyst: Domestic Political Tension

The war in North America has been typically portrayed as very popular, with much of the British populace at least initially. Why not punish the ungrateful rebel colonists? This interpretation has muddled somewhat over the past 30 years, but politically speaking, Lord North's government enjoyed an overwhelming parliamentary majority when it decided to pacify the colonists by force. An overriding desire for punishment rather than reconciliation dominated Parliament. The government's leadership, especially the king and Germain, overwhelmingly favored violent pacification, a dynamic that hampered the Howe brothers, who found their roles as "Peace Commissioners" hamstrung. Little appetite for concession existed in London at the time. There were anti-war Whig politicians like John Wilkes, Charles James Fox, and Charles Watson-Wentworth, the Earl of Rockingham. Wilkes was an avowed anti-American intervention politician, whose radical positions initially made him an outlier. Rockingham, on the other hand, became the political focal point of the anti-war movement. An anti-Lord North and anti-war political group formed around Rockingham's leadership. One of his chief supporters, Edmund Burke, became famous for his opposition to the American War and later the French Revolution. Burke gave an impassioned, four-hour speech to Parliament where he argued against violent pacification of the American colonies. Yet his admonitions were ultimately ignored by a large majority in Parliament, and they voted to maintain a naval blockade along the coasts of all the rebellious colonies.[17]

As the war became prolonged and the hope for a quick, decisive victory faded, opposition to the war widened but became more complicated. Some, like Rockingham, directly opposed the war on the argument that it changed the fundamental relationship between two parts of the empire. If forceful coercion of North America was possible, then the same measures could be inflicted on the Home Islands. A more politically palatable avenue of attack was not to outright oppose the war but to criticize North's government on its financial ramifications. The war's widening expense and the potential tax increases that followed proved two particularly effective issues opponents pointed to as consequences of the fighting in North America.[18]

When the war expanded in 1778 and Britain at war not just with itself but with its traditional foe—France—the nature of opposition to the war also changed. In one sense it became more muddled; fighting a war against France and then a year later, Spain, was familiar to the British people. The threat of invasion in 1778 and 1779, combined with Jones' raids on the British coastline, better focused the attention on taking the fight to their European enemies.[19] Much like British strategy in general, the public's attention shifted from North America to Europe and imperial defense. It was harder to criticize the government for spending money and raising troops when focused on fighting France. Opponents of naval expansion in 1776, for example, were much more willing to accede to a naval buildup and expenditures once France threatened British naval superiority.[20]

Political opponents found it easier to attack the British government's prosecution of the war once it involved France. Troop mobilization and army expansion became volatile subjects. Recruitment options broadened. Impressment, foreign mercenaries or auxiliaries, and Irish Catholic recruitment represented just some of the approaches the government took to bolster military numbers. In a country traditionally opposed to a large standing army, it led to accusations of authoritarianism by opponents of the war.[21]

In the war's early years, if one argued against the use of force in North America, it was a tricky thing to also berate the government for not doing a sufficient job at pacification. Once France, Spain, and the Dutch Republic became fair game, so too did the leadership's strategic decisions. In the time-honored tradition of those not in power, opponents argued that if they were in charge, things would be different.[22] North's government faced a dual problem: the war in North America dragged on with no end in sight while fighting throughout the rest of the empire could charitably be described as stalemated.

The opposition to North's government and the American War coalesced into a serious political challenge in late 1779 and early 1780. There was potential that, as skilled of a politician as he was, North's government could not survive for long. Then everything changed in June 1780 when London violence erupted in what became known as the Gordon Riots.[23] Named after the leader and prime instigator, Lord George Gordon, the rioters were anti-Catholic and reacted to the Papist Act of 1778. The Act was designed to relax restrictions on British Catholics and, among other things make it easier for them to join the army, a policy to mitigate Britain's mobilization problems. But to anti-Catholics like Gordon, it demanded repeal. The riots lasted for a week. Though the mob never expanded beyond London, property damage was significant.[24] Both the regular army and the militia suppressed the mob with force. Hundreds of rioters died, and others were executed after the fact. It resulted in a defining moment for British domestic politics and British society. For the war, however, it meant retention of the status quo. Government's opponents became once again divided in response to the Gordon Riots, and North's administration held onto power.

Stability stemming from fear of further riots proved fleeting; the devastating loss at Yorktown took that away. When news reached London, North suspected that his administration and potentially the war, was over. Still, a disastrously poor wartime leader, he was a canny politician and fought to retain control in an increasingly untenable environment. King George and Germain wanted to continue the fight, but pressure to end the war built in Parliament. Ultimately, it took four months for North's administration to fully unravel. North resigned on 27 March 1782.[25] A coalition of politicians opposed to continuing the war—Fox, Lord Shelburne, and Lord Rockingham—assumed power. Rockingham succeeded North as First Lord of the Treasury and de facto prime minister. He almost immediately opened direct peace negotiations with both the Americans and France. However, Rockingham unexpectedly died from influenza a few months later. Shelburne then took Rockingham's place, and peace negotiations moved forward with both the Americans and their European allies. North's ministry held control during years of stalemate and loss and survived the disaster at Saratoga. Yorktown was the breaking point; the fighting in North America had gone on for too long without a major victory or success. The Battle of the Saintes (April 1782), arguably the biggest victory won by the British during the war, occurred after the collapse of North's ministry. It also had little effect on the American diplomatic position during peace negotiations, even if it did weaken the French.

## Peace Negotiations: The American Deal

The Shelburne ministry's willingness to start peace negotiations was complicated. Part of the issue was the nature of the belligerents. Britain both tried to resolve an internal rebellion and conduct peace negotiations with three different European powers, not just a matter of granting independence to the American colonies and then *c'est finis*. The rebellious American colonies had an alliance with France, which in theory bound them to negotiate a joint peace. France also had an alliance with Spain, which came with its own diplomatic guarantees and requirements. Finally, there was the Dutch Republic, which admittedly had received a tough lot, having been dragged into the fighting by the British in 1780. Nonetheless, an agreement still needed to be signed. Given the complicated potential of peace negotiations, it made sense for Britain to fracture unity and conduct separate agreements with attempts made even before the full negotiations began in Paris. Catherine the Great of Russia, starting December 1780 and going into 1781, tried to act as a mediator to end Britain's global war against France and Spain. Britain agreed to the mediation but insisted that Austria sign on as co-mediator to cause a rift between France and Austria. Sparking conflict in continental Europe would have given much-needed leverage to British negotiators. The whole process fell apart when no party agreed on American participation. Rockingham's ministry also tried in vain to find allies for leverage in the negotiations, even approaching the Dutch to organize a separate peace.[26]

Yorktown changed the calculus: the Americans were now allowed at the negotiation table. Shelburne's ministry reached out to talk with the American rebels. Three primary envoys represented American interests: Benjamin Franklin, John Jay, and John Adams. Franklin had lived in Paris for years, Jay traveled from Madrid, and Adams from Amsterdam. Their instructions from the Continental Congress were quite clear: negotiate a peace alongside Vergennes and the French. It was very fortunate for both the British and the Americans that the peace commissioners chose to outright disobey their orders. Richard Oswald, a Scottish merchant with extensive ties to the American colonies, led the American negotiations for Britain. Similar in age to Franklin, the two men got along well. He was joined by a small team of diplomatic envoys who all operated on a general goal set by Shelburne. They were to negotiate with the Americans and ultimately accede to their independence and if possible, via a separate peace from France.[27]

Franklin, Jay, and Adams were all suspicious of French intentions. Not naïve, they understood that French help came at a potential diplomatic cost. But they also did not wish to see America throw off one European master only to find itself beholden to another. Jay was very suspicious of Vergennes' intentions and did not trust the French to protect American interests.[28] Adams was of a similar mind and worried that trusting Vergennes to negotiate a peace would make America dependent on their French allies. He was also suspicious of Franklin's relationship with Vergennes.[29] But even Franklin, who loved the French and was loved by the French, was willing to agree to a separate peace if possible. Shelburne's ministry stood ready to make concessions and, ultimately, did give the Americans a generous peace deal. To understand why, it is important to look at the strategic focus and overall British objectives. The North American colonies were lost; Shelburne and his cabinet understood that fact even if George III still wanted to fight. Shelburne was also personally invested in maintaining Anglo-American connections. If the colonies would not stay within the empire, he preferred they remain close friends so as to maintain good diplomatic relations and, more importantly, good trade relationships. Most importantly, the colonies were always of secondary importance when compared to the continental balance of power. They could not afford to grant France too much influence and power. In other words, while the loss of much of North America was a severe blow, infinitely worse is if their former colonies fell into the French sphere of influence.[30]

The diplomatic stage was set. On one side, a group distrustful of their allies' intentions and, on the other, a party willing to concede much in favor of turning toward those who they viewed as their true foe. From July through November 1782, British and American negotiators worked toward an agreement. Independence was the ideal starting point, but several important ancillaries needed resolution. Some initial demands were rejected out of hand such as Franklin's suggestion that Canada be given to America. Others, such as compensation for damages Loyalists incurred, proved more difficult sticking points.[31] In October and November, the two parties met almost every day, with the French largely kept in the dark by their American allies. Ultimately, the British and Americans signed a preliminary peace treaty on 30 November 1782. It gave the colonies their independence, clarified boundaries and fishing rights, and removed British troops. Debts owed to British merchants before the war remained intact, but there was no clear agreement on Loyalist damage claims. The most the Americans offered was to suggest that the individual states adopt remuneration policies. Shelburne agreed to the toothless provision, reasoning that it was cheaper for the British government to bear the cost than to continue waging war.[32] Most importantly, the negotiators signed the agreement absent the French, contravening the American's initial alliance agreement and the negotiation team's orders from Congress. Technically it was a preliminary document (the excuse given to Vergennes), but it *de facto* removed the Americans and the American theater from the war. It weakened the European allies' bargaining positions. Finally, it ensured that no matter what the eventual settlement outcome, it was now less likely that Britain would lose its influence over North America to France.

## Peace Negotiations: The European Deals

With Anglo-American negotiations ongoing in Paris, a team of British envoys overseen by Alleyne FitzHerbert negotiated with the French, Spanish, and Dutch but with a substantial difference between the two negotiating groups. Fighting still raged between the belligerents and with British successes. The Battle of the Saintes resulted in a significant naval loss for the French in April 1782, and try as they might, Franco-Spanish forces could not capture Gibraltar. In September, the final grand assault on the fortress failed to force British capitulation. A third relief convoy in November further secured Gibraltar's safety and weakened the French and Spanish negotiating position.

Events on continental Europe also influenced peace negotiations. The lack of fighting on the continent allowed France to focus solely on the maritime domain. In 1780, Russia indirectly aided France with the League of Armed Neutrality. Russia also signed a secret alliance with Austria, a French ally, which helped isolate Britain on the continent.[33] However, while France focused on the maritime war, Russia advanced its interests against the Ottoman Empire, another French ally. In late 1782, Russia signaled that it intended to take Crimea, an Ottoman territory, forcing France to focus its attention eastward.[34]

Vergennes felt pressured by the Anglo-American preliminary peace and angry over the betrayal of the alliance' spirit. He also was frustrated at the probable loss of French influence over America beyond the war, particularly political leverage. But Vergennes' primary objective was always full independence for the American colonies, the clearest way to strike at British prestige and restore the Anglo-French balance of power.[35] The separate agreement did not undercut that objective; it only put unwanted pressure on the European powers to also reach an agreement with Great Britain. Most of the Anglo-French negotiations centered on rebalancing the Seven Years' War peace. Vergennes, for example, initially asked for the territories in India to be restored to their 1754 boundaries. Shelburne refused; he wanted peace but not as generous to France as to the Americans. Instead, Britain offered a number of Indian towns more relevant for their revenue than their strategic value. Other deals included fishery rights in Newfoundland, the return of the Senegal and Goree trade forts, removal of a restriction for France to fortify Dunkirk, and the transfer of Caribbean Islands. Many of these concessions, much like American independence, were designed to recover French honor and restore the balance of power on the continent. The preliminary peace agreement was signed just two months after the American settlement, in January 1783.

Spanish negotiators, initially more stubborn than the French, insisted on the forfeiture of Gibraltar, the primary reason Spain entered into war, as a condition of peace. Even after the last failed assault, they still refused to give up on the effort. In a difficult position, Shelburne demanded severe concessions by both France and Spain, including either Puerto Rico or Dominica and Guadeloupe in the Caribbean. However, Gibraltar's resolute defense over a three-year siege became very popular in London; the price needed to be even higher if one of the few British successes emerged as a bargaining chip. Ultimately, negotiations broke down. Spain decided to extract as many territorial concessions as possible without gaining Gibraltar. Britain ended up ceding West and East Florida and Minorca to the Spanish, leaving only Canada as British North American territory. The Dutch Republic's demands were similarly scoped; they wanted free navigation, return of all the territories captured, and payment for the losses. Shelburne was the least generous with the Dutch, militarily weak with little leverage. He only offered to return the territories, including St Eustatius, and took Negapatam in India as compensation. An additional sign that the Dutch Republic was essentially powerless in the negotiations: their envoys did not negotiate with the British as everything went through Vergennes.[36]

## Treaty Aftermath

When news of the preliminary deals reached London, Shelburne was excoriated both by MPs and the press and by not just former supporters of Lord North but also members of Shelburne's own faction, specifically Fox. They argued that Shelburne and his envoys gave up too much territory and did not properly look after the rights of Loyalists.[37] An unlikely alliance formed between Fox and North, which forced Shelburne out of office. Fox became the first Foreign Secretary, a newly created office. He immediately set about renegotiating the agreements, something he had claimed he could do during the months he criticized Shelburne. But, the final treaties looked very similar, and in some cases identical to the earlier preliminary agreements. Fox failed to gain significant ground and the final documents were signed in September 1783.[38]

There were both immediate and longer-term consequences to the war termination outcome. The fulcrum to the war, France, found itself paying a very high price for a few overseas territories and the restoration of French honor through British misfortune. France's indirect and direct involvement proved very expensive. Rebuilding the French Navy from the ashes of the Seven Years' War was particularly costly. To complicate matters, France chose to pay for the war via loans without increasing taxes. They sold offices to defray the expense, but those offices could not provide a stable long-term solution. France faced a long-term, multi-decade financial challenge; the American war only exacerbated the problem. Attempts in the later war years to be more fiscally transparent only further reduced confidence in the French government.[39] Ultimately, the financial stressors incurred while helping the American rebels became one of the catalysts of the French Revolution later in the 1780s. The French hoped that increased long-term trade with the new United States might counterbalance the war's financial cost, a difficult proposition. Though the political ties were severed, there were still significant American commercial and cultural connections to Britain, a core reason France insisted on a joint peace. But the separately negotiated treaties landed a severe blow to a potential sphere of influence swap. Adding to France's woes was the changing continental geopolitical situation. They were unable to translate the honor they regained into meaningful political or military influence. They failed to stymie Russia's push into the Crimea, nor were they able to dictate the flow of international relations elsewhere in Europe. By 1787, war threatened again with France too far in debt and unable to leverage any more money through borrowing. Lack of funds meant less military power, influence, and trust with other European nations. In short, the costs for France supporting the American War far outweighed the benefits.[40]

The Americans also faced a difficult post-war transition. Reasonably unified during the war, the former British colonies now needed a process for further integration. The states were bound by the Articles of Confederation passed by the Continental Congress in 1777 and ratified by all in 1781, a skeletonized, weak form of central government. The journey between 1783 and the ratification of the US Constitution in 1788 (implemented in 1789) witnessed uncertainty, violence, severe post-war economic difficulties, and above all else, intense, and earnest political debate about the new nation's future. Lack of a strong central government allowed instability as exacerbated by the aftereffects of the Treaty of Paris.

A key tenet of any war termination process is the actual execution of the peace agreement. Diplomacy and negotiation may set the terms, but they mean little if there is no enforcement mechanism. Among two powers of relatively equal strength, the threat of further war mitigates post-peace tensions. A brand-new nation lay in a tougher position. American expansion westward proved a particular problem. American envoys secured all territory from the Appalachian range to the eastern bank of the Mississippi River. Furthermore, they were guaranteed freedom of use for travel and trade on the Mississippi and access to markets in Spanish New Orleans. Spain soon realized that if it restricted physical access, they could choose who might trade on the river, making settlers in territories west of the mountains more beholden to Spain than America. They also built forts from West Florida to Louisiana to dissuade American expansionists.[41] Only by 1795 did the United States have the diplomatic clout to negotiate a treaty with Spain that solved the territorial issues and avoided war.

Britain was also slow in adhering to aspects of the peace treaty. They maintained and garrisoned border forts in the Northwest Territory despite the agreement to evacuate. Lacking a strong federal government, Americans could only diplomatically protest. Much like the Spanish, the British tried to enflame tensions and take advantage of a divided and weak America. Ultimately their intent was to watch it collapse and then scoop back some of the pieces.[42] British policymakers held a robust pessimism about the United States' long-term viability. While governed by the Articles of Confederation, the Americans were not viewed as being on par with European nations when it came to diplomatic negotiations.[43] The new Constitution strengthened the American position in terms of future treaty negotiations and enforcement.

From a British perspective, the loss of so much colonial territory in North America sparked a form of soul-searching. The most immediate question that arose from the Peace of 1783 centered on what happens to American Loyalists. At war's end, Loyalists often faced a stark choice: stay living in a new nation and reject their old country or leave and become war refugees. Those that stayed faced potential discrimination and violence. During the struggle, a civil war engulfed the colonies, particularly in the Carolinas. Those tensions did not disappear once the war ended. Many Loyalists had fled to areas controlled by Crown forces and their property and land were not necessarily intact when and if they returned. Furthermore, despite the Treaty of 1783 specifically prohibiting reprisals against Loyalists, many states ignored that provision. Loyalist property confiscation emerged as an especially burdensome problem, both during the war and after the peace. There were also social and legal questions on how best to reintegrate the Loyalists who decided to stay.[44] A contentious process, it mirrored (or perhaps helped dictate) Anglo-American diplomatic tension following the peace.

Many Loyalists chose to leave, either during the war or in the years following. Exact numbers are difficult to ascertain, but an estimated 60,000 Loyalist refugees fled between 1774 and 1784.[45] Many went north to Canada, choosing at least to stay in the remains of British North America. Others sought new lives in the Caribbean, West Africa, India, or even Spanish territories, particularly heavily Loyalist East and West Florida. Some Loyalists chose to go to the Home Islands.[46] In certain areas of very high Loyalist concentration such as the Cross Creek region of North Carolina (Scottish Highlanders) and the Swiss-German settlements west of Charlotte, North Carolina, Loyalists who paid fines and swore allegiance to the state remained, relatively unmolested. But those exceptions were unusual. Regardless of the location, the overall character of the empire changed. Policymakers in London experimented with the best way to assert more control over the individual parts of the empire while also mitigating the factors that led to the American rebellion.[47]

Refugees or residents, tension ran high between the United States and Britain over Loyalist disputes. The treaty did little to mollify British or American perspectives on the problem. The British demanded compensation for property damage inflicted on Loyalists, and the United States was both unwilling and unable (because of the weak central government) to oblige. The Loyalist plight became a useful justification for Britain's continued interference in North America. Only after the United States created a stronger federal government did negotiations advance. John Jay, one of the original envoys for the 1783 peace, negotiated an Anglo-American treaty (ratified by the Senate in 1795) that diffused much of the tension. It helped solidify the British sphere of influence in American affairs and separate the United States from French and Spanish domination.[48] The Jay treaty did not resolve Loyalist's concerns. The Loyalists remained an awkward, widespread reminder of a great failure of the British Empire. As to the border and territorial tensions, only another war in 1812 finally settled both nations into a pattern of mutual respect and accommodation in North America that blossomed over the decades into the "Special Relationship" based on friendship, a shared culture and value system, and common interests.

## Notes

1 Clausewitz, On War, 92.
2 Fowler, Rebels, 136–40.
3 Volo, Blue Water Patriot, 218.
4 John Paul Jones and Gerard W. Gawalt, ed. and trans., John Paul Jones' Memoir (Washington, DC: U.S. Government Printing Office, 1979), 41.
5 Sheldon S. Cohen, Commodore Abraham Whipple of the Continental Navy (Gainesville, FL: University Press of Florida, 2010), 51, 68, 101, 121.
6 Henning Hillmann and Christina Gathman, "Overseas Trade and the Decline of Privateering," in The Journal of Economic History 71, no. 3 (September 2011): 734–5, 745. France, Spain and The Dutch Republic also empowered their own privateers to harass British commerce.
7 Willis, Struggle, 95.
8 Stephen Conway, The British Isles and the War for American Independence (Oxford: Oxford University Press, 2000), 64.
9 Simon Hill, "The Liverpool Economy during the War of American Independence, 1775–83," in The Journal of Imperial and Commonwealth History 44, no. 6 (2016): 844–5; Hillman and Gathman, "Overseas Trade," 739; Conway, British Isles, 70.
10 Dull, French Navy, 237–8.
11 Hattendorf, Newport, 103–5.
12 Dull, French Navy, 238.
13 Colin Pengelly, Sir Samuel Hood and the Battle of the Chesapeake (Gainesville, FL: University Press of Florida, 2009), 100–2.
14 Ibid., 114–5.
15 Jerome A. Green, The Guns of Independence: The Siege of Yorktown, 1781 (New York: Savas Beatie, 2005), 20–2.
16 For an in-depth analysis and description of the actual engagement, see Carpenter, Southern Gambit.
17 Ferling, Whirlwind, 135–6.
18 Conway, British Isles, 148–9.
19 Simon Lutnick, The American Revolution and the British Press 1775–1783 (Columbia, MO: University of Missouri Press, 1967), 152–3.

20 Conway, *British Isles*, 152.
21 Ibid., 164.
22 Ibid., 149–50.
23 O'Shaughnessy, *Men Who Lost America*, 74.
24 Roy Porter, *English Society in the 18th Century* (New York: Penguin Books, 1990), 101.
25 O'Shaughnessy, *Men Who Lost America*, 74–8.
26 Andrew Stockley, *Britain and France at the Birth of America: The European Powers and the Peace Negotiations of 1782–1783* (Exeter: University of Exeter Press, 2001), 26–8, 30, 42–4.
27 Ferling, *Whirlwind*, 317; Stockley, *Britain and France*, 37–9; Henry Laurens also played a minor role in the discussions.
28 Frank W. Brecher, *Securing American Independence: John Jay and the French Alliance* (Westport, CT: Praeger, 2003), 185, 190.
29 James H. Hutson, *John Adams and the Diplomacy of the American Revolution* (Kentucky: The University Press of Kentucky, 1980), 121, 134.
30 Stockley, *Britain and France*, 53–4.
31 Ibid., 62–3.
32 Ibid., 64–5; Ferling, *Whirlwind*, 315–6.
33 Orville T. Murphy, *The Diplomatic Retreat of France and Public Opinion on the Eve of the Revolution 1783–1789* (Washington, DC: The Catholic University of America Press, 1998), 17.
34 Brendan Simms, *Three Victories and a Defeat; The Rise and Fall of the First British Empire* (New York: Basic Books, 2008) 658–9.
35 Stockley, *Britain and France*, 72–3.
36 Ibid., 109–11, 120, 122–3, 126–8.
37 Lutnick, *American Revolution*, 206–7.
38 Simms, *Three Victories*, 660.
39 Murphy, *Diplomatic Retreat*, 26–8; Brendan Simms, *Europe: The Struggle for Supremacy, from 1453 to the Present* (New York: Basic Books, 2014), 132.
40 Simms, *Europe*, 141–2.
41 Taylor, *American Revolutions*, 345–6.
42 Don Higginbotham, "War and State Formation in Revolutionary America" in *Empire and Nation: The American Revolution in the Atlantic World,* eds. Eliga H. Gould and Peter S. Onuf (Baltimore, MD: The Johns Hopkins University Press, 2005), 66–7.
43 Eliga H. Gould, *Among the Powers of the Earth* (Cambridge, MA: Harvard University Press, 2012), 126–7.
44 Maya Jasanoff, *Liberty's Exiles: American Loyalists in the Revolutionary World* (New York: Vintage Books, 2011), 318–9.
45 Ibid., 357; Keith Mason, "The American Loyalist Diaspora" in Gould and Ounf, *Empire and Nation*, 240. Higher estimates put the number between 80,000 and 100,000.
46 Jasanoff, *Liberty's Exiles*, 351–7.
47 Taylor, *American Revolutions*, 330–3.
48 Gould, *Among the Powers*, 136–7.

# CONCLUSION

## Peril and Delusion

> The mere fact that the British Ministry rested its hopes on the co-operation of American loyalists was sufficient to distract its councils and to vitiate its plans . . . of all foundations on which to build a campaign this is the loosest, the most treacherous, the fullest of peril and delusion. . . . Their purpose being vague and unconfirmed, the Ministers proceeded without any idea of what an army could or could not do, or of the force that was required for any given object.[1]

The eminent British Army Historian, Sir John Fortescue, succinctly sums up the problems of incoherent strategies, poorly executed operations, and misunderstanding of the nature of the conflict that doomed Crown efforts to pacify the rebellious North American colonies and return them to allegiance between 1775 and 1781. Although Fortescue addresses the particular Southern Campaign Loyalist Strategy ("peril and delusion"), the assessment might easily capture the essence of the entire war effort. With that in mind, it is useful to repeat the overarching thesis and themes of this textbook as stated in the opening Introduction.

Throughout the War of American Independence, British leaders failed to develop an effective strategy to quell the discontent and subsequent revolt in the North American colonies and thus failed to restore allegiance to the Crown. By contrast, the American Patriots conducted a successful defensive war of attrition that, in combination with the intervention of European powers, countered and nullified all Crown political, military, economic, and diplomatic efforts to end the rebellion. Despite losing the North American colonies by 1783, British naval and military forces successfully defeated French and allied efforts to conquer either the British homeland or the most significant colonial and imperial possessions.

British political and military measures undertaken in the wake of the Seven Years' War set the stage for conflict between the British colonists and the Crown. With the outbreak of open rebellion in Massachusetts in April 1775, the British

DOI: 10.4324/9781003041276-18

Empire faced a daunting challenge—how does a distant imperial power conduct a war to suppress a colonial rebellion while simultaneously defending against peer competitors? Britain needed an effective military and political strategy to suppress the rebellion and return the colonies to allegiance, particularly after French, Spanish, and Dutch intervention turned the colonial affair into a global, great power conflict. Despite the state of communications, transportation, lack of sufficient naval and military manpower resources and logistics, policy and strategy decision-makers embarked on an offensive strategy of annihilation (pacification by brute force). The result was a series of conventional operations designed to crush the Continental Army, suppress the Patriot militia and insurgents (often called partisans), allow the Loyalists to restore the royal government, and pacify the colonies, thus restoring allegiance. Several variations of this strategy emerged throughout the war, often achieving operational success but ultimately resulting in strategic failure. From the American Patriot viewpoint, the war was largely reactive in that by fighting a strategy of defensive attrition (Fabian Strategy), the Patriots wore down British political will to continue the struggle following the surrender at Yorktown, Virginia, in October 1781. From the French and Spanish perspectives, the war represented revenge for the Seven Years' War humiliation. The war's outcome was neither the result of British errors nor a conflict won by American bravery and strategic insight. It was, rather, a complex mosaic composed of a colonial domestic discontent complicated by a dynamic international situation and an emerging and distinct American culture. A number of key themes and concepts run through this examination of the conflict that resulted in the creation of a new, and totally unique nation, the United States of America.

British authorities, both civil and military, failed to articulate and execute coherent strategies for pacification. Due to the nature of the war administration in transition from the feudal monarchical household pattern to the modern, bureaucratized, industrial state, a successful and cohesive strategy never emerged. While the various stratagems from offensive attrition to divide and conquer to reliance on loyalism all might have worked if superbly executed, given human nature and the inevitable "fog and friction" of warfare, perfect execution was unlikely. Additionally, absent a strong "One Great Director," personalities with differing strategic and operational concepts roiled the decision-making waters. One need look no further than the Clinton-Cornwallis dynamic or the Germain-Sandwich rivalry. In retrospect, there might not have been any strategy, military or political, that would have brought the colonies back into the fold. Perhaps the one with any merit might well be as expressed in 1776 by Sir Henry Clinton when he advocated winning the colonials' "hearts and minds."

The war's events illustrate a dynamic that has complicated great power strategies and operations for thousands of years. Even in the twenty-first century, great or superpowers struggle with how to prosecute a war, especially a low-intensity, irregular, or hybrid war, from afar. In the 1770s, transporting supplies and troops from the British Isles to the colonies might take four weeks or four months. No timely or reliable communications existed, leaving local commanders largely on their own and making critical strategic and operational decisions without tight command, control, and coordination. Civil to military relations (CIVMIL or CMR) are often disrupted by dynamics of personality, ineffective leadership, or service rivalries. In this conflict, while such episodes as the so-called "Conway Cabal" occasionally roiled Patriot CMR, by and large key players such as Washington, Adams, Franklin, and many others kept the Patriot CMR upright and sailing smoothly. For the Crown side, the CMR dynamic played badly. Cabinet rivalries and personality conflicts roiled British war administration and execution. General officer and service rivalries flummoxed operations. Army and navy joint cooperation depended on commanders' personalities, which often undercut military effectiveness. In short, British fielded forces suffered mightily from a CMR breakdown at the highest levels of civil and military authority.

The Patriots, on the other hand, employed a highly successful strategy of defensive attrition or "Fabian Strategy" named for the Roman consul Fabius Maximus, who employed it against the Carthaginian general Hannibal Barca in the 2nd Punic War (3rd century BCE). George Washington evolved through a series of disastrous battlefield defeats and ineffective strategies before finally finding the appropriate Fabian Strategy. Nathanael Greene then employed the strategy against Cornwallis and Crown forces in the South. Essentially, in a classic Fabian Strategy, the weaker side conducts a low-intensity war or "*petit guerre*" against the stronger opponent. Operations include attacks on logistics, communications, outposts, and so on, to achieve small incremental victories and wear down the opponent's resolve or ability to continue the fight. The ultimate expression of the Fabian Strategy is the final, decisive, culminating battle that forces the stronger opponent to end the war. While Crown forces and politicians struggled to find the right strategy, the Patriots executed, often brilliantly, their war-winning strategy.

The War of American Independence that started on a spring day on a Massachusetts village common erupted into yet another global, imperial, maritime conflict between the British Empire and the Bourbon powers, France and Spain. In essence, the struggle was a war within a war within a war. It was a local irregular insurgency fought within a larger regional context that eventually morphed into a global great power war. In this context, alliances and coalitions became critical. The American Patriots could not have prosecuted the war without foreign aid. It is estimated, for example, that perhaps 90 percent of the gunpowder used by the Patriot forces came from France. More specifically, it was French naval power winning temporary "command of the sea" in the Chesapeake Bay and French siege artillery brought from Newport by sea that decided Cornwallis' fate at Yorktown. Had not Spanish General and Governor Don Bernardo de Galvez run amok on the Gulf Coast and West Florida in 1780–1781, might Cornwallis have won his campaign in the South? What if he had the several thousand British and Loyalist troops stationed in East and West Florida to defend against the Spanish? It's an unknown question to be sure. Then what of Britain's normal alliance position in the period?

What if traditional French rivals such as the Dutch, Austrians, or Prussians had seen an opportunity and thrown in their lot with Britain? How might that dynamic have altered the outcome? Thus, the criticality of the alliance and coalition situation played large in the Patriots' ability to not only stay in the fray but ultimately prevail. The war then was one of many peoples. Not only the white male and female colonists and British and German troops but also the African Americans, both free and enslaved, as well as the Native American Indians, all played key roles in the events and the outcome. Much of Europe played a role in some fashion in the American War drama, including French, Spanish, Portuguese, Dutch, and the League of Armed Neutrality kingdoms. Even states such as Austria had roles particularly in the war termination phase. The War of American Independence was truly "A War of Many Peoples."

War termination presents a prickly problem for warring states. Unless one side has been utterly defeated, even conquered, such as in World War II with Germany and Japan, negotiated settlements are typically problematic as each player jockeys to win as much of their policy objectives as possible. Clausewitz was spot on when he declared that no war is ever final. The history of conflict between the mid-seventeenth and early nineteenth centuries between European states certainly underscores his assertion. So it was for the Americans, British, and allies. For that reason, this study devotes considerable attention to the war termination aspects. The outcome of the peace established several dynamics for the participants. The winners were not only the new United States but Great Britain as well. Once the competition for North America, particularly the status of Canada and the Pacific Northwest was established, the two nations became close allies by the twentieth century sharing a common culture, value system, and international interests. France, largely due to the collapse of royal finances aggravated by the war's expenditure, endured the French Revolution turmoil. Spain, already deteriorating, lost most of its American empire in the revolutions of the early nineteenth century. Trade between the former Mother Country and the newborn United States flourished. Finally, freed of the American colonial headaches, the British Empire expanded and dominated the world for the next century and a half.

Through a brief examination of the major dynamics and events, the story of the War of American Independence is analyzed through the major themes of strategy, operational and event narratives, civil to military relations, domestic and international politics, economics, commerce, trade, sea and maritime power, war termination, understanding the nature of a conflict, alliances and coalitions, and winning the support of the people. This work in the Taylor & Francis (Routledge) *Warfare and History* series thus places the War of American Independence in the context of people and societies in conflict. It must always be remembered that most of the great changes in human progression have been brought about by conflict and war. In this regard, the War of American Independence brought forth the modern United States of America and all that that dynamic implies. From it emerged not only Great Britain poised on the verge of world political and economic domination even though losing several colonies but a new republic where sovereign power rested with its citizens and charged with the concepts and philosophy that had evolved over the centuries from Ancient Greece and Rome to the Enlightenment, concepts of the state and the individual in a free society.

## Note

1 Fortescue, *British Army*, part II, vol. 3, 168–9.

# BIBLIOGRAPHY

## Primary Sources—Manuscripts, Collections, and Published Monographs

Adams, John. *The Works of John Adams, Second President of the United States: With a Life of the Author, Notes and Illustrations by His Grandson Charles Francis Adams*, 10 vols. Boston, MA: Little, Brown and Co., 1856.

Adams, John. *The Papers of John Adams*, Edited by Robert J. Taylor et al. Cambridge, MA: Harvard University Press, 1977.

Admiralty, Royal Navy. *Fighting Instructions*, Edited by Sir Julian S. Corbett, Vol. 29. London: Spottswoodie, Publications of the Navy Records Society, 1905.

Allaire, Anthony. *Diary of Lieut. Anthony Allaire (Eyewitness Accounts of the American Revolution)*. New York: New York Times Press, 1968.

Andre, John. *Major Andre's Journal: Operations of the British Army under General Sir William Howe and Sir Henry Clinton, June 1777, to November, 1778*, Edited by William Abbatt. New York: Arno Press, 1968.

Army War College Historical Section. *Historical Statements Concerning the Battle of Kings Mountain and the Battle of the Cowpens, South Carolina*. Washington, DC: Government Printing Office, 1928.

Barnhart, J. D. ed. *Henry Hamilton and George Rogers Clark in the American Revolution: With the Unpublished Journal of Lieut. Gov. Henry Hamilton*. Crawfordsville, IN: R.E. Banta, 1951.

Baurmeister, Carl Leopold. *Revolution in America: Confidential Letters and Journals 1776–1784 of Adj. Gen. Major Baurmeister of the Hessian Forces*, Translated by Bernhard A. Uhlendorf. New Brunswick, NJ: Rutgers University Press, 1957.

Burgoyne, John. *Orderly Book of Lieutenant General John Burgoyne*, Edited by E. B. O'Callaghan. Albany, NY: J. Munsell, 1850.

Campbell, Archibald. *Journal of an Expedition against the Rebels of Georgia in North America*, Edited by Colin Campbell. Darien, GA: Ashantilly Press, 1981.

*Cantonment of His Majesty's Forces in N. America According to the Disposition Now Made & to Be Completed as Soon as Practicable Taken from the General Distribution Dated at New York 29th. March* [1766] Map. Washington, DC: Library of Congress.

*Cantonment of the Forces in North America 11th. Octr.* [1765] Map. Washington, DC: Library of Congress.

Carlton, Guy. *Headquarters Papers of the British Army in North America, 1775–1784* (Dorchester Papers). National Archives, Kew, PRO30/55.

Chadwick, French Ensor. ed. *The Graves Papers and Other Documents Relating to the Naval Operations of the Yorktown Campaign, July to October, 1781.* New York: The Naval History Society, De Vinne Press, 1916.

Chesney, Alexander. *The Journal of Alexander Chesney, a South Carolina Loyalist in the Revolution and After.* The Ohio State University Studies, Contributions in History and Political Science, Number 7, Vol. XXVI, No. 4, Edited by E. Alfred Jones. Columbus, OH: The Ohio State University, 1921.

Clinton, Sir Henry. *Observations on Mr. Stedman's History of the American War.* Farmington Hills, MI: Gale ECCO, 2010a.

Clinton, Sir Henry. *Observations on Some Parts of the Answer of Earl Cornwallis to Sir Henry Clinton's Narrative.* Farmington Hills, MI: Gale ECCO, 2010b.

Clinton, Sir Henry. *Sir Henry Clinton Papers.* Ann Arbor, MI: William L. Clements Library, University of Michigan, 1736–1850.

Clinton, Sir Henry. *The American Rebellion: Sir Henry Clinton's Narrative of His Campaigns, 1775–1782, with an Appendix of Original Documents,* Edited by William B. Willcox. New Haven, CT: Yale University Press, 1954. Reprint, Hamden, CT: Archon, 1971.

Clinton, Sir Henry. *The Narrative of Lieutenant-General Sir Henry Clinton, K.B., Relative to His Conduct During Part of His Command of the King's Troops in North America: Particularly to That Which Respects the Campaign Issue of 1781.* Farmington Hills, MI: Gale ECCO, 2010.

Continental Congress. *Letters of the Delegates of the Continental Congress,* Edited by Paul H. Smith. Washington, DC: Library of Congress, 1981.

Cornwallis Correspondence. National Archives, Kew, PRO 30/11.

Cornwallis, Charles. *The Cornwallis Papers, Abstracts of Americana,* Edited by George H. Reese. 1859. Reprint, Charlottesville, VA: University of Virginia Press, 1970.

Cornwallis, Charles. *An Answer to That Part of the Narrative of Lieutenant-General Sir Henry Clinton, K.B., Which Relates to the Conduct of Lieutenant-General Earl Cornwallis, During the Campaign in North America, in the Year 1781.* Farmington Hills, MI: Gale ECCO, 2010.

Cornwallis, Charles. *The Cornwallis Papers: The Campaigns of 1780 and 1781 in the Southern Theatre of the American Revolutionary War,* Edited by Ian Saberton, 6 vols. Uckfield: Naval and Military Press, 2010.

Cornwallis, Charles. *Correspondence of Charles, First Marquis Cornwallis,* Edited by Charles Derek Ross. Cambridge: Cambridge University Press, 2011.

Dann, John C. ed. *The Revolution Remembered: Eyewitness Accounts of the War for Independence.* Chicago, IL: University of Chicago Press, 1980.

Davies, K. G. ed. *Documents of the American Revolution 1770–1783,* 20 vols. Shannon: Irish Universities Press, 1976.

Döhla, Johann Conrad. *A Hessian Diary of the American Revolution,* Translated and Edited by Bruce E. Burgoyne. Norman, OK: University of Oklahoma Press, 1990.

Donop, Wilhelm Gottlieb Levin von. *Des Obermarschalls und Drosten Wilhelm Gottlieb Levin von Donop zu Lüdershofen, Maspe Nachricht von dem Geschlecht der von Donop.* Paderborn, 1796.

Donop, Wilhelm Gottlieb Levin von. "Letters from a Hessian Mercenary." Translated and Edited by C. V. Easum and Hans Huth. *PMBH* 62, no. 4 (October 1938): 499.

Drake, Francis S. ed. *Tea Leaves: Being a Collection of Letters and Documents Relating to the Shipment of Tea to the American Colonies in the Year 1773, by the East India Tea Company.* Boston, MA: A.O. Crane, 1884.

Drayton, John. *Memoirs of the American Revolution*, 2 vols. Charleston, SC: A.E. Miller, 1821.

Edmunds, Albert J. "Letters of a French Officer, Written at Easton, Penna., in 1777–1778." *PMBH* 35, no. 1 (1911): 90–102.

Egle, William H. *Pennsylvania Archives*, Series 2, Vols. 10–15. Harrisburg, PA: E.K. Meyers, State Printers, 1887–1907.

Ewald, Johann von. *Diary of the American War: A Hessian Journal*, Translated and Edited by Joseph P. Tustin. New Haven, CT: Yale University Press, 1979.

Ewald, Johann von. *Treatise on Partisan Warfare*, Translated and Annotated by Robert A. Selig and David Curtis Skaggs. Westport, CT: Greenwood Press, 1991.

Fonblanque, Edward Barrington. *Political and Military Episodes in the Latter Half of the Eighteenth Century: Derived from the Life and Correspondence of the Right Hon. John Burgoyne, General, Statesman, Dramatist*. London: Macmillan, 1876.

Force, Peter. ed. *American Archives*, Vol. 2, 1775. Washington, DC: M. St. Clair Clarke and Peter Force, 1839.

Freeholders of Fincastle County, Virginia, Committee of Safety. *Address of the People of Fincastle County, Virginia, to the Delegates from that Colony, Who Attended the Continental Congress*. Chicago, IL: University of Chicago American Archives Documents of the American Revolution; *The Virginia Gazette*, no. 2, 10 February 1775.

Gage, Thomas. *Thomas Gage Papers. William L. Clements Library*. Ann Arbor, MI: University of Michigan.

Gilder Lehrman Collection. *Pennsylvania Journal and Weekly Advertiser*. New York: The Gilder Lehrman Institute of American History, December 6, 1775.

Graham, Samuel. *Memoir of General [Samuel] Graham: With Notices of the Campaigns in Which He Was Engaged from 1779 to 1801*, Edited by His Son, Colonel J. J. Graham. Edinburgh: R. and R. Clark, 1862.

Great Britain, House of Commons. *The Parliamentary Register; or, History of the Proceedings and Debates of the House of Commons: Containing an Account of the Most Interesting Speeches and Motions; Accurate Copies of the Most Honourable Letters and Papers; of the Most Material Evidence, Petitions &c Laid Before and Offered to the House, During the Fifth Session of the Fourteenth Parliament of Great Britain*, Edited by John Stockdale. London: Wilson and Co., 1802.

Great Britain, Office of the Secretary of State. *Original Correspondence of the Secretary of State (Letter Books of the Colonial Office) (America and West Indies)*, National Archives, Kew. CO/5.

Greene, Nathanael. *The Papers of Nathanael Greene*, Edited by Richard K. Showman, Dennis M. Conrad, Roger N. Parks, and Elizabeth C. Stevens, 9 vols. Chapel Hill, NC: University of North Carolina Press, 1991.

Guelph, George William Frederick, King George III. *The Correspondence of King George the Third from 1760 to December 1783, Printed from the Original Papers in the Royal Archives at Windsor Castle, Arranged and Edited by the Hon. Sir John Fortescue*, Edited by Sir John Fortescue. London: Macmillan, 1927–1928.

Guelph, George William Frederick, King George III. *The Correspondence of King George the Third*, Edited by Sir John Fortescue. London: Macmillan and Co., 1928.

Hamilton, Alexander. *The Papers of Alexander Hamilton*, Edited by Harold C. Syrett and Jacob E. Cooke, 27 vols. New York: Columbia University Press, 1961–1979.

Hanger, George. *The Life, Adventures, and Opinions of Colonel George Hanger*, 2 vols. Charleston, SC: Nabu, 2010.

Harcourt, William. *The Harcourt Papers*. Edited by Edward Harcourt, Vol. 11. Oxford: Oxford University Press, 1880–1885.

Hardman, John and Munro Price. eds. *Louis XVI and the comte de Vergennes: Correspondence 1774–1787*. Oxford: Voltaire Foundation, 1998.

Hood, Sir Samuel. *Hood Letters*. Greenwich; London: National Maritime Museum.

Hood, Sir Samuel. *Letters of Sir Samuel Hood*, Edited by David Hannay. London: Navy Records Society, 1895.

Hough, Franklin Benjamin. *The Siege of Savannah by the Combined American and French Forces under the Command of Gen. Lincoln and the Count D'Estaing in the Autumn of 1779.* 1866. Reprint, New York: Da Capo Press, 1974.

Howe, William. *The Narrative of Lt. Gen. Sir William Howe to a Committee in the House of Commons on the 29th of April, 1779.* London: H. Baldwin, 1779.

Howe, William. *General Sir William Howe's Orderly Book at Charlestown, Boston and Halifax, June 17 1775 through 1776 26 May*, Edited by Benjamin Franklin Stevens. London: Benjamin Franklin Stevens, 1890.

Hunter, Martin. *The Journal of Gen. Sir Martin Hunter and Some Letters of his Wife, Lady Hunter*, Edited by A. Hunter. Edinburgh: Edinburgh Press, 1894.

Jefferson, Thomas. *The Papers of Thomas Jefferson*, Edited by Julian P. Boyd et al., 45 vols. Princeton, NJ: Princeton University Press, 1950–2021.

Jones, John Paul. *John Paul Jones' Memoir*, Edited and Translated by Gerard W. Gawalt. Washington, DC: U.S. Government Printing Office, 1979.

*Journals of the Continental Congress, 1774–1789*, 34 vols, Edited by Worthington C. Ford et al. Washington, DC: Library of Congress, 1904–1937.

Lamb, Roger. *An Original and Authentic Journal of Occurrences During the Late American War from Its Commencement to the Year 1783.* Dublin: Wilkinson and Courtney, 1809.

Lee, Charles. *The Life and Memoirs of the Late Major General Lee, Second in Command to General Washington, During the American Revolution, to Which Are Added, His Political and Military Essays.* New York: Richard Scott, 1813.

Lincoln County Assizes. *Confiscation Papers and Lincoln County Court Minutes for 1782 and 1783.* Raleigh, NC: North Carolina State Archives, 1783.

Mackenzie, Roderick. *Strictures on Lt. Col. Tarleton's "History of the Campaigns of 1780 and 1781, in the Southern Provinces of North America."* Farmington Hills, MI: Gale ECCO, 2010.

Molyneux, Thomas More. *Conjunct Expeditions, or Expeditions That Have Been Carried on Jointly by the Fleet and Army: With a Commentary on Littoral Warfare.* London: R. and J. Dodsley, 1759.

Montague, John, Earl of Sandwich. *The Private Papers of John, Earl of Sandwich, First Lord of the Admiralty, 1771–1781*, Edited by G. R. Barnes and J. H. Owens. London: Navy Records Society, 1932–38.

Morgan, Edmund S. ed. *Prologue to Revolution: Sources and Documents on the Stamp Act Crisis, 1764–1766.* Chapel Hill, NC: University of North Carolina Press, 1959.

Motier, Gilbert. *Lafayette in the Age of the American Revolution: Selected Letters and Papers, 1776–1790.* Edited by Stanley J. Idzerda, 5 vols. Ithaca, NY: Cornell University Press, 1977–1983.

North Carolina Office of Archives and History. *North Carolina Colonial Records*, Edited by Robert J. Cain, Vol. 10. Raleigh, NC: North Carolina State Archives, 1999.

O'Hara, Charles. Grafton Papers, Suffolk Record Office, Bury St Edmunds, UK, 1781.

Peebles, John. *John Peebles' American War: The Diary of a Scottish Grenadier, 1776–1782*, Edited by Ira D. Gruber. Mechanicsburg, PA: Stackpole Books, 1998.

Roberts, Kenneth. ed. *March to Quebec, Journals of the Members of Arnold's Expedition.* Garden City, NY: Doubleday, 1938.

Rodney, Sir George. *Sailing and Fighting Instructions.* London: National Archives, Kew.

Royal Commission on Historical Manuscripts. *Historical Manuscripts Commission, Fourteenth Report, Appendix, Part X, "The Manuscripts of the Earl of Dartmouth Volume II, American Papers."* London: His Majesty's Stationary Office, 1895.

Royal Commission on Historical Manuscripts. "Headquarters Papers of the British Army in North America." In *Report on American Manuscripts in the Royal Institution of Great Britain (Dorchester Papers)*, Edited by Benjamin Franklin Stevens and Henry J. Brown, Vol. 1. London: His Majesty's Stationery Office, 1904.

Royal Commission on Historical Manuscripts. *Historical Manuscripts Commission, Stopford-Sackville Papers: Report on the Manuscripts of Mrs. Stopford-Sackville, of Drayton House, Northamptonshire*, 2 vols. London: His Majesty's Stationary Office, 1904–10.

Royal Commission on Historical Manuscripts. *Historical Manuscripts Commission, Report on Manuscripts in Various Collections, VI: The Manuscripts of Miss M. Eyre Matcham, Captain H. V. Knox, Cornwallis-Wykeham-Martin.* London: His Majesty's Stationary Office, 1909.

Royal Commission on Historical Manuscripts. *Historical Manuscripts Commission, Hastings Manuscripts, Report on the Manuscripts of the Late Reginald Rawdon Hastings, HMC 78*, Vol. 3. London: His Majesty's Stationary Office, 1928–1947.

Royal Commission on Historical Manuscripts. *Orderly Book: H.B.M. 43d Regiment of Foot General Orders: From 23 May to 25 Aug 1781. Additional Manuscripts, 42,449.* London: British Library.

Royal French Navy. *The Siege of Savannah in 1779, as Described in Two Contemporaneous Journals of French Officers in the Fleet of Count D'Estaing*, Edited by Charles C. Jones, Jr., 1874. Reprint, New York: The New York Times & Arno Press, 1968.

Royal Navy, Admiralty. *Admiralty Papers.* London: The National Archives, Kew, 1700 to 1799.

Stedman, Charles. *The History of the Origin, Progress, and Termination of the American War*, 2 vols. 1794. Reprint, Charleston, SC: Nabu, 2010.

Stevens, Benjamin Franklin. ed. *Facsimiles of Manuscripts in European Archives Relating to America, 1773–1783*, 25 vols. London: Malby & Sons, 1889–95.

Stevens, Benjamin Franklin. ed. *The Campaign in Virginia 1781: Clinton-Cornwallis Controversy.* 2 vols. 1888. Reprint, Charleston, SC: Nabu, 2010.

Sullivan, John. *The Letters and Papers of Major-General John Sullivan, Continental Army*, Edited by Otis G. Hammond, 3 vols. Concord, NH: New Hampshire Historical Society, 1930–9.

Swinson, Arthur. *A Register of Regiments and Corps of the British Army.* London: Archive Press, 1972.

Syrett, David. ed. *The Rodney Papers: Selections from the Correspondence of Admiral Lord Rodney, Volume II, 1763–1780.* London: Navy Records Society, 2007.

Tarleton, Banastre. *A History of the Campaigns of 1780 and 1781 in the Southern Provinces of North America.* 1787. Reprint, New York: Arno Press, 1968.

Thacher, James. *A Military Journal During the American Revolutionary War, from 1775 to 1783, Describing Interesting Events and Transactions of this Period with Numerous Historical Facts and Anecdotes.* 1823. Reprint, Cranbury, NJ: The Scholar's Bookshelf, 2005.

Themistocles. *A Reply to Sir Henry Clinton's Narrative. His Numerous Errors Are Pointed Out, Conduct of Lord Cornwallis Vindicated from Aspersion. Includes the Public and Secret Correspondence.* Farmington Hills, MI: Gale ECCO, 2010.

United States Naval History Division. *Naval Documents of the American Revolution*, 15 vols. Washington, DC: U.S. Government Printing Office, 1964–2019.

War Office, Great Britain. *War Office Papers.* National Archives, Kew, UK. WO 34.

Washington, George. *The Writings of George Washington: Being His Correspondence, Addresses, Messages and Other Papers, Private and Public*, Edited by Jared Sparks, Vol. 8. Boston, MA: Russell, Odiorne, and Metcalf, 1835.

Washington, George. *The Writings of Washington*, Edited by John C. Fitzpatrick et al., 39 vols. Washington, DC: United States Government Printing Office, 1931–1944.

Washington, George. *George Washington Papers at the Library of Congress, 1741–1799: Series 8b*, Manuscript Division. Washington, DC: Library of Congress, 1973.

Washington, George. *The Papers of George Washington, Revolutionary War Series*, Edited by W. W. Abbot and Dorothy Twohig, 16 vols. Charlottesville, VA: University of Virginia Press, 1985–2006.

Woodmason, Charles. *The Carolina Backcountry on the Eve of the Revolution*, Edited by Richard J. Hooker. Chapel Hill, NC: University of North Carolina Press, 1953.

## Secondary Sources—Journal Articles, Academic Papers, Dissertations

Adams, George R. "The Carolina Regulators: A Note on Changing Interpretations." *The North Carolina Historical Review* 49, no. 4 (1972): 345–52.

Atkinson, C. T. "British Forces in North America, 1774–1781: Their Distribution and Strength, Part 1." *Journal of the Society for Army Historical Research* 16 (1937): 3–23.

Babits, Lawrence E. "Greene's Strategy in the Southern Campaign, 1780–1781." *Air Force Journal of Logistics* 8, no. 1 (Winter 1984): 10–4.

Bayse, Arthur Herbert. "The Secretary of State for the Colonies, 1768–1782." *The American Historical Review* 28, no. 1 (1922): 13–23.

Bennett, Thomas B. "Early Operational Art: Nathanael Greene's Carolina Campaign, 1780–1781." Fort Leavenworth, KS: School of Advanced Military Studies, United States Army Command and General Staff College, 1993.

Berg, Richard H. "The Southern Campaigns: The British Effort to Retake the South, 1778–1781." *Strategy and Tactics* 104 (1985): 14–23.

Bodle, Wayne. "Generals and 'Gentlemen': Pennsylvania Politics and the Decision for Valley Forge." *Pennsylvania History* 62, no. 1 (January 1995): 59–89.

Breen, Kenneth. "Graves and Hood at the Chesapeake." *Mariners' Mirror* 66 (1980): 63–4.

Brown, Alan S. "James Simpson's Reports on the Carolina Loyalists, 1779–1780." *Journal of Southern History* 21, no. 4 (November 1955): 518–9.

Brown, Gerald S. "The Anglo-French Naval Crisis: A Study of Conflict in the North Cabinet." *William and Mary Quarterly*, 3d ser., 9, no. 3 (July 1952): 317–37.

Browne, Gregory M. "Fort Mercer and Fort Mifflin: The Battle for the Delaware River and the Importance of American Riverine Defenses during Washington's Siege of Philadelphia." MA Thesis, Western Illinois University, 1996.

Burne, A. H. "Cornwallis at Yorktown." *Journal of the Society for Army Historical Research* 17 (Summer 1938): 71–6.

Carpenter, Charles F. "The Southern Loyalists in British Strategic Military Planning for the American War of Independence." BA Honors Thesis, University of North Carolina, 1979.

Carpenter, James L. "The Army of Cornwallis: A Study of Logistics Inadequacies." *Logistics Spectrum* 10, no. 3 (Fall 1976): 5–13.

Carpenter, Stanley D. M. "Patterns of Recruitment of the Highland Regiments of the British Army, 1756 to 1815." M.Litt Thesis, Department of Modern History, University of St Andrews, 1978.

Carpenter, William L. *The Battle of Ramsour's Mill*. Lincolnton, NC: Lincoln County Historical Association and Lincoln County Museum of History, 1995.

Cavanaugh, John C. "The Military Career of Major General Lincoln in the War of the American Revolution." PhD Dissertation, Duke University, 1969.

Cave, Alfred A. "The Delaware Prophet Neolin: A Reappraisal." *Ethnohistory* 46, no. 2 (1999): 265–90.

Clover, J. P. *The British Southern Campaign in the Revolutionary War: Implications for Contemporary Counter-Insurgency*. Carlisle, PA: US Army War College, 2006.

Coburn, Frank Warren. *The Battle of April 19, 1775*. Lexington, MA: Lexington Historical Society, 1922.

Comtois, Pierre. "Virginia Under Threat." *Military History* 11, no. 4 (1994): 54–60.

Conway, Stephen. "To Subdue America: British Army Officers and the Conduct of the Revolutionary War." *William and Mary Quarterly*, 3d ser., 43, no. 3 (1986): 381–407.

Conway, Stephen. "The Politics of British Military and Naval Mobilization, 1775–83." *The English Historical Review* 112, no. 449 (November 1997): 1179–203.

Crawford, Michael J. "New Light on the Battle Off the Virginia Capes: Graves vs. Hood." *The Mariner's Mirror* 103, no. 3 (2017): 337–40.

Curtis, Thomas D. "Riches, Real Estate, and Resistance: How Land Speculation, Debt, and Trade Monopolies Led to the American Revolution." *The American Journal of Economics and Sociology* 73, no. 3 (2014): 474–626.

Davis, Andrew M. "The Employment of Indian Auxiliaries in the American War." *The English Historical Review* 2, no. 8 (October 1887): 709–28.

Davis, Robert S., Jr. "The British Invasion of Georgia in 1778." *Atlanta Historical Journal* 24 (1980): 5–25.

Del Papa, Eugene M. "The Royal Proclamation of 1763: Its Effect upon Virginia Land Companies." *The Virginia Magazine of History and Biography* 83, no. 4 (1975): 406–11.

Dukes, Richard Sears, Jr. "Anatomy of a Failure: British Military Policy in the Southern Campaign of the American Revolution, 1775–1781." PhD Dissertation, University of South Carolina, 1993.

Elmer, Ebenezer. "Excerpts from the Journal of Surgeon Ebenezer Elmer of the New Jersey Continental Line, September 11–19, 1777." *The Pennsylvania Magazine of History and Biography* 35, no. 1 (1911): 104.

Farley, M. Foster. "The 'Old Wagoner' and the 'Green Dragoon.'" *History Today* 25, no. 3 (1975): 190–5.

Frasché, Louis D. F. "Problems of Command: Cornwallis, Partisans and Militia, 1780." *Military Review* 57, no. 4 (April 1977): 60–74.

Gathman, Christina and Henning Hillmann. "Overseas Trade and the Decline of Privateering." *The Journal of Economic History* 71, no. 3 (September 2011): 625–61.

Graham, William. "The Battle of Ramsour's Mill, June 20, 1780." *The North Carolina Booklet* 4 (1904).

Green, Stuart A. "The Origins of British Strategy in the War for American Independence." In *Military History of the American Revolution: The Proceedings of the 6th Military History Symposium, United States Air Force Academy, 10–11 October 1974*. Edited by Stanley J. Underdal. Washington, DC: Office of Air Force History, Headquarters USAF and United States Air Force Academy, 1974.

Green, Stuart A. "Notes and Documents: Repeal of the Stamp Act: The Merchants' and Manufacturers' Testimonies." *The Pennsylvania Magazine of History and Biography* 128, no. 2 (2004): 179–97.

Hamer, Philip M. "John Stuart's Indian Policy during the Early Months of the American Revolution." *The Mississippi Valley Historical Review* 17, no. 3 (December 1930): 351–66.

Hatch, Charles E., Jr. "Gloucester Point in the Siege of Yorktown, 1781." *William and Mary Quarterly*, 2d ser., 20 (April 1940): 265–84.

Hill, Simon. "The Liverpool Economy During the War of American Independence, 1775–83." *The Journal of Imperial and Commonwealth History* 44, no. 6 (2016): 835–56.

Hoffer, Edward E. *Operational Art and Insurgency War: Nathanael Greene's Campaign in the Carolinas.* Fort Leavenworth, KS: School of Advanced Military Studies, US Army Command and General Staff College, 1988.

Johnson, Donald F. "The Failure of Restored British Rule in Revolutionary Charleston, South Carolina." *The Journal of Imperial and Commonwealth History* 42, no. 1 (2014): 22–40.

Kyte, George W. "Strategic Blunder: Lord Cornwallis Abandons the Carolinas, 1781." *The Historian* 22, no. 2 (1960): 129–44.

Larrabee, Harold A. "A Near Thing at Yorktown." *American Heritage* 12, no. 6 (1961): 56–64, 69–73.

Lawrence, Alexander A. "General Robert Howe and the British Capture of Savannah in 1778." *Georgia Historical Quarterly* 36 (1952): 303–27.

Leach, Douglas Edward. *Arms for Empire: A Military History of the British Colonies in North America.* New York: Macmillan and Company, 1973.

Leech, Timothy. "'Crossing the Rubicon: The Establishment of the Continental Army and American State Formation, 1774–1776." PhD Dissertation, Ohio State University, 2017.

Lumpkin, Henry. "The Battle off the Capes." *Virginia Cavalcade* 31, no. 2 (1981): 68–77.

Lutnick, Solomon M. "The Defeat at Yorktown: A View from the British Press." *Virginia Magazine of History and Biography* 72, no. 4 (1964): 471–8.

Mackesy, Piers. "British Strategy in the War of American Independence." *Yale Review* 52, no. 4 (1963): 539–57.

Mahnken, Thomas. "A Strategy for Protracted War." In *Unrestricted Warfare Symposium, 2006: Proceedings on Strategy, Analysis and Technology.* Laurel, MD: Johns Hopkins University Applied Physics Laboratory, 2006, 35–64.

Mallahan, Richard A. *The Siege of Yorktown: Washington vs. Cornwallis.* Maxwell Air Force Base, AL: Air University, Air Command and Staff College, 1985.

Massey, Gregory De Van. "The British Expedition to Wilmington, January-November, 1781." *North Carolina Historical Review* 66, no. 4 (1989): 387–411.

Middleton, Richard. "Pontiac: Local Warrior or Pan-Indian Leader?" *Michigan Historical Review* 32, no. 2 (2006): 1–32.

Miller, John C. "The Massachusetts Convention 1768." *The New England Quarterly* 7, no. 3 (1934): 445–74.

Nelson, Paul David. "Horatio Gates in the Southern Department, 1780: Serious Errors and a Costly Defeat." *North Carolina Historical Review* 50, no. 3 (1973): 256–72.

New England Historical Society. *The Red, Black, and White Men of Glover's Regiment Take Washington across the Delaware.* Stonington, ME: New England Historical Society.

Novotny, Jan M. "Stamp Duties," *The Journal of Economic History* 15, no. 3 (1955): 288–90.

Olson, Gary D. "Thomas Brown, Loyalist Partisan and the Revolutionary War in Georgia, 1777–1782." *Georgia Historical Quarterly* 54 (1970): 1–19.

Pearson, Jesse T. *The Failure of British Strategy During the Southern Campaign of the American Revolutionary War, 1780–81.* Fort Leavenworth, KS: US Army Command and General Staff College, 2005.

Rankin, Hugh F. "The Moore's Creek Bridge Campaign, 1776." *The North Carolina Historical Review* 30 (1953): 23–60.

Rhinesmith, W. Donald. "October 1781: The Southern Campaign Ends at Yorktown." *Virginia Cavalcade* 31, no. 2 (1981): 52–67.

Rogers, George C. "The Charleston Tea Party: The Significance of December 3, 1773." *South Carolina Historical Magazine* 75, no. 3 (1974): 153–68.

Rogers, Shelly. *Francis Marion, The Swamp Fox: American Military in Low Intensity Conflict.* Quantico, VA: Marine Corps Command and Staff College, 1988.

Schlesinger, Arthur M. "The Colonial Newspapers and the Stamp Act." *The New England Quarterly* 8, no. 1 (1935): 63–83.

Selig, Robert. "Francois Joseph Paul Comte de Grasse, the Battle off the Virginia Capes, and the American Victory at Yorktown." *Journal of the Colonial Williamsburg Foundation* 21, no. 5 (October—November 1999): 26–32.

Smith, Bradley W. *Decision at Wilmington: Cornwallis Abandons the Carolinas, 1781.* Fort Leavenworth, KA: School of Advanced Military Studies, US Army Command and General Staff College, 1982.

Smith, Glenn Curtis. "An Era of Non-Importation Associations, 1768–73." *William and Mary Quarterly* 20, no. 1 (1940): 84–98.

Smith, Michael. *Lord Charles Cornwallis: A Study in Strategic Leadership Failure.* Carlisle, PA: US Army War College, 2001.

Smith, Paul H. "The American Loyalists: Notes on Their Organization and Numerical Strength." *William and Mary Quarterly* 25 (April 1968): 259–7.

Stanley, H. Palmer. "The Military, the Law, and Public Order in England, 1650–1850." *Journal of the Society for Army Historical Research* 56, no. 228 (1978): 198–214.

Thomas, Joseph M. "Swift and the Stamp Act of 1712." *PMLA* 31, no. 2 (1916): 247–63.

Thomas, Peter D. G. "The Cost of the British Army in North America, 1763–1775." *William and Mary Quarterly* 45, no. 3 (1988): 510–6.

Tiedemann, Joseph S. "A Tumultuous People: The Rage for Liberty and the Ambiance of Violence in the Middle Colonies in the Years Preceding the American Revolution." *Pennsylvania History: A Journal of Mid-Atlantic Studies* 77, no. 4 (2010): 387–431.

Tokar, John R. *Redcoat Resupply: Strategic Logistics and Operational Indecision in the American Revolutionary War, 1775–1783.* Fort Leavenworth, KS: School of Advanced Military Studies, United States Army Command and General Staff College, 1999.

Urwin, Gregory J. W. "Cornwallis and the Slaves of Virginia: A New Look at the Yorktown Campaign." *International Commission of Military History Proceedings* (2002): 172–92.

Weddle, Kevin J. "A Change of Both Men and Measures: British Reassessment of Military Strategy after Saratoga, 1770–1778." *The Journal of Military History* 77, no. 3 (July 2013): 837–65.

Whittenburg, James P. "Planters, Merchants, and Lawyers: Social Change and the Origins of the North Carolina Regulation." *William and Mary Quarterly* 34, no. 2 (1977): 215–38.

Wight, Frank R. *Nathanael Greene, Major General of the American Revolution.* Maxwell Air Force Base, AL: Air University, Air Command and Staff College, 1965.

Willcox, William B. "The British Road to Yorktown: A Study in Divided Command." *American Historical Review* 52, no. 1 (October 1946): 1–35.

Willcox, William B. "British Strategy in America, 1778." *Journal of Modern History* 19, no. 2 (June 1947): 103.

Wright, John W. "Notes on the Siege of Yorktown in 1781 with Special Reference to the Conduct of a Siege in the Eighteenth Century." *William and Mary Quarterly*, 2d ser., 12 (October 1932): 229–49.

Wright, Robert K. "A Crisis of Faith: Three Defeats that Cost a Reputation." *The Hessians: Journal of the Johannes Schwalm Historical Association* 21 (2018): 52.

York, Neil L. "Pennsylvania Rifle: Revolutionary Weapon in a Conventional War." *Pennsylvania Magazine of History and Biography*, July 1979. University Park, PA.


## Secondary Sources—Monographs

Alden, John R. *John Stuart and the Southern Colonial Frontier: A Study of Indian Relations, War, Trade, and Land Problems in the Southern Wilderness, 1754–1775*, University of Michigan Publications, History and Political Science, Vol. XV. Ann Arbor, MI: University of Michigan Press, 1944.

Alden, John R. *The South in the Revolution, 1763–1789*. Baton Rouge, LA: Louisiana State University Press, 1957.

Alexander, Bevin. *How Great Generals Win*. New York: W. W. Norton, 1993.

Allen, Thomas B. *Tories: Fighting for the King in America's First Civil War*. New York: Harper, 2010.

Anderson, Fred. *Crucible of War: The Seven Years' War and the Fate of Empire in British North America, 1754–1766*. New York: Alfred A. Knopf, 2000.

Anderson, Troyer Steele. *The Command of the Howe Brothers During the American Revolution*. New York: Oxford University Press, 1936.

Archer, Richard. *As If an Enemy's Country: The British Occupation of Boston and the Origins of Revolution*. New York: Oxford University Press, 2010.

Arthur, Robert. *The Sieges of Yorktown 1781 and 1862*. Fort Monroe, VA: Coast Artillery School, 1927.

Atwood, Rodney. *The Hessians*. Cambridge: Cambridge University Press, 1980.

Axelrod, Alex. *Blooding at Great Meadows: Young George Washington and the Battle That Shaped the Man*. Philadelphia, PA: Running Press, 2007.

Babits, Lawrence E. *A Devil of a Whipping: The Battle of Cowpens*. Chapel Hill, NC: University of North Carolina Press, 1998.

Babits, Lawrence E. and Joshua B. Howard. *Long, Obstinate, and Bloody: The Battle of Guilford Courthouse*. Chapel Hill, NC: University of North Carolina Press, 2009.

Bailyn, Bernard. *The Ideological Origins of the American Revolution*. Cambridge, MA: Harvard University Press, 1967.

Baker, Norman. *Government and Contractors: The British Treasury and War Supplies, 1775–83*. London: Athlone Press, 1971.

Bargar, B. D. *Lord Dartmouth and the American Revolution*. Columbia, SC: University of South Carolina Press, 1965.

Barrento, António. *Guerra Fantástica: The Portuguese Army and the Seven Years' War*. Warwick: Helion and Company, 2020.

Barrow, Thomas C. *Trade and Empire: The British Customs Service in Colonial America, 1660–1775*. Cambridge, MA: Harvard University Press, 1967.

Bass, Robert D. *Swamp Fox: The Life and Campaigns of General Francis Marion*. New York: Holt, 1959.

Bass, Robert D. *The Green Dragoon*. Orangeburg, SC: Sandlapper, 2003.

Batson, Douglas E. *Registering the Human Terrain: A Valuation of Cadastre*. Washington, DC: National Defense Intelligence College, 2008.

Baugh, Daniel. *The Global Seven Years' War, 1754–1763*. New York: Pearson Education, 2011.

Billias, George A. *George Washington's Opponents: British Generals and Admirals in the American Revolution*. New York: William Morrow, 1969.

Billias, George A. *George Washington's Generals and Opponents*. Cambridge, MA: Da Capo, 1994.

Black, Jeremy. *War for America: The Fight for Independence, 1775–1783*. New York: St. Martin's, 1991.

Black, Jeremy. *Parliament and Foreign Policy in the Eighteenth Century*. Cambridge: Cambridge University Press, 2004a.

Black, Jeremy. *The British Seaborne Empire*. New Haven, CT: Yale University Press, 2004.

Bodle Wayne W. and Jacqueline Thibaut. *Valley Forge Historical Research Report, Vol. 1* Valley Forge, PA: United States Department of the Interior, National Park Service, 1980.

Borick, Carl P. *A Gallant Defense: The Siege of Charleston, 1780*. Columbia, SC: University of South Carolina Press, 2003.

Bowler, R. Arthur. *Logistics and the Failure of the British Army in America, 1775–1783*. Princeton, NJ: Princeton University Press, 1975.

Brecher, Frank W. *Securing American Independence: John Jay and the French Alliance*. Westport, CT: Praeger, 2003.

Brewer, John. *The Sinews of Power: War, Money and the English State, 1688–1783*. New York: Alfred A. Knopf, 1989.

Brinkley, W. David. *Back to the Future: The British Southern Campaign, 1780–1781*. Fort Leavenworth, KS: School of Advanced Military Studies, United States Army Command and General Staff College, 1998.

Brown, Gerald S. *The American Secretary: The Colonial Policy of Lord George Germain, 1775–1778*. Ann Arbor, MI: University of Michigan Press, 1963.

Brown, Marion Marsh. *The Swamp Fox*. Philadelphia, PA: Westminster, 1950.

Brown, Robert W., Jr. *Kings Mountain and Cowpens: Our Victory Was Complete*. Charleston, SC: History Press, 2009.

Brown, Wallace. *The King's Friends: The Composition and Motives of the American Loyalist Claimants*. Providence, RI: Brown University Press, 1965.

Brumwell, Stephen. *Redcoats: The British Soldier and the War in the Americas, 1775–1763*. Cambridge: Cambridge University Press, 2002.

Buchanan, John. *The Road to Guilford Courthouse: The American Revolution in the Carolinas*. New York: Wiley, 1999.

Buchanan, John. *The Road to Valley Forge: How Washington Built the Army That Won the Revolution*. New York: Barnes and Noble, 2007.

Bunker, Nick. *An Empire on the Edge: How Britain Came to Fight America*. New York: Alfred A. Knopf, 2014.

Calloway, Colin G. *The American Revolution in Indian Country: Crisis and Diversity in Native American Communities*. New York: Cambridge University Press, 1995.

Calloway, Colin G. *The Scratch of a Pen: 1763 and the Transformation of North America*. New York: Oxford University Press, 2006.

Carp, E. Wayne. *To Starve the Army at Pleasure: Continental Army Administration and American Political Culture, 1775–1783*. Chapel Hill, NC: UNC Press, 1984.

Carpenter, Stanley D. M. *Military Leadership in the British Civil Wars, 1642–1651: 'The Genius of This Age.'* London: Frank Cass, 2005.

Carpenter, Stanley D. M. *Southern Gambit: Cornwallis and the British March to Yorktown*. Norman, OK: University of Oklahoma Press, 2019.

Chernow, Ron. *Washington: A Life*. New York: Penguin Press, 2010.

Christie, Ian R. and Benjamin W. Labaree. *Empire or Independence, 1760–1776: A British-American Dialogue on the Coming of the American Revolution*. New York: W. W. Norton, 1976.

Clary, David A. *George Washington's First War: His Early Military Adventures*. New York: Simon & Schuster, 2011.

Clausewitz, Carl von. *On War*, Indexed Edition, Edited and translated by Michael Howard and Peter Paret. Princeton, NJ: Princeton University Press, 1984.

Cohen, Eliot A. *Conquered into Liberty: Two Centuries of Battles along the Great Warpath That Made the American Way of War*. New York: Free Press, 2011.

Cohen, Sheldon S. *Commodore Abraham Whipple of the Continental Navy*. Gainesville, FL: University Press of Florida, 2010.

Coker, William S. and Robert R. Rea. *Anglo-Spanish Confrontation on the Gulf Coast During the American Revolution*. Pensacola, FL: Gulf Coast History and Humanities Conference, 1982.

Commager, Henry Steele and Richard B. Morris. *The Spirit of Seventy-Six: The Story of the American Revolution as Told by Its Participants*. New York: HarperCollins, 1967.

Conway, Stephen. *The British Isles and the War for American Independence*. Oxford: Oxford University Press, 2000.

Cook, Don. *The Long Fuse: How England Lost the American Colonies, 1760–1785*. New York: The Atlantic Monthly Press, 1995.

Corbett, Julian S. *Fighting Instructions. Publications of the Navy Records Society*, Vol. 29. London: Spottswoodie, 1905.

Corbett, Julian S. *Some Principles of Maritime Strategy*. London: Longmans Green, 1911 Reprint, Annapolis: Naval Institute Press, 1988.

Corbett, Theodore. *No Turning Point: The Saratoga Campaign in Perspective*. Norman, OK: University of Oklahoma Press, 2012.

Crow, Jeffrey J. and Larry E. Tise. eds. *The Southern Experience in the American Revolution*. Chapel Hill, NC: University of North Carolina Press, 1978.

Cummins, Joseph A. *Ten Tea Parties: Patriotic Protests That History Forgot*. Philadelphia, PA: Quirk Books, 2012.

Dameron, David. *Kings Mountain: The Defeat of the Loyalists October 7, 1780*. Cambridge, MA: Da Capo, 2003.

Danley, Mark H. and Patrick J. Speelman. *The Seven Years' War: Global Views*. Boston, MA: Brill, 2012.

Daughan, George C. *If by Sea: The Forging of the American Navy from the Revolution to the War of 1812*. New York: Basic Books, 2008.

Davis, Burke. *The Campaign That Won America: The Story of Yorktown*. New York: Eastern Acorn, 1989.

Davis, Burke. *The Cowpens-Guilford Courthouse Campaign*. Philadelphia, PA: University of Pennsylvania Press, 2002.

Davis, Robert S., Jr. *Georgians in the Revolution: At Kettle Creek (Wilkes Co.) and Burke County*. Easley, SC: Southern Historical Press, 1986.

De Fonblanque, Edward Barrington. *Political and Military Episodes in the Latter Half of the Eighteenth Century: Derived from the Life and Correspondence of the Right Hon. John Burgoyne, General, Statesman, Dramatist*. London: Macmillan, 1876.

De Vorsey, Jr. Louis. *The Indian Boundary in the Southern Colonies, 1763–1775*. Chapel Hill, NC: University of North Carolina Press, 1966.

Dearden, Paul F. *The Rhode Island Campaign of 1778*. Providence, RI: Rhode Island Bicentennial Federation, 1980.

DeMond, Robert O. *The Loyalists in North Carolina during the Revolution*. 1930. Reprint, Baltimore, MD: Clearfield, 2009.

Desjardin, Thomas A. *Through a Howling Wilderness: Benedict Arnold's March to Quebec, 1775.* New York: St. Martin's Press, 2006.

Dickinson, H. T. ed. *A Companion to Eighteenth-Century Britain.* Oxford: Blackwell, 2002.

Donoughue, Bernard. *British Politics and the American Revolution: The Path to War, 1773–75.* London: Macmillan, 1964.

Draper, Lyman C. *King's Mountain and Its Heroes: History of the Battle of King's Mountain, October 7th, 1780, and the Events Which Led to It.* 1881. Reprint, Charleston, SC: Nabu, 2010.

Dull, Jonathan R. *The French Navy and American Independence: A Study of Arms and Diplomacy, 1774–1787.* Princeton, NJ: Princeton University Press, 1975.

Dull, Jonathan R. *The Age of the Ship of the Line: The British & French Navies, 1650–1815.* Lincoln, NE: University of Nebraska Press, 2009.

Edgar, Walter. *South Carolina: A History.* Columbia, SC: University of South Carolina Press, 1998.

Falkner, James. *Fire over the Rock: The Great Siege of Gibraltar, 1779–1783.* Barnsley: Pen and Sword Military, 2009.

Fenn, Elizabeth A. *Pox Americana: The Great Smallpox Epidemic of 1775–82.* Boston, MA: Hill and Wang, 2002.

Ferling, John. *A Leap in the Dark: The Struggle to Create the American Republic.* New York: Oxford University Press, 2003.

Ferling, John. *Almost a Miracle: The American Victory in the War of Independence.* Oxford: Oxford University Press, 2007.

Ferling, John. *Independence: The Struggle to Set America Free.* New York: Bloomsbury, 2011.

Ferling, John. *Whirlwind: The American Revolution and the War that Won It.* London: Bloomsbury, 2016.

Ferreiro, Larrie D. *Brother at Arms: American Independence and the Men of France & Spain Who Saved It.* New York: Alfred A. Knopf, 2016.

Fischer, David Hackett. *Albion's Seed: Four British Folkways in America.* New York: Oxford University Press, 1989.

Fischer, David Hackett. *Paul Revere's Ride.* New York: Oxford University Press, 1994.

Fischer, David Hackett. *Washington's Crossing.* New York: Oxford University Press, 2004.

Fischer, David Hackett. *Champlain's Dream: The European Founding of North America.* New York: Simon & Schuster, 2008.

Flavell, Julie. *The Howe Dynasty: The Untold Story of a Military Family and the Women Behind Britain's Wars for America.* New York: Liveright, 2021.

Fleming, Thomas. *Washington's Secret War: The Hidden History of Valley Forge.* Washington, DC: Smithsonian, 2005.

Ford, Worthington C. ed. *Defenses of Philadelphia in 1777.* Brooklyn, NY: Historical Printing Club, 1897. Reprint, De Capo Press, 1971.

Forrest, Alan. *The Death of the French Atlantic: Trade, War, and Slavery in the Age of Revolution.* Oxford: Oxford University Press, 2021.

Fortescue, Sir John. *The War of Independence: The British Army in North America, 1775–1783.* 1911. Reprint, London: Greenhill Books, 2001.

Fortescue, Sir John. *A History of the British Army,* 20 Vol. 1902. Reprint, East Essex: Naval and Military Press, 2004.

Fowler Jr., William M. *Rebels Under Sail: The American Navy During the Revolution.* New York: Charles Scribner's Sons, 1974.

Frentzos, Christos G. and Antonio S. Thompson. ed. *The Routledge Handbook of American Military and Diplomatic History: The Colonial Period to 1877.* New York: Routledge, 2015.

Gallagher, John J. *The Battle of Brooklyn 1776.* New York: Perseus Books, Da Capo Press, 1995; reprint, Edison, NJ: Castle Books, 2002.

Gilbert, Alan. *Black Patriots and Loyalists: Fighting for Emancipation in the War for Independence.* Chicago, IL: University of Chicago Press, 2012.

Gleig, G. R. *Lives of the Most Eminent British Military Commanders.* London: Longman, 1831–1832.

Golway, Terry. *Washington's General: Nathanael Greene and the Triumph of the American Revolution.* New York: Henry Holt and Company, 2005.

Gordon, John W. *South Carolina and the American Revolution: A Battlefield History.* Columbia, SC: University of South Carolina Press, 2003.

Gould, Eliga H. *Among the Powers of the Earth.* Cambridge, MA: Harvard University Press, 2012.

Gould, Eliga H. and Peter S. Ounf. eds. *Empire and Nation: The American Revolution in the Atlantic World.* Baltimore, MD: Johns Hopkins University Press, 2015.

Greene, Jerome A. *The Guns of Independence: The Siege of Yorktown, 1781.* New York: Savas Beatie, 2009.

Grenier, John. *The First Way of War: American War Making on the Frontier.* Cambridge: Cambridge University Press, 2005.

Griffin, Clarence W. *The History of Old Tryon and Rutherford Counties, North Carolina, 1730–1936.* Spartanburg, SC: The Reprint Company Publishers, 1982.

Gruber, Ira D. *The Howe Brothers and the American Revolution.* Chapel Hill, NC: University of North Carolina Press, 2014.

Hagan, Kenneth J. and William R. Roberts, eds. *Against All Enemies: Interpretations of American Military History from Colonial Times to the Present.* New York: Greenwood Press, 1986.

Hairr, John. *Guilford Courthouse: Nathanael Greene's Victory in Defeat, March 15, 1781.* Cambridge, MA: Da Capo, 2002.

Handel, Michael I. *Masters of War: Classics of Strategic Thought.* 3rd Edition. London: Frank Cass, 2001.

Harris, Michael C. *Brandywine: A Military History of the Battle That Lost Philadelphia But Saved America, September 11, 1775.* El Dorado Hills, CA: Savas Beatie, 2014.

Harris, Michael C. *Germantown: A Military History of the Battle for Philadelphia, October 4, 1777.* El Dorado Hills, CA: Savas Beatie, 2020.

Hart, Basil H. L. *The British Way in Warfare.* New York: Macmillan, 1933.

Hart, Basil H. L. *Strategy,* 2nd Revised Edition. New York: Frederick A. Praeger, 1967.

Hatch, Robert McConnell. *Thrust for Canada: The American Attempt on Quebec in 1775–1776.* Boston, MA: Houghton Mifflin, 1979.

Hattendorf, John B. *Newport, the French Navy, and American Independence.* Newport, RI: The Redwood Press, 2005.

Hibbert, Christopher. *Redcoats and Rebels.* New York: W. W. Norton, 1990.

Higginbotham, Don. ed. *Reconsiderations on the Revolutionary War: Selected Essays: Contributions in Military History, Number 14.* Westport, CT: Greenwood Press, 1978.

Higginbotham, Don. *Daniel Morgan: Revolutionary Rifleman.* Chapel Hill, NC: University of North Carolina Press, 1979.

Higginbotham, Don. *The War of American Independence: Military Attitudes, Policies, and Practices, 1763–1789.* Bloomington, IN: Indiana University Press, 1971.

Higginbotham, Don. *George Washington and the American Military Tradition.* Athens, GA: University of Georgia Press, 1985.

Higgins, W. Robert. ed. *The Revolutionary War in the South: Power, Conflict, and Leadership, Essays in Honor of John Richard Alden.* Durham, NC: Duke University Press, 1979.

Hoffman, Ronald and Peter J. Albert. eds. *Arms and Independence: The Military Character of the Revolution.* Charlottesville, VA: University Press of Virginia, 1984.

Holmes, Richard. *Redcoat: The British Soldier in the Age of Horse and Musket.* New York: W. W. Norton & Company, 2001.

Hutson, James H. *John Adams and the Diplomacy of the American Revolution.* Kentucky: University Press of Kentucky, 1980.

Jackson, John W. *The Pennsylvania Navy 1775–1781: The Defense of the Delaware.* New Brunswick, NJ: Rutgers University Press, 1974.

Jackson, John W. *The Delaware Bay and River Defenses of Philadelphia, 1775–1777.* Philadelphia, PA: Philadelphia Maritime Museum, 1977.

Jackson, John W. *With the British Army in Philadelphia 1777–1778.* San Rafael, CA: Presidio Press, 1979.

Jackson, John W. *Fort Mercer, Guardian of the Delaware.* Gloucester, NJ: Gloucester County Cultural and Heritage Commission, 1986a.

Jackson, John W. *Fort Mifflin Valiant Defender of the Delaware.* Philadelphia, PA: Old Fort Mifflin Historical Society Preservation Committee, 1986.

Jasanoff, Maya. *Liberty's Exiles: American Loyalists in the Revolutionary World.* New York: Alfred A. Knopf, 2011.

Johnson, William. *Sketches of the Life and Correspondence of Nathanael Greene,* 2 vols. 1822. Reprint, New York: Da Capo Press, 1973.

Johnston, Henry P. *The Yorktown Campaign and the Surrender of Cornwallis, 1781.* 1881. Reprint, Spartanburg, SC: The Reprint Company, 1973.

Kain, Henry C. *The Military and Naval Operations on the Delaware in 1777.* Philadelphia, PA: The City History Society of Philadelphia, 1910.

Katcher, Philip R. N. *Encyclopedia of British, Provincial, and German Army Units 1775–1783.* Harrisburg, PA: Stackpole Books, 1973.

Kennedy, Paul M. *The Rise and Fall of British Naval Mastery.* London: A. Lane, 1976.

Kenny, Kevin. *Peaceable Kingdom Lost: The Paxton Boys and the Destruction of William Penn's Holy Experiment.* New York: Oxford University Press, 2009.

Ketchum, Richard M. *Decisive Day: The Battle for Bunker Hill.* New York: American Heritage, 1962.

Ketchum, Richard M. *Divided Loyalties: How the American Revolution Came to New York.* New York: Henry Holt, 2002.

Ketchum, Richard M. *Victory at Yorktown: The Campaign That Won the Revolution.* New York: Henry Holt, 2004.

Kohn, Richard H. *Eagle and Sword: The Beginnings of the Military Establishment in America.* New York: The Free Press, 1975.

Labourdette, J. F. *Vergennes, Ministre principal de Louis XVI.* Paris: Editions Desjonquières, 1990.

Lambert, Robert Stansbury. *South Carolina Loyalists in the American Revolution.* Columbia, SC: University of South Carolina Press, 1987.

Landers, H. L. *The Battle of Camden.* Washington, DC: Government Printing Office, 1929.

Landers, H. L. *The Virginia Campaign and the Blockade and Siege of Yorktown, 1781: Including a Brief Narrative of the French Participation in the Revolution Prior to the Southern Campaign.* Washington, DC: U.S. Army War College, 1931.

Lanning, Michael. *African Americans in the Revolutionary War.* New York: Kensington Publishing, 2000.

Leckie, Robert. *George Washington's War: The Saga of the American Revolution.* New York: Harper Perennial, 1993.

Lender, Mark E. *The River War*. Trenton, NJ: New Jersey Historical Commission, 1979.

Lender, Mark E. and Gary Wheeler Stone. *Fatal Sunday: George Washington, the Monmouth Campaign and the Politics of Battle*. Norman, OK: University of Oklahoma Press, 2016.

Lender, Mark E. *Cabal! The Plot against General Washington*. Yardley, PA: Westholme Publishing, 2019.

Lengel, Edward G. *General George Washington: A Military Life*. New York: Random House, 2005.

Liell, Scott. *46 Pages: Thomas Paine, Common Sense, and the Turning Point to Independence*. New York: MJF Books, 2003.

Lockhart, Paul. *The Drillmaster of Valley Forge: The Baron de Steuben and the Making of the American Army*. New York: Harper Collins, 2008.

Lockhart, Paul. *The Whites of Their Eyes: Bunker Hill, the First American Army, and the Emergence of George Washington*. New York: HarperCollins, 2011.

Lumpkin, Henry. *From Savannah to Yorktown: The American Revolution in the South*. Columbia, SC: University of South Carolina Press, 1981.

Lunt, James. *The Duke of Wellington's Regiment (West Riding)*. London: Leo Cooper, 1971.

Lutnick, Simon. *The American Revolution and the British Press, 1775–1783*. Columbia, MO: University of Missouri Press, 1967.

Luzader, John F. *Saratoga: A Military History of the Decisive Campaign of the American Revolution*. New York: SavasBeatie, 2008.

Machiavelli, Niccolo. *Discourses on Livy*, Translated by Harvey Mansfield and Nathan Tarcov. Chicago, IL: University of Chicago, 1996.

Mackesy, Piers. *The War for America, 1775–1783*. Lincoln, NE: University of Nebraska Press, 1992.

Magill, Frank N. ed. *Great Lives from History: British and Commonwealth Series*, Vol. 2. Pasadena, CA: Salem, 1987.

Mahan, Alfred T. *The Major Operations of the Navies in the War of American Independence*. London: Sampson Low, Marsten, 1913.

Mahan, Alfred T. *The Influence of Sea Power Upon History 1660–1783*. New York: Dover, 1987.

Maier, Pauline. *From Resistance to Revolution: Colonial Radicals and the Development of American Opposition to Britain, 1765–1776*. London: Routledge & Keegan Paul, 1973.

Maier, Pauline. *American Scripture: Making the Declaration of Independence*. New York: Alfred A. Knopf, 1997.

Malone, Patrick M. *The Skulking Way of War: Technology and Tactics among the New England Indians*. Baltimore, MD: John Hopkins University Press, 1993.

Mao Tse-Tung [Mao Zedong]. *On Protracted War*. Peking [Beijing]: Foreign Languages Press, 1967.

Marlow, Louis. *Sackville of Drayton*. Totowa, NJ: Rowman and Littlefield, 1973.

Marshall, P. J. *The Making and Unmaking of Empires: Britain, India and America, c. 1750–1783* Oxford: Oxford University Press, 2005.

Martin, James Kirby and Mark Edward Lender. *A Respectable Army: The Military Origins of the Republic, 1763–1789*. Arlington Heights, IL: Harlan Davidson, 1982.

Mattern, David B. *Benjamin Lincoln and the American Revolution*. Columbia, SC: University of South Carolina Press, 1995.

Mazzagetti, Dominick. *Charles Lee: Self Before Country*. New Brunswick, NJ: Rutgers University Press, 2013.

McBurney, Christian M. *The Rhode Island Campaign: The First Franco-American Operation in the Revolutionary War*. Yardley, PA: Westholme Press, 2011.

McGuffie, T. H. *The Siege of Gibraltar 1779–1783*. Philadelphia, PA: Dufour Editions, 1965.

McGuire, Thomas. *The Philadelphia Campaign*, 2 vols. Mechanicsburg, PA: Stackpole Books, 2006.

McIntyre, James R. *The Development of the British Light Infantry, Continental and American Influences, 1740–1765*. Point Pleasant, NJ: Winged Hussar Publishing, 2015.

McKee, Christopher. *Edward Preble, A Naval Biography, 1761–1807*. Annapolis: Naval Institute Press, 1972.

McLynn, Frank. *1759: The Year Britain Became Master of the World*. New York: Atlantic Monthly Press, 2004.

Merrell, James H. *The Indians' New World: Catawbas and Their Neighbors from European Contact Through the Era of Removal*. Chapel Hill, NC: University of North Carolina Press, 1989.

Messick, Hank. *King's Mountain: The Epic of the Blue Ridge "Mountain Men" in the American Revolution*. Boston, MA: Little, Brown, 1976.

Meyer, Duane. *The Highland Scots of North Carolina, 1732–1776*. Chapel Hill, NC: University of North Carolina Press, 1987.

Middlekauff, Robert. *The Glorious Cause: The American Revolution, 1763–1789*, Revised and Expanded Edition. New York: Oxford University Press, 2005.

Middlekauff, Robert. *Washington's Revolution: The Making of America's First Leader*. New York: Alfred A. Knopf, 2015.

Mintz, Max M. *The Generals of Saratoga*. New Haven, CT: Yale University Press, 1990.

Mintz, Max M. *Seeds of Empire: The American Revolutionary Conquest of the Iroquois*. New York: New York University Press, 1999.

Morgan, Edmund S. *The Stamp Act Crisis: Prologue to Revolution*, 3rd Edition. Chapel Hill, NC: University of North Carolina Press, 1995.

Morton, Brian N. and Donald C. Spinelli. *Beaumarchais and the American Revolution*. Lanham, MD: Lexington Books, 2003.

Murphy, Orville T. *Charles Gravier, Comte de Vergennes: French Diplomacy in the Age of Revolution, 1719–1787*. Albany, NY: State University of New York Press, 1982.

Murphy, Orville T. *The Diplomatic Retreat of France and Public Opinion on the Eve of the Revolution 1783–1789*. Washington, DC: The Catholic University of America Press, 1998.

Murray, Williamson and Peter R. Mansoor. *Hybrid Warfare: Fighting Complex Opponents from the Ancient World to the Present*. New York: Cambridge University Press, 2012.

Nelson, James L. *Benedict Arnold's Navy: The Ragtag Fleet that Lost the Battle of Lake Champlain But Won the American Revolution*. New York: McGraw Hill, 2006.

Nelson, James L. *George Washington's Secret Navy, How the American Revolution Went to Sea*. New York: McGraw Hill, 2008.

Nelson, Paul David. *General Horatio Gates: A Biography*. Baton Rouge, LA: Louisiana State University Press, 1976.

Nelson, Paul David. *Francis Rawdon-Hastings, Marquess of Hastings: Soldier, Peer of the Realm, Governor-General of India*. Madison, NJ: Fairleigh Dickinson University Press, 2005.

Nelson, Paul David. *General Sir Guy Carleton, Lord Dorchester: Soldier-Statesman of Early British Canada*. Plainsboro, NJ: Associated University Presses, 2000.

Nester, William R. *The Frontier War for American Independence*. Mechanicsburg, PA: Stackpole Books, 2004.

Newman, Gerald. ed. *Britain in the Hanoverian Age, 1714–1837*. New York: Garland, 1997.

Norton, Mary Beth. *1774: The Long Year of Revolution*. New York: Alfred A. Knopf, 2020.

O'Donnell, James H. *Southern Indians in the American Revolution*. Knoxville, TN: University of Tennessee Press, 1973.

O'Donnell, Patrick K. *The Indispensables: The Diverse Soldier-Mariners Who Shaped the Country, Formed the Navy, and Rowed Washington Across the Delaware.* New York: Atlantic Monthly Press, 2021.

O'Meara, Walter. *Guns at the Forks.* Englewood Cliffs, NJ: Prentiss-Hall, 1965.

O'Shaughnessy, Andrew Jackson. *An Empire Divided: The American Revolution and the British Caribbean.* Philadelphia, PA: University of Pennsylvania Press, 2000.

O'Shaughnessy, Andrew Jackson. *The Men Who Lost America: British Leadership, the American Revolution, and the Fate of the Empire.* New Haven, CT: Yale University Press, 2013.

Olson, Alison Gilbert and Richard Maxwell Brown. eds. *Anglo-American Political Relations: 1675–1775.* New Brunswick, NJ: Rutgers University Press, 1970.

Padfield, Peter. *Maritime Supremacy and the Opening of the Western Mind: Naval Campaigns that Shaped the Modern World, 1588–1782.* London: John Murray, 1999.

Pancake, John S. *1777: The Year of the Hangman.* Tuscaloosa, AL: University of Alabama Press, 1977.

Park, Steven. *The Burning of His Majesty's Schooner Gaspee: An Attack on Crown Rule before the American Revolution.* Yardley, PA: Westholme, 2016.

Parks, Virginia. *Siege, Spain and Britain: Battle of Pensacola, March 9-May 8, 1781.* Pensacola: Pensacola Historical Society, 1981.

Patterson, Benton Rain. *Washington and Cornwallis: The Battle for America, 1775–1783.* Boulder, CO: Taylor, 2004.

Pearson, Michael. *Those Damned Rebels: The American Revolution as Seen through British Eyes.* Cambridge, MA: Da Capo, 2000.

Peckham, Howard H. *The War for Independence: A Military History.* Chicago, IL: University of Chicago Press, 1958.

Pengelly, Colin. *Sir Samuel Hood and the Battle of the Chesapeake.* Gainesville, FL: University of Florida Press, 2009.

Philbrick, Nathaniel. *Mayflower: A Story of Courage, Community, and War.* New York: Viking, 2007.

Phillips, Kevin. *1775: A Good Year for Revolution.* New York: Viking, 2012.

Piecuch, Jim. *The Battle of Camden: A Documentary History.* Charleston, SC: History Press, 2006.

Piecuch, Jim. *Three Peoples, One King: Loyalists, Indians, and Slaves in the Revolutionary South, 1775–1782.* Columbia, SC: University of South Carolina Press, 2008.

Piecuch, Jim. *The Blood Be Upon Your Head: Tarleton and the Myth of Buford's Massacre, the Battle of the Waxhaws: May 29, 1780.* Lugoff, SC: Woodward Corporation, 2010.

Porter, Roy. *English Society in the 18th Century.* London: Penguin Books, 1990.

Raab, James W. *Spain, Britain and the American Revolution in Florida, 1763–1783.* Jefferson, NC: McFarland, 2007.

Rankin, Hugh F. *North Carolina in the American Revolution.* Raleigh, NC: Historical Publications Section, Division of Historical Resources, Office of Archives and History, North Carolina Department of Cultural Resources, 1959.

Rankin, Hugh F. *Greene and Cornwallis: The Campaign in the Carolinas.* Raleigh, NC: North Carolina Office of Archives and History, 1976.

Rankin, Hugh F. *The North Carolina Continentals.* Chapel Hill, NC: University of North Carolina Press, 1971.

Reed, John F. *Campaign to Valley Forge, July 1, 1777-December 19, 1777.* Philadelphia, PA: University of Pennsylvania Press, 1965.

Rodger, N. A. M. *The Insatiable Earl: A Life of John Montagu, Fourth Earl of Sandwich, 1718–1792.* New York: W. W. Norton & Company, 1993.

Rodger, N. A. M. *The Command of the Ocean: A Naval History of Britain, 1649–1814.* New York: W. W. Norton, 2004.

Royster, Charles. *A Revolutionary People at War: The Continental Army and American Character, 1775–1783.* Chapel Hill, NC: University of North Carolina Press, 1979.

Rush, N. Orwin. *Spain's Final Triumph Over Great Britain in the Gulf of Mexico: The Battle of Pensacola, March 8 to 8 May, 1781.* Tallahassee, FL: Florida State University, 1966.

Scheer, George F. and Hugh F. Rankin. *Rebels and Redcoats.* New York: World Publishing, 1957.

Schwoerer, Lois G. *"No Standing Armies!:" The Anti-Army Ideology in Seventeenth-Century England.* Baltimore, MD: Johns Hopkins University Press, 1974.

Searcy, Martha C. *The Georgia-Florida Contest in the American Revolution, 1776–1778.* Tuscaloosa, AL: University of Alabama Press, 1985.

Seeley, John Robert. *The Expansion of England.* London: Macmillan, 1883.

Selby, John M. *The Road to Yorktown.* New York: St. Martin's, 1976.

Shaw, Helen L. *British Administration of the Southern Indians, 1756–1783.* 1931. Reprint, Norwalk, CT: AMS Press, 1981.

Shy, John. *A People Numerous and Armed: Reflections on the Military Struggle for American Independence,* Revised Edition. Ann Arbor, MI: University of Michigan Press, 1990.

Simms, Brendan. *Three Victories and a Defeat: The Rise and Fall of the First British Empire.* New York: Basic Books, 2009.

Simms, Brendan. *Europe: The Struggle for Supremacy, 1453 to Present.* New York: Basic Books, 2013.

Smith, Paul H. *Loyalists and Redcoats: A Study in British Revolutionary Policy.* Chapel Hill, NC: University of North Carolina Press, 1964.

Snow, Dean. *1777: Tipping Point at Saratoga.* New York: Oxford University Press, 2016.

Spring, Matthew. *With Zeal and with Bayonets Only: The British Army on Campaign in North America, 1775–1783.* Norman, OK: University of Oklahoma Press, 2010.

Stanley, George F. G. *Canada Invaded, 1775–1776.* Toronto: A.M. Hakkert, 1973.

Starr, J. Barton. *Tories, Dons, and Rebels: The American Revolution in British West Florida.* Gainesville, FL: University of Florida Press, 1976.

State of Georgia. *Kettle Creek: The Battle of the Cane Brakes, Wilkes County.* Atlanta, GA: State of Georgia, Department of Natural Resources, Office of Planning and Research, Historic Preservation Section, 1975.

Stempel, Jim. *Valley Forge to Monmouth: Six Transformative Months of the American Revolution.* Jefferson, NC: McFarland, 2021.

Stewart, Frank A. *History of the Battle of Red Bank with Events Prior and Subsequent Thereto.* Woodbury, NJ: Board of Freeholders of Gloucester County, 1927.

Stockley, Andrew. *Britain and France at the Birth of America: The European Powers and the Peace Negotiations of 1782–1783.* Exeter: University of Exeter Press, 2001.

Stoker, Donald J., Kenneth J. Hagan and Michael T. McMaster. eds. *Strategy in the American War of Independence: A Global Approach.* London: Routledge, 2010.

Stone, Lawrence. ed. *An Imperial State at War: Britain from 1689 to 1815.* London: Routledge, 1994.

Stryker, William S. *The Forts on the Delaware in the Revolutionary War.* Trenton, NJ: John L. Murphy Publishing Co., 1901.

Sun Tzu. *The Art of War,* Edited and Translated by Samuel B. Griffith. New York: Oxford University Press, 1963.

Swisher, James K. *The Revolutionary War in the Southern Backcountry.* Gretna, LA: Pelican, 2008.

Syrett, David. *Shipping and the American War 1775–83: A Study of British Transport Organization*. London: Athlone Press, 1970.

Syrett, David. *The Royal Navy in American Waters, 1775–1783*. Aldershot: Scolar, 1989.

Syrett, David. *The Royal Navy in European Waters During the American Revolutionary War*. Columbia, SC: University of South Carolina Press, 1998.

Syrett, David. *Admiral Lord Howe*. Annapolis: Naval Institute Press, 2006.

Taaffe, Stephen R. *The Philadelphia Campaign, 1777–1778*. Lawrence, KS: University of Kansas Press, 2003.

Taylor, Alan. *American Revolutions: A Continental History, 1750–1804*. New York: W. W. Norton & Co., 2016.

Thayer, Theodore. *Nathanael Greene: Strategist of the American Revolution*. New York: Twayne, 1960.

Thayer, Theodore. *Yorktown: Campaign of Strategic Options*. Philadelphia, PA: J. B. Lippincott, 1975.

Tilley, George L. and Thomas Crane. *The British Navy and the American Revolution*. Columbia, SC: University of South Carolina Press, 1987.

Treacy, M. F. *Prelude to Yorktown, the Southern Campaign of Nathanael Greene, 1780–1781*. Chapel Hill, NC: University of North Carolina, 1963.

Tuchman, Barbara W. *The March of Folly from Troy to Vietnam*. New York: Alfred A. Knopf, 1984.

Unger, Harlow Giles. *American Tempest: How the Boston Tea Party Sparked a Revolution*. Cambridge, MA: DaCapo Press, 2011.

Urban, Mark. *Fusiliers: The Saga of a British Redcoat Regiment in the American Revolution*. New York: Walker & Company, 2007.

Valentine, Alan. *Lord George Germain*. Oxford: Clarendon Press, 1962.

Van Creveld, Martin. *Command in War*. Cambridge, MA: Harvard University Press, 1985.

Van Tyne, Claude Halstead. *The Loyalists in the American Revolution*. New York: The Macmillan Company, 1902.

Volo, James M. *Blue Water Patriots: The American Revolution Afloat*. Lanham, MD: Rowman and Littlefield, 2008.

Walling, Karl-Freidrich. *Republican Empire: Alexander Hamilton on War and Free Government*. Lawrence, KS: University Press of Kansas, 1999.

Ward, Christopher. *The War of the Revolution*. New York: Macmillan, 1952.

Watt, Gavin K. *Rebellion in the Mohawk Valley: The St. Leger Expedition of 1777*. Toronto: The Dundurn Group, 2002.

Wickwire, Franklin and Mary Wickwire. *Cornwallis: The American Adventure*. Boston, MA: Houghton Mifflin, 1970.

Willcox, William B. *Portrait of a General: Sir Henry Clinton in the War of Independence*. New York: Knopf, 1964.

Willis, Sam. *The Struggle for Sea Power: A Naval History of the American Revolution*. New York: W. W. Norton, 2016.

Wilson, David K. *The Southern Strategy: Britain's Conquest of South Carolina and Georgia, 1775–1780*. Columbia, SC: University of South Carolina, 2005.

Wood, Gordon. *The Radicalization of the American Revolution*. New York: Alfred A. Knopf, 1992.

Wood, William J. *Battles of the Revolutionary War, 1775–1781*. Cambridge, MA: Da Capo Press, 2003.

Wright, J. Leach, Jr. *Florida in the American Revolution*. Gainesville, FL: University of Florida, 1975.

Wylie, J. C. "Excerpts from "Reflections on the War in the Pacific," Appendix A. In *Military Strategy: A General Theory of Power Control*. Annapolis: Naval Institute Press, 1989.

Zabin, Serena. *The Boston Massacre: A Family History*. Boston, MA and New York: Houghton Mifflin Harcourt, 2020.

Zobel, Hiller B. *The Boston Massacre*. New York: W. W. Norton, 1970.

# INDEX

Note: references to figures, images, illustrations, and maps are indicated by page citations in *italics*.

9780367484996